Constitutional Democracy: Policies and Politics

Little, Brown and Company
Boston   Toronto

Constitutional Democracy
Policies and Politics

Peter Woll
Brandeis University

Copyright © 1982 by Little, Brown and Company (Inc.)

All rights reserved. No part of this book may be reproduced in any form
or by any electronic or mechanical means including information storage
and retrieval systems without permission in writing from the publisher,
except by a reviewer who may quote brief passages in a review.

Library of Congress Catalog Card No. 82-80430

ISBN   0-316-951455

9 8 7 6 5 4 3 2 1

MV

Published simultaneously in Canada by Little, Brown & Company (Canada) Limited

Printed in the United States of America

The author acknowledges permission to quote material from the following
sources:
   The Vantage Point by Lyndon Baines Johnson. Copyright © 1971 by HEC
Public Affairs Foundation. Reprinted by permission of Holt, Rinehart and
Winston, Publishers.
   Elizabeth Drew, "Running," in *The New Yorker* (December 1, 1975).
Reprinted by permission; © 1975 The New Yorker Magazine, Inc.
(Acknowledgments continued on page 477)

For Denise

Contents

Chapter 3   The Dynamics of the Federal System   93

Part II   The Political Process   129

Chapter 5   Interest Groups and Political Participation   189

Part III The Governmental Process   251

Chapter 8   The Bureaucracy   377

Chapter 9   The Courts   413

Preface

This book is designed to be a core text for introductory American government courses. Its chapters cover the major areas of politics generally included in such courses, from the framing of the Constitution to contemporary government practices and policies. The foundations, theories, and practices of American political institutions are analyzed in detail, using extensive illustrations from the real political world to give students a sense of the excitement and diversity in this field.

Chapter 1 focuses on the politics of the Philadelphia Convention of 1787 and the outstanding features of the Constitution. Each article of the Constitution is outlined and discussed, along with the concept of federalism, the separation of powers, checks and balances, and judicial review. The chapter concludes with two contrasting ways of looking at the intentions of the Founding Fathers. The Madisonian model emphasized the importance of a system of separation of powers and checks and balances to restrain the national government from hasty, irrational, and demogogic actions. Madison, one of the strongest nationalists at the Philadelphia Convention, always argued that the national government should have power over state governments, but he wanted a balanced process of government that would be both restrained and effective. Hamilton, on the other hand, stressed the importance of an independent, unified executive branch that would be capable of acting with dispatch to cope with national problems.

Chapter 2 covers civil liberties and civil rights, including the debate over whether or not to attach a separate Bill of Rights to the Constitution, the background and meaning of each provision of the Bill of Rights, and the nationalization of the Bill of Rights. The chapter concludes with an analysis of each citizen's right to equal protection under the law, which, although not originally part of the Bill of Rights, has become an important part of our constitutional system.

Chapter 3 completes the section on constitutional government with a discussion of the dynamics of the federal system. The concept of federalism was crucial to making the Constitution acceptable both to nationalists and to advocates of states' rights. The discussion summarizes the ways in which the Constitution shapes the federal system and the development of constitutional standards governing federalism. The chapter concludes with an examination of the politics of federalism from historical and contemporary perspectives.

Part II proceeds to examine the political process, beginning in Chapter 4 with an analysis of political parties, elections, and electoral behavior. The framers of the Constitution, who wished to control and neutralize "faction," considered parties only in negative terms. Parties developed immediately after the founding of the Republic, however, first to reflect the views of political elites, and then to become a central component of an emerging democratic political process. A description of contemporary party politics and trends in presidential and congressional parties is illustrated with a case study of the presidential election of 1980 to help students answer the question of whether or not electoral choice and party programs make a difference. The images and issues of the 1980 campaign demonstrate the extent to which parties and candidates help to make our government one of rational discussion or emotional manipulation.

Interest groups complement political parties in shaping governmental processes and policies. The text describes the group theory model of government, the context of group action, interest groups in operation, and the recurring problem of whether and how to control interest group activity.

Part III, an account of the government process, includes chapters on the presidency, Congress, the bureaucracy, and the courts.

Chapter 6 considers the context within which the president must function, the responsibilities, powers, and limits of the presidency, the important role played by the White House staff, and other components of the executive office. The chapter ends with a discussion of the relationship between the president and Congress on foreign and domestic policy.

The focus then turns southeastward along Pennsylvania Avenue to the Capitol and an analysis of what the Founding Fathers called the First Branch of the Government—Congress. First, an overview of the legislature stresses its fragmentation, and the way in which legislators influence public policy not only through the passage of bills but also through the many informal networks of power that connect Capitol Hill with the bureaucracy downtown.

Chapter 7 analyzes the constitutional and political contexts of Congress, including bicameralism, the judicial interpretation of congressional authority, and the relationship between Congress on the one hand and the president, the bureaucracy, interest groups, political parties, and the electorate on the other.

The discussion of the external forces that impinge upon the legislature is complemented by an examination of the internal politics of Capitol Hill, including the committee system, congressional parties, and the caucuses and special groups that have gained increasing prominence in legislative politics.

An important aspect of both the internal and external politics of Capitol Hill is the constantly evolving budget process, established by the Budget and Impoundment Control Act of 1974. The text traces the development of budgetary politics on Capitol Hill, describing the successes and failures of the Budget Committees the Ninety-seventh Congress (1981–1982), including a discussion of the "reconciliation" process initially created by the Budget Act of 1974 but used only once before the Ninety-seventh Congress.

Congressional policymaking is illustrated, including an analysis of the impact of Congress upon the broader policy process. A major responsibility of Congress is supervision of the implementation of programs by administrative agencies.

Chapter 8 analyzes the powers, responsibilities, and relationships of the bureaucracy with Congress and the president. Discussion of the constitutional and political contexts of the bureaucracy emphasizes that administrative agencies are not readily subject to presidential or congressional control. Administrative rule making and adjudication are described as important aspects of policymaking. The chapter concludes with an examination of the problem of administrative responsibility.

The important role of the bureaucracy was not foreseen by the Founding Fathers. They concentrated upon establishing a tripartite government consisting of the presidency, Congress, and the judiciary. Chapter 9 concludes the text with an investigation of the important role the judiciary has assumed in government. The ebb and flow of judicial self-restraint and activism are analyzed in terms of the broader political forces that impinge upon the Supreme Court and the lower courts as well. Examples of judicial policymaking are given to illustrate the importance of the political environment within which courts must make decisions. Whether described as conservative or liberal, the Supreme Court cannot for long escape being at the center of political controversies.

The author is indebted in the preparation of this book to Jim Murray, who edited the initial manuscript and made many valuable suggestions. Cynthia Chapin expertly guided the production of the book. Sharon Bryan copyedited the manuscript with unusual skill and insight. Barbara Nagy, as always, cheerfully did the necessary typing. Denise Pollut buoyed the author's spirits throughout the project.

Constitutional Democracy: Policies and Politics

Part I

The Constitutional Context

The Constitution is treated with reverence by the American people.

CHAPTER 1

Constitutional Government

The Constitution has been a beacon that has guided Americans in their quest for self-government from the beginning of the Republic to the present. The Constitution is an unusually frugal document, embodying the visions and hopes of the remarkable men who drafted, redrafted, debated, compromised, and finally agreed upon its major principles.

Benjamin Franklin, at the close of the Convention of 1787, expressed the views of many of his fellow delegates when he declared, "I confess that there are several parts of this Constitution which I do not at present approve, but I am not sure I shall never approve them." Franklin continued, "I agreed to this Constitution with all its faults, if they are such; because I think a general government necessary for us, and there is no form of government but what may be a blessing to the people if well administered, and believe further that this is likely to be well administered for a course of years, and can only end in despotism as other forms have done before it, when the people shall become so corrupted as to need despotic government, being incapable of any other."[1]

While the Constitution was, as John Roche has pointed out, a practical political document that embraced compromises often reluctantly made between the sharply contrasting viewpoints of the state delegations, the final document embodied overarching principles and practices that have profoundly affected the way in which government functions.[2]

[1] Max Farrand, *The Records of the Federal Convention of 1787*, 4 vols. (New Haven: Yale University Press, 1911), 2: 641–42.

[2] John P. Roche, "The Founding Fathers: A Reform Caucus in Action," *American Political Science Review* 55 (December 1961): 799–816.

The Constitution is the most frugal document that has ever been devised to govern successfully the affairs of a great nation. Its apparent simplicity belies its true character, which is a skillful blending of theoretical and practical considerations to forge a new government that would be powerful enough to deal with national concerns but sufficiently limited to protect state sovereignty and the liberties and rights of all citizens.

Federalism, the separation of powers and checks and balances, and judicial review are the central principles of the Constitution. Nowhere does the Constitution explicitly declare that the new system of government was to be federal, or that the three branches of the government were to check and balance each other. Moreover, the important principle of judicial review of congressional, executive, and state actions can only be inferred from the debates of the Constitutional Convention and the explanations of the Constitution written by Alexander Hamilton, James Madison, and John Jay that appeared in *The Federalist*.

Federalism

A federal government is one in which there is a constitutional division of governmental authority between a central government, on the one hand, and constituent or state units on the other. Under the federal form the national government may exercise only those powers explicitly or implicitly granted to it, while the constituent units or states retain all other governmental authority.

The federal character of the Constitution lies in its explicit granting of authority to the national government, most particularly to Congress. The national government is limited to the exercise of the enumerated powers of Congress under Article I, and those that are "necessary and proper" to carry out the expressly stated powers. Specific grants of authority are also made to the president, who, for example, makes treaties by and with the advice and consent of the Senate. Finally, only the Supreme Court is to decide cases and controversies arising under the Constitution, treaties, and the laws of the land. The combined constitutional powers of the three branches of the national government constitute the boundaries beyond which the national government cannot go.

Within its sphere of power the national government is supreme under the terms of Article VI, which binds state judges to respect the Constitution, laws of the United States made in pursuance thereof, and all treaties made under the authority of the United States. Moreover, Article VI provides that no state constitution or law can supersede the federal Constitution or laws.

The federal character of the Constitution is further defined by denying certain powers, such as the authority to pass bills of attainder or ex post facto laws, to both the national and state governments. Some denials of power apply only to the national government (Art. I, sec. 9), while others apply only to states (Art. I, sec. 10).

Finally, the Tenth Amendment adopted in 1791 unequivocally restated the federal character of the new government by providing that the states were to retain all powers that the Constitution neither delegated to the United States nor prohibited to the individual states.

The separation of powers refers to the separation of the three branches of the national government from each other in their exercise of *primary* legislative, executive, and judicial authority. The separation of powers does not mean, however, that the three branches are to be totally separate and distinct. The separation of the three branches can only be maintained by the *sharing* of *secondary* powers as far as is necessary to bring about adequate checks and balances. (See Figure 1.1.)

The separation of the three branches of the government is accomplished not only through separation of powers and checks and balances, but also by giving each branch a separate political constituency. Moreover, Congress itself is divided so that—in the view of the framers—the Senate would act as a check upon the House. The authors of the Constitution hoped to supply the necessary political incentives to maintain the separation of powers: each department would have not only

The Separation of Powers and Checks and Balances

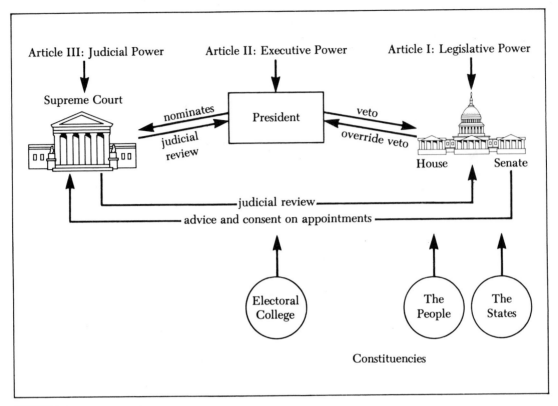

Article III: Judicial Power   Article II: Executive Power   Article I: Legislative Power

Supreme Court

President   House   Senate

nominates

judicial review

veto

override veto

judicial review

advice and consent on appointments

Electoral College   The People   The States

Constituencies

FIGURE 1.1
The Separation of Powers: Checks and Balances. *Separate and shared powers and separate constituencies were designed to guarantee checks and balances among the three branches of the government.*

the *means* to resist encroachments from coordinate branches, but also the *motives* to remain independent.

Important components of the separation of powers and checks and balances system include the presidential veto of congressional laws, the requirement that the president sign all legislation, and the sharing of the treaty-making and appointment powers between the president and the Senate. By implication, the authority of the Supreme Court to overturn executive actions and congressional laws is also an important part of the system.

The separation of powers doctrine prevents the three branches of the government from going beyond constitutional prescriptions in the exercise of the functions of coordinate branches. Moreover, no branch can exercise the "whole" power of another branch, or its primary authority under the Constitution. The president, for example, cannot legislate on

Constitutional Government

his own. Congress cannot take over the function of appointing executive officers. Neither the Supreme Court nor constitutional courts—lower courts created by Congress—can become executive agencies or legislative bodies.

While the theory of the separation of powers seems clear, it is not always easy to interpret in practice. For example, when Congress creates an administrative agency, how far can it go in delegating legislative responsibilities to the agency? At what point does the agency become a legislative body on its own independent of congressional control? Generally the courts have required, in theory at least, that Congress clearly state its intent in delegating legislative authority to the bureaucracy to assure that the will of Congress be carried out.

Judicial review refers to the power of the Supreme Court and lower federal courts to declare congressional or presidential acts unconstitutional, or presidential, administrative, and state actions to be beyond the authority of the Constitution or statutory law. (See Figure 1.2.) This authority is a critical part of the checks and balances system at the national level, and is vital to the preservation of the supremacy of federal law.

Judicial review was not discussed at the Convention of 1787 because the delegates assumed that, once they gave the federal courts jurisdiction to hear cases and controversies arising under the Constitution, treaties, and federal law, they would necessarily have the authority to delcare unconstitutional and unlawful legislation and actions that went beyond constitutional or lawful authority. At the time the Convention met it had been the practice in many states for courts to overturn laws contrary to state constitutions. Several times during the Philadelphia Convention delegates made statements which assumed that the power of judicial review would reside with the federal courts, and no objections were heard. Arguing for the adoption of the Constitution, Alexander Hamilton explicitly stated in *The Federalist* (No. 78) that the Supreme Court would have the power to declare acts of Congress to be unconstitutional. With respect to declaring state actions unconstitutional, it seems clear that the supremacy clause combined with the grant of jurisdiction to the

Judicial Review

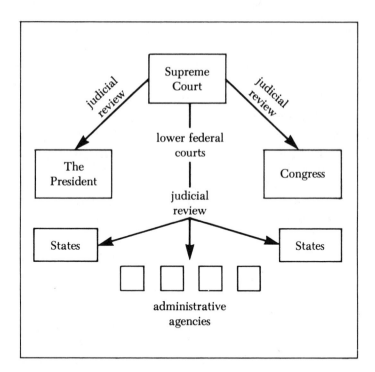

Supreme Court to hear cases arising under the Constitution and federal law implied federal judicial power over the states.

HOW THE GOVERNMENT WORKS UNDER THE CONSTITUTION

The Constitution defines the extent and limits of government power. The first three articles of the Constitution are the "distributing clauses," which define the basic legislative, executive, and judicial powers that are to be exercised by Congress, the president, and the judiciary, respectively.

Article I:
Legislative Power

Article I provides first that:

All legislative powers herein granted shall be vested in a Congress of the United States, which shall consist of a Senate and House of Representatives.

This clause insures that the *primary* legislative authority of the government will reside in a bicameral legislature. The framers of the Constitution recognized that Congress would be the lawmaking body for the nation, although they did delegate to the president veto power over congressional legislation, and the responsibility for recommending laws to Congress. Moreover, the president was given extensive explicit and implicit authority to make foreign policy. But there was no doubt that Congress was to be the supreme legislative body in the domestic sphere. Under constitutional doctrine developed by the courts, Congress can theoretically delegate its legislative authority to the executive and administrative branch only if it clearly states its legislative intent.

The bicameral structure was designed to provide checks and balances within the legislative body itself. The Senate was to act as a check upon the House, which was conceived to be more subject to the ill-considered whims of popular majorities. The representatives of the small states also viewed the Senate as an important federal body in which all states would have equal representation.

Term of Office and Method of Election. Members of the house were to be elected by the people for a term of two years, and those of the Senate were to be chosen by state legislatures for staggered six-year terms—one-third of the Senate is elected every two years.

The two-year term of office was designed to keep members of the House close to the electorate, while the six-year term of the Senate combined with the indirect election of its members was to give the upper body a more conservative and deliberative cast than the popularly elected House. The adoption of the Seventeenth Amendment in 1913 established the popular election of the Senate, but the longer term of office that gives senators a certain degree of protection from direct and constant popular pressures was not changed.

Apportionment of the House. The Constitution provides that: "The number of representatives shall not exceed one for every 30,000, but each state shall have at least one representative." Within this limitation the size of the House is determined by Congress itself, and is now set by law at 435 members. From the beginning, the House was to be apportioned according to the populations of the individual states. Article I, sec. 2 required a census to be taken every ten years and House apportionment to be changed accordingly as population shifted from one state to another. Nothing in the Constitution explicitly required congressional electoral districts to be equal in population, although the framers clearly supported the "one-person-one-vote" principle in general terms. The Three-fifths Compromise diluted voting equality among the states by giving the free inhabitants of slave states a proportionately greater voting strength than their compatriots in the free states, but the Three-fifths Compromise was reluctantly agreed to at the Philadelphia Convention only as a political necessity to save the Constitution.[3]

[3] The Three-fifths Compromise counted slaves as three-fifths of a person in the determination of a state's population, upon which its congressional representation was based.

Qualifications of Members of Congress. Members of both the House and the Senate must be citizens and residents of the states they represent. Representatives must be at least twenty-five years of age, while Senators are required to be at least thirty. The higher age requirement for the Senate was based in part upon the belief of many framers that age begets wisdom. The framers seriously discussed imposing property qualifications for members of Congress, but rejected the idea after extensive debate.

Article I, sec. 5 provides that: "Each house shall be the judge of the elections, returns and qualifications of its own members." Congress cannot extend qualifications for membership beyond those already specified in the Constitution, but can only judge whether or not its members meet the constitutional standards of citizenship, residency, and age.

The Power of Expulsion. Either branch of the national legislature may, under the terms of Article I, sec. 5, "punish its members for disorderly behavior, and, with the concurrence of two-thirds, expel a member." Expulsion may be for failure to meet constitutional qualifications, or for other reasons such as unethical behavior or criminal indictments and convictions. At the outset of the Civil War several Confederate members were expelled for treason, but Congress has otherwise seldom used this power. Most members faced with the

Constitutional Government

prospect of expulsion have resigned before such action was taken.

Congressional Organization and Procedures. Bicameralism is the major organizational feature created by the Constitution. It was established by providing different constituencies for the House and the Senate, the House to be the popular body and the Senate to represent the states. Moreover, the two branches of the legislature exercise different powers in some spheres. For example, the Senate has exclusive authority to advise and consent on treaties by the president with foreign governments, on presidential appointments of "public ministers," and other officials designated by Congress. The House has exclusive authority to originate legislation to raise revenue. The House may impeach civil officers, while the Senate has the ultimate power to convict impeached officials of "high crimes and misdemeanors."

Apart from bicameralism, the Constitution offers few details for congressional organization and procedures. Article I, sec. 2 provides that the House "shall choose their Speaker and other officers," making the Speaker a constitutional officer. In the upper body, the vice-president "shall be President of the Senate, but shall have no vote, unless they be equally divided" (Art. I, sec. 3). The Senate "shall choose their other officers, and also a President Pro Tempore in the absence of the Vice President, or when he shall exercise the office of President of the United States" (Art. I, sec. 3).

Other constitutional provisions require Congress to assemble each year, provide that a majority of each House shall constitute a quorum to do business, and prohibit either branch of the legislature from adjourning for more than three days during a session of Congress without the consent of the other, nor may either House adjourn "to any other place than that in which the two Houses shall be sitting" (Art. I, sec. 5).

Finally, Congress is required to keep an official journal of its proceedings. The journal is a record of bills and resolutions that have been introduced and votes that are taken. The yeas and nays of members must be recorded on any questions at the request of one-fifth of the members present. The journal is separate from the Congressional Record, which includes what is said on the floor of the House and the Senate and whatever matters members choose to put in it. The Record, which began in 1873, contains much of what is in the journal, but also a great deal of extraneous material from newpaper articles to birthday and anniversary congratulations to constituents.

Support and Protection of Congress. The framers of the Constitution provided that Senators and Representatives would be paid out of the federal treasury. The level of pay is to be determined by Congress itself. Many delegates argued against giving the legislature the authority to determine its own pay, but the alternative proposal at the Convention was to allow the states to determine the pay of their representatives. The nationalists, many of them reluctantly, supported the compensation provision of the Constitution because they recognized that state control over congressional pay would give state legislatures too much direct influence over their representatives.

In addition to supporting Congress by giving it the authority to determine its own compensation, the Constitution protects members by providing in Article I, sec. 6 that:

[Members of Congress] shall in all cases, except treason, felony, and breach of the peace, be privileged from arrest during their attendance at the sessions of their respective Houses, and in going to and returning from the same; and for any speech or debate in either House, they shall not be questioned in any other place.

The Constitution does not exempt congressmen from the legal obligations that pertain to other citizens, but merely protects them from arrest while they are attending congressional sessions, and from actions such as libel against them for what they say during the course of congressional proceedings or what they write in committee reports and other documents.

The Powers of Congress. Article I, sec. 8 enumerates the powers of Congress, the most important of which are the powers to lay and collect taxes, provide for the common defense and general welfare, and regulate commerce with foreign nations and among the states. Authors of the Constitution considered each of these powers critical to an effective national government, and over the years Congress has relied upon these provisions to vastly expand the power of the national government over that of the states.

After listing seventeen separate congressional powers, the Constitution gives the legislature the authority to make all laws "which shall be necessary and proper for carrying into execution the foregoing powers, and all other powers vested by this Constitution in the government of the United States, or in any department or officer thereof." The "necessary and proper," or "implied powers" clause, as this section of the Constitution is referred to, has been interpreted from the very beginning of the Republic to broaden the constitutional authority of Congress. The legislature is not limited to the *explicit* powers of Article I, but can exercise authority that derives from the enumerated powers to include whatever reasonable means Congress considers necessary to implement its powers.

Limitations on Congressional Powers. Article· I, sec. 9 provides that Congress cannot suspend the writ of habeas corpus "unless when in cases of rebellion or invasion the public safety may require it." Moreover, the legislature cannot pass a bill of attainder or ex post facto law.[4]

Other limits on Congress include the prohibition upon levying a capitation or other direct tax on individuals or property unless it is proportionately divided among the states in accordance with their populations or respective number of articles to be taxed. Congress is prohibited from taxing articles exported from any state, and the legislature cannot discriminate against particular states in the regulation of foreign and domestic commerce.

Limitations on the States. In order to facilitate the development of national power, the Constitution places both implicit and explicit limitations on the powers of the individual states. Implicitly, the states cannot pass laws which interfere with the exercise of national power under Article I; they may exercise concurrent legislative authority only insofar as their laws do not conflict with national law. Explicitly, the Constitution in

---

[4] A bill of attainder is a legislative act that convicts and punishes a person for committing a crime. An ex post facto law retroactively makes criminal an act which was not a crime when the act was committed, or which increases the punishment for a crime committed in the past beyond the punishment that existed at the time the act was committed.

Article I, sec. 10, prohibits the states from engaging in foreign relations, coining or printing money, and passing bills of attainder, ex post facto laws, or laws impairing the obligation of contracts. No state can lay duties or imposts on the imports or exports of another state "except what may be absolutely necessary for executing its inspection laws." States cannot keep troops, engage in war, or negotiate agreements or compacts with other states.

Article II: Executive Power

James Madison pointed out (*The Federalist*, 48) that under the Constitution the executive power was restrained within a narrower compass and was simpler in its nature than congressional power. Taken at face value, Article II is far more frugal than Article I: it simply vests the executive power in *one* president, to be chosen by electors from each state in proportion to their number of senators and representatives.

The president is required to be a natural-born citizen.

The office of vice-president was created to provide someone who could assume the duties of the presidency in the event of the removal of the president from office, or his death, resignation, or inability to discharge the powers and duties of the office.

Powers of the President. Article II says very little about the powers of the president, which seems especially surprising now that the presidency has become one of the most powerful and important institutions of the federal government. While they are few in number, the powers of Article II are in critical domestic and foreign policy areas.

First, all executive power is delegated to the president, who is to "take care that the laws be faithfully executed." This provision makes the president the chief executive, a responsibility that is further confirmed by his constitutional authority to nominate public ministers and executive officers—by and with the advice and consent of the Senate—and, if necessary, remove executive officials. The Senate may vest in the president sole authority to appoint temporary public officials. The authority of chief executive is an important prerogative power of the office that gives the president wide latitude to choose appropriate means to carry out the law.

Second, the principle of civilian control over the military was established by making the president commander-in-chief of the armed forces. This authority too has been broadly interpreted as a prerogative power of the president, who not only directs the armed forces but also may engage them in wars, or what are euphemistically termed "conflicts" or "police actions."

Third, the role of the president in foreign policymaking is derived from his authority to make treaties by and with the advice and consent of two-thirds of the Senate. In addition, the president appoints ambassadors and consuls subject to Senate confirmation. The president also receives foreign ambassadors. By implication, Article II makes the president chief of state, the representative of the nation abroad and at home in the performance of the ceremonial functions of government.

Finally, the Constitution delegates important legislative responsibilities to the president, not only by giving him the veto power over congressional laws, but also by directing him to recommend legislation to Congress and to give the legislature information on the state of the Union from time to time. Moreover, he may convene Congress on extraordinary occasions, and even adjourn the legislature in cases where the two houses do not agree on a time of adjournment (Art. II, sec. 3).

In summary, Article II establishes a uniquely American institution, a constitutional presidency with an independent constituency and potentially vast powers, but at the same time limited within the framework of the checks and balances system.

At the outset, Article III provides that:

Article III: Judicial Power

The judicial power of the United States, shall be vested in one Supreme Court, and in such inferior courts as the Congress may from time to time ordain and establish.

Judicial power is exercised under Article III by *constitutional* courts—that is, courts created under the terms of Article III and subject to its conditions. The Supreme Court is the only constitutional court required by Article III, although the framers definitely foresaw the creation of additional federal courts by Congress.

The prescribed conditions for federal courts under Article III limit judicial power to cases and controversies arising under the constitution, laws, and treaties. The federal courts cannot initiate cases.

Another important condition of Article III requires judges to have tenure during good behavior, and compensation that cannot be reduced during their continuance in office.

Article III states the original jurisdiction of the Supreme Court—that is, cases which go immediately to the Supreme Court for a decision. The original jurisdiction extends to cases affecting ambassadors, other public (foreign) ministers and consuls, and to cases in which a state is a party. In all other cases the Supreme Court is given appellate jurisdiction under regulations established by Congress.

Article IV: Interstate Relations

Article IV governs various aspects of interstate relations.

Full Faith and Credit. Each state must honor, or give full faith and credit, "to the public acts, records, and judicial proceedings of every other state." This provision requires states, for example, to honor divorce decrees, drivers' licenses, and court judgments of all kinds awarded or given by other states.

Privileges and Immunities. In addition to providing for full faith and credit among the states, the Constitution requires that the citizens "of each state shall be entitled to all privileges and immunities of citizens in the several states." States cannot grant their own citizens different privileges and immunities or fundamental rights from those granted to out-of-state citizens. For example, out-of-state citizens cannot be discriminatorily taxed, or denied access to state courts. Where fundamental rights are not jeopardized, however, states may grant privileges to their own citizens that are not accorded to out-of-state citizens—a state may require residency for voting, for example, and for attending state universities.

Constitutional Government

Extradition. A fugitive from justice in one state that is found in another state "shall on demand of the executive authority of the state from which he fled, be delivered up to be removed to the state having jurisdiction of the crime." Although fugitives are usually returned upon the request of the governor of the state in which the crime has been committed, under unusual circumstances extradition is sometimes refused. There is no formal method to compel a state to return a fugitive from justice.

New States. Congress is given the authority to admit new states to the Union, but no new state can be created within the jurisdiction of an existing state or formed from a combination of two or more states without the consent of the state legislatures involved as well as of Congress.

Guaranteeing Republican Government. The guaranty clause requires the United States to "guarantee to every state in this Union a republican form of government, and shall protect each of them against invasion; and on application of the legislature [of the state] or of the executive (when the legislature cannot be convened) against domestic violence." In the early years of the Republic, Congress delegated to the president the authority to send troops to protect states against domestic violence under the terms of this constitutional provision.

The Constitution establishes two methods of amendment. First, Congress may by a two-thirds vote in both houses propose amendments that are submitted to the states. In order for an amendment to be added to the Constitution, three-fourths of the state legislatures or conventions must approve it. All constitutional amendments that have been adopted have been proposed by Congress, and all but one have been submitted to the legislatures of the states. Only the Twenty-first Amendment, adopted in 1933, which repealed the Eighteenth Amendment (Prohibition), was ratified by state conventions.

Article V:
Amending
the Constitution

The second method of amending the Constitution, which has not yet been used, requires Congress, upon the application of two-thirds of the state legislatures, to call a special constitutional convention for proposing amendments which must then be ratified by two-thirds of the legislatures or conventions of the states.

Although twenty-six amendments have been added to the Constitution, many of them significantly changing its original provisions, more important constitutional change has occurred as a result of judicial interpretation and governmental practices. The ambiguity of many parts of the Constitution has provided great leeway for the courts, the president, and Congress in constitutional interpretation.

Article VI: The Supremacy Clause

The penultimate article of the Constitution is one of its most important:

> This Constitution, and the laws of the United States which shall be made in pursuance thereof; and all treaties made, or which shall be made, under the authority of the United States, shall be the supreme law of the land; and the judges in every state shall be bound thereby, any thing in the Constitution or the laws of any state to the contrary not withstanding.

The supremacy clause unequivocally binds state judges to the terms of the Constitution and requires them to respect the authority of the national government and constitutional prescriptions regarding the states. Within its sphere of action, the national government is supreme.

Article VII: Ratification of the Constitution

The framers of the Constitution carefully provided for its ratification by state conventions rather than state legislatures, recognizing that many state legislatures were dominated by advocates of states' rights who had vested interests in preserving state power. Article VII states that: "The ratification of the conventions of nine states, shall be sufficient for the establishment of this Constitution between the states so ratifying the same."

Perspectives on the Constitution. The theoretical underpinnings of the Constitution were forcefully and eloquently explained by Alexander Hamilton and James Madison in a series of essays that appeared in the newspapers of New York City between October 1787 and August 1788. Hamilton initiated the articles, which were written in the form of letters to the people of New York, and wrote 51 of the 85 essays that were published. James Madison wrote 26 essays, while John Jay, a prominent New York lawyer and political leader, who was to become the first Chief Justice of the Supreme Court, contributed five articles. Collectively the 85 essays were published in one volume entitled *The Federalist,* which, along with the debates of the Convention, became an authoritative source on the meaning of the Constitution.

The Constitution can be viewed from one of two broad perspectives. First, it can be seen as incorporating James Madison's explanation of the constitutional plan that he developed at the Convention and supported in *The Federalist.* Madison emphasized the importance of constitutional limits on government. Second, the Constitution can be interpreted from the strict Federalist perspective of Alexander Hamilton, who helped to shape it at the Convention and who described its grand design in *The Federalist.* Hamilton emphasized the importance of constitutional powers over the limits upon government. He viewed the Constitution as a device that would enable the government, particularly the president, to act forcefully in the national interest.

THE MADISONIAN MODEL OF CONSTITUTIONAL GOVERNMENT

The views James Madison gave in *The Federalist* on the meaning of the Constitution generally followed the positions he had taken at the Convention of 1787.

Throughout the Convention deliberations Madison stressed the importance of a government to be limited by law rather than controlled by popular actions. At the Convention session on 26 June 1787, Madison told his fellow delegates that the purposes of the Constitution were first, "to protect the people

Madison's Views
at the Constitutional
Convention

[5] Farrand, Records, 1:421.

[6] Ibid., pp. 421–22.

[7] Ibid., p. 422.

[8] Ibid.

[9] Ibid.

against their rulers, [and] secondly, to protect the people against the transient impressions into which they themselves might be led."[5] Madison stressed that citizens should always be aware of the possibility of the betrayal of their trust by government. He argued that an "obvious precaution against this danger would be to divide the trust between different bodies of men, who might watch and check each other. In this they would be governed by the same prudence which has prevailed in organizing the subordinate departments of government, where all business liable to abuses is made to pass through separate hands, the one being a check on the other."[6]

Madison went on to point out at the Convention that once the people have established checks and balances to prevent their government from betraying their trust, it "would next occur to such a people, that they themselves were liable to temporary errors, through want of information as to their true interests; and that men chosen for a short term, and employed but a small portion of that in public affairs, might err from the same cause. This reflection would naturally suggest, that the government be so constituted that one of its branches might have an opportunity of acquiring a competent knowledge of the public interests."[7] The Senate was to become the governmental branch that, because it was detached from direct popular control, would be able rationally to determine the national interest. It would not be swayed by temporary popular passions and demands for short-run opportunistic legislation. The Senate would not be controlled by the "fickelness and passion" that was liable to affect the House of Representatives. The "enlightened citizens" elected as senators would "seasonably interpose against impetuous counsels [that might otherwise rule the House of Representatives]."[8]

At the Convention, Madison declared that a political system which preserved liberty raised the danger of majority domination of the minority. The majority "might, under sudden impulses, be tempted to commit injustice on the minority."[9] Madison's discussion of this problem at the Convention was later to find expression in *The Federalist* (10), in which he examined the basis of faction and concluded that it could only be controlled by the kind of republican government estab-

Constitutional Government

lished in the Constitution. "In all civilized countries," Madison stated at the Convention, "the people fall into different classes, having a real or supposed difference of interests. There will be creditors and debtors; farmers, merchants, and manufacturers. There will be, particularly, the distinction of rich and poor."[10] Madison asked the Convention delegates: "How is this danger [of faction] to be guarded against, on the republican principles? How is the danger, in all cases of interested coalitions to oppress the minority, to be guarded against? Among other means, by the establishment of a body, in the government, sufficiently respectable for its wisdom and virtue to aid, on such emergencies, the preponderance of justice, by throwing its weight into that scale."[11] The Senate was to be the body with the wisdom necessary to prevent minority interests from being overwhelmed by majority interests. The wisdom of the Senate was to be cultivated not only by allowing its members freedom to deliberate rationally in an atmosphere unswayed by popular passions, but also by requiring its members to be older than the elected representatives of the House. Madison not only equated age with wisdom, but concluded that the members of the Senate should be in "such a period of life as would render a perpetual disqualification to be reelected, little inconvenient, either in a public or private view."[12]

In general, Madison stressed the need to balance a wide range of interests in government; no one interest was to dominate. Madison favored the advocacy of popular interests in the House of Representatives, and reluctantly accepted the interests of the states that would be defended in the Senate. Like most of the delegates at the Convention, he was concerned about the unbridled rule of the majority. He did not want the path of majority rule to be eased, but wanted to help create a governmental obstacle course that would restrain the majority from taking ill-considered, unjust, unfair action that would trample upon minority interests and rights.

Madison's suspicions of majority rule led him to warn the Convention about the inherently greater power of legislative bodies, particularly unicameral legislatures elected by the people, over other branches of the government. He strongly supported the separation of powers, arguing that the preser-

[10] Ibid.

[11] Ibid., p. 423.

[12] Ibid.

vation of liberty requires the separation of the legislative, executive, and judicial powers and a high degree of independence for each branch of the government. Madison particularly stressed the need to keep legislative and executive powers "distinct and independent of each other."[13]

Madison supported the separation of powers as an important mechanism for curbing the legislature. His fear that the natural domination of the legislative branch would tend to place the president and the judiciary in subordinate positions was one factor that prompted him to back a proposal for a Revisionary Council composed of the president and members of the Supreme Court which would review acts of the legislature and veto, subject to a legislative override, those laws found to be unwise or unconstitutional. Madison feared that in confrontations with the legislature the executive in the new republic would be inherently weak, since it would lack the support and respect accumulated in the history, customs, and traditions of monarchies such as Great Britain. The power of the president to veto acts of Congress would be given more weight and would be more likely to be upheld if the veto decision were a joint one with members of the Supreme Court. In the end, Congress could always override a veto, whether by the president or by a council of revision, but it would be less likely to do so if the legislation had been overturned by a joint presidential-judicial council.[14]

While the model of government supported by Madison at the Convention accentuated the need to balance powers among the national branches of the government, there was no doubt in Madison's mind that the national government should be strong in relation to the states. Madison was a committed nationalist, as were a majority of the delegates. The underlying purpose of the Convention was to adopt a plan of government that would correct the weaknesses of the Articles of Confederation, which had allowed the states to control and cripple the national government. The government of the Articles of Confederation was really no government at all. In evaluating the Madisonian perspective on the new government, it is important to keep in mind the essential nationalist thrust of Madison's views. Madison was con-

[13] Ibid., 2:35.

[14] Edmund Randolph of Virginia originally proposed the Council of Revision as part of the comprehensive Randolph plan for the Constitution that was laid before the delegates at the outset of the Convention. The proposal was: "Resolved, that the executive, and a convenient number of the national judiciary, ought to compose a Council of Revision, with authority to examine every act of the National Legislature, before it shall operate, and every act of a particular Legislature before a negative thereon shall be final; and that the dissent of the said Council shall amount to a rejection, unless the act of the National Legislature be again passed, or that of a particular Legislature be again negatived by—of the members of each branch." Ibid., 1:21.

cerned about unchecked popular rule, the protection of minority interests, and the prevention of demogogic government. At the same time he had an overriding concern that the institutions of government be capable of developing a national interest that would be independent of factions, and that would not yield to the centrifugal forces of state sovereignty.

During the Convention debates, while Madison was proclaiming the urgency of checks and balances at the national level, he was also voicing deep concerns about the potential power of the states to render the new national government impotent. He stressed the fact that "in spite of every precaution, the general government would be in perpetual danger of encroachments from the state governments."[15] Madison was a strong supporter of federalism as a device to *increase* the authority of the national government over the states. Under the federal form, the national government would be able to act *directly* upon citizens of the states within the sphere of national power. Although in *The Federalist* (No. 39) Madison had emphasized the importance of the constitutional balance between national and state powers, at the Convention he in fact worked diligently for a predominant national government. While he was warning the delegates about the natural superiority of legislatures that threatened a proper balance of powers among the branches of government at the national level, he supported delegating extensive authority to Congress over matters that previously had been within the jurisdiction of the states. He wanted Congress to be vested with a veto power over state laws, and argued for a strong national government to protect civil liberties and rights against incursions by the states. He argued the necessity of giving the national government powers that would enable it to provide "more effectually for the security of private rights, and the studied dispensation of justice. Interferences [by the states] with these were evils which had, more perhaps than anything else, produced this Convention. Was it to be supposed, that republican liberty could long exist under the abuses of it practised in some of the states?"[16] Madison was not proposing a separate bill of rights that would limit state action, but expansive national powers that would be exercised in the national inter-

[15] Farrand, *Records*, 1:356.

[16] Ibid., p. 134.

est to prevent political majorities in the states from trampling upon the rights of minorities.

The prevailing viewpoint among delegates to the Convention was that minority rights should be protected. Madison's views on this issue lend credibility to those who have argued that the Constitution was drafted by a political and economic elite concerned primarily with the protection of property interests against expropriation by the debtor classes.[17] Madison seemed particularly concerned about the distinctions between rich and poor, creditors and debtors, and property owners and nonowners as the basis of political factions that might lead to the disintegration of society. More particularly, he seemed to be concerned that property owners were in a minority whose interests would not be respected by the nonowner majority. But he was also concerned about one type of property-holding majority imposing its will upon other property owners. Madison asked, "What has been the source of those unjust laws complained of among ourselves? Has it not been the real or supposed interest of the major number? Debtors have defrauded their creditors. The landed interest has borne heavily on the mercantile interest. The holders of one species of property have thrown a disproportion of taxes on the holders of another species."[18]

The remedy for this problem, Madison argued at the Convention and later reiterated (*The Federalist*, 10), is to "enlarge the sphere [of government], and thereby divide the community into so great a number of interests and parties, that, in the first place, the majority will not be likely, at the same moment, to have a common interest separate from that of the whole, or of the minority; and in the second place, that in case they should have such an interest, they may not be so apt to unite in the pursuit of it."[19] Madison concluded that it was necessary "to frame a republican system on such a scale, and in such a form, as will control all the evils [of faction] which have been experienced."[20]

Madison's contributions to *The Federalist* repeated and refined the views he had expressed at the Convention. Though they added nothing new, they did explain in somewhat greater detail the premises upon which the Constitution was based and how the new national government was supposed to work.

[17] This is the major argument advanced by Charles A. Beard in *An Economic Interpretation of the Constitution* (New York: Macmillan, 1913). Beard argued that the Constitution was rigged to protect the interests of the framers in personal property, particularly public securities. For a critical comment upon Beard's work see Robert E. Brown, *Charles A. Beard and the Constitution: A Critical Analysis of An Economic Interpretation of the Constitution* (Princeton, N.J.: Princeton University Press, 1966).

[18] Farrand, *Records*, 1:135.

[19] Ibid., p. 136.

[20] Ibid.

Madison states the premise of the separation of powers in *The Federalist* (47) as follows: "The accumulation of all powers, legislative, executive, and judiciary, in the same hands, whether of one, a few, or many, or whether hereditary, self-appointed, or elective, may justly be pronounced the very definition of tyranny." Madison was quick to point out, however, that the principle of separation of powers did not require the three branches of the government to be absolutely independent of one another. Madison pointed out that Montesquieu, who had written about the need for a separation of powers in his famous political treatise, *Spirit of the Laws* (1748), and whose views were widely known and respected in eighteenth century America, did not mean that under the separation of powers the branches of government "ought to have no *partial agency* in, or no *control* over, the acts of each other. His meaning . . . can amount to no more than this, that where the *whole* power of one department is exercised by the same hands which possess the *whole* power of another department, the fundamental principles of a free constitution are subverted." Madison emphasized that the principle of the separation of powers, which had been so widely adopted in the new state constitutions, was not absolute, but permitted a sufficient degree of contact among the branches of government to sustain governmental checks and balances.

The principle of checks and balances was an essential component of the separation of powers. Each branch of the government was to possess adequate and sufficient *motives* to resist encroachment by coordinate branches. Madison emphasized in *The Federalist,* as he had previously stated at the Constitutional Convention, his opinion that the three branches of the government were not inherently equal in power. The legislature was inevitably the dominant branch, being the repository of a wide range of legislative authority that traditionally and customarily had been placed in its hands. Moreover, the legislature represented the people, who collectively had delegated their sovereign powers to it. Madison concluded that: "In a representative republic, where the executive magistracy is carefully limited, both in the extent and the duration of its power; and where the legislative [power] is exercised by an assembly, which is inspired by a supposed influence over the people, with an intrepid confidence in its own strength; which is sufficiently numerous to feel all the passions which actuate a multitude; yet not so numerous as to be incapable of pursuing the objects of its passions, by means which reason prescribes; it is against the enterprising ambition of this department, that the people ought to indulge all their jealousy and exhaust all their precautions" (*The Federalist*, 48). The natural tendency of legislative bodies is to extend their powers into spheres that properly should be reserved to the executive or judiciary.

Madison had expressed concern at the Convention about the potential weakness of executive power, and his writings in *The Federalist* accentuated his view that the natural limits upon both the executive and the judiciary would act automatically to curb encroachments from these sources upon each other or into the legislative sphere. The executive power, "being restrained within a narrower compass, and being more simple in its nature; and the judiciary being described by landmarks, still left uncertain, projects of usurpation by either of these departments would immediately betray and defeat themselves" (48). Madison did not foresee the possibility of an "imperial presidency" nor the likelihood of a Supreme Court that through its authority to exercise judicial review would become a super-legislature.

Madison's strong advocacy of the principle of bicameralism was an extension of his concern over the possibility of legislative encroachments upon coordinate branches. Moreover, as Madison had emphasized at the Convention, the bicameral legislature would serve the goals of dampening unwarranted actions by popular majorities, and would provide in the Senate a body that could uphold the national interest against the parochial demands of specialized groups that might temporarily find themselves in a political majority capable of dominating the House of Representatives.

Throughout Madison's discussion of the premises, means, and ends of government, there is an assumption that politics inevitably involves a quest for power by individuals and groups that may or may not serve the national interest. Madison, like most of the framers of the Constitution, believed in original political sin. Politicians were not to be trusted, and government could not be structured on the premise that those seeking power always possessed good political motives. It should be assumed that the political process would more often than not be used for selfish personal or group interests. In commenting upon the need for a separation of powers and checks and balances system, Madison declared that it "may be a reflection on human nature, that such devices should be necessary to control the abuses of government. But what is government itself, but the greatest of all reflections on human nature? If men were angels, no government would be necessary. If angels were to govern men, neither external nor internal controls on government would be necessary. In framing a government, which is to be administered by men over men, the great difficulty lies in this: You must first enable the government to control the governed; and in the next place, oblige it to control itself. A dependence on the people is, no doubt, the primary control on the government; but experience has taught mankind the necessity of auxiliary precautions" (*The Federalist,* 51).

Madison also reiterated his nationalism in his contributions to *The Federalist.* His support of the separation of powers and checks and balances system to provide internal governmental checks among the three branches did not imply a weak national government overall, particularly in relation to the states. To placate the fears of proponents of state power, Madison stressed perhaps more than he believed the limits upon the new national government relative to the powers of the states: "The adversaries to the plan of the Convention, instead of considering in the first place what degree of power was absolutely necessary for the purposes of the federal government, have exhausted themselves in a secondary inquiry into the possible consequences of the proposed degree of power to the governments of the particular states" (*The Federalist,* 45). Madison went on to point out, however, that the states have nothing to fear from the reach of national power. The states exercise direct sovereignty over their people within their own spheres, and naturally have more popular support than the national government. The state governments "may be regarded as constituent and essential parts of the federal government; whilst the latter is nowise essential to the operation or organization of the former. Without the intervention of the state legislatures, the President of the United States cannot be elected at all." Moreover, the number of individuals employed by the national government "will be much smaller than the number employed under the particular states. There will consequently be less of personal influence on the side of the former than of the latter." The "powers delegated by the proposed constitution to the federal government are few and defined. Those which are to remain in the state governments are numerous and indefinite." The powers of the national government will be most extensive during times of war and of danger. During peacetime the states will tend to predominate. Madison pointed to all of these reasons to assure the readers of *The Federalist* that the states would have nothing to fear from the national government, but that the national government might very well be subject to state domination.

While Madison was attempting in *The Federalist* to soothe the opposition to a strong national government, he supported the wide-ranging powers that had been delegated to Congress in Article I. He, like Hamilton, backed national control of commerce, taxation, and the armed forces. Madison joined the other nationalists at the Constitutional Convention in support of granting to the national government all of the authority that was required to meet the exigencies of the Union. All of the powers that the Constitution had granted to the national government were, according to Madison, necessary and proper to preserve the Union. In *The Federalist,* he discussed the war power at length, supporting the "indefinite power of raising troops, as well as providing fleets; and of maintaining both in peace as well as in war" (41). He advocated the complete power of the national government to regulate foreign commerce and commerce among the states (*The Federalist,* 42). The power of raising revenue through taxation and borrowing money, he argued, had "been clearly shown to be necessary , both in the extent and form given to it by the Constitution" (*The Federalist,* 41). As Madison continued his review in *The Federalist* of each power that had been delegated to the national government, he pointed out why it was necessary to achieving the goal of Union.

Madison concluded his discussion of the powers granted to Congress by Article I with an analysis of the final clause of that article, which delegates to Congress the authority to "make all laws which shall be necessary and proper for carrying into execution the foregoing powers, and all other powers vested by this Constitution in the government of the United States, or in any department or officer thereof." Madison wrote: "Few parts of the Constitution have been assailed with more intemperance than this [necessary and proper clause]; yet on a fair investigation of it, as has been elsewhere shown, no part can appear more completely invulnerable. Without the *substance* of this power, the whole Constitution would be a dead letter" (*The Federalist,* 44). Madison declared that even if the Constitution had not contained such a clause, "there can be no doubt that all the particular powers requisite as means of executing the general powers would have resulted to the government by unavoidable implication. No axiom is more clearly established in law, than that wherever the end is required, the means are authorized; wherever a general power to do a thing is given, every particular power necessary for doing it is included."

A careful reading of Madison's views at the Convention and in *The Federalist* reveals that the Madisonian model is one of internal governmental limits and checks on the one hand, and of extensive national powers over the states on the other. Madison wanted a national government that would be forced to operate with restraint in response to the temporary and passionate demands of popular majorities advancing their own interests at the expense of minority rights and interests. But he also wanted a national government that had the incentive and capability to act swiftly, rationally, and with firmness to advance the national interest.

THE HAMILTONIAN MODEL OF THE CONSTITUTION

The Constitution, viewed from a Hamiltonian perspective, considers the separation of powers more important a buttress for the strength of the presidency and the Supreme Court than as a source of checks and balances among the three branches of government. Differences between the Madisonian and Hamiltonian models of government derived from the Constitution are ones of degree rather than kind, but nevertheless reflect important contrasting opinions on the way in which the government under the Constitution is supposed to work. Hamilton emphasized the importance of executive power, and stressed the significance of the independence of the Supreme Court and its implicit authority to overrule acts of Congress. He saw the separation of powers as expanding rather than limiting executive power, on the basis of the independent authority and constituency given to the president.

At the Constitutional Convention Hamilton particularly stressed the inherent power of the states, which could only be balanced by a constitutional framework that granted adequate powers to the national government and created an effective executive.

Hamilton declared in his major opening address to the Convention that an effective government must be based upon certain principles and a recognition of the incentives of politics. There must be an "active and constant interest in supporting" a national government, a principle that would be difficult to attain because of the high degree of esprit de corps that existed in the states that backed state sovereignty.[21] The states "constantly pursue internal interests adverse to those of the whole. They have their particular debts, their particular plans of finance, etc. All of these, when opposed to, invariably prevail over, the requisitions and plans of Congress [under the Articles of Confederation]."[22] There must be a "habitual attachment of the people" to government, and the "whole force of this tie is on the side of the state government. Its sovereignty is immediately before the eyes of the people; its protection is immediately enjoyed by them."[23]

A viable government, he continued, must possess the necessary force, by which he meant "a coercion of laws or coercion of arms," to impose its will upon the people and to deal with challenges from foreign powers. Government also requires influence, "a dispensation of those regular honors and emoluments which produce an attachment to the government."[24] Hamilton felt at the time of the Constitutional Con-

[21] Farrand, *Records,* 1:284.

[22] Ibid.

[23] Ibid.

[24] Ibid., p. 285.

Constitutional Government

vention that all of the influence stemming from government resided in the hands of the states.

Hamilton emphasized that the underlying incentive of politics was the "love of power." Because men love power, it would be particularly difficult to persuade the states to delegate the powers they already retained to a new national government.[25] Somehow, he felt, the new national government must be given the requisite powers to establish, preserve, and develop the union.

[25] Ibid., p. 284.

Hamilton strongly advocated the creation of an executive that would be independent of the legislature, in terms of both executive powers and mode of election. At the outset Hamilton derided the Patterson, or New Jersey, plan for the new Constitution that essentially would have continued the dominance of Congress and the states that had existed under the Articles of Confederation. The Patterson plan, like the Randolph or Virginia plan, provided for the election of the executive by Congress, for a term that would not be renewable. The Patterson plan thus went farther than the Articles of Confederation by at least creating an executive. One of the major defects of the Articles had been their lack of an executive, with all authority residing in a Congress in which each state had an equal vote. Hamilton objected to the provisions in both the Patterson and Randolph plans that required legislative election of the president. But more importantly, Hamilton opposed the dominant Congress and its control by the states that would have resulted from the Patterson plan. Under that plan, no independent powers were given to the president and each state had an equal vote in Congress, as it had under the Articles of Confederation.

Hamilton proposed a national government with wide powers over the states, with a Congress, president, and judiciary that would not be subject to state domination. Commenting upon the Patterson plan, Hamilton noted that the general power of the national government, "whatever be its form, if it preserves itself, must swallow up the state powers. Otherwise, it will be swallowed up by them."[26] Not only must the national government have extensive powers, but to execute them effectively it must have an independent and powerful execu-

[26] Ibid., p. 287.

tive. Hamilton declared: "It is against all the principles of a good government, to vest the requisite [national] powers in such a body as Congress. Two sovereignties cannot co-exist within the same limits. Giving powers to Congress must eventuate in a bad government, or in no government."[27]

At the Convention Hamilton boldly proposed at least the possibility of eliminating the states altogether and the creation of a unitary form of government in which all constitutional power would reside in the hands of the national government. If the state governments were "extinguished," argued Hamilton, he was "persuaded that great economy might be obtained by substituting a general government."[28] Hamilton "did not mean, however, to shock the public opinion by proposing such a measure. On the other hand, he saw no *other* necessity for declining. They [the states] are not necessary for any of the great purposes of commerce, revenue, or agriculture."[29]

Hamilton unabashedly declared that "the British government was the best in the world," and he "doubted much whether anything short of it would do in America."[30] The unified system of government that prevailed in Great Britain, with all constitutional authority originally residing in the hands of the central government, dealt effectively with the problem of faction. The checks and balances of the British government, declared Hamilton, adequately protected minority interests against the incursions from the majority. The bicameral Parliament reflected a balance of interests, and the hereditary monarchy bolstered the authority of the executive, which at the time Hamilton wrote consisted both of the king and the cabinet elected by the Parliament. Hamilton extolled the virtues of the hereditary monarchy as characteristic of executive power in Great Britain even though the prime minister and the cabinet had become the dominant executive force since the Glorious Revolution of 1688.

Hamilton argued before the Convention that no good executive "could be established on republican principles."[31] Hamilton stressed that there could be no good government without a good executive. Further, the "English model was the only good one on this subject. The hereditary interest of the king was so interwoven with that of the nation, and his personal emolument so great, that he was placed above the

---

[27] Ibid.

[28] Ibid.

[29] Ibid.

[30] Ibid., p. 288.

[31] Ibid., p. 289.

Constitutional Government

danger of being corrupted from abroad; and at the same time was both sufficiently independent and sufficiently controlled, to answer the purpose of the institution [of the executive] at home."[32]

To establish firm leadership at the national level, Hamilton wanted a Senate that would be elected for life, or at least during good behavior, and an executive who would serve for life. Any lesser term for the executive, particularly one as short as the seven years being proposed at the Convention, would give the chief executive an incentive to devote his time primarily to political machinations to preserve and extend his power, particularly to secure his reelection. Not permitting the reelection of the president would, in Hamilton's view, create a weakness in the office that would be intolerable. A lifetime executive would not forget his responsibility to uphold the national interest, and "will therefore be a safer depository of power. It will be objected, probably, that such an executive will be an *elective monarch,* and will give birth to the tumults which characterize that form of government."[33] Hamilton argued that under certain circumstances elective monarchies were the best form of government, and he proposed that the executive authority of the national government "be vested in a governor, to be elected to serve during good behavior; the election to be made by electors chosen by the people in the election districts aforesaid."[34] Hamilton's plan provided:

The authorities and functions of the executive to be as follows: to have a negative on all laws about to be passed, and the execution of all laws passed; to have the direction of war when authorized or begun; to have, with the advice and approbation of the Senate, the power of making all treaties; to have the sole appointment of the heads or chief officers of the departments of finance, war, and foreign affairs; to have the nomination of all other officers (ambassadors to foreign nations included), subject to the approbation or rejection of the Senate; to have the power of pardoning all offenses except treason, which he shall not pardon without the approbation of the Senate.[35]

Hamilton also proposed a lifetime Senate to serve during good behavior and to be elected from districts within the states by the people rather than by state legislatures. He did not specify the number of senators to represent each state in

[32] Ibid.

[33] Ibid., p. 290.

[34] Ibid., p. 292.

[35] Ibid.

his original plan. Hamilton clearly saw the Senate as the most important body of the national legislature, and specified powers that it was to exercise exclusively, particularly in the area of foreign affairs where it was given the sole power to declare war, and the power to approve of treaties. Hamilton also would have given the Senate "the power of approving or rejecting all appointments of officers, except the heads or chiefs of the departments of finance, war, and foreign affairs."[36]

Hamilton proposed the "supreme judicial authority to be vested in judges, to hold their offices during good behavior, with adequate and permanent salaries."[37] While Madison was later to proclaim the authority of the Supreme Court to overturn acts of Congress, that provision was not part of his proposal at the Constitutional Convention.

Hamilton left no doubt about his belief that the national government should be supreme over the states. He wanted a national government that would be more capable of acting quickly and efficiently than that supported by Madison. The separation of powers and checks and balances devices were less important to Hamilton as internal regulators than they were to Madison. Madison was a strong nationalist, and he, too, unequivocally backed the supremacy of the national government; Hamilton, however, spelled out national supremacy even more explicitly. Hamilton's plan concluded with the provision: "All laws of the particular states contrary to the Constitution or laws of the United States to be utterly void; and the better to prevent such laws being passed, the governor or president of each state shall be appointed by the general government, and shall have a negative upon the laws about to be passed in the state of which he is the governor or president."[38]

As the drafting of the Constitution proceeded, Hamilton's influence was particularly important in forging a presidency independent of the legislature and possessed of significant prerogative powers. It was Hamilton's idea to establish an electoral college to select the president, composed of electors that would be separate from members of state legislatures. The final plan of the Convention provided for the appointment of presidential electors in accordance with the directions

[36] Ibid.

[37] Ibid.

[38] Ibid., p. 293.

Constitutional Government

of the state legislatures, to be equal for each state to the number of senators and representatives it had in Congress. Until the very end of the Convention the recommendation of the Randolph plan that the president be chosen by the Congress looked as if it might be accepted by the majority; with the help of others, however, Hamilton turned the tide in favor of an independently elected president. Although Hamilton's recommendation for a lifetime presidency was not given serious consideration by the other delegates, proposals for the limitation of the term of the presidency to a set number of years—usually seven—were ultimately defeated. Hamilton could at least take comfort in the fact that while Article II limited the president to a term of four years, the president could be reelected for a succession of terms without limitation. A president with long tenure was at least a possibility, which gave the executive a potential degree of permanency that Hamilton supported.

Perhaps the best synthesis of Hamilton's views on the separation of powers can be found in his discussions in *The Federalist* of the presidency (70) and of the Supreme Court (78).

The Hamiltonian Perspective on the Separation of Powers

Hamilton opened his discussion of the separation of powers by referring to a point he had made at the Convention: "There is an idea, which is not without its advocates, that a vigorous executive is inconsistent with the genius of republican government. The enlightened well-wishers to this species of government must at least hope that the supposition is destitute of foundation; since they can never admit its truth, without, at the same time, admitting the condemnation of their own principles." Hamilton then went on to state the fundamental premise of his model of government: "Energy in the executive is a leading character in the definition of good government. It is essential to the protection of the community against foreign attacks; it is not less essential to the steady administration of the laws, to the protection of property against those irregular and high-handed combinations, which sometimes interrupt the ordinary course of justice, to the security of liberty against the enterprises and assaults of ambition, of faction, and of anarchy." Hamilton found that the "ingredients which constitute energy in the executive are: unity; duration; and adequate provision for its support; competent powers." And, the "ingredients which constitute safety in the republican sense are: a due dependence on the people; a due responsibility." The Constitution, largely because of Hamilton's own efforts, provided for both an energetic and responsible executive. The unity of the presidency, its independent powers, and indirect popular election that did not depend upon Congress guaranteed that it would possess the attributes of energy and safety which Hamilton sought. While Madison considered the separation of powers to be a critical check upon ill-advised popular majorities and the evil effects of faction, Hamilton saw in the powerful presidency which he considered the separation of powers to have established the answer to good government and control of faction. Not only could the president check the legislature through his veto power, but he also could take independent action to advance the national interest.

The Scope of
National Power in
the Hamiltonian Model

Hamilton, like Madison, advocated wide national power over the states. Hamilton carried his argument favoring the subordination of the states to the national government farther than any of the other delegates to the convention, as can be observed in his recommendation that it would be a good idea to eliminate the states altogether. Recognizing that the states were and would remain formidable powers, Hamilton stressed the importance of granting to the federal government the broadest authority that was politically feasible to achieve the purposes of the Union.

Hamilton was the precursor of Chief Justice John Marshall in backing a "loose construction" of the powers that the Constitution had delegated to the national government. Hamilton was one of the original federalists who championed the unequivocal supremacy of the national government over the states. Madison, too—who was to become a leader of the Jeffersonian or Republican party and its first president—agreed with Hamilton that the powers of the national government should be broadly interpreted. The differences between the two men on the reach of national powers over the states were insignificant, especially in comparison to their diverging interpretations of the separation of powers.

Hamilton interpreted the enumerated powers of Congress to be *unlimited* within their respective spheres. For example, the power granted in Article I to raise and support armies and provide for the national defense implied the absolute authority of Congress to take whatever measures it considered necessary to achieve the common defense. Hamilton wrote:

> The authorities essential to the common defense are these: to raise armies, to build and equip fleets; to prescribe rules for the government of both; to direct their operation; to provide for their support. These powers ought to exist without limitation, *because it is impossible to foresee or to define the extent and variety of national exigencies, and the correspondent extent and variety of the means which may be necessary to satisfy them.* The circumstances that endanger the safety of nations are infinite, and for this reason no constitutional shackles can wisely be imposed on the power to which the care of it is committed.[39]

[39] *The Federalist*, 23.

Hamilton emphasized that Congress must possess the necessary means to carry out all of the enumerated powers. This would be true, Hamilton stressed, even in the absence of the implied powers or necessary and proper clause of Article I. Hamilton did not view Congress as different from the other branches of the national government in terms of the reach of their powers over the states. The powers the Constitution granted to each of the three branches of the government, he argued, were complete, and implied the means for their execution. A strong Congress, an energetic executive, and an independently powerful Supreme Court are all necessary to an effective national government capable of acting in the national interest. Each of the branches of the government must be given "the most ample authority for fulfilling objects committed to its charge."[40]

[40] Ibid.

"A government," concluded Hamilton, "the constitution of which renders it unfit to be trusted with all the powers which a free people *ought to delegate to any government,* would be an unsafe and improper depository of the *national interests.*"[41]

[41] Ibid.

Since Hamilton viewed all of the powers delegated by the Constitution to the national government as intrinsically containing the means of their execution, he considered the necessary and proper clause to be essentially redundant. He asked: "What is a power but the ability or faculty of doing a thing? What is the ability to do a thing but a power of employing the *means* necessary to its execution?" (*The Federalist,* 33). All delegated powers include the authority to take the necessary and proper action to carry them out. Why, then, was the necessary and proper clause included as part of Article I? "The answer," stated Hamilton, "is that it could only have been done for greater caution, and to guard against all cavilling refinement in those who might hereafter feel a disposition to curtail and evade the legitimate authority of the Union."[42] Hamilton then asked, "Who is to judge of the necessity and propriety of the laws to be passed for executing the powers of the Union?" The national government "must judge, in the first instance, of the proper exercise of its powers, and its constituents in the last period. If the federal government should overpass the just bounds of its authority and make a tyrannical use of its powers, the people, whose creature it is, must appeal to the standard they have formed, and take such measures to redress the injury done to the Constitution as the exigency may suggest and prudence justify."[43]

Hamilton's arguments for expansive and complete national powers were raised in a practical context in 1791 after Congress had passed its first legislation creating a national bank. Nothing could be dearer to Hamilton's heart than a national bank. Washington had appointed him to be the first secretary of the treasury, a position he held with relish, and which he considered made him responsible for the financial stability of the new republic.[44] After Congress passed the bank legislation, President George Washington, apparently doubtful of its constitutionality, requested the views of Hamilton and Jefferson on the matter. Predictably, there was no doubt in Hamilton's mind that the law was constitutional. Reiterating the views he had previously expressed in *The Federalist* and applying them to the legislation, Hamilton wrote to the President:

. . . It is conceded that *implied powers* are to be considered as delegated equally with *expressed ones*. Then it follows, that as a power of erecting a corporation may as well be *implied* as any other

---

[42] *The Federalist,* 33.

[43] Ibid.

[44] The Treasury Department building at the White House end of Pennsylvania Avenue is guarded by a statue of Alexander Hamilton, whose stern countenance serves as a reminder to those within that they should act responsibly and conservatively to protect the solvency and credibility of the nation in financial affairs.

Constitutional Government

thing, it may as well be employed as an *instrument* or *means* of carrying into execution any of the specified powers, as any other *instrument* or *means* whatever. The only question must be in this, as in every other case, whether the means to be employed, or, in this instance the corporation to be erected, has a natural relation to any of the acknowledged objects or lawful ends of the government. Thus a corporation may not be directed by Congress for superintending the police of the city of Philadelphia, because they are not authorized to *regulate* the *police* of that city. But one may be erected in relation to the collection of taxes, or to the trade with foreign nations, or to the trade between the states, or with the Indian tribes; because it is the province of the federal government to *regulate* those objects, and because it is incident to a general *sovereign* or *legislative* power to *regulate* a thing, to employ all the means which relate to its regulation to the best and greatest advantage.[45]

In contrast to Hamilton, Jefferson took the strict constructionist stance in his letter to the President:

I considered the foundation of the Constitution as laid on this ground: That "all powers not delegated to the United States, by the Constitution, nor prohibited by it to the states, are reserved to the states or to the people. . . . To take a single step beyond the boundaries thus specially drawn around the powers of Congress, is to take possession of a boundless field of power, no longer susceptible of any definition.

The incorporation of a bank, and the powers assumed by this bill, have not, in my opinion, been delegated to the United States by the Constitution.[46]

Jefferson narrowly interpreted the constitutional powers of the national government, finding nowhere in Article I the explicit or implied authority to incorporate a national bank.

Hamilton's views prevailed in 1791 when George Washington agreed with him on the constitutionality of the legislation and signed the bill creating the first bank of the United States. With the help of the early Federalist Supreme Court led by Chief Justice John Marshall, it was the Hamiltonian position that prevailed overall in constitutional interpretation.

[45] Gerald Gunther, *Cases and Materials on Constitutional Law*, 9th ed. (Mineola, N.Y.: The Foundation Press, Inc., 1975), p. 101.

[46] Ibid., p. 100.

CONCLUSION

The ebb and flow of politics throughout American history has reflected and emphasized the contrasting approaches to government taken by Madison and Hamilton. The long-term political trend favors the strong and independent Hamiltonian presidency, capable in times of crisis of rising above the limiting effects of the separation of powers to govern in the national interest effectively and with dispatch. The "imperial presidency," which stresses the importance of the prerogative powers of the president over checks and balances, and the need for cooperation with Congress, is distinctly Hamiltonian in character. Times of crisis in American history have produced presidents that have acted independently to deal with national crises. Presidents Abraham Lincoln, Woodrow Wilson, and Franklin D. Roosevelt, for example, established important precedents for vigorous and independent presidential actions, precedents that later were followed by presidents such as Harry S. Truman, Lyndon B. Johnson, and Richard M. Nixon.

The same separation of powers that has produced independent and powerful presidents has also forged a political system characterized by checks and balances that has, on occasion, even stalemated governments. Even the strongest presidents have been frustrated by an assertive Congress.

The survival of the nation and the supremacy of the national government were goals strongly supported by Hamilton and Madison. The flexibility of the Constitution they helped to draft has provided a basis for forceful presidential action to meet national crises, at the same time that it has established checks and balances which have prevented the president from becoming a constitutional dictator. In the long run, it has served the broad purposes of constitutional democracy—effective but limited government.

Suggestions for Further Reading

Beard, Charles A. *An Economic Interpretation of the Constitution.* New York: Macmillan, 1913. In this controversial work, the author argues that the Constitution was written by an economic elite to protect its financial interests.

Ferrand, Max. *The Framing of the Constitution of the United States.* New Haven: Yale University Press, 1913. A brief work covering the highlights of the Philadelphia Convention by the editor of the definitive volumes on the Convention proceedings that feature Madison's Notes.

Hamilton, Alexander; Madison, James; and Jay, John. *The Federalist Papers*. New York: New American Library, 1961. Originally published as newspaper articles in 1787–88. The best current edition of *The Federalist* is that by Clinton Rossiter.

Rossiter, Clinton. *1787: The Grand Convention*. New York: Macmillan, 1956. A lucid writer provides an absorbing account of the Philadelphia Convention and the subsequent ratification campaign.

Wills, Garry. *Inventing America*. Garden City, N.Y.: Doubleday, 1978. An innovative and challenging account of the origins of the Declaration of Independence.

————. *Explaining America: The Federalist*. Garden City, N.Y.: Doubleday, 1981. The author gives his view of the "real" Madison, stressing the Virginian's support of a strong national government.

Citizens have the right to speak, write, and associate freely to express their beliefs.

CHAPTER 2

Civil Liberties and Civil Rights Under the Constitution

The Bill of Rights, which every citizen now takes for granted, was not part of the original Constitution of 1787. Its omission did not mean that the delegates to the Convention considered civil liberties and civil rights to be of minor importance; quite the contrary was the case. The men who drafted the Constitution assumed the existence of inalienable civil liberties and civil rights, and many believed these rights to be based upon a natural law that was superior to the laws of men. Theoretical considerations aside, all of the delegates had been molded in one way or another by the Anglo-American legal tradition which up to the time of the writing of the Constitution had strongly emphasized the importance of independent rights and liberties of citizens that could not be curtailed by government.

The framers of the Constitution, like all American colonists, assumed that the rights of Englishmen did not stop at the borders of Great Britain, but followed them to the shores of America. The delegates to the Convention of 1787 could cite chapter and verse from the Magna Charta of 1215, the English Bill of Rights of 1689, and the numerous common law precedents that upheld the rights and liberties of citizens. It was the assumption of the existence of pervasive civil liberties and civil rights possessed by all citizens that made the addition of a separate Bill of Rights to the Constitution seem redundant, superfluous, and even dangerous because it would imply a national authority to curtail rights and liberties that were not specifically included in the Bill of Rights.

The subject of civil liberties and rights was rarely mentioned during the debates at the Constitutional Convention in 1787. Because they assumed the existence of broad rights and liberties of citizens, the delegates did not think it necessary to make explicit that which was already implied. Moreover, the rights and obligations of citizens of the states in relation to their state governments was a matter to be resolved by state political processes and constitutions.

Significantly, the new state constitutions that were written during the revolutionary period did not uniformly contain explicit protections of civil liberties and civil rights. The political leaders who drafted the state constitutions, like the delegates to the national convention, often did not see a need to protect expressly rights and liberties which were taken for granted. Only seven of the new state constitutions contained separate bills of rights. Six states incorporated various rights in the main bodies of their constitutions.

The Virginia Bill of Rights, drafted by George Mason, preceded the Declaration of Independence and included the fundamental right of revolution in addition to the more traditional Anglo-American rights and liberties. The state constitutions, whether in separate bills of rights or incorporated in their general provisions, collectively contained wide-ranging rights and liberties that later were used as reference points in drafting the Bill of Rights, as well as in those provisions of the Constitution itself which protected rights, such as the prohibition upon the suspension of the writ of habeas corpus unless required by a national emergency. The state constitutions contained such rights and liberties as the freedoms of speech and press, and the rights of assembly and petition, all of which became part of the First Amendment. Each provision of the national Bill of Rights had one or more precedents in the state constitutions.

CIVIL RIGHTS IN THE ORIGINAL CONSTITUTION

The provisions in the Constitution that guarantee civil rights include the protection against the suspension of the writ of habeas corpus and the prohibitions upon ex post facto laws and bills of attainder.[1] In Article III, sec. 2, the Constitution provides for jury trials "of all crimes," and that "such trials shall be held in the state where the said crimes shall have been committed." This section guarantees the right to a jury trial to persons accused of crime by the *national* government.

As fundamental as were the protections of civil rights contained in the original provisions of the Constitution pertaining to habeas corpus, bills of attainder, ex post facto laws, and jury trials, they were not all included without some debate. The framers agreed without dissent on the importance of the writ of habeas corpus and the right to a jury trial. The only debate over the habeas corpus provision concerned whether or not the Constitution should authorize suspension under any circumstances. It was Gouverneur Morris of Pennsylvania who moved the Constitutional provision allowing for suspension in cases of rebellion or invasion, which passed on a state vote of seven to three. There was little debate over the jury trial provision, although several delegates wanted the right to a jury trial extended to civil as well as criminal cases.

Massachusetts delegate Elbridge Gerry introduced the motion to prohibit Congress from passing bills of attainder or ex post facto laws. There was no objection to the prohibition upon bills of attainder, which passed unanimously, but the proscription upon ex post facto laws received only a seven to three state vote in favor. Some delegates thought the ex post facto proscription would be confusing unless it was explicitly limited to criminal law, although by common usage such a limitation was already implied. The most interesting argument against the ex post facto law prohibition was that of Pennsylvania delegate James Wilson, who later was to argue before the Pennsylvania ratifying convention that a separate bill of rights was entirely unnecessary. His arguments at the Constitutional Convention against the inclusion of the ex post facto clause suggested the position he later would take in opposition to a separate bill of rights. He told the Convention that inserting anything in the Constitution regarding ex post facto laws "will bring reflections on the Constitution, and proclaim that we are ignorant of the first principles of legislation, or are constituting a government that will be so."[2] Wilson felt that it should be assumed that ex post facto laws

[1] The *writ of habeas corpus* is a court order to an arresting officer requiring the defendant to be brought before the court and a statement of why the defendant is being held in custody. Although the Constitution authorizes the suspension of the writ of habeas corpus in cases of rebellion or invasion where the public safety requires it, congressional laws or presidential actions suspending the writ are subject to judicial review. A *bill of attainder* is legislation that convicts and punishes a person. An *ex post facto law* retroactively makes a particular act a crime that was not a crime when it was committed, or subsequent to the commission of a crime increases the punishment for it. Ex post facto laws by definition impose *criminal* penalties. Retroactive civil laws are not prohibited by the Article I, sec. 9 proscription upon ex post facto laws.

[2] Farrand, *Records*, 2:376.

were unconstitutional. Connecticut delegate Oliver Ellsworth agreed with Wilson, asserting that "there was no lawyer, no civilian, who would not say, that ex post facto laws were void of themselves. It cannot, then, be necessary to prohibit them."[3] The major argument that was later to be used against the ratification of the Bill of Rights was essentially the same as those of Wilson and Ellsworth against the ex post facto provision—that it made the framers of the Constitution look foolhardy because they were stating the obvious. What kind of men would insert into the Constitution the protection of rights that everyone knew already existed? Surely, in the view of James Wilson and others, such a course of action by the delegates would reduce their credibility and that of the Constitution among the states whose support was crucial to the success of the new plan of government.

The Convention never seriously considered the addition of rights beyond those few it inserted, nor was the need for a separate bill of rights seriously contemplated. South Carolina delegate Charles Pinckney, who was one of the younger and more active members of the Convention, but who does not seem to have had a great deal of influence, introduced his own plan to the Convention after Edmund Randolph had submitted his proposal. Under the Pinckney plan: "The legislature of the United States shall pass no law on the subject of religion; nor touching or abridging the liberty of the press; nor shall the privilege of the writ of habeas corpus ever be suspended, except in cases of rebellion or invasion."[4] The Pinckney plan was never taken seriously by the Convention. Unlike the Randolph plan, Pinckney's proposals, many of which overlapped those of Randolph, were not considered and voted upon by the delegates. The Pinckney plan is the only mention of freedom of the press in the Convention deliberations, and the only proposal to bar the national government from passing a law on the subject of religion.

A brief discussion of the possibility of adding a separate bill of rights took place during the waning days of the Convention. Virginia delegate George Mason, an articulate member of his delegation who ended up being dissatisfied with the final plan and voting against it for what he considered an excessive concentration of power in the hands of the national

[3] Ibid.

[4] Ibid., 3:599.

Civil Liberties and Civil Rights Under the Constitution

government, proposed that a bill of rights be drafted based upon the rights contained in state constitutions. His motion was seconded by Elbridge Gerry. Connecticut delegate Roger Sherman expressed the feelings of a majority of the delegates when he briefly responded to Mason's proposal for a separate bill of rights by declaring that the state declarations of rights were entirely sufficient, and that there was no reason to distrust the national legislature. Mason responded that the "laws of the United States are to be paramount to state bills of rights."[5] The proposal for a separate bill of rights failed on a five to five state vote, with Massachusetts recorded as absent.[6]

The failure of the framers of the Constitution to include a separate bill of rights, which was barely discussed during the Convention proceedings, caused concern among some of the political leaders in the states. After all, the states had in their own constitutions extensively set forth the rights of their citizens. Why should not the federal government do the same? Opponents of the Constitution used the lack of a separate bill of rights as an argument against its adoption, and even proponents of the Constitution suggested that it would be wise to add a bill of rights.

Thomas Jefferson, who strongly supported the Constitution, nevertheless felt that the omission of a bill of rights was a major deficiency in it. Writing to James Madison shortly after the Constitution had been sent to the states for ratification, Jefferson stressed his belief that a bill of rights should be attached to the Constitution that would provide for "freedom of religion, freedom of the press, protection against standing armies, restriction of monopoly, the eternal and unremitting force of the habeas corpus laws, and trials by jury in all matters of fact triable by the laws of the land, and not by the laws of nations."[7] Jefferson referred to the arguments of James Wilson of Pennsylvania, who claimed the addition of a separate bill of rights would be dangerous because it would imply the authority of the national government to abridge rights that were not expressly listed, "a *gratis dictum,* the reverse of which might just as well be said; and it [Wilson's argument] is opposed by strong inferences from the body of

[5] Ibid., 2:588.

[6] Ibid.

The Debate Over the Bill of Rights

[7] Jefferson, who was in Paris during the framing of the Constitution, and who later was to become an advocate of strict constructionism that would limit the reach of national power, supported the Constitution but expressed several reservations. In addition to suggesting the need for a bill of rights, Jefferson also felt that the Constitu-

tion should limit the presidency to two terms, which in effect became the informal practice of the Republic until Franklin Roosevelt ran for a third term in 1940. Jefferson's discussion of his approbations and misgivings with regard to the Constitution may be found in his letter to James Madison, 20 December 1787, in *The Life and Selected Writings of Thomas Jefferson*, ed. Adrienne Koch and William Peden (New York: Random House, Modern Library ed., 1944), pp. 436–41.

---

[8] Ibid.

the [national Constitution], as well as from the omission of the cause of our present confederation, which had made the reservation in expressed terms."[8] Jefferson was referring to the fact that the Constitution did proscribe the abridgement of certain rights, and that the Articles of Confederation explicitly provided that each state retained those freedoms and rights that were not expressly delegated by the Articles to Congress.

The arguments against a separate bill of rights expressed by James Wilson were also echoed by Alexander Hamilton (*The Federalist,* 84). Hamilton, like Wilson, argued that the addition of a bill of rights would be redundant and dangerous. It would imply that a national government would have the authority to abridge the very rights that were enumerated if there were no explicit statement to the contrary in a bill of rights. By the same reasoning, Hamilton concluded that a bill of rights would make it easier for the national government to abridge rights that were not expressly listed. The Constitution was drafted in good faith, declared Hamilton, and the government to be established under it would also act responsibly. Indeed, he argued, no bill of rights could prevent the abridgment of rights by a government bent upon destroying the civil liberties and rights of the people.

The arguments of Wilson and Hamilton did not assuage the fears of those proponents of a bill of rights who wanted the same formal protections of civil liberties and civil rights to be included in the national Constitution that commonly had been incorporated into state constitutions. Although many state constitutions did not have separate bills of rights, generally their declarations of rights were far more extensive than the statements incorporated in the national Constitution. The delegates to the national Convention clearly saw the extensive rights embodied in state constitutions as adequate protections of civil liberties and civil rights generally. Although the declarations of rights in state constitutions limited only state governments, the rights that had been listed reflected what were generally considered to be the inalienable natural and common law rights of all citizens.

The closeness of the ratification campaigns in several states made the promise of the advocates of the new Constitution to draft a bill of rights an important trade-off for votes in the

Civil Liberties and Civil Rights Under the Constitution

ratifying conventions of several states. Many of the delegates to the first Congress considered themselves to be under an obligation to honor promises that had been made during the ratification campaigns. In his first inaugural address, President George Washington called upon Congress to consider carefully the addition of a bill of rights to the Constitution. Under the leadership of James Madison, Congress rose to the occasion, drafting twelve amendments, ten of which were finally submitted to the states for ratification to become the Bill of Rights of the new national government.

Today the Bill of Rights is not only taken for granted, but its provisions are considered by most citizens to embody historical, traditional, immutable rights and liberties. But as the debate over the inclusion of a bill of rights in the Constitution suggests, the issue of civil liberties and civil rights was highly political and at the same time involved considerations of jurisprudence and philosophy.

Drafting the Bill of Rights

What rights and liberties were to be included in a bill of rights was a highly debated topic in the first Congress. At first, under the leadership of Congressman James Madison, an effort was made to amend the original text of the Constitution to incorporate new rights and liberties, including prohibitions upon congressional abridgement of freedom of speech and press, religion, assembly, and the bearing of arms. An attempt was made to amend Article III to extend its jury trial protection to include more fully the principles of common law. Although the House voted to add civil liberties and civil rights protections by amending the original constitutional text, the Senate did not go along, and finally a separate Bill of Rights was agreed to that encompassed most of the provisions of the original House plan.

During the drafting of the Bill of Rights by the first Congress, the question of its applicability to the states themselves was not explicitly raised. It was clearly the intent of the drafters of the Bill of Rights, however, that its provisions would apply only to the national government. The debates in the first Congress focused solely upon questions concerning the proper limitations of the national government. Significantly, the Senate defeated a House proposal which provided that "No state shall infringe the right of trial by jury in criminal cases, nor the rights of conscience, nor the freedom of speech or of the press." The rejection of this provision unequivocally proves the intent of the first Congress that drafted the Bill of Rights to have its provisions apply only as limitations upon the national government. The First Amendment sets the tone for the entire Bill of Rights in its opening words, "*Congress* shall make no law . . ." (my emphasis).

Twelve amendments to the Constitution were approved by Congress in 1789 and sent to the states, where the first ten amendments were ratified by the requisite three-fourths of the states in 1791.[9]

[9] Connecticut, Massachusetts, and Georgia failed to ratify the amendments. On the hundred and fiftieth anniversary of the adoption of the Bill of Rights in 1941, the legislatures of the three states voted their approval of it.

AN OVERVIEW OF THE BILL OF RIGHTS

The First Amendment: Freedoms of Speech, Press, Religion and the Rights of Assembly and Petition

The First Amendment embodies fundamental liberties which many consider to be the most important in the Bill of Rights. The amendment provides that:

Congress shall make no law respecting an establishment of religion, or prohibiting the free exercise thereof; or abridging the freedom of speech, or of the press; or the right of the people peaceably to assemble, and to petition the government for a redress of grievances.

The First Amendment guarantees of freedom of speech, press, assembly, and petition are essential underpinnings of the democratic process. The fundamental importance of the freedoms of speech and press led the Supreme Court to nationalize them early, making them applicable as safeguards against state action under the due process clause of the Fourteenth Amendment, which provides that no state shall deprive any person of life, liberty, or property, without due process of law. The opinion in *Gitlow* v. *New York* (1925) and the ruling in *Near* v. *Minnesota* (1931) defined the "liberty" of the due process clause to include the freedoms of speech and press.

In addition to guaranteeing freedoms essential to the democratic process, the First Amendment religion clauses proscribe Congress from passing legislation that would establish an official government church or aid a particular religion, and from interfering in the free exercise of religion through legislation that prevents people from practicing their religious beliefs. The freedom to practice religion is not absolute and may be curtailed on the basis of a compelling governmental interest. For example, the Constitution does not require Congress to exempt all persons from the draft who claim a religious conscientious objection to war. Congress has set conditions of conscientious objector status which do interfere with the free exercise of some religions.

The Second Amendment states that:

A well regulated militia, being necessary to the security of a free state, the right of the people to keep and bear arms, shall not be infringed.

This amendment was passed because of the fear that Congress might disarm the state militias.[10] One of the more controversial provisions of the Constitution was the Article I power of Congress to regulate state militias, with the provision that the appointment of militia officers would be reserved to the states as well as the authority of training the militia in accordance with the discipline prescribed by Congress. Alexander Hamilton wrote (in *The Federalist,* 29) that if it were "possible seriously to indulge a jealousy of the militia upon a conceivable establishment under the federal government, the circumstance of the officers being in the appointment of the states ought at once to extinguish it. There can be no doubt that this circumstance will always secure to them a preponderating influence over the militia."

[10] The word "state" in the amendment is used in the generic sense and does not refer to the states of the Union. This does not affect the intent of the amendment, however, which was to protect the states against federal action disarming their militias.

The states did not accept Hamilton's argument that they would have nothing to fear from national control over their militias, which many state leaders felt might lead to a standing national army without any countervailing force in the states. Elbridge Gerry of Massachusetts spoke to this point in his defense of the Second Amendment in the first Congress:

What, Sir, is the use of a militia? It is to prevent the establishment of a standing Army, the bane of liberty. Now, it must be evident, that under this provision, together with their other powers, Congress could take such measures with respect to a militia, as to make a standing army necessary. Whenever governments mean to invade the rights and liberties of the people, they always attempt to destroy the militia, in order to raise an army upon their ruins.[11]

[11] Cited in A. F. Dick Howard, *Commentaries on the Constitution of Virginia* (Charlottesville: University Press of Virginia, 1974), p. 273.

Since the intent of the Second Amendment was clearly to prevent national disarmament of state militias, to what extent is the *constitutional* authority of Congress to regulate guns limited? Clearly, Congress cannot regulate guns in such a way as to disarm state militias. But there would seem to be no constitutional impediments to general gun control legislation aimed at protecting individuals against violence. For example, in *United States* v. *Miller* (1939), the Court upheld the National Firearms Act, which required the registration of certain types of guns including sawed-off shotguns, against a Second Amendment challenge that it violated the individual's rights to bear arms. Justice McReynolds wrote for the Court that in the absence of evidence that the possession of a sawed-off shotgun "at this time has some reasonable relationship to the preservation or efficiency of a well-regulated militia, we cannot say that the Second Amendment guarantees the right to keep and bear such an instrument. Certainly it is not within judicial notice that this weapon is any part of the ordinary military equipment or that its use could contribute to the common defense."[12] The *Miller* ruling did not answer the question of the extent to which individuals have a Second Amendment right to bear arms that ordinarily would be appropriate to military forces. Since the *Miller* case is the only one pertaining to the constitutionality of a federal law challenged on Second Amendment grounds, some doubt remains regarding the validity of comprehensive federal gun control legislation.

[12] United States v. Miller, 307 U.S. 174, 178 (1939).

The Third Amendment: Limits on Quartering of Soldiers

The eighteenth century fear of standing armies in the colonies and the new states was amply justified, since such armies had been employed by Great Britain to suppress colonial resistance and enforce unpopular laws. The Third Amendment was directed at the unpopular British practice of quartering soldiers in private homes, an exploitation of citizens that both nationalists and states' rights advocates agreed was intolerable. The Third Amendment provides that:

Civil Liberties and Civil Rights Under the Constitution

No soldier shall, in time of peace, be quartered in any house, without the consent of the owner, nor in time of war, but in a manner to be prescribed by law.

The Third Amendment has not required judicial exposition or comment because there is no ambiguity in nor has there been any debate over its terms.

The Fourth Amendment is deeply rooted in the Anglo-American legal tradition. It was a common practice in Great Britain, beginning in the fourteenth century, to have agents of the government conduct searches of homes and persons to ferret out materials that were, in the view of the king and his ministers, seditious and against the public interest. The unbridled power of the king to authorize searches and seizures was curbed somewhat after the Glorious Revolution of 1688 and the establishment of parliamentary supremacy.

After 1688 the English government, with the support of the monarchy, began to limit governmental authority to search and seize because unreasonable searches and seizures were considered to be a violation of the fundamental rights of English citizens. The enforcement of tax laws through abusive searches and seizures was specifically curbed by Parliament in the eighteenth century. Parliamentary action did not establish standards limiting searches and seizures generally, however, and the common law courts took it upon themselves to develop common law standards that would restrict searches and seizures that had been authorized by the king and Parliament.

While Englishmen in Britain were being given increased protections by the courts against unreasonable searches and seizures, their compatriots in the American colonies were increasingly being subjected to searches and seizures by agents of the British government seeking to enforce customs and tax laws. Great Britain was attempting to impose its rigid mercantile system of economic controls over the colonies through whatever means it considered to be necessary, regardless of the "rights" of the colonists. Officers of the Crown in the colonies conducted searches for smuggled goods simply on the basis of the authority derived from their commissions. When they met opposition, they obtained "writs of assistance" is-

The Fourth Amendment: Protection Against Unreasonable Searches and Seizures

sued by colonial governors or courts under the authority of Parliament in the name of the king. The authority of Parliament to issue such writs was directly challenged in the Colony of Massachusetts in the famous Writs of Assistance case in 1761. A group of Boston merchants employed a brilliant young attorney, James Otis, Jr., to argue their position that the writs should not be issued. Otis told the court that the writs violated the fundamental constitutional rights of Englishmen and that Parliament had no authority to authorize them. The writs were issued, although Otis had persuaded some of the justices to his side, and they continued to be granted until the outbreak of the Revolutionary War.

The colonial experience with arbitrary searches and seizures by agents of the Crown in violation of what the colonists considered to be fundamental principles of English law was the historical background of the Fourth Amendment, which provides that:

The right of the people to be secure in their persons, houses, papers, and effects, against unreasonable searches and seizures, shall not be violated, and no warrants shall issue, but upon probable cause, supported by oath or affirmation, and particularly describing the place to be searched, and the persons or things to be seized.

The Fourth Amendment requirement for search warrants establishes an important judicial check upon the search and seizure actions of police and government officers. Although the initiative for searches and seizures always lies with police agents, they must obtain court approval before acting. Although courts more often than not readily grant police requests for search warrants, the involvement of the courts prevents totally independent police action. Perhaps the most important limitation of all on searches and seizures is that evidence which a court finds was obtained through an unreasonable search and seizure is inadmissible in both federal and state courts.[13]

The Fourth Amendment, like most constitutional provisions, contains a great deal of ambiguity. What is a "search and seizure"? What is an "unreasonable" search and seizure? Both of these questions have been answered in contrasting ways by different courts and justices. For example, in *Olmstead* v. *United States* in 1928, Chief Justice Taft wrote

[13] The Supreme Court extended the full protections of the Fourth Amendment to the states in Mapp v. Ohio, 367 U.S. 643 (1961).

Civil Liberties and Civil Rights Under the Constitution

the Court's majority opinion holding that wiretapping did not constitute a "search" under the terms of the Fourth Amendment. To be covered by the Fourth Amendment, declared Taft, a search must be accompanied by the seizure of physical objects or the physical entry into the premises that are searched. The case itself involved, in the words of the Court, a massive conspiracy to sell liquor unlawfully. The discovery of the conspiracy was made through wiretapping. Four justices dissented in separate opinions. Justice Louis Brandeis wrote one of his most famous dissents, in which he linked the Fourth Amendment protection against unreasonable searches and seizures with the Fifth Amendment safeguard against compulsory self-incrimination. He stated:

When the Fourth and Fifth Amendments were adopted, the "form that evil had theretofore taken" had been necessarily simple. Force and violence were then the only means known to man by which a government could directly effect self-incrimination. It could compel the individual to testify—a compulsion effected, if need be, by torture. It could secure possession of his papers and other articles incident to his private life—a seizure effected, if need be, by breaking and entry. Protection against such invasion of "the sanctity of a man's home and the privacies of life" was provided in the Fourth and Fifth Amendments by specific language.[14]

After noting the original conditions that led to the Fourth Amendment defense against unreasonable searches and seizures and the Fifth Amendment protection against self-incrimination, Brandeis pointed out that the Fourth and Fifth Amendment safeguards should be extended to meet new problems of government invasion of privacy: "Subtler and more far-reaching means of invading privacy have become available to the government. . . . Discovery and invention have made it possible for the government, by means far more effective than stretching upon the rack, to obtain disclosure in court of what is whispered in the closet."[15] Brandeis concluded that:

The makers of our Constitution undertook to secure conditions favorable to the pursuit of happiness. They recognized the significance of man's spiritual nature, of his feelings, and of his intellect. They knew that only a part of the pain, pleasure, and satisfactions of life are to be found in material things. They sought to protect Americans in their beliefs, their thoughts, their emotions, and their sensations. They conferred, as against the government, the right to be let alone—the most comprehensive of rights and the right most

[14] Olmstead v. United States, 277 U.S. 438, 473 (1928).

[15] Ibid.

valued by civilized men. To protect that right, every unjustifiable intrusion by the government upon the privacy of the individual, whatever the means employed, must be deemed a violation of the Fourth Amendment.[16]

[16] Ibid., p. 478.

Brandeis particularly emphasized that the Fourth Amendment proscription upon unreasonable searches and seizures may buttress the Fifth Amendment protection against self-incrimination. Under such circumstances the Fourth Amendment should be broadly interpreted to limit government action.

The disagreement on the Supreme Court in the *Olmstead* case reflected the contrasting ways in which the Fourth Amendment could be interpreted. Disagreement over the reach of the Fourth Amendment continued. In *Katz* v. *United States* (1967) the Court, with Justice Black registering the only dissent, extended the safeguards of the Fourth Amendment to require search warrants before police officers can eavesdrop, even in semipublic places (in this case a telephone booth). Justice Black, dissenting, would have strictly interpreted the Fourth Amendment. Taking a position similar to that of the majority in the *Olmstead* case, he argued that the Fourth Amendment protections cover only objects that can be physically seized. Black's dissent concluded that eavesdropping on a conversation held in a telephone booth cannot in any literal sense be considered a "search and seizure."

The question concerning the extent to which searches and seizures can be conducted with and without warrant has not been definitively answered by the Supreme Court. The *Katz* ruling somewhat ambiguously extended the shield of the Fourth Amendment to electronic eavesdropping, but at the same time permitted such eavesdropping and, by implication, wiretapping if law enforcement officers first obtained a warrant. The Supreme Court and the lower federal judiciary continue to grapple with the problem of defining Fourth Amendment standards on a case-by-case basis.

The Fifth Amendment: Grand Juries, Double Jeopardy, Self-Incrimination, Due Process, and Eminent Domain

The Fifth Amendment is one of the most comprehensive and eclectic parts of the Bill of Rights. It is best considered by breaking it down into its components.

Civil Liberties and Civil Rights Under the Constitution

Grand Juries. First, it provides for grand juries:

No person shall be held to answer for a capital, or otherwise infamous crime, unless on a presentment or indictment by a grand jury.

The grand jury, one of the oldest institutions in Anglo-American law, is a jury of inquiry in criminal cases that hears evidence presented by the government prosecuting officer to determine whether or not a presentment should be made or an indictment returned. A *presentment* is a written notice of an offense, based upon reasonable grounds for believing that the individual named has committed it, and is made by the grand jury on its own motion. An *indictment* is also a written accusation charging a person with having committed a criminal act, but, unlike the presentment, an indictment is made at the request of the government and usually framed first by the prosecuting officer. Grand juries do not try persons, their function being limited to accusing individuals of crimes. The proceedings are secret, and only the government is represented. The term *grand* jury is derived from its greater size relative to the ordinary trial, or *petit* jury. At common law, grand juries consisted of not fewer than twelve nor more than forty-three persons. In American practice these numbers have been altered by statute in some states. The ordinary *petit* jury consisted of twelve persons, but this number has also been altered by statute in some states.

While the grand jury is an ancient common law institution, the right to indictment by a grand jury remains one of the handful of provisions of the Bill of Rights that have not been nationalized under the due process clause of the Fourteenth Amendment and made applicable to state action.[17] The Supreme Court has not changed Justice Cardozo's opinion in *Palko* v. *Connecticut* (1937) that the right to indictment by a grand jury, although of "value and importance," is not a "principle of justice so rooted in the traditions and the conscience of our people as to be ranked as fundamental," nor is it "implicit in the concept of ordered liberty."[18]

The Fifth Amendment requires grand jury indictment:

except in cases arising in the land or naval forces or in the militia, when in actual service in time of war or public danger . . .

The Supreme Court has construed the exemption to the

[17] The other parts of the Bill of Rights that have not been nationalized under the due process clause of the Fourteenth Amendment are: trial by a jury in civil cases; prohibition against excessive bail and fines; the right to bear arms; and the Third Amendment prohibition upon the quartering of troops in private homes.

[18] Palko v. Connecticut, 302 U.S. 319, 325 (1937).

grand jury requirement to extend only to persons serving in the military forces. Civilian dependents or employees of the military cannot be tried for capital crimes by military tribunals, but must be given full protections of the Bill of Rights.[19]

Double Jeopardy. In addition to the grand jury safeguard in capital cases, the Fifth Amendment provides protection against double jeopardy:

Nor shall any person be subject for the same offense to be twice put in jeopardy of life or limb . . .

The double jeopardy provision of the Fifth Amendment applies only to criminal cases, and, until 1968, the protection against double jeopardy under the Fifth Amendment extended only to federal crimes.[20] What constitutes "double jeopardy" is not always easily answered. A defendant is put into jeopardy when he or she has been indicted and brought to trial. If the defendant is acquitted, or if the prosecutor agrees to a dismissal of the case, the defendant cannot be tried again. The double jeopardy restriction, however, does not prevent the retrial of a defendant if the jury was unable to reach a verdict during the first trial. Moreover, the double jeopardy shield does not prevent both the federal government and the states from separately trying an individual who has committed an offense that violates both federal and state laws. A person may also be subject to civil proceedings in addition to a criminal trial for the same offense.

Self-incrimination. Perhaps the most historic and widely cited provision of the Fifth Amendment is its protection against self-incrimination:

nor shall [any person] be compelled in any criminal case to be a witness against himself . . .

The Fifth Amendment safeguard against self-incrimination has a long and complicated history. The origin of the privilege dates to the twelfth century, and arose from disputes between the monarchy and the church. The kings in their struggle with the church sought to limit the authority of the bishops to compel testimony from citizens of the realm with regard to

[19] See Kinsella v. United States ex rel Singleton, 361 U.S. 234 (1960); Reid v. Covert, 354 U.S. 1 (1957).

[20] The double jeopardy safeguard of the Fifth Amendment was incorporated into the due process clause of the Fourteenth Amendment in Benton v. Maryland, 392 U.S. 925 (1968).

alleged offenses. The privilege against self-incrimination, however, did not become operative in the common law until centuries later. During the sixteenth and seventeenth centuries it was not an uncommon practice to use torture to extract confessions from alleged criminals. But by the end of the seventeenth century the privilege against self-incrimination was incorporated into the common law largely as a result of an action of Parliament that voted to overturn a conviction by the king's council of the Star Chamber on the ground that the king's court had violated the individual's right to refuse to testify against himself.[21]

Although the privilege against self-incrimination had deep historical roots, the Supreme Court did not consider it to be one of those fundamental and historic rights required to be included under the due process clause of the Fourteenth Amendment as a limitation upon state action until 1964.[22] The protection against self-incrimination as strictly interpreted by the courts applies only to criminal cases. A major question regarding the reach of the Fifth Amendment self-incrimination shield was raised during the 1950s when congressional investigations by the House Committee on Un-American Activities and by Senator Joseph McCarthy who was chairman of the Government Operations Committee, cast a broad net to catch and expose Communist subversives. Many witnesses before these congressional committees refused to answer questions on self-incrimination grounds as well as First Amendment grounds of freedom of speech, press, and association. Congressional questioning could not only expose a witness to possible criminal prosecution for violation of subversive control statutes, but also cast a chilling effect upon the willingness of persons to express political views or join associations that might possibly be considered subversive. Regardless of the claims of witnesses to the contrary, their rights before congressional committees conducting legitimate investigations are determined by Congress, and not by the courts. The rules of congressional committees may and usually did permit witnesses to "take the Fifth" in their refusal to answer questions. On more than one occasion, however, frustrated committee chairmen and members sought contempt citations to be voted by Congress against what they consid-

[21] See Erwin N. Griswold, *The Fifth Amendment Today* (Cambridge, Mass.: Harvard University Press, 1955), p. 3.

[22] See Mallory v. Hogan, 378 U.S. 1 (1964); and Murphy v. Waterfront Commission of New York Harbor, 378 U.S. 52 (1964).

ered to be obstreperous witnesses. Several rulings of the Supreme Court did require that committee investigations have a legitimate legislative purpose, but the Court did not extend the self-incrimination protection of the Fifth Amendment to witnesses before congressional committees.[23]

Congress has passed legislation that allows federal prosecutors under certain circumstances—for example, in connection with narcotics violations—to grant immunity from both federal and state prosecution in return for compelled testimony. Once immunity is granted to a person he or she may not refuse to answer questions.

Due Process. After the self-incrimination clause the Fifth Amendment includes the due process clause, which provides:

nor [shall any person] be deprived of life, liberty, or property, without due process of law . . .

The due process clause of the Fifth Amendment should be contrasted with the due process clause of the Fourteenth Amendment, which provides that *no state* may deprive a person of life, liberty, or property without due process of law. As we will see below, the due process clause of the Fourteenth Amendment has been interpreted to include all of the protections afforded by the Fifth Amendment due process clause and many more as well.

The term "due process of law" is a highly subjective one, requiring judicial interpretation for clarification. The difficulty comes from the fact that judges and legal scholars often define due process in contrasting ways. What, then, is the meaning of the Fifth Amendment due process clause? In one of the few cases in which the Supreme Court attempted to define the reach of the due process clause, *Murray's Lessee* v. *Hoboken Land and Improvement Company* (1856), Justice Curtis wrote:

The words "due process of law," were undoubtedly intended to convey the same meaning as the words, "by the law of the land," in Magna Charta. . . . The Constitution contains no description of those processes which it was intended to allow or forbid. It does not even declare what principles are to be applied to ascertain whether it be due process. It is manifest that it was not left to the legislative power to enact any process which might be devised. The article is a restraint on the legislative as well as on the executive and judicial powers of

[23] See Watkins v. United States, 354 U.S. 178 (1957); and Barenblatt v. United States, 360 U.S. 109 (1959).

Civil Liberties and Civil Rights Under the Constitution

government, and cannot be so construed as to leave Congress free to make any process "due process of law" by its mere will. To what principles, then, are we to resort to ascertain whether this process, enacted by Congress, is due process? To this the answer must be twofold. We must examine the Constitution itself, to see whether this process be in conflict with any of its provisions [such as the Bill of Rights]. If not found to be so, we must look to those settled usages and modes of proceeding existing in the common and statute law of England, before the emigration of our ancestors, and which are shown not to have been unsuited to their civil and political condition by having been acted on by them after the settlement of this country. . . . [T]hough "due process of law" generally implies and includes . . . regular allegations, opportunity to answer, and a trial according to some settled course of judicial proceedings . . . yet, this is not universally true.[24]

[24] Murray's Lessee v. Hoboken Land and Improvement Company, 18 Howard 272, 276–80 (1856).

The formula for determining the content of the Fifth Amendment due process clause announced by Justice Curtis in the *Murray's Lessee* case allowed the Court broad discretion in developing due process standards. The Court was to refer to the Constitution, the Bill of Rights, and "those settled usages and modes of proceeding existing in the common law and statute law of England" to define due process. Using such an approach, the definition of due process arrived at by the Court would necessarily contain a highly subjective element.

The inclusion of the due process clause in the Fifth Amendment implies that the framers of the Bill of Rights thought that "due process of law" had a meaning that went beyond the procedural protections included in the other parts of the Bill of Rights. For example, the Fifth Amendment incorporates the protection against self-incrimination directly before the due process clause. Unless the due process clause is to be thought of as being completely redundant, due process presumably was intended to mean something different from the procedural safeguard against self-incrimination and the other procedural protections of the Bill of Rights. The Supreme Court, however, generally has interpreted *procedural* due process of the Fifth Amendment as essentially embodying the procedural protections that are stated elsewhere in the Bill of Rights. But the Court has, at times, gone beyond the explicit provisions of the Bill of Rights in interpreting Fifth Amendment due process. It has held, for example, that the due process law gives aliens the right to a hearing in deportation cases.[25]

[25] *Wong Yang Sung v. McGrath*, 339

stated that since deportations may deprive aliens of liberty and even of life, they must be given due process, which requires a hearing before an impartial administrative judge or tribunal.

While the due process clause of the Fifth Amendment was largely redundant in the protection of procedural rights, since such rights had been included in other parts of the Bill of Rights, a conservative Supreme Court did in the early twentieth century use the due process clause to review the *substantive* content of congressional legislation and overturn it if the Court felt that Congress had intruded upon the liberty and property rights of individuals. For example, in *Atkins* v. *Children's Hospital* in 1923, the Court overturned a congressional statute that prescribed minimum wages for women in the District of Columbia on Fifth Amendment due process grounds. The Court ruled that the law interfered with the constitutional freedom of contract, which was a liberty guaranteed by the due process clause. The *Adkins* case was an example at the national level of due process review which reached to the substance of legislation to determine its fairness. Substantive due process review, which essentially involved the Court in making legislative judgments, was exercised primarily over *state* laws under the due process clause of the Fourteenth Amendment. The subjectivity of substantive due process review comes from the wide range of possible interpretations of the words "liberty" and "property" in the due process clause. In giving substance to these words, the Court essentially had to exercise its own judgment without grounding its opinions in explicit provisions of the Constitution, such as the Bill of Rights, or in historic customs, traditions, and common law precedents, all of which were used to define *procedural* due process.

A development of major importance in the interpretation of the due process clause of the Fifth Amendment was the Court's decision in *Bolling* v. *Sharpe* in 1954 to include equal protection of the laws as part of due process. The Court, essentially employing the method of substantive due process review, defined "liberty" of due process to include equal protection. Equal protection of the laws is explicitly guaranteed in the Constitution only in the Fourteenth Amendment, which governs *state* rather than national action. In the *Bolling* case the Court held that the Fourteenth Amendment equal protection clause was incorporated into the due process clause of the Fifth Amendment, a ruling that extended equal protection to national action.

Eminent Domain. The final provision of the Fifth Amendment states:

nor shall private property be taken for public use, without just compensation.

The just compensation clause restricts the government's power of eminent (prominent, superior) domain (territory). This is the power all governments have to control the territory of the state for public use in the public interest. In time of peace, for example, the power of eminent domain is used primarily by state governments to take private property for public highways. In time of war, the national government may find it in the public interest to seize territory for the common safety. The power of eminent domain is based upon the ultimate authority of the sovereign to deploy any and all of the state's wealth in cases of public necessity and safety. The power of eminent domain applies only to private property, since the government automatically has control over its own property.

The Fifth Amendment does not limit the power of eminent domain, but does require that the government pay "just compensation" when it takes private property for public use. Generally what constitutes "taking" private property is clear, as when the government seizes the land of an individual and transfers title to itself. The courts have not defined the taking of private property to include government action that indirectly reduces the value of such property—for example, government regulatory measures that reduce the rates of return that individuals could otherwise receive from their property are not covered by eminent domain. Most government regulation reduces the profit-making opportunities of private individuals in some way, but clearly the government could not function if it were required to compensate citizens for the indirect effects of controlling the environment, food and drugs, consumer product safety, health and safety in the workplace, and so on.

Perhaps because the Fifth Amendment limitation upon the power of eminent domain was taken for granted as a proper control of government it was the first provision of the Bill of Rights to be incorporated under the due process clause of the Fourteenth Amendment in 1890.[26]

[26] Chicago, Milwaukee and St. Paul Ry. Co. v. Minnesota, 134 U.S. 418 (1890).

The Sixth Amendment: The Rights of the Accused in Federal Criminal Trials

The Sixth Amendment prescribes the fundamental rights of those accused of federal crimes. First:

In all criminal prosecutions, the accused shall enjoy the right to a speedy and public trial, by an impartial jury of the state and district wherein the crime shall have been committed, which district shall have previously been ascertained by law . . .

Speedy Trial. The Sixth Amendment's requirement that jury trials take place in the state where the crime was committed repeats the jury trial provision of Article III. The delegates at the 1787 Constitutional Convention considered the right to a trial by jury in criminal cases to be so important that they included it as one of the very few civil rights explicitly protected by the Constitution. The reaffirmation of the right to a jury trial in the Sixth Amendment stresses the late eighteenth century view of the primary importance of the right to a jury trial. It is interesting, however, that the fundamental right to a jury trial that was so widely accepted at the time the Constitution was adopted was not applied by the Supreme Court in its interpretation of the due process clause of the Fourteenth Amendment until 1968.[27]

[27] Duncan v. Louisiana, 391 U.S. 145 (1968).

In *Duncan* v. *Louisiana* (1968), the Court finally ruled that the right to a jury trial was a fundamental principle of liberty and justice, and essential to a fair trial. The *Duncan* decision overruled prior decisions of the Supreme Court that had supported the authority of the states to dispense with jury trials in criminal cases. The decision to incorporate the right to a jury trial under the Fourteenth Amendment due process clause was not unanimous. Justice Harlan, joined by Justice Stewart, strongly dissented from the majority opinion. Considerations of federalism were paramount to the dissenting justices, who argued that the Supreme Court should not fasten on the states "federal notions of criminal justice."[28] The major point

[28] Ibid., 173.

Civil Liberties and Civil Rights Under the Constitution

stressed by the dissenting justices was not that the right to a jury trial was unimportant, but that the states should be granted leeway in legislating their own criminal procedures to try cases falling within their jurisdictions. The dissenters particularly objected to the way in which the Supreme Court selectively incorporated certain provisions of the Bill of Rights under the due process clause of the Fourteenth Amendment while excluding others. The Court had not conclusively proven, Harlan argued, that the right to a jury trial was any more or less "fundamental" than other provisions of the Bill of Rights that had not yet been incorporated.

The majority opinion in the *Duncan* case clearly signalled a new approach by the Supreme Court to the whole question of incorporating provisions of the Bill of Rights under the due process clause of the Fourteenth Amendment. The opinion itself, supporting the right to a jury trial, virtually completed the process of incorporating the procedural protections of the Bill of Rights under the Fourteenth Amendment. Moreover, the *Duncan* opinion firmly signalled that the Supreme Court was going to interpret the procedural protections afforded by the Fourteenth Amendment due process clause primarily in terms of the Bill of Rights, applying federal protections derived from the Bill of Rights to the states. The Court's approach was intended to establish consistency between federal and state jurisdictions in constitutionally guaranteed criminal procedures.

The jury trial provision of the Sixth Amendment, seemingly simple on its face, is in certain respects difficult to interpret. For example, what exactly constitutes the right to a "speedy" and "public" trial?

The Supreme Court squarely confronted the question of the right to a speedy trial in *Klopfer* v. *North Carolina* (1967). The appellant, a professor of zoology at Duke University, had been indicted by the State of North Carolina for criminal trespass after he had taken part in a sit-in demonstration at a Chapel Hill restaurant. Klopfer was tried after his indictment, but the jury failed to agree on a verdict and the judge declared a mistrial, which gave the state the opportunity to try the professor again or drop all charges against him. However, the state prosecutors were apparently unable to make up their minds on whether or not to proceed to a second trial, and after a year had passed the defendant demanded to be tried forthwith or have his case dismissed. The state court denied the professor's request to have action taken one way or another on his case, and instead granted the state prosecutor's motion to place the indictment on an inactive status that would allow the state to prosecute the defendant at any future time. Klopfer claimed that his Sixth Amendment right to a speedy trial was violated by the North Carolina procedure, which, at the time, was allowed by thirty states. The defendant appealed to the North Carolina Supreme Court, which ruled against him, declaring that the right to a speedy trial did not compel the state to prosecute a defendant. Klopfer took his case to the Supreme Court, which reversed the North Carolina decision on the ground that it violated the speedy trial provision of the Sixth Amendment. Chief Justice Warren wrote the opinion for a unanimous Supreme Court, stating that the delay and uncertainty caused by the North Carolina procedure deprived the defendant of his life and liberty without due process of law that was guaranteed by the Fourteenth Amendment. "The pendency of the indictment," declared Warren, "may subject him [the defendant] to public scorn and deprive him of employment, and almost certainly will force curtailment of his speech, associations, and participation in unpopular causes. By indefinitely prolonging this oppression, as well as the 'anxiety and concern accompanying public accusation,' the criminal procedure condoned in this case by the Supreme Court of North Carolina clearly denies the petitioner the right to a speedy trial which we hold is guaranteed to him by the Sixth Amendment of the Constitution of the United States."[29]

[29] Klopfer v. North Carolina, 386 U.S. 213, 222 (1967).

Public Trial. The Supreme Court has had more difficulty interpreting the public trial requirement of the Sixth Amendment than in defining the right to a speedy trial. The Burger Court in particular has been unable to agree on exactly what constitutes the right to a public trial. Under certain circumstances the right to a public trial is clear and unequivocal: The Court has held, for example, that a person is deprived of the right where a criminal trial is conducted by a court that is entirely closed to the public.[30]

Undoubtedly the most difficult question confronting the Court with regard to the Sixth Amendment's right to a public trial concerns the extent to which public trials may be curtailed in the interests of and at the request of criminal defendants themselves, on the ground that prejudicial press accounts would deny them their Sixth Amendment right to trial by an impartial jury. Not only does the defendant have the right to a fair trial under the Sixth Amendment, but the state, acting as prosecutor, also has an interest in guaranteeing criminal defendants fair trials.

The Sixth Amendment's guarantee of a fair public trial may conflict with the freedom of the press guaranteed by the First Amendment. The right of the press to cover criminal trials is not absolute, and may be curtailed in the interest of justice. Courts must balance the rights of defendants against the First Amendment freedom of the press in cases where the right of the press to cover a criminal trial freely is challenged. In 1966 the Supreme Court reversed the murder conviction of Dr. Sam Sheppard, who had been accused of killing his wife, on the ground that the media coverage of the trial created an atmosphere of severe prejudice to the defendant.[31] Justice Clark wrote the opinion of the Court reversing the conviction, pointing out that from "the cases coming here we note that unfair and prejudicial news comment on pending trials has become increasingly prevalent. Due process requires that the accused receive a trial by an impartial jury free from outside influences. Given the pervasiveness of modern communications and the difficulty of effacing prejudicial publicity from the minds of the jurors, the trial courts must take strong measures to insure that the balance is never weighed against the accused."[32] Clark concluded that trial judges must take all necessary measures to prevent an atmosphere of prejudice to criminal defendants. The *Sheppard* decision did not hold that trial judges should censor press accounts of criminal trials, but merely that they should take necessary action to deter the media from prejudicing the jury. The courts stressed in the *Sheppard* case that trial judges have a wide range of options

[30] See In re Oliver, 333 U.S. 257 (1948). But a defendant's right to a public trial is not absolute, and may be curtailed by the state for a number of compelling reasons, one of which is the protection of witnesses, including young witnesses in rape cases, and undercover agents.

[31] Sheppard v. Maxwell, 384 U.S. 333 (1966).

[32] Ibid., p. 351.

available to them to prevent the media from undermining fair trials without having to resort to outright censorship.

The Burger Court confronted the question of the constitutionality of direct trial court censorship of the press in *Nebraska Press Association* v. *Stuart* in 1976. The case involved a particularly brutal crime in which six members of a family were murdered in cold blood. The crime attracted widespread media coverage that resulted in pretrial publicity that was prejudicial to the defendant. The trial court judge issued an order that prohibited the public release of any testimony given or evidence produced at the *preliminary* hearing for the defendant. The Nebraska Press Association challenged the order in the higher state courts, but the order was sustained with certain modifications that listed the pretrial events allowed to be reported. The final restrictive order detailing exactly what the press could and could not report from the pretrial hearing was a clear example of prior censorship of the press. On appeal to the Supreme Court, the order was overturned. Chief Justice Burger wrote the majority opinion for the court in the *Nebraska Press Association* case, stressing that since the Nebraska trial court had not invoked closure at the outset of the pretrial proceedings the pretrial hearing was open to the public and to the press, making the restrictive order one of prior censorship of what could be reported. Nothing proscribed the press, Burger declared, from reporting events that transpire in the courtroom.

There was an implication in Chief Justice Burger's opinion that under certain circumstances the Supreme Court might uphold the closure of pretrial proceedings in the interest of justice to a criminal defendant. The Court did not confront the question of closure in the *Nebraska Press Association* case, however, and the issue of the extent to which trial judges could close pretrial proceedings remained open. While the majority opinion suggested that the closure of pretrial proceedings might under certain circumstances be justifiable, Justices White, Brennan, and Stevens wrote separate concurring opinions that stressed their view that prior censorship of the press is not justified under any circumstances. The three concurring justices agreed that trial judges have the authority to take adequate measures to deal with prejudicial press accounts of criminal trials without having to resort to the extreme measure of censorship of the press. Such measures might include warning newspapers to check the accuracy of their accounts and suggesting to the media that it not publish or broadcast prejudicial stories and material that was not introduced during the hearing. Disobedience of judicial warnings not to engage in out-of-court statements prejudicial to defendants may be punishable as contempt if it is found that the actions of the media constitute a clear and present danger to the conduct of a fair trial. Judicial warnings and citations for contempt may have an adverse effect upon media coverage of trials, but they do not constitute direct censorship of the press.

The constitutionality of the closure of a pretrial criminal proceeding came before the Court in *Gannett Company* v. *DePasquale* in 1979. Justice Stewart delivered the opinion of the Court, declaring that the public does not have an independent constitutional right to insist upon access to a pretrial judicial proceeding when the accused, the prosecutor, and the trial judge all have agreed to the closure of that proceeding in order to assure a fair trial. The issue, Stewart stated, "is whether members of the public have an enforceable right to a public trial that can be asserted independently of the parties in the litigation."[33] Stewart pointed out that while there is a strong societal interest in public trials, "there is a strong societal interest in other constitutional guarantees extended to the accused as well. The public, for example, has a definite and concrete interest in seeing that justice is swiftly and fairly administered. . . . Similarly, the public has an interest in having a criminal case heard by a jury, an interest distinct from the defendant's interest in being tried by a jury of his peers."[34] He went on to point out, however, that the public interest in the constitutional guarantees of the Sixth Amendment does not give the public a constitutional right to enforce those guarantees. Moreover, under the Sixth Amendment, the public does not have a constitutional right to attend a criminal trial, although there is a common law rule of open proceedings that "permits and even presumes open trial as a norm."[35] "But," continued Stewart, "even if the Sixth and Fourteenth Amendments could properly be viewed as embodying com-

[33] Gannett Company v. DePasquale, 443 U.S. 368, 382–83 (1979).

[34] Ibid., p. 383.

[35] Ibid., p. 385.

mon law right of the public to attend criminal trials, it would not necessarily follow that the petitioner would have a right of access under the circumstances of this case. For there exists no persuasive evidence that at common law members of the public have any right to attend *pretrial* proceedings; indeed, there is substantial evidence to the contrary."[36]

The *Gannett Company* decision was a highly controversial one, supported by only five justices, three of whom—Burger, Powell, and Rehnquist—felt compelled to write separate concurring opinions of their own because they did not fully agree with the reasoning of Justice Stewart, who had delivered the opinion of the Court. Chief Justice Burger emphasized that the Court's opinion applied only to pretrial processes, a point that he did not feel was entirely clear in Stewart's opinion. Powell stressed the point that excluding all members of the press from the courtroom, which was done by the lower trial court in the *Gannett Company* case, "differs substantially from the 'gag order' at issue in *Nebraska Press,* as the latter involved a classic prior restraint."[37] Justice Rehnquist would have gone further than his colleagues in the majority in support of the authority of trial courts to exclude the press. Rehnquist stated that "the trial court is not required by the Sixth Amendment to advance any reason whatsoever for declining to open a pretrial hearing or trial to the public."[38]

Justice Blackmun, joined by Justices Brennan, White, and Marshall, wrote a vigorous dissenting opinion in the *Gannett Company* case. He contended that the Sixth and Fourteenth Amendments guarantee the right to a public trial not only to the accused but also to the public. The Sixth Amendment, although on its face securing the right to a public trial only to the accused, does not "permit the inference that the accused may compel a private proceeding simply by waiving the right [to a public trial]."[39] Blackmun did not suggest that the Sixth Amendment imposes an absolute requirement that courts be open at all times; however, trial courts should impose rigid standards to justify the closure of criminal proceedings. The standards that Blackmun would have applied would have required the accused to demonstrate to the satisfaction of the trial judge that irreparable damage to the defense would result from the proceedings being open, and moreover to support

[36] Ibid. Emphasis added.

[37] Ibid., p. 399.

[38] Ibid., p. 404.

[39] Ibid., p. 418.

Civil Liberties and Civil Rights Under the Constitution

the conclusion that alternatives to closure would not adequately protect the defendant's right to a fair trial. Finally, Blackmun would have required the accused to demonstrate that closure would be effective in protecting against the perceived harm.[40]

The *Gannett Company* decision was widely perceived by the press to constitute a significant threat to its right of access to criminal trials. The pessimistic view of the press was supported by the actions of trial judges throughout the country who began to issue closure orders in pretrial and even trial proceedings that would never have been given before the *Gannett Company* decision. Chief Justice Burger went to great lengths to explain what he perceived to be the limited nature of the decision, emphasizing that it pertained only to pretrial and not to trial hearings.

The Sixth Amendment's provision for a public trial by an impartial jury requires the trial court not only to conduct criminal proceedings in a nonprejudicial atmosphere, but also to guarantee a jury that is not selected on the basis of gender discrimination. In the 1975 case of *Taylor* v. *Louisiana*, the Supreme Court invalidated a state jury selection system that excluded women, holding that women are "sufficiently numerous and distinct from men and . . . if they are systematically eliminated from jury panels, the Sixth Amendment's fair cross-section requirement cannot be satisfied."[41] A century earlier the Supreme Court had used the equal protection clause of the Fourteenth Amendment to proscribe racial discrimination in jury selection by invalidating a state law that limited eligibility for juries to white males who were twenty-one years of age or older.[42] Generally, where state action is concerned, the equal protection clause has been relied on more often than the Sixth Amendment to prevent discrimination in the selection of juries. In addition to gender and race, nationality and religion are also excluded as criteria for jury selection.

Local Juries. After providing for speedy and public trials by impartial juries, the Sixth Amendment required that the trial take place in and the jury be drawn from the state and district where the crime was committed. Like many of the provisions

[40] Ibid., p. 441–42.

[41] Taylor v. Louisiana, 419 U.S. 522, 531 (1975).

[42] Shroeder v. West Virginia, 100 U.S. 303 (1880). Contrast Virginia v. Rives, 100 U.S. 339 (1880), holding that the mere absence of blacks from a jury did not on its face constitute a denial of equal protection under the Fourteenth Amendment.

of the Bill of Rights, this part of the Sixth Amendment was included because of the history of dissatisfaction among the colonists with the practices of George III, who had forced colonists accused of committing crimes in America to stand trial in England. The framers of the Bill of Rights were worried that the new national government might be tempted to use the same practice by removing individuals accused of crimes in the states to a separate national jurisdiction. The Sixth Amendment's provision for conducting criminal trials in the district where the crime was committed does not prevent a defendant from seeking to have the trial moved on the ground that it would be impossible to have a fair trial in that community.

Additional Procedural Rights. Having prescribed the right to a speedy and public trial, and the setting of criminal proceedings, the Sixth Amendment grants certain procedural rights to criminal defendants, providing that in all criminal prosecutions the accused shall enjoy the right:

to be informed of the nature and cause of the accusation; to be confronted with the witnesses against him; to have compulsory process for obtaining witnesses in his favor, and to have the assistance of counsel for his defence.

The procedural protections afforded to criminal defendants by the concluding clauses of the Sixth Amendment were, in the eighteenth century, considered in the broadest sense to be fundamental to due process of law. Like all of the provisions of the Bill of Rights, however, they were originally intended only to apply within federal jurisdiction. And, as was the case with other procedural protections afforded by the Bill of Rights, the safeguards of the Sixth Amendment were listed separately from the due process clause of the Fifth Amendment. Due process under the Fourteenth Amendment could also be considered separately from the Bill of Rights. According to numerous Supreme Court rulings after 1868, due process in the generic sense did not automatically include the procedural safeguards of the Bill of Rights. The Warren Court, however, in addition to incorporating the rights to a speedy and public jury trial under the due process clause of the Fourteenth Amendment, added the remaining procedural protections of the Sixth Amendment as well. In the famous case of *Gideon* v. *Wainwright* in 1963, the Court unequivocally extended the right to counsel in *all* criminal cases to the states under the Fourteenth Amendment due process clause; in 1965 incorporated the right to confrontation of adverse witnesses;[43] and in 1967 extended the right of accused persons to obtain witnesses in their favor to the states.[44] states.[44]

The Sixth Amendment rights given to criminal defendants to know the charges against them, to be confronted with adverse witnesses, to have the opportunity to obtain favorable witnesses, and to have the assistance of counsel are essential to making the machinery of justice work. There is a presumption of the innocence of the accused in criminal trials, and defendants are given every opportunity to prove their innocence. Criminal proceedings are fundamentally designed to determine accurately the facts of individual cases, facts that pertain to the actions of the accused and to other parties indirectly involved in the case as well.

[43] Pointer v. Texas, 380 U.S. 400 (1965).

[44] Washington v. Texas, 388 U.S. 14 (1967).

The Seventh Amendment provides:

The Seventh Amendment: Trial by Jury in Common Law Cases

In suits at common law, where the value in controversy shall exceed twenty dollars, the right of trial by jury shall be preserved, and no fact tried by a jury, shall be otherwise re-examined in any court of the United States than according to the rules of the common law.

The Seventh Amendment remains one of the few parts of the Bill of Rights that has not been incorporated under the due process clause of the Fourteenth Amendment as a fundamental right. It applies to *civil* suits at common law, not to suits arising out of statutory law. While the Seventh Amendment gives parties to civil common law suits the right to a trial by jury where the value of the controversies exceeds twenty dollars, a jury may be waived with the consent of both parties.

The Eighth Amendment provides:

The Eighth Amendment: Prohibition of Excessive Bail, Fines, and Cruel and Unusual Punishments

Excessive bail shall not be required, nor excessive fines imposed, nor cruel and unusual punishments inflicted.

The excessive bail and fine safeguards of the Eighth

Amendment have been applied by the Supreme Court at the *federal* level to prevent setting of bail at a figure higher than is reasonable to assure the presence of a defendant at his or her trial. In determining the reasonableness of bail a court may take into account, for example, such considerations as the reputation of the offender and his or her ability to pay. Bail may be denied for some crimes, such as those for which the penalty is death. Moreover, bail may be denied if the court considers that under no circumstances will it insure the presence of the accused at trial. Bail may also be denied to persons the courts feel will commit other crimes pending their trials. While the excessive bail provision applies to federal jurisdiction, it has not been extended to the states under the due process clause of the Fourteenth Amendment.

The Eighth Amendment prohibition upon excessive fines has rarely raised a controversy in the courts. The Supreme Court has held that the failure to pay a fine due to indigency cannot be used as the reason for sentencing a defendant to prison.[45] Moreover, the Court has ruled that indigents cannot be detained for failure to pay a fine for an offense that is not otherwise punishable by imprisonment.[46]

By far the most important provision of the Eighth Amendment is its prohibition upon the infliction of cruel and unusual punishments. This prohibition generally pertains to the sentencing of criminal offenders and to punishments suffered after incarceration.[47]

The framers of the Eighth Amendment inserted the cruel and unusual punishment prohibition to ban punishments such as branding and whipping, which still existed in certain parts of the country at the time the Bill of Rights was adopted. It was clearly the intent of the framers of the amendment to prevent torture and other forms of "barbarous" punishments, but they did not intend to abolish what was obviously the most extreme example of a "cruel" punishment—capital punishment. Capital punishment was not "unusual" at the time the Eighth Amendment was framed, and was an accepted punishment in the states for murder, rape, and other crimes as well. In an early death penalty case, Justice Black wrote a concurring opinion expressing his view of the intent of the Eighth Amendment with regard to capital punishment:

[45] Williams v. Illinois, 399 U.S. 235 (1970).

[46] Tate v. Short, 401 U.S. 395 (1971).

[47] In Ingraham v. Wright, 430 U.S. 651 (1977), a majority opinion by Justice Powell joined by Justices Burger, Stewart, Blackmun, and Rehnquist specifically stated that the Eighth Amendment applied only to those convicted of a crime, and did not cover the disciplinary corporal punishment of public school children; however, Justice White, joined by Brennan, Marshall, and Stevens, dissented, declaring that the Eighth Amendment prohibition upon cruel and unusual punishment should not be restricted to those convicted of crimes but should prohibit all barbaric punishments regardless of the nature of the offense for which the punishment was given. The dissenters would have applied the Eighth Amendment to the disciplinary spanking of schoolchildren.

. . . The Eighth Amendment forbids "cruel and unusual punishments." In my view, these words cannot be read to outlaw capital
punishment because that penalty was in common use and authorized
by law here and in the countries from which our ancestors came at
the time the amendment was adopted. . . . Although some people
have urged that this Court should amend the Constitution by interpretation to keep it abreast of modern ideas, I have never believed
that lifetime judges in our system have any such legislative power.[48]

[48] McGautha v. California, 402 U.S.
183, 226 (1971).

Justice Black's view that the Eighth Amendment did not
apply to capital punishment was accepted by the Court until
the historic case of *Furman* v. *Georgia*, decided in 1972. The
Furman case, in which the petitioner had been convicted of
murder during a burglary and sentenced to death, was joined
with two other cases, one in Georgia and the other in Texas, in
which the defendants had been convicted of rape and sentenced to death. All of the defendants were black, and the
women in the rape cases were white.

The Supreme Court invalidated the death sentences in the
Furman and related cases, but the grounds for the invalidation
varied, and each of the majority justices wrote a separate
opinion. The dissenters were also unable to agree on the
constitutionality of the death penalty, and wrote separate
opinions expressing their views.

Justice Douglas, one of the five justices in the majority that
invalidated the death penalty, stated that it was cruel and
unusual punishment to apply the death penalty selectively to
minorities as was the case in the states involved in the *Furman*
case. Justice Brennan declared that the cruel and unusual
punishment provision of the Eighth Amendment was not limited to torture and other forms of punishment that were
considered cruel and unusual at the time the amendment was
adopted. Arbitrarily subjecting persons to capital punishment
which had not been proven to serve any penal purpose was,
concluded Brennan, an affront to human dignity that violated
the Eighth Amendment. Justice Stewart agreed with his colleagues in the majority that the capricious way in which the
death penalty was imposed was unconstitutional cruel and
unusual punishment. Justice White voted to invalidate the
death penalty because in the states involved in the *Furman*
and related cases, Georgia and Texas, the death penalty had

been so infrequently used that it could not be demonstrated to serve the purpose of criminal justice. Finally, in the majority, Justice Marshall flatly stated that the death penalty violated the Eighth Amendment because it was excessive, unnecessary, and morally unacceptable.

Chief Justice Burger led the four dissenting justices whose separate opinions sounded a strong tone of judicial self-restraint. Joining Burger in dissent were Justices Blackmun, Powell, and Rehnquist, all of whom argued that regardless of whether or not members of the Court considered the death penalty to be personally distasteful, it was not the proper role of the Supreme Court to prevent the states from imposing the death penalty, which clearly was not considered to be "cruel" nor "unusual" at the time the Eighth Amendment was adopted. They concluded that the death penalty was no more cruel in the twentieth century than it had been at the time the Eighth Amendment was adopted; therefore, there was no constitutional justification for overturning the use of the death penalty in the states.

In addition to finding the *capricious* imposition of the death penalty a violation of the Eighth Amendment, the Court has found other punishments to be impermissibly cruel and unusual. Long before the *Furman* case in 1972, the Court held in a bizarre case that it was cruel and unusual punishment to subject a person to the process of execution a second time, after the first execution failed because of technical difficulties.[49] In other cases not related to the death penalty the Court has invalidated on Eighth Amendment grounds a state law making narcotic addiction a crime punishable by a short term in jail,[50] and overturned a congressional statute that prescribed the loss of citizenship as part of the punishment for members of the armed forces who had been convicted and dishonorably discharged for desertion during wartime.[51] The Court has also reviewed prison conditions and practices to determine whether or not they are in conformity with judicial standards required under the Eighth Amendment. For example, the Court has ruled that the deliberate indifference of prison officials to the serious medical needs of a prisoner is cruel and unusual punishment.[52]

[49] Louisiana ex rel Francis V. Resweber, Sherf, et al., 329 U.S. 459 (1947), holding that it was cruel and unusual punishment to reschedule a convicted murderer for electrocution after the first attempt had failed because the apparatus malfunctioned and did not deliver sufficient electric current to result in death.

[50] Robinson v. California, 370 U.S. 660 (1962).

[51] Trop v. Dulles, 356 U.S. 86 (1958).

[52] Estelle v. Gamble, 429 U.S. 97 (1976).

Civil Liberties and Civil Rights Under the Constitution

The Ninth Amendment was added to the Bill of Rights to answer one of the most important objections that was raised during the debate over the inclusion of a separate Bill of Rights in the Constitution. One of the principal arguments of Alexander Hamilton and others who opposed a separate Bill of Rights was that it would imply the authority of the national government to abridge rights that were not explicitly enumerated in a Bill of Rights. The Ninth Amendment expressly bars such an inference:

The enumeration in the Constitution, of certain rights, shall not be construed to deny or disparage others retained by the people.

The Ninth Amendment is based upon the widespread eighteenth century belief in natural law and natural rights. Thomas Jefferson articulated in the Declaration of Independence the general philosophy that all men "are endowed by their creator with certain inalienable rights." Jefferson listed life, liberty, and the pursuit of happiness as among the most fundamental natural rights, and believed in natural rights that went far beyond those he had explicitly put into the Declaration of Independence. Jefferson's views reflected those of most eighteenth century Americans, who assumed the existence of natural rights that were conferred by the "laws of nature and of nature's god," and not by government. Jefferson and others considered a separate Bill of Rights important simply to reinforce the protection of citizens against governmental intrusion into clearly important areas of civil liberties and civil rights. But the framers of the Bill of Rights did not intend that its enumeration would be inclusive of all natural rights and liberties, a point that was made explicit by the Ninth Amendment.

The concept of natural law and natural rights, accepted at the time the Constitution, the Bill of Rights, and the Ninth Amendment were framed and adopted, poses difficulties for those who interpret and implement law. Defining the content of natural law and the natural rights derived from it is necessarily a highly subjective process. The framers of the Constitution apparently did not want to grapple with the issue of enumerating the rights and liberties of citizens apart from the very few rights they included in the main body of the Constitution, on which there was no disagreement. James Madison and his colleagues in the first Congress that framed the Bill of Rights recognized that it was only a partial listing of the fundamental rights and liberties of citizens.

The Supreme Court has periodically recognized that there is a universe of rights that extends beyond the explicit provisions of the Bill of Rights. The due process clause of the Fourteenth Amendment in particular has been used not only to incorporate most of the provisions of the Bill of Rights, but also, in several important cases, to extend the right of privacy, a right that was not enumerated in the Bill of Rights. The right of privacy was defended in *Griswold* v. *Connecticut* (1965), in which the Court ruled that a Connecticut statute which made it a criminal act to prescribe or *use* birth control devices was an unconstitutional invasion of personal privacy. Justice William O. Douglas wrote the majority opinion in the *Griswold* case, citing the Ninth Amendment as justification for extending rights to citizens that were not part of the Bill of Rights. Douglas stated that the

> guarantees in the Bill of Rights have penumbras, formed by emanations from those guarantees that help give them life and substance. . . . Various guarantees create zones of privacy. The right of association contained in the penumbra of the First Amendment is one. . . . The Third Amendment in its prohibition against the quartering of soldiers "in any house" in time of peace without the consent of the owner is another facet of that privacy. The Fourth Amendment explicitly affirms the "right of the people to be secure in their persons, houses, papers, and effects, against unreasonable searches and seizures." The Fifth Amendment in its self-incrimination clause enables the citizen to create a zone of privacy which government may not force him to surrender to his detriment.[53]

In the *Griswold* case the Court used the due process clause of the Fourteenth Amendment to incorporate a new right of privacy that had never before been explicitly upheld against intrusion by the states.

Justice Goldberg emphasized the importance of the Ninth Amendment in granting the Court freedom to go beyond the Bill of Rights in defining the protections afforded to citizens:

> . . . The Ninth Amendment to the Constitution may be regarded by some as a recent discovery and may be forgotten by others, but since 1791 it has been a basic part of the Constitution which we are sworn

[53] Griswold v. Connecticut, 381 U.S. 479, 484 (1965).

Civil Liberties and Civil Rights Under the Constitution

to uphold. To hold that a right so basic and fundamental and so deep-rooted in our society as the right of privacy in marriage may be infringed because that right is not guaranteed in so many words by the first eight amendments to the Constitution is to ignore the Ninth Amendment and to give it no effect whatsoever. Moreover, a judicial construction that this fundamental right is not protected by the Constitution because it is not mentioned in explicit terms by one of the first eight amendments or elsewhere in the Constitution, would violate the Ninth Amendment, which specifically states that "The enumeration in the Constitution, of certain rights, shall not be *construed* to deny or disparage others retained by the people."[54]

The *Griswold* case was a launching ground for a major debate in constitutional law regarding the authority of the Supreme Court to go beyond the Bill of Rights in defining the due process clause of the Fourteenth Amendment. Justice Black, dissenting, became the leading spokesman for the point of view that the Court should limit itself to upholding only those rights that were explicitly enumerated in the Bill of Rights. Black took the historically questionable position that the Ninth Amendment was "intended to limit the federal government to the powers granted expressly or by necessary implication."[55] The Ninth Amendment, concluded Black, should not be used in combination with the due process clause of the Fourteenth Amendment to limit state action beyond the constraints expressly stated in the Bill of Rights.[56]

The Ninth Amendment was again used by some of the justices of the Supreme Court as a ground for supporting the interventionist approach of the Court in recognizing a right to personal privacy that included, within limits, the right to abortion. Justice Blackmun's opinion for the Court stated that the right of privacy, "whether it be founded in the Fourteenth Amendment's concept of personal liberty and restrictions upon state action, as we feel it is, or as the district court determined in the Ninth Amendment's reservation of rights to the people, is broad enough to encompass a woman's decision whether or not to terminate her pregnancy."[57] Justice Blackmun was pointing out that the Ninth Amendment could be used as a basis for the Court's decision, although the majority of justices in the *Roe* case held that the abortion statutes under consideration invaded the liberty that was protected by the due process clause of the Fourteenth Amendment. In a concurring opinion, Justice Douglas noted that the

[54] Ibid., pp. 491–92. Emphasis added.

[55] Ibid., p. 520.

[56] Black had consistently taken the position that the due process clause of the Fourteenth Amendment fully incorporated the provisions of the Bill of Rights. In the context of the 1940s and 1950s Black's position—in contrast to that of Justice Frankfurter, for example—was considered to be one of judicial intervention. Frankfurter, unlike Black, favored only selective incorporation of certain provisions of the Bill of Rights as part of due process under the Fourteenth Amendment.

[57] Roe v. Wade, 410 U.S. 113, 153 (1973).

Ninth Amendment "obviously does not create federally enforceable rights. . . . But a catalog of these rights includes customary, traditional, and time-honored rights, amenities, privileges, and immunities that come within the sweep of 'the blessings of liberty' mentioned in the Preamble to the Constitution. Many of them, in my view, come within the meaning of the term 'liberty' as used in the Fourteenth Amendment."[58]

[58] Ibid., pp. 210–11.

The Tenth Amendment: The Reserved Powers of the States

The Tenth Amendment adds nothing to the intent of the framers of the Constitution, which clearly was to establish a national government with enumerated and implied powers while reserving to the states all powers that were not delegated to the national government. The 1787 Constitution, however, did not explicitly provide a reserved powers clause guaranteeing to state governments all those powers not delegated to the national government. Reassurances by proponents of the Constitution during the ratification campaign, stating that the new national government would be limited to those powers defined in the Constitution, were not accepted by advocates of states rights and by those fearful of an overbearing national government. Alexander Hamilton, for example, pointed out that the "powers delegated by the proposed constitution to the federal government are few and defined. Those which are to remain in the state governments are numerous and indefinite." Hamilton, perhaps the strongest nationalist of the time, was nevertheless willing to declare unequivocally that "the powers *reserved* to the several states would extend to all the objects which, in the ordinary course of affairs, concern the lives, liberties, and properties of the people, and the internal order, improvement, and prosperity of the states."[59]

[59] *The Federalist*, 45. Emphasis added.

The Tenth Amendment was added to the Bill of Rights to assuage the fears of the advocates of states' rights. The amendment provides:

The powers not delegated to the United States by the Constitution, nor prohibited by it to the states, are reserved to the states respectively, or the people.

The proponents of states' rights had, during the debate over

Civil Liberties and Civil Rights Under the Constitution

the Tenth Amendment, attempted to limit more explicitly the authority of the national government by limiting its powers to those "expressly" delegated by the Constitution. The nationalists, led by Madison, defeated the end-run attempt by the champions of states' rights in the first Congress, for they recognized, as they had during the Constitutional Convention itself and the ratification campaign, that a viable national government had to be given the flexibility to employ whatever means were necessary and proper for the implementation of its enumerated powers.

While the Tenth Amendment was a redundant addition to the Constitution, it was later to be cited from time to time by the Supreme Court and by the advocates of states' rights as an important limitation upon the authority of the national government. In the early twentieth century the Court used the Tenth Amendment to support the doctrine of dual federalism, which held that the national government could not use its authority under Article I to invade the reserved powers of the states. For example, an attempt by Congress in 1916 to regulate the conditions of child labor in the states by using its commerce power to prevent the shipment in interstate commerce of goods produced by children under proscribed conditions was invalidated by the Court in *Hammer* v. *Dagenhart* in 1918. The Court simply held that the control over the conditions of production was a matter of local concern and fell within the sphere of the reserved police powers of the states that could not be invaded by the national government.[60] The doctrine of dual federalism survived until the middle of Franklin D. Roosevelt's second term. The Court earlier had frustrated many of the major programs of the New Deal and in some cases used the Tenth Amendment as the basis for its decisions. In 1936 the Court overturned a major piece of New Deal legislation regulating the conditions of agricultural production on the ground that the power to regulate agriculture was reserved to the states.[61]

The Court's abandonment of the doctrine of dual federalism after 1937 was a return to the nationalist position on the scope of federal power that had been taken by Chief Justice John Marshall at the outset of the nineteenth century. In a number of wide-ranging opinions, Marshall rejected the

[60] Hammer v. Dagenhart, 247 U.S. 251 (1918).

[61] United States v. Butler, 297 U.S. 1 (1936).

argument made by the proponents of states' rights that the Tenth Amendment limited the authority of the national government to powers that had been expressly enumerated in the Constitution. In *McCulloch* v. *Maryland* (1819) and in *Gibbons* v. *Ogden* (1824), he argued that Congress has the authority not only to employ whatever means it considers necessary to implement its enumerated powers, but also to exercise exclusive jurisdiction in cases of conflict between federal and state laws. The abandonment by the Supreme Court of the doctrine of dual federalism in 1937 was accompanied by a return to the firm nationalistic tone of the opinions of the Marshall Court.

THE PROCESS OF NATIONALIZATION OF THE BILL OF RIGHTS

The preceding overview of the Bill of Rights lists the dates for the inclusion of particular rights under the due process clause of the Fourteenth Amendment, making them applicable to state action. Most of these provisions were not finally incorporated under the Fourteenth Amendment until the end of the Warren Court era in 1968. The process of incorporation was a gradual one that reflected shifting views on the Supreme Court and changing responses to what were considered by many justices to be conditions in the states requiring judicial intervention rather than self-restraint.

Applying the Bill of Rights Under the Due Process Clause

The process of nationalization involved the Court in a delicate and often controversial process of applying its own values in defining the content of the due process clause of the Fourteenth Amendment. The intent of the congressional framers of the Fourteenth Amendment was very likely to make the entire Bill of Rights applicable to the states under the amendment's privileges and immunities clause, which provided that no state "shall make or enforce any law which shall abridge the privileges or immunities of citizens of the United States."[62] Five years after the adoption of the Fourteenth Amendment, however, the Supreme Court in the historic *Slaughterhouse Cases* ruled that the privileges and immunities clause of the Four-

[62] The radical republicans in Congress who authored and sponsored the Fourteenth Amendment stated explicitly that the privileges and immunities clause incorporated the entire

Civil Liberties and Civil Rights Under the Constitution

teenth Amendment did not in any way alter the constitutional balance between the national government and the states that had existed before the amendment was adopted.[63] The "privileges and immunities" of citizens of the United States, the Court held, consisted of the same privileges and immunities that had originally been incorporated into the Constitution, such as the privilege to possess property. The Court concluded that the rights of citizens insofar as they were exclusively within state jurisdictions were determined solely by state constitutions and laws. The effect of the *Slaughterhouse* opinion was to establish two classes of citizens, those of the United States on the one hand, and those of the states on the other. The rights and obligations of each class of citizen were determined, respectively, by the federal Constitution and laws and by state constitutions and laws.

The *Slaughterhouse* decision essentially struck the privileges and immunities clause from the Fourteenth Amendment as a viable weapon for judicial protection of civil liberties and rights. When, in the twentieth century, the Court was challenged to extend the protections of the Bill of Rights to the states, the means it had for doing this was the due process clause of the Fourteenth Amendment, unless it chose explicitly to overrule the *Slaughterhouse* decision and resurrect the privileges and immunities clause. The Court found the due process clause to be easily adaptable to applying the Bill of Rights within state jurisdictions; moreover, by using the admittedly vague concept of due process the Court had discretion to impose its own interpretation of exactly what constituted Fourteenth Amendment due process. The due process clause readily accommodated the ebb and flow of judicial opinion concerning how far the standards of the Bill of Rights should reach into the states. (See Figure 2.1.)

The process of incorporation of most of the provisions of the Bill of Rights was a long and often tortuous one. In deciding whether or not to incorporate certain provisions under due process, the Court was essentially engaging in substantive due process review. That is, the Court frequently injected its own values into its definitions of what constituted "liberty," just as it had in determining under what circumstances "property" could be regulated under the due process

Bill of Rights as a limitation upon the states. Even those in Congress who opposed the Fourteenth Amendment agreed that its privileges and immunities clause would have the effect of nationalizing the Bill of Rights. Historical evidence, however, does not clearly establish that the state legislatures which adopted the amendment agreed that it would nationalize the Bill of Rights.

---

[63] Slaughterhouse Cases, 16 Wallace 36 (1873).

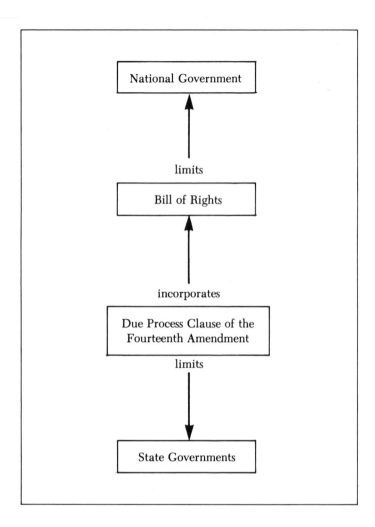

FIGURE 2.1
The Application of the Bill of Rights.
The Bill of Rights limits state action only through the due process clause of the Fourteenth Amendment.

clause. For example, when the Court decided in *Gitlow* v. *New York* that the "liberty" of the Fourteenth Amendment incorporated the freedom of speech and press of the First Amendment, it was simply applying its own notions of what the Fourteenth Amendment due process clause should protect. Moreover, the Court's method of giving procedural substance to the due process clause was as subjective as its formula for determining the liberty and property rights.

Early in the twentieth century the Court declared that its standard for determining what freedoms and rights were to be included under the due process clause was to be whether or

Civil Liberties and Civil Rights Under the Constitution

not a freedom or right was fundamental to the protection of liberty and justice, historical, and "implicit in the concept of ordered liberty."[64]

The standards of due process that the Court began to develop as early as 1908, in *Twining* v. *New Jersey,* at first resulted only in a highly selective process of incorporation of the Bill of Rights. By the time of the benchmark case of *Palko* v. *Connecticut* in 1937, in which Justice Cardozo spelled out the selective incorporation approach that had become and was to remain the basis of interpreting the due process clause by a majority of justices, only a few of the safeguards of the Bill of Rights had been incorporated. These included all of the freedoms of the First Amendment, with the exception of the right of petition; the eminent domain safeguards of the Fifth Amendment; a watered down right to counsel drawn from the Sixth Amendment, which applied only to capital cases; and a general right to a fair trial based upon the Seventh and Eighth Amendments, but not fully applying the provisions of those amendments. The long process of incorporating most of the remainder of the Bill of Rights was finally completed in 1968.

During the incorporation process there were frequently sharp disagreements on the Court regarding the proper formula to be used in defining Fourteenth Amendment due process. The selective incorporation approach, articulated by Justice Cardozo in the *Palko* opinion, was the most widely accepted and required that the definition of the various components of the Fourteenth Amendment due process clause be drawn explicitly from the provisions of the Bill of Rights. Usually this meant that the incorporation of a provision of the Bill of Rights would make it applicable to the states in the same way that it applied in federal jurisdiction. The incorporation of the right of privacy under due process in the *Griswold* case in 1965 added an important new dimension to the selective incorporation formula under which the Court expressed its willingness to go beyond the Bill of Rights in defining due process. This approach has been described as "selective incorporation *plus*."[65]

A more flexible and subjective approach to defining due process than resulted from selective incorporation was advocated by Justice Felix Frankfurter and a minority of the

[64] These standards are enunciated in Palko v. Connecticut, 302 U.S. 319 (1937); and Twining v. New Jersey, 211 U.S. 78 (1908).

[65] Henry J. Abraham, *Freedom and the Court,* 3rd ed. (New York: Oxford University Press, 1977), pp. 97, 100–102.

[66] Ibid., pp. 97–99.

[67] An excellent and interesting example of the Frankfurter approach may be found in Rochin v. California, 342 U.S. 165 (1952), in which Frankfurter wrote the Court's opinion holding that stomach-pumping to produce evidence for a criminal trial was a violation of due process because the conduct "shocks the conscience," and offends even "hardened sensibilities." The methods were "too close to the rack and the screw to permit of constitutional differentiation."

Court.[66] The Frankfurter approach has often been referred to as one of "natural law," under which due process was defined on the basis of the same general standards used in selective incorporation—namely, the fundamental, historical, and essential nature of a freedom or right. The Bill of Rights would not itself be used as the major reference point in the process of definition. Under the Frankfurter method, a right or freedom would be incorporated under the Fourteenth Amendment not because it was in the Bill of Rights, but because regardless of the Bill of Rights it could be considered of a fundamental nature.[67]

Another minority approach to defining Fourteenth Amendment due process was espoused by Justice Black, who argued that it was the clear intent of the framers of the Fourteenth Amendment to apply the Bill of Rights to the states, and that therefore *all* of the provisions of the Bill of Rights should be incorporated under the due process clause. Black forcefully argued against the position that more freedoms and rights than were explicitly included in the Bill of Rights could be extended to the states under the rubric of due process. His dissent in the *Griswold* case argued that since there was no express right to privacy in the Bill of Rights, the Connecticut birth control law—which Black considered to be "uncommonly silly"—could not be invalidated on the ground that it violated a right of personal privacy that was protected by due process of law.

The essential completion of the incorporation of the Bill of Rights by the end of the Warren Court era in 1968 did not finally resolve controversy over the meaning of due process within and without the Court. In the middle decades of the twentieth century, considerations of federalism were an important basis for judicial self-restraint in limiting the extension of the protections afforded citizens at the national level to the states. The Warren Court's adoption of the "incorporation-plus" approach in the *Griswold* case raised the possibility of the Court's becoming a super legislature over the states in important areas of public policy. The Court's decision to invalidate state abortion laws in *Roe* v. *Wade* in 1973, on the ground that they violated personal privacy protected by the Fourteenth Amendment, was heralded by many

Civil Liberties and Civil Rights Under the Constitution

as a defense of freedom of choice, but criticized by some as an outrage. The political controversy over the abortion decision continued into the 1980s, when right-to-life groups pushed for a constitutional amendment that would overturn the Court's decision.

The history of incorporation continually involved the Court in controversies regarding the extent to which national standards should control the states. The incorporation-plus position that has been taken by the Court has extended the controversy to involve the question of how far the justices should go in imposing their own values of due process of law beyond what is explicitly part of the Bill of Rights.

A NOTE ON EQUAL PROTECTION OF THE LAWS

The Bill of Rights does not explicitly require equal protection under the laws. The constitutional prescription of equality is first found in the Fourteenth Amendment equal protection clause, which provides: "No state shall . . . deny to any person in its jurisdiction the equal protection of the laws." The principle of equality was first applied to the states to protect the newly freed blacks from discrimination. Requirements for equal protection are also found in the Thirteenth Amendment, prohibiting slavery and involuntary servitude, and in the Fifteenth Amendment, forbidding the government to deny citizens of the United States the right to vote "on account of race, color, or previous condition of servitude."

With the exception of the privileges and immunities clause in the original Constitution, which, in the words of Alexander Hamilton, was designed to assure "that equality of privileges and immunities to which the citizens of the Union will be entitled,"[68] equal protection did not exist as an operative concept before it became an explicit part of the Fourteenth Amendment in 1868. The framers of the Constitution assumed that all citizens would be equal before the law; they did not consider it necessary to state or even discuss the obvious. Insofar as the framers discussed equality, they were concerned with the equality of the vote of each state in the Senate, the equality of representation in the House, based upon popula-

[68] *The Federalist*, 80.

tion, and the equality of states in voting for the president. The issue of equality at the Convention, then, focused upon the equality of states, not of citizens, except insofar as they were represented by states. The framers of the Constitution knew, in the words of South Carolina delegate Charles Pinckney, that among the people of the United States, "there are fewer distinctions of fortune and less of rank than among the inhabitants of any other nation. Every freeman has a right to the same protection and security and a very moderate share of property entitles them to the possession of all the honors and privileges the public can bestow. Hence arises a greater equality, than used to be found among the people of any other country, an equality which is more likely to continue."[69]

While the states are required to provide equal protection under the Civil War amendments, particularly the Fourteenth, and under the privileges and immunities clause of Article IV, sec. 2, equal protection standards have been extended to the national government as well.[70] In *Bolling* v. *Sharpe* (1954), the Court found an equal protection command in the due process clause of the Fifth Amendment.[71] Again, in *Wesberry* v. *Sanders* (1964), the Court held that the requirement of Article I, sec. 2 that representatives be chosen "by the people of the several states" means "that as nearly as is practicable one man's vote in a congressional election is to be worth as much as another's."[72]

The standards of equal protection, which have been principally developed and applied under the Fourteenth Amendment equal protection clause for the states and under the due process clause of the Fifth Amendment for the national government, have varied over time. Until the Warren Court era the states were given broad discretion to enact laws that treated separate groups of people differently. Considerations of federalism were paramount in the minds of most justices in reviewing state action challenged on equal protection grounds. The interventionist stance of the Warren Court radically altered the way in which equal protection was judicially determined.

How the Problem of Equal Protection Arises

A potential problem of equal protection arises when legislation treats two groups of people differently in pursuit of a

[69] Farrand, *Records,* 1:398.

[70] Under the privileges and immunities clause, states are required to grant equal treatment under their laws to citizens of other states. See, for example, Toomer v. Witsell, 334 U.S. 385, 395 (1948).

[71] Bolling v. Sharpe, 347 U.S. 497 (1954).

[72] Wesberry v. Sanders, 376 U.S. 1, 7–8 (1964).

Civil Liberties and Civil Rights Under the Constitution

particular legislative goal. For example, benefits under the Social Security system may not be allocated to men and women on the same basis, reflecting a congressional premise that the economic needs of men and women differ. In a section of the Social Security law that was declared unconstitutional in 1975, Congress provided greater benefits to women than to men similarly situated.[73] A variety of provisions of federal and state laws have granted women greater economic benefits than men in the same position. This results in "unequal treatment" in the generic sense, but is not necessarily in violation of constitutional standards of equal protection applied by the courts. For example, the Court has upheld tax exemptions for widows that were not granted to widowers,[74] and exempting women from jury duty unless they volunteered.[75] Increasingly, however, the unequal treatment of men and women in law has been disallowed by the Supreme Court. In addition to eliminating gender differentiation in the Social Security law, the Court has voided laws which exclude women from being appointed the administrators of estates,[76] deny military dependency allowances to the male spouses of female members of the armed services,[77] and which require husbands but not wives to pay alimony following divorce.[78]

The process of differentiating groups of people in legislation is one of *classification* of those groups for the purposes of the law. Since the decision of the Warren Court in *Brown* v. *Board of Education* in 1954, racial classifications have been overturned, even those designed to remedy the effects of past discrimination.[79] In the *Brown* case itself the Court unanimously declared unconstitutional the de jure segregation of the races in seventeen southern and border states. Other classifications in law that the Court has viewed with suspicion but has not always voided include the separate classification and differential treatment of "illegitimate" children,[80] aliens,[81] and poor people.[82]

Strengthening equal protection of the laws has been a major movement in both federal and state courts since the era of the Warren Court, which extended from 1953 to 1968. The Warren Court was particularly anxious to protect the right of racial minorities to equal treatment under the law. Complementing the decisions of the Supreme Court during the War-

[73] Weinberger v. Weisenfeld, 420 U.S. 636 (1975).

[74] Kahn v. Shevin, 416 U.S. 351 (1974), upholding a Florida law giving more favorable tax exemptions to widows than to widowers on the grounds that the legislative classification was substantially related to a legitimate legislative goal, namely remedying the subordinate economic position of women in society.

[75] Hoyt v. Florida, 368 U.S. 57 (1961), sustaining the Florida law that exempted women from jury duty but required men to serve on the grounds that the separate treatment of men and women was justified because "woman is still regarded as the center of home and family life." Ibid., pp. 61–62.

[76] Reed v. Reed, 404 U.S. 71 (1971).

[77] Frontiero v. Richardson, 411 U.S. 677 (1973).

[78] Orr v. Orr, 440 U.S. 268 (1979).

[79] Regents of the University of California v. Bakke, 438 U.S. 265 (1978).

[80] See, for example, Labine v. Vincent, 401 U.S. 532 (1971), upholding a Louisiana law subordinating the rights of acknowledged illegitimate children to legitimate children and relatives of the parents in claims upon an estate left without a will; and Weber v. Aetna Casualty and Surety Co., 406 U.S. 164 (1972), overturning a Louisiana workers compensation law that subordinated the claims of illegitimate to those of legitimate children.

[81] See, for example, Gram v. Richardson, 403 U.S. 365 (1971), voiding a state law that denied welfare benefits to all noncitizens and to aliens who had not resided in the country for a period of fifteen years; and In re Griffiths, 413 U.S. 717 (1973), invalidating the New York law that limited permanent positions in the state civil service to American citizens.

[82] In San Antonio v. Rodriguez, 411 U.S. 1 (1973), the Court sustained a Texas law under which the property tax was used by local communities as the basis of financing public education. The law had been challenged as a violation of the equal protection clause of the Fourteenth Amendment on the grounds that it operated to the disadvantage of the poorer school districts.

ren period were congressional and presidential actions that vastly extended equal protection of the laws under the Civil Rights Act of 1964, the Voting Rights Act of 1965, and a major affirmative action program initiated by President Lyndon B. Johnson. Under affirmative action the government required its own agencies, as well as groups in the private sector receiving federal funds, to take measures to remedy the effects of past discrimination. Affirmative action programs became commonplace throughout the federal bureaucracy and among universities, labor unions, and private employers to encourage the hiring of blacks and other racial minorities, as well as women—groups that had been subject to past discrimination.

Both the Supreme Court and the political arms of government retreated from the firm commitment to affirmative action made by the Court, Congress, and the president in the 1960s. The 1978 Bakke decision in particular questioned the very basis of affirmative action by holding that the University of California, Davis, medical school could not establish quotas for the admission of members of racial minorities. Such a practice, stated the Court's majority, was unconstitutional "reverse discrimination" against whites. The conservative approach of the Burger Court toward equal protection was complemented by the Reagan administration, which moved immediately to soften affirmative action programs in the federal government and the private sector. The Reagan administration also opposed continuation of provisions of the Voting Rights Act of 1965, which authorized the Justice Department to intervene actively within state and local jurisdictions to prevent discrimination in voting.

While there has been a shift away from governmental activism in affirmative action and other areas of equal protection, the fundamental right to equality under the law remains an outstanding feature of the American polity, one that has strengthened democracy and constitutional government.

Suggestions for Further Reading

Abraham, Henry J. *Freedom and the Court.* 3rd edition. New York: Oxford University Press, 1977. The author discusses the development of civil liberties and civil rights through an examination of leading Supreme Court cases.

Higginbotham, A. Leon, Jr. *In the Matter of Color.* New York: Oxford University Press, 1978. An award-winning study of the role of law in the subjugation of black Americans during the colonial period.

Kluger, Richard. *Simple Justice.* New York: Random House, 1977. The history of school desegregation from the adoption of the Fourteenth Amendment in 1868 to the *Brown* cases in 1954 and 1955.

Orfield, Gary. *Congressional Power: Congress and Social Change.* New York: Harcourt Brace Jovanovich, 1975. An examination of the legislative politics of civil rights legislation.

Sindler, Allan P. *Bakke, Defunis, and Minority Admissions.* New York: Longman, 1978. An absorbing account of the Bakke case and the history of affirmative action.

Woodward, C. Van. *The Strange Career of Jim Crow.* New York: Oxford University Press, 1957. A brief account of the background and flavor of segregation as it was practiced in the South.

The national government and the states are partners in the political process. (The Colorado, South Carolina, and Massachusetts state houses are depicted below the U.S. Capitol.)

CHAPTER 3

The Dynamics of the Federal System

The history of American politics is to a very large extent a reflection of the changing balance between national and state power. The struggle for freedom in America began with the colonies attempting to free themselves from England's yoke. Although the colonial governments were legally directly under the control of the British government, in practice the enormous distance in space and time between the mother country and America enabled the colonies to have wide discretion in determining how they were to govern themselves. The quest for freedom that drew the colonists to America was nurtured on its shores, and eventually led to the Revolution and the Declaration of Independence.

The Revolution and the Declaration of Independence reflected the desire of the former colonies that had now become independent states to retain their sovereignty as *states*. The Declaration of Independence is somewhat misleading in its title: "A Declaration by the representatives of the United States of America in Congress assembled." While the Declaration seems to be referring to a union of the states, in fact each of the states considered itself an independent, sovereign body. The signing of the Declaration represented approval by the states themselves as well as a mutual pledge by its signers to support its principles and the boycott and embargo actions that already had been taken against Great Britain. Although the signing was a tentative first step toward union, Garry Wills points out that "The 'we' of the Declaration is neither the 'we the people' of the Constitution nor the 'we as individuals' who signed as a promise of observing the embargos. The

[1] Garry Wills, *Inventing America* (Garden City, N.Y.: Doubleday 1978), p. 340.

Declaration speaks for the thirteen United *States*. These new *states* pledged to each other their honor, that honor accruing to sovereignties as they take their 'free and equal station' with other nations."[1]

While the Articles of Confederation, submitted to the states by Congress in 1777 and finally ratified by all of the states in 1781, moved tentatively and timidly in the direction of establishing a central government, they left the sovereignty of the states largely untouched. Under the Articles, all national governmental authority resided in a Congress in which each state had one vote. The powers delegated by the Articles to the national government were very limited, and did not include the authority to tax or to regulate commerce. Given their recent experience with Great Britain, whose taxes and commercial regulations upon the colonists had led to so much unhappiness that it was a major cause of the break with the mother country, the states had no intention of relinquishing these powers to the national government.

The lack of an explicit executive and judicial authority under the Articles was a major weakness, to say the least, in the national government, but it would have been unthinkable at such an early stage in the development of the new government to create the kind of strong executive authority that eventually emerged under Article II of the Constitution. Too many colonists perceived a strong executive as a threat to their fundamental rights of life, liberty, and property.

The weakness of the national government under the Articles was reflected in their provision that: "Each state retains its sovereignty, freedom and independence, and every power, jurisdiction and right, which is not by this confederation expressly delegated to the United States, in Congress assembled." The inclusion of this caveat was a victory for the advocates of states' rights. Its terms provide an interesting background to the debate that occurred after the adoption of the Constitution over the proper interpretation of the authority of Congress under Article I. It was clearly the intent of the federalists at the Convention to allow the extension of congressional authority beyond the explicit powers of Article I to incorporate whatever reasonable means Congress considered necessary to execute its powers. The Articles of Confederation

The Dynamics of the Federal System

were based upon the acceptance of the supremacy of states' rights, whereas the Constitution was unequivocally nationalist in its thrust.

From the perspective of the 1980s it is easy to forget that the emergence of a real union of the states came only after long and bitter conflict between proponents of national power and advocates of states' rights. It is remarkable that in the atmosphere of the postrevolutionary period, when state sovereignty was widely accepted without question, a constitution clearly nationalist in tone was drafted in the first place and ratified by the states. It took men of vision—not just men of property out to protect their interests, as Charles Beard claims—to see the importance of the nationalist cause as the failure of the government under the Articles of Confederation became increasingly evident. The need to provide for a strong national defense, which could only come about through the common action of the states, was an important motivating factor in the adoption of the Constitution of 1787, as was the evident need for the national regulation of commerce among the states and with foreign nations. Under the Articles the states continued to act as free and independent nations, but they had already become too intertwined commercially to permit each to go its own way. Foreign commercial and military threats to the interests of the individual states could be met only by the establishment of a national government capable of insuring the national defense and the regulation of foreign commerce.

As the federal system evolved, it was profoundly shaped by the development of constitutional doctrines of federalism and by changing political forces.

THE CONSTITUTIONAL BACKGROUND OF FEDERALISM

Federalism is defined as a system in which there is a constitutional division of authority between a central government and, collectively, constituent units that in the United States are the individual states.[2] Federalism contrasts with a unitary form of government in which all constitutional authority remains with the national government. (See Figure 3.1.) The

Definition of Federalism

[2] The constituent units in federal systems are referred to in different ways. In the Canadian system, for example, the constituent units are called provinces.

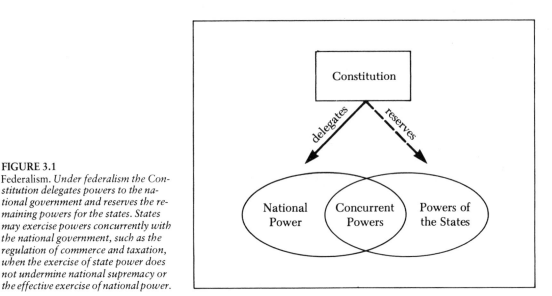

FIGURE 3.1
Federalism. *Under federalism the Constitution delegates powers to the national government and reserves the remaining powers for the states. States may exercise powers concurrently with the national government, such as the regulation of commerce and taxation, when the exercise of state power does not undermine national supremacy or the effective exercise of national power.*

constitutional division of authority between national and constituent units in federal or unitary systems does not have to be based upon written constitutions, but may stem from parliamentary legislation. In Great Britain, for example, which is a unitary government, the actions of Parliament are supreme, and insofar as they affect the basic structures of government and determine the rights and liberties of the British people, they form the unwritten constitution of the country. Laws of Parliament may also determine Commonwealth relationships, and, in the case of Canada, the British–North American Act of 1867 became the "constitution" of Canada. The Canadian government remains without a formal written constitution similar to the American Constitution of 1787. Whether by formal constitution or informal constitutional arrangements adopted through statutory law, all of the federal systems of the world—which consist primarily of systems arising from former British colonies—grant by law a degree of governmental autonomy to constituent units.[3]

The constitutional division of authority between national and state governments in a federal system is a meaningful one in which the states independently or concurrently with the national government exercise substantial powers. In the focus of our study, the United States, the constitutional powers

[3] Federal systems that were former British colonies, in addition to the United States, are: Australia, Canada, India, Malaysia, Nigeria, and Pakistan. The British West Indies, New Zealand, and Rhodesia tried federalism but failed. The only former self-governing British colonies that never tried federalism are Burma and the Union of South Africa.

The Dynamics of the Federal System

granted to the federal government by the delegates at the 1787 Convention represented the extreme to which the nationalists could go in strengthening the central government and at the same time secure the support of Convention moderates and advocates of states' rights. While Alexander Hamilton boldly suggested the possibility of abolishing the states altogether, neither he nor any of the other delegates saw such a course of action as a practical possibility.

Establishing Federalism

The constitutional overview given in Chapter 1 stresses the nationalistic character of the Convention of 1787, and the fact that both James Madison and Alexander Hamilton, whose views of the Constitution are used to reflect two important contrasting ways in which the Constitution may be interpreted, agreed fundamentally on the principle of national dominion over the states. Madison was as much a nationalist as Hamilton in advocating a strong national government in relation to the states.

The Madisonian and Hamiltonian perspectives reflected the views of an overwhelming majority of the Convention delegates. After all, the Convention had been called specifically to remedy deficiencies in the Articles of Confederation, and to strengthen the weaknesses of the federated government under the Articles, particularly in relation to the regulation of commerce and providing for the common defense.

Virginia delegate Edmund Randolph, whose plan provided the basis for the Constitution itself, laid three propositions before the Convention early in its proceedings that suggested "a union of the states merely federal will not accomplish the objects proposed by the Articles of Confederation, namely, common defense, security of liberty, and general welfare."[4] Randolph stressed that "a *national* government ought to be established, consisting of a *supreme* legislative, executive, and judiciary."[5]

Charles Pinckney was shocked at what he considered to be the implication of Randolph's remarks, which he saw as favoring the abolition of state governments altogether. He asked Randolph if that was his intent, and the Virginian replied that he merely wished to advocate the adoption of the

[4] Farrand, *Records,* 1:30.

[5] Ibid. The emphasis is in the original text.

[6] Ibid., pp. 18–19, 30.

[7] A rump session is an illegal gathering of individuals who refuse to disband according to law. William Safire points out that the word "rump" is "from the Scandinavian word for the hind quarters of an animal, its meaning crossing over to 'remnant' or 'tail end.' " See William Safire, *Safire's Political Dictionary* (New York: Random House, 1978), p. 623.

plan he had submitted to the Convention, which did not call for the abolition of the states but for a national government powerful enough to cope with the pressing national concerns of an adequate defense, the development of commerce, and the prevention of quarreling among the states that could lead to disintegration of the country.[6]

The opponents of the Randolph plan backed that of William Patterson of New Jersey, who wanted to preserve the system of government under the Articles of Confederation, with only minor changes that would increase the authority of Congress. Under the Patterson plan, the national government could not act directly upon *individuals* within states, but only upon the states themselves. Moreover, the people would have no direct representative in the national government, but could only be indirectly represented through the states. As under the Articles of Confederation, each state would have a single vote in a unicameral national legislature. The states were the focal point of the Patterson plan, which expanded the powers of the Congress to include the right to tax and to regulate commerce, but did not provide the national government with instruments of enforcement. A fundamental premise of Patterson's approach was that the Convention lacked the authority to alter drastically the Articles of Confederation. Although Patterson did not go so far as to proclaim the Convention a rump session,[7] he did suggest that the Randolph plan would be essentially illegal because its provisions went beyond the authorized powers of the Convention.

The majority of Convention delegates readily defeated the Patterson plan and ignored its author's admonition regarding the extent of the Convention's authority by adopting a modified form of the Randolph plan. William Patterson, however, represented an important states' rights group at the Convention, which above all did not wish to see the interests of the smaller states ignored by a new national government that would be controlled by such large states as Virginia and New York. Delegates from the smaller states, such as New Jersey, Connecticut, and Massachusetts, worked to secure the "great compromise" between large and small states that secured equal representation for all states in the Senate regardless of their populations.

The Dynamics of the Federal System

By July the Convention was threatened with stalemate over the issue of the proper boundaries between national and state authority, and in particular the representation of the small states in the Senate. Randolph himself had become distinctly disenchanted with the proceedings, and proposed the adjournment of the Convention to enable the large states to regroup their forces to work out a compromise with the small states. Patterson went one step farther than Randolph and proposed the indefinite adjournment of the Convention, stating that: "No conciliation could be admissible on the part of the smaller states, on any other ground than that of an equality of votes in the second branch [the Senate]."[8]

[8] Farrand, *Records,* 2:18.

Ironically, although Randolph supported the "great compromise" which gave equal representation to large and small states in the Senate, he did not support the final draft of the Constitution and refused to sign it. Randolph, who originally had been instrumental in developing a plan that laid the groundwork for the establishment of a national government with the authority to take direct action upon the people of the United States and to act for the nation in foreign affairs, saw his original plan amended to grant even greater powers to the national government than Randolph wished. He opposed the enlargement of the undefined powers of Congress, which he considered to be an unwarranted threat to the states. He rose in the final days of the Convention to voice his objections to the Constitution, among which was "the want of a more definite boundary between the general and state legislatures, and between the general and state judiciaries."[9] Randolph stated that he could not promote the establishment of a plan which he "verily believed would end in tyranny."[10] He called for the initiation of a new constitutional process that would begin with the adoption of a constitutional plan by Congress, after which it would go to the state legislatures and proceed through state conventions to a general convention "with full power to adopt or reject the alterations proposed by the state conventions, and to establish finally the government."[11]

[9] Ibid., p. 564.

[10] Ibid.

[11] Ibid.

While Randolph considered himself to have been overtaken by the nationalists at the Convention who were willing to go further than he was in establishing a powerful national government, William Patterson of New Jersey and most of the

Federalism in the Context in Which the Constitution Was Ratified

be generally unlimited and would be able to exercise excessive power on the basis of the necessary and proper clause. Virginia delegate George Mason also refused to sign because of what he considered to be too broad authority given to the president and unwarranted congressional authority over the states in some areas.

13 It was the skillful parliamentary maneuvering of Benjamin Franklin that secured the adoption of the clause stating that the Constitution had been unanimously approved by the states. This was of course correct, but it did overlook the dissent of Randolph, Mason, and Gerry, and the doubts of other members of the Convention as well regarding the viability of the new Constitution.

14 Farrand, *Records,* I:89.

other delegates from the smaller states at the Convention supported the final plan.12 The Constitution was finally "done in Convention by the unanimous consent of the states present" (Article VII) on 17 September 1787, and submitted to the states to be ratified by *conventions,* with nine states sufficient for ratification.13

The ratification campaign for the Constitution took place in a political environment in which states' rights and state sovereignty were taken for granted. Nationalists at the Convention did not by any means reflect the views of the majority of state leaders. The Convention had been a self-chosen body of nationalists, as the call for the Convention reflected a nationalist bias and the selection of delegates largely resulted in a preponderance of those who favored strengthening the Articles of Confederation. The Convention was a gathering of important political leaders whose views did not always represent the concerns of leaders in the states, many of whom wanted to preserve their own power, and who saw the proposal for a new national government as a distinct threat to their interests.

The delegates to the 1787 Convention knew fully well the difficulties they would face in attempting to secure the approval of the new Constitution in the states. They recognized that state political leaders would more than likely oppose the Constitution. The framers agreed that it was important to bypass state legislatures in particular in the ratification process, and therefore provided for the approval of the Constitution by state conventions.

Edmund Randolph expressed the views of most of the delegates on the importance of ratification by state conventions. "One idea," he declared, "has pervaded all our proceedings, to wit, that opposition as well from the states as from individuals, will be made to the system to be proposed. Will it not then be highly imprudent to furnish any unnecessary pretext by the mode of ratifying it?"14 Ratification by Congress and by state legislatures, he argued, would raise the objection that the Constitution had not been approved by the people directly. Moreover, the state legislative bodies have a vested interest in opposing the Constitution. "Whose opposition will be most likely to be excited against the system?" asked Randolph: "That of the local demagogues who will be degraded by it, from the importance they now hold. They will spare no efforts to impede that progress in the popular mind, which will be necessary to the adoption of the plan."[15] Randolph concluded: "It is of great importance . . . that the consideration of this subject should be transferred from the [state] legislatures, where this class of men have their full influence, to a field in which their efforts can be less mischievous."[16] The power of state politicians would be reduced in conventions elected by the people.

Jame Madison, who agreed with Randolph's political observations on the importance of state conventions, added that state legislatures would not have the legal authority to ratify the new Constitution because the changes it would bring about "would make essential inroads on state constitutions; and it would be a novel and dangerous doctrine, that a legislature could change the constitution under which it held its existence."[17]

The establishment of state conventions for the ratification of the Constitution was a critical first step in securing its approval. Once such approval was obtained, the legitimacy of the Constitution could not be questioned because it would have been accepted by the people directly.

[15] Ibid.

[16] Ibid.

[17] Ibid., pp. 92–93.

The opposition to the Constitution that had been foreseen by its framers, and which led them to attempt to circumvent state political leaders by providing for Convention ratification, materialized with a vengeance. The debate over the Constitution focused upon the issue of federalism, and the proper boundaries of national and state powers. Proponents of the Constitution became known as the Federalists, later to become a political party, while the opponents of the Constitution were called the anti-Federalists.

Prominent among the Federalists were Alexander Hamilton and James Madison, who had been instrumental in sponsoring the call for the Constitutional Convention in the first place, and in drafting its provisions. Hamilton and Madison

Alexander Hamilton and James Madison Explain the New "Federal" Constitution

[18] *The Federalist* consists of eighty-five letters that appeared in the newspapers of New York City from 27 October 1787 through 16 August 1788. See Chapter 1.

were the principal authors of *The Federalist,* essays first published as newspaper articles advocating the adoption of the Constitution in New York.[18]

The Federalist Supreme Court under John Marshall shaped the Constitution in terms that were entirely consistent with the theme of *The Federalist* essays, which supported a strong national government and extensive national powers. Just as the standards of the Marshall Court that buttressed national power became, with only intermittent interruptions, the basis of constitutional interpretation, so the philosophy of *The Federalist* writings provided an important underpinning for the expansion of national power.

Alexander Hamilton was well aware that the Federalists would have to fight for the ratification of the Constitution in New York. For this reason he did not suggest in *The Federalist* that the new national government would dominate the states, as he hoped it would, but attempted to alleviate the fears of the anti-Federalists that the states would lose their sovereignty under the new Constitution. Madison, too, emphasized that the Constitution respected state sovereignty, granting the national government only the necessary powers to deal with national concerns while reserving to the states power over state matters.

While both Hamilton and Madison moderated their nationalistic views in *The Federalist* from those they had expressed at the Convention, the essays in *The Federalist* consistently and unremittingly stressed the need for a strong national government. As indicated in Chapter 1, Hamilton and Madison stressed the importance of a flexible interpretation of national powers, and the need for Congress to have the authority to determine the means for the execution of its enumerated powers. Hamilton argued that the powers of Congress are to be complete and unlimited within the sphere of national powers outlined in Article I.

In The Federalist, Hamilton and Madison underlined one of the most important characteristics of the new Constitution, its delegation to the national government of the authority to act directly upon the citizens of the states without the state governments acting as intermediaries. Hamilton declared that: "A federal government capable of regulating the common concerns and preserving the general tranquility" must be able to "carry its agency [directly] to the persons of the citizens. It must stand in need of no intermediate legislation; but must itself be empowered to employ the arm of the ordinary magistrate to execute its own resolutions. The majesty of the national authority must be manifested through the medium of the courts of justice."[19] If state legislatures were given the authority to act as intermediaries between the national government and the people, a weak and ineffective national government would result.

[19] *The Federalist*, 16.

Hamilton recognized that the new power granted to the national government to act directly upon citizens was considered by the anti-Federalists to be a major threat to state sovereignty. What would prevent the national government from absorbing the power of the states even over local matters? Hamilton attempted to assuage that fear: "Allowing the utmost latitude to the love of power, which any reasonable man can require, I confess I am at a loss to discover what temptation the persons entrusted with the administration of the general government could ever feel to divest the states of [control over local concerns]. The regulation of the mere domestic police of a state, appears to me to hold out slender allurements to ambition. Commerce, finance, negotiation, and war, seem to comprehend all the objects which have charms for minds governed by the passion; and all the powers necessary to those objects, ought, in the first instance, to be lodged in the national depository."[20] In any event, stated Hamilton, the states will be more likely to control the national government than vice versa. Not only are the states directly represented in Congress, but they stand in a dominant position in relation to their own citizens. The loyalty of citizens is first to their state governments, and only secondarily to the national government. Since the loyalty of people is divided by states, a collective national will cannot be formed that would use the instruments of the national government, particularly Congress, to subvert state interests.

[20] *The Federalist*, 17.

Madison, like Hamilton, emphasized in *The Federalist* the balance the new Constitution struck between national and state interests. Madison stressed that the character of the Constitution was both national and "federal." Madison pointed out that the Constitution is national insofar as it regards the Union as a consolidation of states and "federal" in the ways in which the Union is considered to be a confederacy of sovereign states. The ratification of the Constitution itself, he declared is a federal rather than a national act because it requires the participation of the people of each state taken separately. The House of Representatives is national in character, whereas the Senate is federal. Madison stressed the importance of the power of the national government to act directly upon the people. But he concluded that in the extent of its powers the new government is federal, since the jurisdiction of the government "extends to certain enumerated objects only, and leaves to the several states a residuary and inviolable sovereignty over all other objects."[21]

Madison continued his list of national and federal attributes of the Constitution, finding the election of the president to be federal because of the role of the states *qua* states in the electoral college. Finally, Madison observed that the amendment process was a mixture of national and federal traits. It is federal insofar as amendments must be approved by states, not by the collective body of citizens of the nation, and national insofar as fewer than all of the states are required for the ratification of an amendment. Madison concluded that:

> The proposed Constitution, therefore, even when tested by the rules laid down by its antagonists, is, in strictness, neither a national nor a federal constitution, but a composition of both. In its foundation it is federal, not national; in the sources from which the ordinary powers of the government are drawn, it is partly federal and partly national; in the operation of these powers, it is national, not federal; in the extent of them again, it is federal, not national; and, finally in the authoritative mode of introducing amendments, it is neither wholly federal nor wholly national.[22]

The arguments in *The Federalist* that at once backed a strong national government but pointed out the balanced nature of the Constitution and its respect for state power over local matters reflected the position Alexander Hamilton took at the New York Convention, in which his skillful political bargaining and persistence finally produced a vote of 30–27 in favor of ratification. The vote was close in other states as well, but by July 1788 all of the states but North Carolina and Rhode Island had ratified the Constitution.[23]

[21] *The Federalist*, 39.

[22] *The Federalist*, 39.

[23] North Carolina finally ratified the

The Dynamics of the Federal System

With the ratification of the Constitution, the federalists had won an important victory that created a national government with the potential to dominate the states. The early Federalist administrations of George Washington and John Adams, coupled with a Supreme Court dominated by the Federalist philosophy and by a strong adherence to the tenets of strong national power even after the Republicans took control of the Court, assured the establishment of strong national foundations for the new Republic.

Constitution in November 1789, after the new government was operating, and Rhode Island in 1790.

HOW THE CONSTITUTION SHAPES THE FEDERAL SYSTEM

The Constitution determines the formal relationships between the national government and the states, and governs the formal linkages among the states themselves. Constitutional interpretation over the almost two centuries of the existence of the Republic has of course profoundly affected the constitutional standards that govern the federal system.

Early Constitutional Interpretation of Federalism

The federalist and nationalist framers of the Constitution clearly intended to create a national government with powers adequate to deal with the scope of national concerns, and with supremacy over the states within the sphere of national power. The intentions of such key Convention figures as Alexander Hamilton, James Madison, and Edmund Randolph that have been discussed at length above were unequivocally in support of a dominant national government, although there were naturally disagreements among these and other members of the Convention on the proper scope and reach of national power.

The early interpretation of the Constitution by the Supreme Court before and during the era of the Federalist Chief Justice John Marshall articulated and implemented the principles of the flexibility and completeness of congressional authority coupled with national supremacy. The opinions of Chief Justice Marshall in *McCulloch* v. *Maryland* (1819) and in *Gibbons* v. *Ogden* (1824) completed a trend of Court rulings that upheld the broad construction of congressional power under

Article I, and the supremacy of national over state law. The Court left no doubt that it would uphold Article VI of the Constitution, which states: "This Constitution and the laws of the United States which shall be made in pursuance thereof; and all treaties made . . . under the authority of the United States, shall be the supreme law of the land; and the judges in every state shall be bound thereby, anything in the Constitution or laws of any state to the contrary notwithstanding." The Supreme Court made it clear that it would not only uphold national law and void state legislation contrary to it, but would also extend its jurisdiction to state courts to assure the compliance of state judges with national law.[24]

The early rulings of the Supreme Court that buttressed national power made it clear that although the intentions of the framers of the Constitution were clearly in favor of a strong national government, the ambiguity of much of the language of the Constitution opened the way to state challenges to national power. It was not too difficult for the advocates of states' rights to construct a constitutional rationale that supported a weak rather than a strong national government. Even the supremacy clause itself, which on its face seemed to be an absolutely clear statement of the predominance of national law, could be construed narrowly, as it was by the lawyers speaking for the states in the *McCulloch* and *Gibbons* cases, to extend only to those powers of Congress *explicitly* mentioned in Article I. The proponents of states' rights simply argued that the sphere of state sovereignty encompassed many of the powers that the federalists included under Article I on the basis of the necessary and proper clause. The plain language of the Constitution did not resolve many of the questions concerning the proper boundaries of state and national power. What were considered the reserved powers of the states became a matter of constitutional interpretation.

Constitutional prescriptions concerning federalism extended beyond the delineation of national power and the supremacy of national law. Article I, sec. 10 proscribes states from entering into "any treaty, alliance, or confederation," and from granting letters of marque and reprisal. Moreover, states are forbidden from coining money and issuing bills of

---

[24] See, for example, Chisholm v. Georgia, 2 Dallas 419 (1793).

credit. States cannot "pass any bill of attainder, ex post facto law, or law impairing the obligation of contracts, or grant any title of nobility."

The Constitution forbids the establishment of trade barriers among the states, providing: "No state shall, without the consent of Congress, lay any imposts or duties on imports or exports, except what may be absolutely necessary for executing its inspection laws."

Finally, Article I provides: "No state shall, without the consent of Congress, lay any duty of tonnage, keep troops, or ships of war in time of peace, enter into any agreement or compact with another state, or with a foreign power, or engage in war, unless actually invaded, or in such imminent danger as will not admit of delay."

While the Constitution prohibits certain state acts, it also defines national obligations to the states in several areas. Congress was forbidden to prohibit the importation of slaves until 1808, although the national legislature was authorized to impose a tax or duty upon the importation of slaves not to exceed ten dollars per person. Congress was given the authority to admit new states to the Union, "but no new state shall be formed or erected within the jurisdiction of any other state; nor any state be formed by the junction of two or more states, or parts of states, without the consent of the legislatures concerned as well as of Congress" (Article IV, sec. 3).[25]

The important guaranty clause of the Constitution provided: "The United States shall guarantee to every state in this Union a republican form of government, and shall protect each of them against invasion; and on application of the legislature, or of the executive (when the legislature cannot be convened) against domestic violence" (Article IV, sec. 4).

The Constitution defined certain relationships among the states themselves as well as between the states and the national government. According to Article IV: "Full faith and credit shall be given in each state to the public acts, records, and judicial proceedings of every other state." Congress was given the authority by general legislation to "prescribe the manner in which such acts, records, and proceedings shall be proved, and the effect thereof."

In regulating interstate relationships the Constitution also

[25] Five states have been formed out of other states with the consent of their legislatures and of Congress: Vermont from New York (1791); Kentucky from Virginia (1792); Tennessee from North Carolina (1796); Maine from Massachusetts (1820); and West Virginia from Virginia (1863).

provided that the "citizens of each state shall be entitled to all privileges and immunities of citizens in the several states" (Article IV, sec. 2). States were obligated to respect the laws of other states regulating crime and slavery.

The early interpretation of the Constitution by the Supreme Court through the era of Chief Justice John Marshall focused primarily on defining the extent of the authority of Congress and of the federal courts over the states, and establishing the principle of national supremacy in domestic affairs, leaving delicate questions of interpretation of the constitutional provisions regulating federalism to a later time, when appropriate cases and controversies arose. Marshall did consider one other aspect of federalism under the Constitution when, on two occasions, he used the provision forbidding the state impairment of the obligation of contracts to invalidate state laws.[26]

Marshall broadly interpreted the proscription of the contract clause in a way that limited state action even more than the framers of the Constitution had intended. The clause was put into the Constitution essentially because the framers did not want property rights to be overturned by popularly elected majorities in state legislatures, and was aimed at debtor relief laws that had been passed by many states. Marshall held in *Fletcher* v. *Peck* (1810) that the contract clause prohibition extended beyond the protection of private contractual rights to public contracts as well.[27] In *Dartmouth College* v. *Woodward* (1819), Marshall reaffirmed the Court's position that the contract clause did not govern private debtors and creditors only, but precluded the legislature of New Hampshire from abrogating what in effect was a public contract.[28]

While the early Supreme Court, and the Marshall Court in particular, upheld national power and broadly interpreted the constitutional proscription of state impairment of contracts, two years before his death Marshall wrote the opinion in *Barron* v. *Baltimore* (1833) that held the protections of the Bill of Rights inapplicable to the states. The ruling did not excite the great interest that had been aroused by such major cases as *McCulloch* and *Gibbons,* which to both the nationalists and the advocates of states' rights involved crucial ques-

[26] Fletcher v. Peck, 6 Cranch 87 (1810); Dartmouth College v. Woodward, 4 Wheaton 518 (1819). Chief Justice John Jay, acting as a federal circuit court judge, had earlier used the contract clause to void a Rhode Island statute.

[27] Marshall held in Fletcher v. Peck that the contract clause prevented the Georgia legislature from rescinding a previous act that had granted land titles.

[28] Marshall did not extend the prohibitions of the contract clause to include all public contracts, but only those that affected property interests.

The Dynamics of the Federal System

tions of constitutional law and vital state interests. Given the historical context within which the Bill of Rights was framed and adopted, there was virtually no rationale that Marshall could have used to support a decision contrary to his ruling in the *Barron* case. Neither the framers of the Constitution nor the congressional contingent that had drafted the Bill of Rights, led by James Madison, intended that it be a limitation upon state action. The constitutional ambiguity surrounding the questions of national power and supremacy involved in the earlier decisions of the Marshall Court did not pertain to the question of applicability of the Bill of Rights to the states. Although Marshall had little choice but to make the ruling he did, the constitutional historian Charles Warren found that it was "a striking fact that this last of Marshall's opinions on this branch of law should have been delivered in limitation of the operation of the Constitution, whose undue extension he had been so long charged with seeking."[29]

[29] Warren, *The Supreme Court in United States History*, 2: 240–41.

While the Marshall Court and its predecessor had resolved the major constitutional question of federalism concerning the reach of national power and its supremacy over the states, other important issues of constitutional provisions pertaining to federalism remained to be resolved at a later time. The Court had yet to face questions concerning the extent to which it could become involved in political controversies relating to the constitutional charge to the national government that it guarantee states a republican form of government. And, in other areas, it would have to decide on questions of the supremacy of the national government in foreign affairs in cases that did not arise until the twentieth century. Throughout its history the Supreme Court also has had to refine and expand upon the doctrines of the Marshall Court governing the reach of national power and the supremacy of national law. Moreover, the Court has continually confronted cases requiring the resolution of conflict among the states.

Finally, although *Barron* v. *Baltimore* made the issue of the applicability of the Bill of Rights to the states temporarily moot, the passage of the Fourteenth Amendment in 1868 laid the groundwork for major developments in constitutional law that placed the Court squarely in the center of what seemed to be an endless controversy over the meaning of the due process and equal protection clauses. Perhaps the most significant aspect of the constitutional law of federalism in the twentieth century was the gradual inclusion of the protections of the Bill of Rights in the Fourteenth Amendment's due process clause, making them applicable to state action. The early interventionist approach of the Marshall Court in expanding national power under Article I, particularly in the regulation of commerce, was more than matched by the activist Warren Court in the 1950s and 1960s when it applied national standards of civil liberties and civil rights to the states under the Fourteenth Amendment.

THE DEVELOPMENT OF CONSTITUTIONAL STANDARDS GOVERNING FEDERALISM

Restricting National Power

The strong support given to doctrines of nationalism by the Supreme Court through the era of Chief Justice John Marshall was not continued after Marshall's death in 1835. Marshall had interpreted the Constitution as being in support of strong national regulation of commerce, but the Court soon was to define the commerce power of Congress more narrowly, in a way that vastly expanded the sphere of state sovereignty.[30] The post–Marshall Court also reduced the reach of national power that had prevailed during the Marshall era under the contract clause by narrowly interpreting the clause to allow states greater freedom to take action that changed contractual obligations.[31]

The trend in constitutional interpretation that began at the end of the Marshall era in 1835, which supported expanded state police powers and powers to regulate commerce concurrently with the national government, continued with certain mutations well into President Franklin D. Roosevelt's New Deal in the 1930s. The Court not only adopted standards that expanded state power in relation to the national government, but which also expanded the sphere of private corporate rights in relation to both the states and the national government at the turn of the twentieth century.

[30] See, for example, New York v. Miln, in which the Court upheld 5–2 as a legitimate exercise of the state police power a New York law that required ships' masters to report specified data about passengers on vessels arriving at New York ports; and Cooley v. Board of Wardens, 12 Howard 299 (1851), upholding a Pennsylvania statute regulating pilots in the Port of Philadelphia on the ground that the subject of the regulation was local in character. The Cooley case in particular changed the Court's interpretation of the commerce clause that had provided the basis for sweeping national power in Gibbons v. Ogden, 9 Wheaton 1 (1824). Under the Cooley test, national power could not extend to objects of commerce that were local in nature and demanded a

The decision of the Supreme Court in *Lochner* v. *New York* in 1905 reflected what could be called a new approach to federalism, one that supported not only the decentralization of power to the states but, in reality, to corporate interests as well. In the *Lochner* case the Court held that a New York law prohibiting bakery employees from working more than ten hours a day or sixty hours a week violated the "freedom to contract" of both employers and employees. The right to contract, stated the Court, is one of those fundamental liberties protected by the due process clause of the Fourteenth Amendment. While the liberty to contract, concluded the Court, is not absolute, any state interference with the exercise of the right must be demonstrated to be a fair, reasonable, and appropriate exercise of the state police power.[32]

The ruling in *Lochner* v. *New York* began what was called the *Lochner* era of substantive due process, during which the Supreme Court imposed its own values upon both national and state legislatures to limit the scope of economic regulation.[33] While more state and federal laws were upheld than were struck down during the *Lochner* era, the Court's substantive due process approach did act as a limit upon both national and state governments. The states as well as the national government were subject to close judicial scrutiny over laws regulating working conditions, setting rates that could be charged by railroads, and other types of economic regulation as well. Both national and state sovereignty suffered, and a new sovereignty of economic interests began to emerge which could have led, if the trend had continued, to a new form of federalism.

The crisis of the Depression, and the concomitant political development that saw a reinvigorated and more broadly based Democratic party rise under the leadership of Franklin D. Roosevelt, brought an end to the *Lochner* era and the interventionist approach of the Supreme Court in reviewing economic legislation at both national and state levels. During Roosevelt's first term in office, the Supreme Court, under the Chief Justiceship of Charles Evans Hughes, valiantly fought against what it considered to be an excessive expansion of

The Lochner Era: Emphasis upon State Powers

diversity of local regulations. Under the Gibbons doctrine, on the other hand, the test was not whether or not the objects of regulation were local or national in character, but whether or not the matter regulated affected interstate commerce in any way.

---

[31] See Charles River Bridge v. Warren Bridge, 11 Peters 420 (1837), in which Chief Justice Taney upheld wide state powers to take action in the public interest even though it affected private interests based upon the state charter. Taney's opinion was in marked contrast to Marshall's doctrine in the Dartmouth College case and in Fletcher v. Peck, that bound states to honor the terms of contracts they had entered into in the past.

---

[32] Lochner v. New York, 198 U.S. 45 (1905). The Lochner case was a classic example of the Court using a "substantive due process" formula to overturn a state law. The substantive due process approach involved the Court in reviewing state laws under the due process clause of the Fourteenth Amendment and national laws under the due process clause of the Fifth Amendment to determine whether, in the view of the Court, they were "reasonable." Under the substantive due

The End of the Lochner Era: Resurgence of National Power

process approach, the Courts imposed their own values upon state and national legislatures.

---

[33] Substantive due process as a method was also employed in the nationaliza-

tion of the protections in the Bill of Rights, and in the extension of civil liberties and rights beyond the explicit provisions of the Bill of Rights. See Chapter 3.

---

[34] Another major consideration of the Court was its conclusion that the NIRA delegated excessive legislative authority to the president and therefore violated the principle of separation of powers which requires that primary legislative authority reside in Congress.

---

[35] The Roosevelt administration itself had become disenchanted with the NIRA and was not unhappy to see the political controversy in which it had become embroiled solved in one stroke by the Court's decision.

---

[36] In 1936 there were six septuagenarian justices. If Roosevelt had been authorized to appoint one new justice for each of them, he could have had enormous influence over the Court's philosophy.

---

[37] See, for example, National Labor Relations Board v. Jones and Laughlin Steel Corporation, 301 U.S. 1 (1937), upholding the National Labor Relations Act of 1935 on the ground that it was properly based upon the commerce power of Congress; and West Coast Hotel Company v. Parrish, 300 U.S. 379 (1937), in which the Court upheld the validity of a Washington

national power over the states and over private interests. The Hughes Court at first wanted to continue a decentralized federal system that emphasized state sovereignty and private economic rights. In one prominent New Deal case, *Schechter v. United States* (1935), a unanimous Supreme Court struck down the keystone of the early New Deal program, the National Industrial Recovery Act of 1933. The principal ground upon which the law was declared unconstitutional was that it exceeded the commerce power of Congress.[34] Hughes, who wrote the majority opinion, ruled that Congress could not, as it had in the Recovery Act, regulate business activities that only indirectly affected interstate commerce.

While the *Schechter* case was an extreme one, involving an extraordinarily sweeping national law that had become unpopular by the time the *Schechter* decision was handed down, the strict constructionist approach of the Court that was used to overturn the NIRA was also used to nullify less controversial New Deal legislation.[35] By the end of his first term, Roosevelt and his advisers were planning a political coup against the Supreme Court, which involved a court-packing scheme that would allow the President to appoint one new justice for each justice over seventy years of age.[36] Roosevelt's plan was submitted to Congress after his overwhelming victory in 1936. Although it had no chance of passage, since it was seen by conservatives and many liberals alike as an unwarranted attack upon judicial independence, the Supreme Court could not help but realize that its insistence upon narrowly interpreting federal power during a time of national emergency made it increasingly unpopular and placed it into political jeopardy. Finally, in a series of decisions beginning in 1937, a majority of the Court supported both New Deal and state legislation regulating economic activity that it would have declared unconstitutional on the basis of the standards it had applied during the early New Deal.[37]

The New Deal was a watershed both for constitutional law and the politics of federalism. The early doctrines of the Marshall Court, which had supported a strong national government but which subsequently had been weakened, had now come full circle to support once again expansive federal power over states, private individuals, and corporate interests. The constitutional law of federalism was complemented by political developments that reflected a widespread national trend in support of an increased role for the federal government in policymaking affecting state and local interests. The states' resources had been inadequate to meet the crisis of the Depression, which demanded a national solution—a full use of national powers and resources to cope with problems of unemployment, social security, labor relations, and economic regulation. The demise of state sovereignty and power in both constitutional law and politics that the New Deal represented was much later to be temporarily altered, although a predominant national government has remained the central feature of American federalism into the 1980s.

state minimum wage law on the ground that it was enacted within the state police power. Significantly, Chief Justice Hughes wrote the majority opinions in both cases.

The year 1937 marked the end of the Supreme Court's application of the substantive due process formula in reviewing national and state legislation in the *economic* sphere. This shift paved the way for the expansion of national power over the states, largely based upon the commerce power, and gave the states freedom to regulate their own economic affairs provided their laws did not conflict with federal legislation.

Constitutional Doctrines Affecting Federalism After the New Deal

While the post-1937 Court allowed the federal government to regulate virtually every facet of economic activity on the basis of the commerce power, the concept of state sovereignty did not die completely. In the 1970s the Burger court held that under certain circumstances state sovereignty acts as a limit upon the commerce power of Congress. The Court noted in *Fry* v. *United States* (1975) that federal power cannot be exercised "in a fashion that impairs the states' integrity or their ability to function effectively in a federal system."[38] The Fry case involved a challenge to the application of a national wage freeze under the Economic Stabilization Act of 1970 to state employees. The employees contended that the Act interfered with sovereign state functions in violation of the Tenth Amendment. Although the Court upheld the law, on the ground that it was emergency legislation designed to reduce rather than increase pressures on state budgets, it warned that it would not permit unwarranted national intrusions into the

[38] Fry v. United States, 421 U.S. 542, 547–48 n. 7 (1975).

[39] Justice William Rehnquist dissented in the Fry case, asserting that the national law improperly interfered with the exercise of traditional state functions involving the determination of the pay for public employees.

[40] National League of Cities v. Usery, 426 U.S. 833 (1976).

[41] Ibid., p. 842.

sphere of state sovereignty. Exactly what constituted state sovereignty remained undefined.[39]

A majority of the Burger Court finally applied the concept of state sovereignty to limit the national commerce power in *National League of Cities* v. *Usery* in 1976.[40] As in the *Fry* case, *National League of Cities* involved a challenge to federal legislation on the ground that it unconstitutionally breached state sovereignty. Congress had broadened the coverage of the Fair Labor Standards Act by extending its wage and hour provisions to state employees. The National League of Cities challenged the law on the ground that it intruded upon the states' performance of essential governmental functions. Justice William Rehnquist wrote the Court's opinion that sustained the challenge. Rehnquist noted the plenary authority of Congress under the commerce clause, citing Marshall's opinion in *Gibbons* v. *Ogden,* but he also emphasized that: "There are limits upon the power of Congress to override state sovereignty, even when exercising its otherwise plenary powers to tax or to regulate commerce."[41] Rehnquist concluded that extension of the wage and hour provisions of the Fair Labor Standards Act to state employees invaded the sovereign authority of the states to determine the wages to be paid to their employees. The national legislation also unconstitutionally interfered with the power of states to determine how they will deliver governmental services to their citizens. Overriding considerations of national policy may support federal legislation that invades state sovereignty, as the Court found in the *Fry* case. In *National League of Cities* v. *Usery,* however, Rehnquist found no compelling reasons to uphold the federal legislation.

The *National League of Cities* ruling was a controversial one within and without the Court. Justice William Brennan, joined by Justices White and Marshall, wrote a strong dissenting opinion emphasizing that the broad reach of the commerce power that had been supported in a long line of cases beginning with *Gibbons* v. *Ogden* supported the federal legislation. The three also argued that the Court should exercise judicial self-restraint in reviewing cases concerning the proper balance between national and state power. A reasonable exercise of the national commerce power should be upheld, for it is not the responsibility of the judiciary to determine how the federal system should be structured.

The *Fry* and *National League of Cities* cases illustrate that considerations of state sovereignty are taken seriously by the Court, and may even be applied to limit the national commerce power. Nevertheless, the ruling of the Court in the *National League of Cities* case was an unusual one, and the dissenters from the decision accurately pointed out that the question of the scope of the national commerce power had been resolved in support of virtually total national power. Challenges to the exercise of the commerce power on the ground of invasion of state sovereignty must necessarily be narrow. In the economic sphere, the ruling of the Court in *Schechter* v. *United States* in 1935 was the last major case upholding a commerce clause challenge to the exercise of national power on the ground that Congress had exceeded its Article I authority.

Although after 1937 the Court allowed the political process to resolve the balance of national and state power in the sphere of economic policy, the Court was to become an active force in applying national standards of civil liberties and civil rights to the states. The New Deal marked a shift in the balance of power in economic policymaking from the states to the national government. This shift in the federal system was, after the Court adopted a posture of self-restraint, the result of political demands upon the president and Congress to take action to meet the national economic emergency. National economic policy was determined by the president and Congress, and not by the courts. In the sphere of civil liberties and civil rights, however, the Supreme Court became the focal point of policymaking that ultimately was to alter the constitutional landscape of the federal system in a profound way.

The process of nationalization of civil liberties and civil rights was a slow one that began with the court's declaration in *Gitlow* v. *New York* in 1925 that the freedom of speech and press guaranteed by the First Amendment applied to the states. The *Gitlow* decision itself, however, gave the constitutional benefit of the doubt to the New York legislature in

Judicial Activism in Defining National Standards for Civil Liberties and Civil Rights

reviewing its criminal anarchy statute that had been challenged in the case. The result was that the Court upheld the New York law. In 1931, in *Near* v. *Minnesota*, the Court for the first time overturned a state law on the ground that it violated the *national* standard of freedom of the press in the First Amendment that was part of the "liberty" protected by the due process clause of the Fourteenth Amendment.

The process of nationalization of civil liberties and civil rights that began with the *Gitlow* and *Near* cases did not continue in earnest until the era of the Warren Court. When Chief Justice Earl Warren retired in 1968, most of the protections of the Bill of Rights had been nationalized under the due process clause of the Fourteenth Amendment, and the Court had adopted a substantive due process stance that it now was applying to the sphere of civil liberties and civil rights. This position laid the groundwork for the expansion of national standards even beyond those of the Bill of Rights. The Court had held in *Griswold* v. *Connecticut* in 1965 that a Connecticut birth control statute violated a national right to privacy—one that was not explicitly spelled out in the Bill of Rights, but which could be implied from it. In 1973, in *Roe* v. *Wade,* the Burger Court was to use the newly articulated right of privacy as the basis for its decision granting women the right to obtain abortions. The *Roe* v. *Wade* decision signalled that the Burger Court was not going to turn the clock back to the time when the Court had cited considerations of federalism as the basis for judicial self-restraint in applying national standards of civil liberties and civil rights to the states.

THE POLITICS OF FEDERALISM

Political forces have helped shape the constitutional context within which the federal system functions, and have also informally shaped intergovernmental relations. The politics as well as the constitutional law of federalism reflect the ebb and flow of forces and themes of centralization and decentralization. The politics of the colonies, the Revolution, and the Articles of Confederation reflected strong forces of decentralization. In contrast, the Constitutional Convention of 1787, the Constitution itself, and its early interpretation by the Supreme Court through the Marshall era represented the politics of nationalism and the centralization of power.

While the Constitution and its early interpretation were remarkable victories for the proponents of a dominant national government with broad powers, the nineteenth century was characterized more by the dominance of the states than the national government over the political and economic life of the country. The constitutional underpinnings of a strong national government could not alone support such a government without the acquiesence and coalescence of political forces moving in the same direction. The politics of the nineteenth century, as well as the dispersed character of the economic system of the period, buttressed state sovereignty and the dispersion of political power.

The victory of the North in the Civil War established the authority of the Union, but it did not lead to an immediate expansion of national power. The states dominated the federal system after the Civil War as they had done before. The apparent congressional intent behind the Fourteenth and Fifteenth Amendments, which was to extend national policies of civil liberties and civil rights to the states, was not realized until a century after the amendments had been ratified. The constitutional law and politics of the post–Civil War period put aside the amendments and, with respect to some provisions, temporarily nullified them.

Throughout the nineteenth century the components of the political process were largely decentralized and dispersed. The principal interest groups were privilege-seekers focusing upon state legislatures for such largesse as corporate charters and land grants. The state legislatures had more bounty to distribute to private interests than did Congress. It was not until post–Civil War industrialization and the development of national economic interdependence that national business, labor, and agricultural interest groups arose to lobby the national as well as the state governments. The nationalization of interest groups was not completed until well into the twentieth century.

The political parties of the nineteenth century also buttressed the decentralization of the federal system. While the philosophies of the parties often were oriented to national problems, their organizations were state and local rather than national in character. The disintegration of national parties began after the demise of the original Federalist and Republican (Jeffersonian) parties that had reflected, respectively, the nationalist and states' rights views of the Constitution. Neither the Federalist nor the original Republican parties were national in scope, but were dominated by political elites that determined the positions of the parties and selected their leaders primarily on the basis of congressional caucuses of party members. The Democratic party of Andrew Jackson was the first to approximate a national party based upon a broad membership and the nomination of its candidate for president by a convention, which was considered to be far more democratic than the nomination by the "King Caucus," the caucus of the members of the congressional party. Although the Democratic party and the opposition party, the Whigs, developed a high degree of party uniformity on national issues, the organizations of both were necessarily confederations of state and local interests. It was these interests that dominated not only the parties, but the Congress as well. Their representatives gathered once very four years for the purpose of nominating a candidate for the presidency, but the seeming unity of the parties in presidential election years belied their real diversity.

Similarly, the parties of the twentieth century remained essentially broad confederations of state and local interests, even as they developed more comprehensive party programs dealing with national issues. American parties have from the very beginning helped to aggregate political interests, but the political and economic diversity of the country, reflected in the constitutional structure of federalism, have always buttressed the dispersion and decentralization of power.

The centrifugal forces of the nineteenth century continually changed the character of the party system. There was no lasting coalition of interests that could form the base of a long-term national party. From the beginning of the Republic until the Civil War, the country saw parties come and go, with no single party reflecting the national interest. The Federalists and the early Republicans were replaced by the Jacksonian Democrats and the Whigs, which in turn metamorphosed into other parties. The split between the North and the South over the issue of slavery profoundly affected the party system as the Civil War approached, splitting the Democrats into northern and southern factions and giving rise to several new parties. The most important of these was the Republican party, which held its first national convention in 1856, and which four years later nominated as its second candidate for the presidency Abraham Lincoln.

The post-Civil War period saw the parties shift once again in organization and policy orientation in response to the war itself. These changes solidified the Democratic party in the South, which became its most important base of support. The Republican party that had led the nation to victory was to dominate the national political scene with very few interruptions until the election of Franklin Roosevelt in 1932, and the Grand Old Party also developed effective political machines that dominated the politics of the rising urban areas as well as the Northern states. The party founded solely to oppose slavery became, by the turn of the twentieth century, largely the party of corporate interests, which it advanced at national, state, and local levels of government.

The industrialization and general economic advancement of the country began to shape the character of the Democratic and the Republican parties. In the nineteenth century the Democrats were rooted in the agrarian sections of the country, but gradually the party began as well to reflect the interests of factory workers in small cities and larger urban communities. A pooling of interests that began to develop between farmers and workers in opposition to corporate interests was represented in the Democratic party that elected Franklin Roosevelt in 1932. During the New Deal the axis between farmers and labor became the base of the Roosevelt coalition that transformed what once had been a minority party into a dominant national party that was to prevail for decades to come.

The politics of the New Deal fundamentally altered the character of the federal system. The Great Depression was an economic emergency that was national in scope and clearly required national action. Roosevelt moved quickly to meet the emergency, and was eventually successful in securing the passage of legislation to channel federal funds to the states to deal with unemployment, and with welfare problems generally. The states and localities had demonstrated their inability to cope with the massive unemployment, which required a vast enlargement of governmental assistance. The Social Security Act of 1935 marked the beginning of federal legislation that gradually took income security and welfare responsibilities away from the states and located them unequivocally in the hands of the national government.

The Social Security legislation of the New Deal represented the important shift in power that took place in the federal system during the first two administrations of President Franklin D. Roosevelt. New and more subtle forms of federal taxation complemented the income tax to bolster the federal treasury at the expense of the states, and to create what Daniel P. Moynihan refers to as a predominant federal fisc.[42] Beginning with the New Deal, the federal government did not hesitate to use its superior revenue-raising power to dominate many facets of state and local government. Federal grant-in-aid programs were instrumental in the progressive increase in federal power over the states. Categorical grant programs are those in which the federal government stipulates conditions that state and local governments must meet in order to receive federal funds. Until the early 1970s, federal aid was channelled to the states solely through categorical grant programs which expanded from 30 providing $800 million of aid to the states in 1938 to 379 dispersing $15.2 billion of aid by 1968. The centralism represented by the categorical grant programs, which was the backbone of federal policy from the New Deal through the Great Society of President Lyndon B. Johnson, was reduced somewhat by the revenue-sharing policies of the Nixon administration; however, the "New Federalism" of the Nixon era was unable to stem the tide of centralization through categorical grants because of the interest on the part of many members of Congress in continuing them. More than

[42] Daniel P. Moynihan, "The Future of Federalism," in *American Federalism: Toward a More Effective Partnership* (Washington, D.C.: Advisory Commission on Intergovernmental Relations, 1975).

a hundred categorical grant programs were added during the decade of the 1970s concurrently with a growth in federal aid through revenue-sharing.[43]

While the centralism of the New Deal changed the nature of intergovernmental relations by shifting relatively more power to the national government than it had previously exercised over the states, state and local, particularly urban, governments continued to grow in importance and assumed many new responsibilities of their own. Cities such as New York and Los Angeles represented the trends and problems of urban government in dozens of other communities throughout the nation. Just as the national government had expanded during the New Deal in response to political demands that it cope with the problems of the Depression, state and local—primarily urban—governments later concurrently expanded as well to meet the pressing needs of their communities. The resurgence of state and local governments ultimately challenged the national government for a greater share of public revenues beginning in the 1960s. The new stirring among state and local governments in the 1960s resulted first in the Great Society and increased centralism of the Johnson Administration and, second, in a reaction to the increasing dominance of the federal government that led to the "New Federalism" of the 1970s.

[43] The nature of federal aid to state and local governments is detailed in the yearly reports of the Advisory Commission on Intergovernmental Relations, Washington, D.C., which also issues valuable periodic reports on various aspects of intergovernmental relations.

The Changing Federal System of the 1960s

The federal system in the 1960s reflected a new and more focused centralism than was represented by the New Deal. During the 1960s, the problems of state and city governments in such areas as welfare, education, rapid transit, crime, assistance to the elderly, and even sewage were studied and restudied by an army of federal and state bureaucrats, by such research groups as the Brookings Institution, and by advisory commissions and congressional committees. At first there seemed to be an abiding faith that whatever the problem it could be solved by professional analysis and federal-state cooperation, which would be characterized by the use of federal resources to solve state and local problems. No area was considered off limits to federal jurisdiction. During the years of the Great Society programs, the federal government boldly moved into the most cherished sphere of state sovereignty, education, to implement policies formulated at the national level by the use of the categorical grant technique.

As the federal government forthrightly—or, as some would say, arrogantly—moved increasingly in the 1960s to create programs to deal with poverty, health, urban renewal, and a host of other problems in local communities, the politics of federalism became chaotic. Each new linkage between the federal bureaucracy and its local counterparts, established in order to bring about federal-state cooperation in the dozens of areas that the national government had entered for the first time, created a new bureaucratic power base and intensified political conflict within and among bureaucratic enclaves. Power seekers at the local level built political constituencies of their own to give them leverage at both state and national levels of government. Local political leaders were often infuriated by upstart challengers whose constituencies had been fueled by federal funds. The federal Office of Economic Opportunity, for example, spawned local community agencies that frequently challenged mayors and other members of local political establishments. The famous "Model Cities" program, under which the federal government sought to eliminate urban blight and encourage city planning, was another example of an area in which intense bureaucratic rivalries developed. The principal federal department involved, Housing and Urban Development, encouraged local participation in city planning without defining how it was to be accomplished. Inevitably, "citizen participation" was transformed in various ways into the development of political constituencies representing the viewpoints of bureaucrats and politicians. The same kind of confusion and conflict that surrounded the poverty program administered by the Office of Economic Opportunity accompanied HUD's Model Cities program.

The centralism of the 1960s ultimately produced more confusion than coordination in intergovernmental relations. The many attempts by federal bureaucrats to dictate local policies, and particularly their encouragement—tacit or otherwise—of the development of local political leaders with their own constituencies capable of challenging both the elected and non-elected local political establishments resulted in a backlash from many of the regular state and local politicians. Both the presidency and Congress were the recipients of widespread demands from governors, mayors, and other local political leaders to reduce the power of the federal government, and of its bureaucracy in particular, in state and local affairs. State and local political establishments quite naturally wanted to be in charge of programs administered within their jurisdictions. At the same time, they wanted the federal government to put unrestricted funds at their disposal. Their demands ultimately resulted in what the Nixon administration called "revenue-sharing." Nixon's sponsorship of the program helped him to gain important support from state and local leaders that helped to nudge him into the White House after the very close election of 1968.

The New Federalism that began during Nixon's first term called for a revitalization of state and local governments, which meant a reduction in the direct control of the federal government over local programs. State and local governments still wanted federal funds, but without the kinds of strings that were attached in the categorical grant programs. At first a major goal of proponents of the New Federalism was to remove the increasing welfare burden of state governments that was beginning to cripple their finances. They hoped to do this by federalizing welfare through a family assistance plan that would provide direct grants to welfare recipients who met federal standards. The keystone of the New Federalism was revenue-sharing, which was to include both the general provision of undesignated federal funds to state and local governments and special revenue-sharing that consolidated major federal grant programs under which earmarked funds would go to the states, but without burdensome federal controls.

The New Federalism was conservative in tone, and aimed at equipping state and local governments to meet such traditional responsibilities as welfare, but which had grown and changed in ways that made it impossible for state and local governments with limited resources to meet them. The con-

The "New Federalism" of the 1970s

servatism of the New Federalism fit nicely into the philosophy of the Republican party; many Democrats as well, having become disenchanted with the failure of the liberal programs of the Great Society, saw value in the restoration of local initiatives and means to cope with public responsibilities.

Although early proponents of the New Federalism and its central component of revenue-sharing saw the possibility of a distinct reduction in the role of the federal government in state and local affairs, the forces of centralism kept pace with those of decentralization. During the 1970s almost a hundred new categorical grant programs were added, and by the end of the decade these programs constituted 72 percent of the total federal aid. This was a reduction from the past, when categorical grant programs encompassed all federal aid to the states; however, the continued importance of the categorical grants made it clear that centralism would remain the dominant characteristic of intergovernmental relations.

The politics of the New Federalism stressed the importance of local governments at the expense of the states, particularly the urban areas whose pressures for aid were felt and responded to in Washington. The bypassing of state governments during the 1970s was even more thorough-going than it had been during the years of the Great Society programs, when the standard method of federal aid involved grants to states that in turn might be dispersed to local governments.

Washington Politics and Federalism

Washington politics is essentially a centripetal force in the federal system. The incentives of Washington politicians and administrators are primarily to draw into their vortex as much power as possible, which does not mean ignoring state and local interests, but does mean retaining in Washington as much control as possible over the largesse of the federal government. Local constituencies are built to buttress power on Capitol Hill and in the administrative agencies downtown. This encourages the dispersion of power within Washington, but does not lead to the relinquishment of power by political actors in Washington to their local counterparts. The centripetal force exerted by the Washington community was a major reason that the Republican presidencies of Richard

Nixon and Gerald Ford did not succeed, despite their best efforts, in subordinating the categorical grant programs to the revenue-sharing of the New Federalism. Neither Nixon nor Ford had a Republican Congress, but even if they had had one, it is doubtful that Republican chairmen of powerful committees on Capitol Hill would have played the Washington power game differently from the way the Democrats did. In general, revenue-sharing does not allow Congressmen to claim credit for benefits distributed to local districts—credit that often is a major reason for their reelection. President Reagan's block grant program, similar to revenue sharing, was not unanimously embraced by Republican committee chairmen in the Senate. Congress significantly scaled down Reagan's proposals by excluding many major categorical grant programs.

The Constitution provided the basis for the centralization of power in Washington. The balance that Madison saw in the Constitution between national and state (federal) interests was clearly skewed, with a little help from the Federalists, in favor of national over state power. Both the power and the political ability of Washington politicians to bypass state governments in building local power bases is rooted in the Constitution. The nationalist framers saw clearly that if the states were made the intermediaries between the national government and the people, meaningful national power would be a fiction. Providing the national government with the authority to act directly upon the people constructed the framework for an eventual dominant national government. The coalescence of constitutional and political realities doomed the New Federalist movement of the 1970s from the start.

The struggle between the forces of centralism and those of decentralization, which has always been a part of American politics, continues in the 1980s, but without the intensity that accompanied the political conflict over the Great Society programs of the 1960s and the New Federalism of the 1970s. The issue of the proper balance between the national government and state and local governments has receded, to be replaced

Federalism in the 1980s

by political debate over such pressing national concerns as inflation, unemployment, energy, and foreign and military policies.

Neither the Democrats nor the Republicans particularly stressed issues pertaining to intergovernmental relations in their 1980 presidential and congressional campaigns. The party platforms did not contain planks that covered federalism per se, and dealt with the issue of intergovernmental relations primarily through platitudes rather than specific recommendations. Republicans opposed the federalization of welfare, and generally supported state and local initiatives. The Democrats advocated somewhat greater national action to deal with state and local problems, but, like the Republicans, did not raise problems of intergovernmental relations to a major level of debate.

The view of the proper balance of power between national, state, and local governments remains in limbo under the Reagan administration. At the same time, the usual power struggles over who is to administer federal programs continues, as do the programs themselves that are rooted in Congress and the bureaucracy. The trend toward centralization of power may be temporarily halted or slowed under the Reagan administration. At the same time, the usual power cal grant programs that were spawned in previous administrations and Congresses remain in effect, and will continue to buttress the centralized nature of the federal system.

Suggestions for Further Reading

Banfield, Edward C. *The Unheavenly City.* Boston: Little, Brown and Co., 1968. An examination of the social, political, and economic problems of cities and their role in the federal system.

Diamond, Martin. "The Federalist's View of Federalism." In *Essays in Federalism*, edited by George C. S. Benson, pp. 21–64. Claremont, Calif.: Institute for Studies in Federalism of Claremont Men's College, 1961. A discussion of the meaning of federalism to the founding fathers.

Grodzins, Morton. *The American System.* Chicago: Rand McNally, 1966. A classic treatment of federalism which argues that there has always been an extensive overlapping of functions between national and state governments.

Pressman, Jeffrey L., and Wildavsky, Aaron B. *Implementation.* Berkeley: University of California Press, 1973. A case study of the ways in which federalism affects the implementation of public policy.

Reagan, Michael D., and Sanzone, John G. *The New Federalism.* New York: Oxford University Press, 1981. An overview of federalism, including grants-in-aid, revenue-sharing, and block grants.

Riker, William H. *Federalism: Origin, Operation, Significance.* Boston: Little, Brown and Co., 1964. A comparative study of the theoretical and practical aspects of federalism.

Part II

The Political Process

National party conventions reflect the drama and excitement of democratic politics.

CHAPTER 4

Political Parties, Elections, and the Electorate

Political parties are, in democratic theory at least, the cement that holds the political process together and gives it meaning. The Constitution was not framed with parties in mind, and in fact the Founding Fathers viewed political parties with suspicion. One of James Madison's principal arguments in support of the Constitution was that the system of federalism and the separation of powers would prevent any one "faction" from controlling the apparatus of the national government. Faction, to Madison, included both political parties and interest groups.

Madison defined faction as "a number of citizens, whether amounting to a majority or minority of the whole, who are united and actuated by some common impulse of passion, or of interest, adverse to the rights of other citizens, or to the permanent and aggregate interest of the community." He declared that one of the great advantages of the Constitution and the Union established under it would be "its tendency to break and control the violence of faction. The friend of popular governments never finds himself so much alarmed for their character and faith as when he contemplates their propensity to this dangerous vice [of faction]."[1]

Madison told his countrymen that under the new Constitution factions would not be able to control the national government, since the Republican principle of representation

The Problem of Faction

---

[1] *The Federalist*, 10.

would disperse and refine the demands of faction. No one group would be able to elect a sufficient number of representatives to control Congress. Moreover, the checks and balances at the national level would prevent unbridled majority rule, which would eliminate the possibility of any one party dominating the governmental process.

Madison also viewed Federalism as an important check upon faction. "The influence of factious leaders," he wrote, "may kindle a flame within their particular states, but will be unable to spread a general conflagration through the other states; a religious sect may degenerate into a political faction in a part of the Confederacy; but the variety of sects dispersed over the entire face of it must secure the national councils against any danger from that source. A rage for paper money, for an abolition of debts, for an equal division of property, or for any other improper or wicked project, will be less apt to pervade the whole body of the Union than a particular member [state] of it, in the same proportion as such a malady is more likely to taint a particular county or district than an entire state."[2]

The antiparty bias of the framers of the Constitution reflected in *The Federalist* was understandable at the time. The process that had led to the framing of the Constitution had been one of constant tension between centripetal and centrifugal forces, between the nationalists who dominated the Philadelphia convention and the advocates of states' rights who saw in the proposed Constitution a threat to their interests. The new nation was faced with the possibility of disintegration, and "faction" was at the time a direct threat to the national interest embodied in the Constitution. In the view of the Founding Fathers, the nation simply could not afford the luxury of uncontrolled pluralism of interests. Pluralistic disintegration was the vice that the Constitution was supposed to cure, not by eliminating faction but by constructing a government in which faction could not dominate the policymaking process.

While the Constitution and the theory underlying it contain an antiparty bias, none of the provisions of the Constitution directly limit the growth of parties in any way. The freedoms of speech, press, association, and the right to petition gov-

[2] Ibid.

Political Parties, Elections, and the Electorate

ernment for a redress of grievances embodied in the First Amendment—but also assumed by the framers of the original Constitution—created an environment in which both parties and interest groups could and did flourish.

Madison recognized that while faction may be undesirable, constitutional government requires preservation of the liberty essential to the existence of parties and interest groups: "Liberty is to faction what air is to fire, an aliment, without which it instantly expires. But it could not be less folly to abolish liberty, which is essential to political life because it nourishes faction, than it would be to wish the annihilation of air, which is essential to animal life, because it imparts to fire its destructive agency."

The Federalist and Republican parties emerged within a decade after the founding of the Republic, and from that day to the present, political parties have always been at the center of the political life of the nation, helping to aggregate interests, shape public policies, provide leadership, and offer choices to the people during elections that have helped to channel popular aspirations into government policies. Parties have not by any means been perfect instruments to organize the collective will of a majority of the nation and translate it into public policy, but given the pluralism of the polity, the parties have gone about as far as they can in helping to organize and direct clashing interests and opposing views of the role of government and the policies that should prevail.

THE LIBERAL-DEMOCRATIC MODEL OF PARTY GOVERNMENT

The skeptical eighteenth century view of parties as factions antagonistic to the national interest gave way in the nineteenth and twentieth centuries to a recognition among many theorists that effective parties were essential to democracy. There is some tension between the premises of constitutional government and what is best termed the liberal-democratic model of party government, in which parties assume a pivotal position in the political process.

As the somewhat elitist government of eighteenth century America began to emerge as a mass democracy in the nineteenth century, it was inevitable that parties would develop to reflect, shape, and capitalize upon the demands of an ever-increasing and diverse electorate. Jacksonian Democracy marked the beginning of a new era of party politics, in which a mass electorate would be courted by political leaders who found it both necessary and profitable to build party organizations to compete effectively in the political marketplace.

As political parties became a prominent fixture of democratic politics, serving the power-oriented goals of politicians and raising the political aspirations of large numbers of people, democratic theorists began increasingly to concern themselves with defining the appropriate role of parties in the democratic polity. Parties could no longer be simply dismissed as undesirable factions opposed to the national interest.

The Role of Parties

What *should* be the role of parties in democratic government? The question has been answered eloquently by theorists who have developed what can best be described as the liberal-democratic model of party government, in which the parties become an integral part of the government, acting as the primary force shaping public policy. At the same time, parties bridge the gap between people and the government by providing the electorate with rational policy alternatives at election time. In the liberal-democratic model the function of parties is primarily to create an environment in which the electorate can make a *rational choice* between *policy* alternatives. Parties become, in a sense, modern-day instruments of the Enlightenment ideals of rationality and progress. The model assumes that the individual voter is rational and both desirous and capable of making political choices based upon an accurate assessment of individual interests.

Party government at its best has been called "government by discussion."[3] The model of government by discussion assumes the existence of a rational and responsible electorate, and political leaders who recognize that their fate at the polls will be determined by the attractiveness to the voters of policies they present. The model of government by discussion is in sharp contrast to the modern public relations approach to political campaigning, which is based upon the premise that

[3] For the best elaboration of the liberal-democratic model of party government see Sir Ernest Barker, *Reflections on Government* (London: Oxford University Press, 1942). Barker's book was written as a passionate defense of democracy against the challenge of fascism, which posited a theory of government that ridiculed the premises and practices of democracy.

the electorate is irrational, and will make its electoral choice on the basis of images of candidates rather than a rational consideration of issues of public policy.

Four stages of discussion occur in the ideal party model of government. First, it is the responsibility of each major political party to formulate and sharpen issues of public policy for debate and for consideration by the electorate. The first stage of discussion takes place within the party organization, among party activists. At this stage interest groups make their demands known, testifying, for example, before the platform committees of the parties on such issues as civil rights, the minimum wage, and a wide range of economic and social concerns. In the party model, interest groups channel their demands to government through political parties, which have a virtual monopoly over the presentation of major policy proposals within government. Because the demands of the political system are to be channeled first to the parties and then to government, public policy deliberations have a consistency, continuity, and visibility they would not where groups outside of the parties have free rein to pressure the institutions of government. The party model assumes disciplined party organizations, in which the members, once elected, strive to achieve the goals of the party and always vote together in the legislature in support of party programs. If the party model were strictly followed in the United States, for example, the Republican majority in the Senate would consistently support the programs of President Reagan, who himself would base his legislative recommendations on the policies that had been agreed upon at the Republican National Convention. The first stage of discussion would be completed at the party conventions if the party model were applicable to American politics.

Once the parties have agreed on their platforms to be presented to the public, the stage of discussion moves to the electorate, where the voters are given a chance to analyze the contrasting programs of the parties on the basis of rational presentations of issues by party candidates. The electoral process extends the arena of rational debate from the parties to the voters. If the parties carried out their task of formulating

Stages of Discussion

contrasting policy proposals, rational choice by the electorate based upon different perceptions of which party program best meets the interests of individual voters would be possible. Theoretically, serious debates are to take place among party candidates, from which all relevant information to make a rational electoral choice is given to the voters. Once the electoral process is completed, the electorate chooses one *party* or the other by voting for its candidate.

The third stage of discussion comes about after the election at the *governmental* level in Congress and the executive. Together the members of the majority and minority parties set their legislative agendas on the basis of the party programs that have been agreed to in the preceding party and electoral stages of discussion. Ideally, the executive is of the same party as the majority of the legislature and acts as a leader in setting the legislative agenda and guiding legislation through Congress. Members of the legislature in the minority act collectively as an *opposition party*, constantly criticizing the policies of the majority, recommending proposals of their own based upon the party platform in order to sharpen national political debate and make the electorate aware of alternatives to the policies of the majority.

| Parties as Policy Instruments | Party government stresses the role of parties at all stages of the policy process. It is the parties that collectively formulate policy proposals, set the legislative agenda, and determine the timing of legislative enactments. It is the parties that make electoral choice meaningful through legislation and executive actions that are responsive to the choices that have been made by the voters. Disciplined parties are the necessary bridges between the people and the government, over which the electorate transmits its will to government, and the mechanism by which policy is made responsive once public choice has been made at the ballot box. In a two-party system, with single-member districts, the party that wins usually represents a majority of those who vote. Party government therefore means rule of the majority, which contrasts with the constitutional model of separation of powers and federalism, as well as with the concept of "concurrent majorities," which de- |

Political Parties, Elections, and the Electorate

scribes a political process that is dominated by different majorities of interest groups in separate policy spheres.

Why are political parties so essential to the realization of majority rule? The assumption is that only political parties can give the necessary degree of definition, coherence, and unity to the process of formulation and implementation of policy based upon majority choice. Without parties, the selection of candidates becomes haphazard, and although individual candidates may run their campaigns on the basis of policy issues, once elected they will be powerless within the maze of government to implement their promises to the electorate in the absence of party support. Therefore, although political campaigns may raise policy issues, where political parties are not functioning in any disciplined manner the public will be deceived if it feels that candidates can meaningfully connect policy preferences with government action.

In the American system, however, party backing is not necessary for elected politicians to exercise power. The president has independent prerogative powers in both the domestic and foreign policy spheres that enable him to act independently in many instances. Presidential authority often has been delegated by Congress. Clever lawyers can more often than not find a statutory or constitutional justification for the exercise of independent presidential power. President Reagan's first act after he took the oath of office, administered by Chief Justice Warren Burger on the West Front terrace of the Capitol, was to enter the Capitol building and, in the presence of Speaker Thomas P. (Tip) O'Neill and Senate Majority Leader Howard Baker, sign a hiring freeze for all federal employment. In the ensuing weeks his director of the Office of Management and Budget, David Stockman, was to wield a budget ax that startled even some Reaganites as it cut scores of federal programs across the board, including a major water project in Howard Baker's Tennessee and Russell Long's Louisiana. Congressional approval will have to follow to make the cuts a reality; however, the initiative was clearly with the president and his new budget director.

While the president can take both domestic and foreign policy initiative without congressional approval, in the domestic sphere the support of both Congress and the bu-

[4] See, for example, United States v. Curtiss-Wright Corp., 299 U.S. 304 (1936).

reaucracy is required if the White House is to have a strong policy impact. In foreign policy, the president is the supreme power, and his authority has been recognized by the Court.[4] But even in foreign policy it behooves a president desirous of maintaining his power to seek the approval of Congress for major foreign policy actions, as President Johnson did in securing the passage of the Gulf of Tonkin Resolution that gave him carte blanche to engage in military action in Vietnam. White House leadership in foreign policy, however, is usually respected by Congress if not given acclamation. For example, President Carter's recognition of the mainland Chinese government after President Nixon and his secretary of state, Henry Kissinger, had paved the way, raised a storm of criticism on Capitol Hill. This was led by Senator Goldwater and others who felt that the United States had betrayed Taiwan, its trusted ally. But the policy of recognition of the People's Republic of China, once made in the White House, was not reversed. Even President Reagan, a staunch supporter of Taiwan, who had during the presidential campaign of 1980 strongly criticized President Carter's recognition of Communist China, was persuaded to continue the formal ties between mainland China and the United States that had been established with great effort.

In the ideal model of party government, a major function of the party is to bind the executive and the legislative branches. This takes place readily in parliamentary systems such as that of Great Britain, where the executive is the cabinet, a committee of the majority party of the legislature. American parties are too diversified, however, to bring about cooperation between the president and Congress, and the constitutional system of separation of powers virtually guarantees conflict rather than agreement between the White House and Capitol Hill. The occupants of each end of Pennsylvania Avenue have different political constituencies and interests that often clash. The president and powerful members of Congress are constantly striving for power, and the struggle more often than not transcends party lines. President Reagan soon found that he could not rely upon the Republican majority in the Senate, in which the senior members of his own party had for the first time in their careers assumed committee chairmanships. For

Political Parties, Elections, and the Electorate

example, Utah Senator Orrin Hatch, the new chairman of the Labor and Human Resources Committee, did not support all of the Reagan proposals for cuts in social programs, including aid to the handicapped. Republican Senator Robert Dole, the new chairman of the powerful Finance Committee, was highly skeptical of Reagan's tax cut proposals because of the likelihood, in Dole's view, that they would increase budget deficits. Reagan represented a particular group within the Republican party, but the Republican members of Congress were by no means all Reaganites. The party label was an insufficient glue to bind its members together.

PARTIES AND THE ELECTORAL PROCESS

It is interesting and valuable to contrast the American party process with the ideal model of party government to determine the extent to which parties have contributed to the achievement of a rational and responsible politics. The focus of our analysis will be upon the national presidential and congressional parties. It should always be remembered, however, that there are literally hundreds of parties throughout the United States which, although classified as Democrats or Republicans, have separate constituencies and often contrasting policy orientations. (See Figure 4.1.) State and local leaders in New England, for example, whether labeled Republicans or Democrats, have little in common with their party brethren in Texas on the critical policy issue of energy. The New England states are consumers of energy, whereas Texas, particularly in its more rural parts, is a producing state. Even within Texas, however, Democrats and Republicans are split on the energy issue, those from such consuming areas as Houston favoring the regulation of oil and natural gas prices, while representatives from producing areas support deregulation of the energy industry.

From the earliest days of the Republic, presidential politics has been, every four years, the focus of the attention of voters throughout the country. More recently, because of the atten-

Presidential Parties

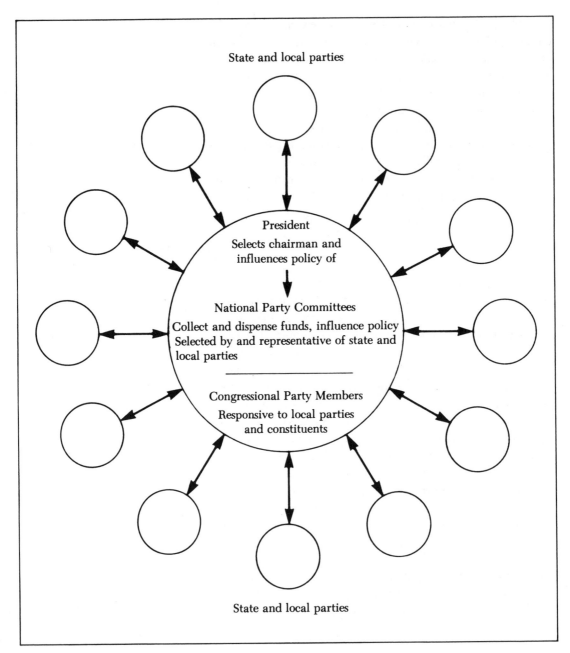

State and local parties

President
Selects chairman and
influences policy of

National Party Committees
Collect and dispense funds, influence policy
Selected by and representative of state and
local parties

Congressional Party Members
Responsive to local parties
and constituents

State and local parties

FIGURE 4.1
National Political Parties. *National
parties are confederations of national,
state, and local interests.*

tion the media give to the game of presidential politics, the race for the presidency seems to be a continual one that begins within weeks after a presidential election. The incumbent apparently begins immediately to prepare for victory in the next election, while challengers test the political waters and begin to line up backers and establish organizations they hope will propel them into the lead in the race for the presidential nomination of their party.

Capturing the presidency is, in the minds of politicians, equivalent to winning the Nobel Prize in their field. The White House is the grand prize for members of the victorious party, as well, since it elevates the power and status of party adherents who have supported the winning candidate.

Whether or not the president supports the favorite policies of particular politicians, the White House is symbolically the most powerful office in the country and one with which all politicians want to be associated—if only in social terms. In what may appear to outsiders to be the somewhat byzantine world of Washington politics, being invited to the state dinners at the White House or to breakfast with the president signals that the favored politician has arrived politically and his spouse (the same is not true for *her* spouse) has arrived socially. One of President Reagan's first acts in the opening weeks of his administration, for example, was to invite the freshman Republicans of the House to a "working breakfast," where their pictures could be taken for hometown consumption and for the Washington press and media sitting or standing next to the president, apparently in confidential conversation about high matters of state. Even before his inauguration, Reagan went to Capitol Hill to lunch with the Republican members of the Senate, and to hold bipartisan sessions that included House Speaker Thomas (Tip) O'Neill and Senate Minority Leader Robert Byrd. Whether in partisan or bipartisan meetings, the presence of the president always elevates the power as well as the spirit of members of his own party who attend.

Because of the importance of the presidency to each party, both Republicans and Democrats have national organizations that have been primarily oriented to bringing the diverse elements of the party together once every four years for the purpose of electing the president. In recent years, the national organizations have also become involved in increasing party strength throughout the country by providing financial support and political expertise to party candidates. Former Senator Bill Brock of Tennessee, after he was defeated in 1976 and became chairman of the Republican National Committee, organized a highly effective national effort to channel Republican resources to congressional as well as to state and local candidates. Brock's goal was not only to use the Republican National Committee to help the Republican candidates for the White House, but also to increase Republican strength both in Congress and in state legislatures. Brock particularly had in mind that after the 1980 census the state legislatures would control redistricting throughout the nation, and he wanted the Republicans to have as much power as possible in the upcoming apportionment battle, which would go a long way toward determining the balance of strength between Democrats and Republicans at the state level for the next ten years.

While both the Republican and Democratic National Committees and the congressional campaign committees of those parties began to expand their party goals to include the election of candidates at all levels of government, the presidency remained the primary target of the national efforts of the parties. The "presidential party" is best defined as those groups and leaders within the party whose backing is necessary for the election of the president. To be nominated in the past, candidates had to have the support of the power brokers of the party, which included party bosses in key cities throughout the country who could deliver the urban vote in the large industrialized states such as California, Illinois, New York, Ohio, and Pennsylvania. The electoral votes of these states were often the key to winning the presidency in tight races. Franklin Roosevelt, Harry Truman, John F. Kennedy, and Lyndon Johnson all had the backing of powerful state and local party leaders, as did Richard M. Nixon and Gerald Ford in the Republican party. The "Roosevelt coalition" of labor union leaders, urban political bosses, workers, farmers, and intellectuals continued to be the presidential constituency of the Democratic party well after the Roosevelt era. Blacks and other minority groups began to be drawn into the Democratic party during Truman's administration, and by the time of Lyndon Johnson's Great Society the Democrats had corralled the votes of minorities throughout the country. The Vietnam War, however, caused a political trauma that threatened to disperse the national coalition of Democrats that had successfully elected presidents in the past. The nomination of North Dakota Senator George McGovern in 1972 that marked a new era in presidential politics had had its roots in changes in the nomination processes that began in the 1960s—processes which contained the seeds of party disintegration.

The choice of George McGovern as the Democratic nominee at the 1972 convention reflected a profound change in the presidential wing of the Democratic party. McGovern had been instrumental in guiding rule changes for the selection of delegates to the national nominating convention. These changes, and the expertise of his astute campaign manager Gary Hart, made it possible for McGovern himself to capture the nomination.

The McGovern Revolution

The 1972 Democratic convention changed the composition of the presidential party from one largely controlled by party power brokers at state and local levels, such as then Mayor Richard Daley of Chicago, and by labor leaders such as George Meany, to a grassroots party that represented a broad cross section of party members.

The immediate cause of the change in the Democratic presidential party was the strife-ridden convention of 1968 in Chicago, which selected Vice-President Hubert Humphrey to be the presidential nominee after President Lyndon B. Johnson had announced, in the face of what he considered to be insurmountable opposition within his party to his pursuit of the Vietnam War, that he would not run for another term. President Johnson and the power brokers of the party had been able to control the selection of the majority of the delegates, and they dominated the convention proceedings from the opening gavel to the end. The ability of the power brokers to control the party was facilitated by the fact that only 40 percent of the delegates were selected in seventeen primary states, the remainder being chosen by state committees or conventions that were dominated by state and local party leaders.

The antiwar forces knew that they were defeated before the convention began. They rallied around the minority candidacy of Senator Eugene J. McCarthy of Minnesota, who had boldly challenged President Johnson in the New Hampshire primary, and who was declared to be the "winner" by the press because of his good showing even though he did not achieve a majority of the votes. Some delegates backed South Dakota Senator George McGovern, who was also a strong opponent of the war.

As the 1968 Democratic Convention proceeded, the Johnson and antiwar forces of the party engaged in political battles within the convention hall and physical conflict on the streets of Chicago. Senator Eugene McCarthy challenged delegations in fifteen states before the Credentials Committee, which is in charge of determining whether or not a delegate has been validly selected in accordance with party rules. McGovern joined McCarthy in attacking the seating of state delegations that primarily supported Hubert Humphrey.

As the Democrats within the convention hall staged acrimonious debates that threatened to disintegrate the presidential party and jeopardize the election of its candidate, outside the hall Mayor Daley had directed the mobilization of a massive physical force, consisting of approximately twelve thousand Chicago police, over seven thousand army regulars, seventy-five hundred Illinois national guardsmen, and a thousand FBI and Secret Service agents to keep the peace in the face of violent demonstrations. Police clubbings of demonstrators and violent physical retaliation by the demonstrators themselves took place before the eyes of tens of millions of television viewers throughout the country. Hundreds of persons were injured on both sides, and hundreds more were arrested.

Meanwhile, within the hall, Humphrey easily won on the first ballot with over 1700 votes, McCarthy receiving only 601 votes and McGovern 146 votes. The big-city bosses and the Southern conservatives were jubilant in victory, which was made unanimous for Humphrey after a final bitter and tumultuous debate on the floor. Humphrey chose as his running mate Maine Senator Edmund Muskie. However, the sharp party divisions exhibited at the convention reflected an underlying disintegration of party forces that helped to defeat Humphrey in his campaign against the Republican presidential nominee, Richard M. Nixon. Humphrey had the support of the power brokers, but many Democratic liberals, particularly younger people and minorities that make up the antiwar faction of the party, felt excluded and were bitter in defeat.

The defeat of the McCarthy and antiwar forces at the 1968 convention was not complete, however, as they did win their battle over some important changes in party rules, particularly the elimination of the mandatory unit rule for the 1968 and subsequent conventions. Under the unit rule a majority of any unit of the party—local and state committees, for example, and state delegations to the national convention—could determine the final decision of the group. The unit rule had the obvious effect of excluding minority members from exerting power over party policy and actions. The greatest concession made to the minority forces of the 1968 convention was an agreement to establish two special commissions to draft reforms for the selection of delegates to the national convention. Senator George McGovern was chosen to head one of these, which became known as the McGovern Commission and was to recommend procedural changes for the 1972 convention that changed the face of the Democratic presidential party.

The McGovern Commission recommended eighteen guidelines for delegate selection to the 1972 convention, the most important of which proposed the abolition of the unit rule at all levels of the delegate selection process; the representation of minority *political* views at each stage of the process; and an affirmative action policy that would guarantee blacks, other minorities, women, and youth (defined as persons under thirty years of age) representation at the convention roughly in proportion to their numbers in the party.

Although the McGovern Commission's recommendations

The McGovern Commission and the 1972 Convention

were merely guidelines for the 1972 convention, in fact most state Democratic parties went along with the recommendations, and in a number of states the primary laws were changed to conform to the Democratic party rules. For example, "winner-take-all primaries," which granted all of the delegate representation of a state to the person who received a plurality of its vote, were in many states changed to conform to the McGovern guidelines that opposed the unit rule.

A Commission on Rules, also created by the 1968 convention to deal with proceedings of future conventions, wrote guidelines that were adopted by the Democratic National Committee which paralleled those of the McGovern Commission. Recommendations were made that men and women be equally represented on the committees of the convention, that convention committee meetings be open, that minority views be represented, and that delegate strength among the states be allotted on the basis of a formula that took into account the electoral college vote of the state in recent presidential elections.

The 1972 Democratic Convention in Action

The changes recommended by the McGovern Commission brought about a sharp change from the past broker-dominated conventions. The composition of the 1972 convention was entirely different from that of the convention of 1968, and from any previous ones. In 1972, 38 percent of the delegates were women, in contrast to only 13 percent in 1968. Youths numbered 21 percent, compared to only 4 percent in 1968. Blacks and other minorities, however, did not significantly increase their strength. The most important difference was the decrease in the number of professional politicians selected as delegates. Even the Democratic Speaker of the House, Carl Albert of Oklahoma, found that he was a stranger to most of the delegates that had been selected at the grassroots level in accordance with the McGovern formula. Mayor Richard J. Daley of Chicago and his delegation, which in past Democratic conventions had been one of the most significant power blocs, were not even seated after the delegation was challenged before the credentials committee for having been chosen in violation of McGovern rules. Union leaders, too, such as George Meany, found themselves outsiders in an arena of power within which they previously had exerted strong influence.

In place of the professionals of past conventions, the McGovern convention of 1972 was controlled by amateurs. The young people, minorities, women, and others at the convention represented professional people (22 percent), teachers (10 percent), students (9 percent), housewives (13 percent), business people (13 percent), farmers (1 percent), laborers (4 percent), clerical workers (4 percent), union members (14 percent), union leaders (5 percent).

George McGovern, the nominee, reflected the victory of those opposed to the war and to party establishment forces. The McGovern victory was to set a precedent for both the Democratic and Republican parties that encouraged ambitious politicians to use the primary route to gain the nominations of their parties. Presidential preference primaries, in which delegates were selected for the conventions, had grown from a mere handful in the early 1960s to twenty-four in 1972. By 1972, nearly two-thirds of the delegates to the convention were chosen in primaries, in contrast to the 41 percent that had been elected by the primary system in 1968. The seventeen state primaries of 1968 had increased to twenty-five in 1972. By 1976 there were thirty state primaries, and in 1980 there were thirty-four state primaries (in addition to one in the District of Columbia) that selected 80 percent of the Democratic and 76 percent of the Republican delegates.

The McGovern revolution spilled over into the Republican party as state primaries increased and Republican candidates found that they too would have to run the primary gauntlet in order to gain the nomination of their party. While the Republican party did not go as far as the Democratic in requiring proportional representation and affirmative action in the delegate selection process, they too saw a lessening of the influence of traditional power brokers. The growth of presidential preference primaries made each election season an open one for challengers wanting to test their skills in running for the presidency. Even incumbent presidents, who in the

Selection of
Presidential Candidates
at the Grassroots Level

past have always been able to control the party to gain a nomination for a second term, could not be assured of an easy victory at the nominating conventions. Incumbent presidents now have to be supported by the grassroots voters of their own parties to win the necessary number of primaries to gain renomination. In 1976, for example, President Gerald Ford was startled to find Ronald Reagan making an end run around party regulars in an attempt to gain the nomination. Reagan entered the Republican primaries and came within a handful of votes of defeating Ford. The Reaganites used their experience to capture the nomination in 1980.

In 1980, incumbent President Jimmy Carter, like Gerald Ford before him, was challenged for the renomination by Senator Edward M. Kennedy of Massachusetts. Kennedy was unsuccessful, but he managed to gain 1,225 delegates, largely by running in the party's primaries. Carter, however, came to the convention with 1,981 votes, 315 more than he needed for the nomination. Carter, like Ford, had to run in the primaries to retain his power within the party. His grassroots support in states such as Iowa (which uses caucuses and not primaries), throughout the South, and in major industrial areas such as Pennsylvania guaranteed him the renomination. Kennedy's primary and caucus victories enabled him to control thirteen delegations at the convention. During the roll call of delegates, Kennedy gained uncommitted delegates from eight additional states, but his total vote was far short of a convention majority.

Effects of Grassroots Participation on the Presidential Parties

Running for the presidency has become a marathon. Like all marathons, the race tests the mental, emotional, and physical resources of candidates. The presidential party, once a broad based but fairly cohesive group of party insiders that had a fair degree of consistency from one election to the next, is now shaped in an ad hoc fashion by the candidates themselves. Presidential parties are becoming "candidate-parties." They are organized around the personality and policy preferences of the candidates first, and only secondarily around the traditional power bastions of the parties. Each candidate has a separate organization that may or may not include party

Political Parties, Elections, and the Electorate

regulars, but is certainly not dominated by them. George McGovern was a party outsider, if one defines the presidential party in traditional terms. His appeal was to the grassroots electorate of the Democratic party, not to its power brokers. Jimmy Carter, too, was an outsider if one thinks of the Democratic party establishment in traditional terms—labor union leaders, machine bosses, civil rights leaders, and the leaders of various pressure groups such as environmentalists and consumer advocates. Many of these leaders jumped on the Carter bandwagon once it became clear to them that he would capture the nomination; however, their support was often less than enthusiastic. By 1980 many had turned to Kennedy, who they felt was more in line with the traditional liberal Democratic view of the role of government.

The nomination of presidential candidates through the grassroots electoral process has important implications for the role of presidential parties in the polity. The party is far more subject to the whims of individual party voters than where power brokers select the nominees, and the voters whose whims must be catered to often represent a minority of the broader electorate that identifies with the party and ultimately will help to elect its candidates. Turnout in primaries generally is notoriously low, rarely going above 40 percent and often falling as low as 25–30 percent of those eligible to participate. Those who do turn out tend to represent the more active members of the party, who often hold more extreme views on issues of public policy than do the majority of voters. The candidates selected in the primary process can easily turn out to be extremists within their own parties, as was the case with George McGovern in 1972. Ronald Reagan, too, was once considered to reflect more extreme views on issues of public policy than were acceptable to moderate Republicans, who backed Gerald Ford in 1976 against the Reagan candidacy. Reagan's nomination in 1980 was greatly aided by a coterie of enthusiastic supporters who had not represented a majority of the party in the past, but who were cohesive enough to win the Republican primaries easily with the help of a small increment of support from newly converted Reaganites.

The marathon preconvention race for the presidency has narrowed the role of presidential parties in policy development. Many candidates who have tested presidential waters by running in primaries have decried the grassroots method of selecting party nominees. John Anderson, who made a quixotic run for the Republican nomination in 1980, before he was forced to become a third-party candidate, called the system that required him to shake hands at factory gates at sunrise in order to corral a few votes "a crazy way to select the leader of the greatest nation on earth."

President Carter attempted to use the "rose garden strategy," sticking close to the grounds directly outside the Oval Office in making his public appearances. Unlike Anderson, however, Carter enjoyed campaigning, and his 1980 preconvention strategy was designed to take advantage of incumbency and avoid the inevitable pitfalls of the campaign trail. The president chose to avoid open debate with Senator Kennedy, a strategy that certainly did not hurt him and probably helped his quest for renomination.

Reagan also chose to approach the primaries and caucuses cautiously in 1980, relaxing as much as possible in his Pacific Palisades home and on his Santa Barbara ranch, often leaving to his lieutenants and surrogates the responsibilities for campaign details and public appearances. Reagan avoided the Iowa caucuses altogether, which was considered by many to be a mark against him, and even after Iowa engaged in a relatively relaxed campaign for the nomination. Reagan and his organization had carefully prepared the groundwork for the nomination over many years, and could count upon support without having to make a maximum last minute effort in many states.

Many candidates wince when asked about their experiences in the grueling race for the presidency. Rarely do they have time to think about "the party," or important issues of public policy. They generally do not have the time or inclination to cast their campaigns in policy terms, to approach the electorate as a rational body interested in making a responsible choice between the parties on the basis of the voters' policy preferences. Issues of public policy generally take a back seat to concerns about image.

Most campaigners and their advisers agree with Marshall

McLuhan that "the medium is the message," and concentrate accordingly upon the projection of their personalities rather than the content of issues. Messages to the public are cast in the simplest and catchiest terms to attract attention and encourage voters to think superficially rather than in depth about matters of public policy.

All candidates, like Reagan in the 1980 campaign, have a set "speech," given with only minor variations to each and every audience before which they appear. In 1976, presidential candidate Jimmy Carter promised to reduce the sprawling bureaucracy without firing any civil servants, to bring honesty and integrity to government—and "you can count on that," he told his listeners eager for change. Gerald Ford was portrayed as the president who had made the nation proud again, who had restored integrity to government after the Republican debacle of Watergate that had forced the resignation of President Nixon in 1974.

In 1980 the candidates of the two major parties, both before and after the conventions, did little to raise the level of public discourse and understanding of what they and their *parties* would do for the nation if elected. Reagan pledged to cut taxes and to reduce the number of federal employees and programs, but no one could have determined from his public statements the extent to which a new Reagan administration would go in attempting to reverse the tide of increasing government expenditures and taxes. It would have been instructive if David Stockman, who advised Reagan during his campaign and was to become his budget director, had outlined in advance the drastic measures the new administration would take to cut federal expenditures across the board, including reductions in social programs, farm and business subsidies, and veterans' benefits. And President Carter, instead of concentrating on calling Reagan a warmonger and a dangerous person, could have articulated what changes he would make in his second administration to deal with the major problems of inflation, low productivity, a runaway federal budget, and higher taxes, all of which were laid by the public at the doorstep of his White House. John Anderson and Liberal party candidate Ed Clark dealt more specifically with issues than Carter or Reagan, a strategy that is more easily adopted by underdogs than major contenders because the former often feel they have little to lose and much to gain.

Walter Mondale, who immediately began gearing up for the 1984 presidential race after his candidate was defeated in 1980, has commented that to win the nomination and the White House, the candidate must be "willing to go through fire," something Mondale openly admitted he was not prepared to do when he first revealed presidential ambitions in 1974. The growth of the grassroots nominating system, said Mondale, "has been malignant almost. It is anarchy."[5] "When you're running for president it's like a series of one-night stands in vaudeville—you have to have a good act every night. The good act may carry you farther than the good program."[6] Mondale concluded:

The feeling that bothered me more than anything else was that we were in the control of events we were unable to stop or do anything about. Experts are coming and telling you what you have to do, what positions you have to take—usually it's what they want. Then there are the people who want you to get a speech coach and cut your hair differently. None of that's very important. What's really important is that the goddamn news media won't pay you much attention until you've become big. You have to spend years on the road until you get enough percentage points in the polls. The national media won't give you a break until then, and their eyes turn glassy when you talk to them about it. They don't want to hear about it. That's because their business isn't electing presidents—it's competing with their competitors. The result is that the nation is denied a look at new leadership. If you want to get on the evening news, you have to escalate your rhetoric in order to merit the time. If you're saying something rational and restrained, that's not news. That's one of the reasons politicians look so bad. They're always saying something wild. The news programs don't want to put someone unknown on because their competitor might be putting someone well known on. It's understandable, but why shouldn't there be some national forum where who our next president might be is considered and among those considered are those who are not well known but who have great merit?[7]

There is little disagreement with Washington attorney Fred Dutton's statement that a presidential campaign "is a frenetic, superficial, compulsive, neurotic process."[8] While the campaign tests the physical and emotional stamina of the candidates, their organizations, staff, financial backing, and ability to deal with the media—all of which are important in the

[5] Elizabeth Drew, "Running," *The New Yorker*, 1 December 1975, p. 64.

[6] Ibid., p. 66.

[7] Ibid., pp. 66–67.

[8] Ibid., p. 82.

proper handling of the presidency—campaigns do not and perhaps cannot raise all of the substantive policy issues that the people would like to know about because, ironically, the people themselves are too involved in the nomination process itself. Much can be hidden from public view in a political campaign, even many attributes of the personalities of the candidates themselves, which can be glossed over much as their physical appearances can be changed by clever makeup before they appear in front of the television cameras.

The "party" of the successful candidate is composed first of his closest personal advisers, and second of the broader organization that has been created specifically to elect him. The presidential party of Edward Kennedy, for example, was different from that of Jimmy Carter. The party of Gerald Ford was different in many respects from that of Ronald Reagan. The relative narrowness of the candidate parties of contemporary presidents makes it more difficult than ever for them to use their party as a major prop in the construction of their scenario of leadership once they have won the cherished prize of the White House. The position papers they so earnestly seek from experts in their coterie of supporters often recommend policies that have little or no relationship to the party platform or to the policies supported by important party groups throughout the nation. A new president must begin immediately after his election to forge new power alliances within and without Washington which go beyond the presidential party that secured him the nomination and election if he is to provide effective leadership for the nation.

ELECTORAL CHOICE, PARTIES, AND PUBLIC POLICY

While political candidates are important representatives of the political parties, and their actions significant in terms of the role of the party in formulating and implementing public policy, the parties themselves play an important role in setting the policy agenda that goes far beyond that played by candidates and campaigns. Even though American parties are loosely organized confederations of diverse interests, they have become an important link between the people and government. Parties provide an important arena within which policy issues are debated intensely by political leaders and the representatives of powerful pressure groups.

Parties and Issue Identification

If one were to ask voters in any part of the country whether or not there are differences between the Democratic and Republican parties, the answer would most often be yes. Regardless of regional differences between the parties, Democrats are generally identified with programs aimed at the redistribution of wealth, Social Security, and the use of government as a positive instrument to solve economic and social problems. Everyone "knows" that the Democrats are the party of the people, and the Republicans represent the rich. These perceptions are clichés, and like all clichés they are trite and overused expressions that often have little relationship to the truth. The fact remains, however, that people perceive fundamental differences between the parties. Those who identify with the Democratic party have different viewpoints on many issues of public policy than do those who identify with Republicans. This does not mean that those who identify with one party or the other necessarily vote for the candidates of that party under all circumstances. Ticket-splitting has become a common voting habit, one that is frequently cited as evidence of the decline of party politics.

Party differences over public policy are sharper at national than at state and local levels. Only at the national level are the parties forced to accommodate wide-ranging and often conflicting interests in writing the party platforms every four years. The disintegration and personalization of presidential parties that began in earnest in the 1970s, accompanied by political campaigns that stress images more than issues, has blurred party policy distinctions in the minds of many voters.

Voters have also been confused about party differences because of the sharp splits within the ranks of each party over important issues of public policy. In the past, for example, Southern Democrats were diametrically opposed to their Northern brethren on the issue of civil rights. Liberal Northern Republicans favored free trade, while midwestern members of the party were isolationist and advocated trade barriers. The Republican party of Dwight Eisenhower was different from that of his challenger, conservative Senator Robert Taft of Ohio. Franklin Roosevelt was able to keep the Democratic party together while he occupied the White House, but in 1948 his successor, Harry Truman, confronted massive defections of Northern liberals and Southern conservatives. At the 1948 convention, the Mississippi delegation and members of the Alabama delegation simply withdrew after the balloting began, to express their opposition to the civil rights stance of the party. At the same time, Northern liberals argued that the party platform had not gone far enough in supporting civil rights. Southern Democrats eventually formed the Dixiecrat party and nominated Democratic Governor Strom Thurmond of South Carolina for president in a special convention held in Birmingham, Alabama. The Democrats were further split when Henry A. Wallace, who had been Roosevelt's vice-president from 1941 to 1944, became the presidential candidate of a new liberal Progressive party.

The divisions within parties of the past continue along different lines in the 1980s. John Anderson was a leading Republican in Congress, heading the Republican conference in the House of Representatives, which includes all Republican members of the House, before he made his presidential attempt first in the Republican party and then as an Independent in 1980. Anderson and Reagan were at opposite ends of the political spectrum on such issues as equal rights for women, abortion, economic policy, and national defense. Which was the real Republican party, that of Reagan or of Anderson? Anderson's inability to make virtually any headway in the Republican primaries suggested that the Reagan philosophy would be the prevailing one for the Republican party in the 1980s. On the Democratic side, voters were equally confused between the active liberalism of Senator Edward Kennedy and the cautious conservatism of Jimmy Carter. Kennedy pushed for a more active governmental role than Carter supported in promoting civil rights and job opportunities.

As each party seeks a new identity in the 1980s, party leaders
are building upon the past at the same time they are developing new policies for the future.

The origins of the current differences between the two
national parties are to be found in the crisis of the Depression
and the response of the parties to it. President Franklin D.
Roosevelt formed what was called the "Roosevelt coalition"
within the Democratic party, consisting of laborers, farmers,
older Americans, the poor, and liberal intellectuals. The coalition became the basis of Roosevelt's electoral support, returning him to office for an unprecedented four terms. Roosevelt's
New Deal programs were responsive to the interests and
concerns of each of the groups within his coalition. An underlying assumption of the New Deal was that government
should be used to solve economic and social problems.
Roosevelt formed what was called a "brain trust" of academic
and other experts that encouraged him in his interventionist
stance. The New Dealers were what political philosophers
have called "positivists," those who believe that government
can and should solve human problems. The Keynesian econ-
omists were part of Roosevelt's brain trust, urging deficit
government spending to stimulate the economy. Roosevelt,
who had promised a balanced budget in his 1932 campaign,
seized upon the Keynesian philosophy as a justification for
increased government expenditures to cope with the overwhelming economic problems of the Depression.

In a nutshell, Roosevelt's New Deal program advocated the
redistribution of wealth through increasing progressive taxation and welfare programs supported by government expenditures. The Social Security system was created in 1935 in
response to the needs of the elderly and poor. Although it was
supported in part by private contributions from individuals,
general revenue funds were used from the very beginning. The
Roosevelt administration also increased direct government
subsidies to the nation's agricultural and industrial sectors.
Farm price supports became a major underpinning of the New
Deal agricultural program. Finally, the Roosevelt administration spawned the greatest increase in regulatory legislation in
history. New agencies were created to regulate the stock ex-
changes, commodity markets, labor relations, public utility

holding companies, the telephone and telegraph industry, the emerging broadcasting industry, airlines, truckers, agricultural marketing, and other spheres of economic activity. Distributive or subsidy policies became a mainstay of the New Deal. Inevitably, the expansion of the role of government during the New Deal created a vast bureaucracy that was itself to become a major political issue.

The Republican response to the New Deal set the tone of future party deliberations and policies for years to come. The Republican party of the 1930s and 1940s, however, was the "out-party," the party that was a minority in Congress and excluded from the White House. Just as the Democrats in 1980 are having difficulty in defining a national party program in the absence of an incumbent president to provide leadership, the Republicans of the 1930s and 1940s were a rudderless ship seeking a port in the political storm that threatened to destroy the Grand Old Party once and for all. Because the out-party does not have a recognized leader, it tends to fragment into the interests that compose it and that are by themselves unable to agree upon alternatives to the program of the party in power. Roosevelt could well have said, as Reagan did at the outset of his administration, "If you don't like what I am doing you have a responsibility to come up with an alternative to meet the national economic emergency." About all the Republicans could do was attack the New Deal, which they considered, in the words of their 1936 platform, to be a "peril to the nation." Under Roosevelt, they claimed, the powers of Congress had been usurped, the integrity and authority of the Supreme Court undermined, and the rights and liberties of citizens violated. They advocated returning responsibility for the welfare of the community to state and local governments and, in words that remind one of Ronald Reagan and David Stockman, advocated balancing the budget "not by increasing taxes but by cutting expenditures, drastically and immediately." The 1936 Republicans urged, as did Ronald Reagan in his opening address to the nation, that a sound currency be preserved "at all hazards. The first requisite of a sound and stable currency is a balanced budget." The Republican party of the New Deal had not yet articulated the concept of "supply-side" economics, under

Electoral Choice, Parties, and Public Policy

which tax cuts are used to increase incentives for productivity, but they certainly would have agreed with the principle. The roots of the Reagan philosophy of government are to be found in Republican policies of the past, and it is not insignificant that Reagan ordered Calvin Coolidge's pictures to be hung in the Oval Office.

The national Democratic and Republican parties of the Roosevelt era differed as sharply on foreign policy as on domestic policy. Isolationism characterized the Republican approach to world affairs, in sharp contrast to Roosevelt's interventionist stance. The foreign policy differences between the parties blurred after World War II, with the emergence of bipartisan foreign policy. Both Democrats and Republicans became "cold warriors," who considered the Soviet Union to be the principal threat to world peace and the security of the nation. Although bipartisanship was practiced in the formulation and conduct of foreign policy, the Republicans as the out-party did not hesitate to seize every opportunity to criticize the Democrats for being weak in confrontation with the Soviet Union and world communism. With the help of the China Lobby, a group representing the interests of Chinese President Chiang Kai-shek, the Republicans charged the Democrats with the betrayal of China and of being responsible for the victory of the Chinese Communists in 1949. In their 1952 platform, the Republicans accused the Democrats of denying "the military aid that had been authorized by Congress and which was crucially needed if China were to be saved. Thus they substituted on our Pacific flank a murderous enemy for an ally and friend."

The programs of both parties during the 1930s and early 1940s failed to include a civil rights policy. Note should be taken, however, of the women's rights plank in the 1940 Republican platform that favored an equal rights amendment. No such provision was found in the Democratic platform. By 1944 both parties were beginning to pay attention to the issue of civil rights, and their platforms included strong statements supporting civil rights. In 1944 the Republicans called for a congressional inquiry into segregation in the armed services, and urged the adoption of corrective legislation. They supported a fair employment practices commission, the abolition of the poll tax, and legislation against lynching. In 1944 the Democrats, taking a cue from the Republican platform of 1940, proposed an equal rights amendment to protect the rights of women. On civil rights generally, the Democrats simply stated: "We believe that racial and religious minorities have the right to live, develop and vote equally with all citizens and share the rights that are guaranteed by our Constitution. Congress should exert its full constitutional powers to protect those rights."

The year 1944 marked the beginning of the articulation of civil rights policies by both parties that finally culminated in the passage of the Civil Rights Act of 1964 and the Voting Rights Act of 1965. Beginning with the Eisenhower administration, the Republicans proposed a less interventionist role for the federal government in protecting civil rights, but nevertheless always supported the principle of equality under the law. The Republicans were more in favor of leaving the resolution of civil rights issues to the states than were the Democrats. In 1952, however, the Republicans did call for federal legislation to end segregation in the District of Columbia.

The Eisenhower period was one of retrenchment for the Democrats, who continued to retain a slim majority of 54 percent of the electorate in congressional, state, and local elections. The Eisenhower victory did not result in a policy shift along Republican lines, because, with the exception of the Eighty-third Congress (1953–1954), in which the Democrats outnumbered the Republicans by one member in the Senate and eight in the House, Eisenhower had to deal with a Democratic Congress throughout his administration. The Democrats made significant comebacks throughout the country in 1954, and regained control of Capitol Hill. The Eisenhower administration was, however, able to achieve some important Republican goals, such as balancing the budget, reducing taxation, and curbing inflation. In foreign policy, Eisenhower's secretary of state, John Foster Dulles, implemented the Republican hard line policy against the Soviet Union.

During the 1950s the Democratic party continued the

rhetoric of the Roosevelt administration, and did little to reshape the policy proposals of the New Deal. Adlai Stevenson, the Democratic presidential candidate in 1952 and 1956, represented the liberal wing of the party that found its major support in the northeast. The split continued in the Democratic party between the southern Dixiecrat wing, the northern liberals, and the more moderate midwest and far west Democratic politicians. Although Stevenson was highly liberal in his orientation, the fact that he came from Illinois gave him a midwest base and the support of prominent politicians from that area. Significantly, the Democratic convention was held in Mayor Daley's Chicago, and the mayor was a strong supporter of Stevenson, who had the backing of the Chicago machine even though he had captured the governorship of Illinois as a reform candidate. While Stevenson was the choice of the Democratic power brokers, Tennessee Senator Estes Kefauver, who was well known to the public because of his nationally televised crime hearings in 1951, was the favorite of the rank and file of the party. Kefauver had defeated Truman in the New Hampshire primary, won the Wisconsin and Nebraska primaries by overwhelming margins, and had primary victories as well in Massachusetts, Pennsylvania, New Jersey, Maryland, Oregon, South Dakota, California, and Ohio. There is little doubt that if a majority of delegates in 1952 had been selected by the presidential primary process, Kefauver would have been the nominee.

The Democratic platforms of 1952 and 1956 promised to continue the New Deal programs and increase government subsidies, aid to education, and Social Security coverage. In addition, the party favored civil rights legislation to guarantee equal employment opportunity, equal political participation, and the elimination of discrimination. The Republicans, while supporting civil rights and government subsidies in areas such as agriculture, stressed what had become the traditional Republican theme of fiscal responsibility, stressing the need to balance the federal budget and to return governmental responsibilities as much as possible to the states. At the same time, the Republicans committed themselves to reductions in federal expenditures, and to decreasing the national debt and taxation.

The policy themes of the national Democratic and Republican parties that originated in the New Deal continued with only slight variations in the early 1960s, but the winds of change were being felt by both parties. The comfortable Roosevelt coalition, which in the late 1940s had been threatened by growing southern sentiment opposing the stand of other party groups on civil rights, became even more shaky as the civil rights movement began to grow and reach a crescendo in the mid and late 1960s. Black and minority support for the Democratic party had been unimportant to Roosevelt, but as these groups increasingly participated in politics they found a more comfortable home in the Democratic than in the Republican party. Most blacks were poor, and did not fit into the establishment circles of the Republicans. The economic programs of the Democrats appealed to blacks because the programs emphasized the importance of federal aid for welfare, education, housing, a minimum wage law, expanded Social Security benefits, and national health insurance. With the exception of many conservative southern Democrats, the party welcomed blacks and minority groups as an important electoral constituency, and responded to their needs in the Great Society program, the Civil Rights Act of 1964, and the Voting Rights Act of 1965.

The expansion of the base of the Democratic party to include blacks and other minorities, and the perception of groups espousing liberal programs that the Democratic party was the only available vehicle for important political, social, and economic change, laid the groundwork for the more eclectic party that emerged between 1968 and 1972. The Roosevelt coalition had been expanded, and was now threatened unless the party could accommodate the diverse and often contrasting interests it had welcomed under its umbrella. The purpose of the McGovern revolution was to facilitate the accommodation by widening the base of participation in party affairs; the party failed, however, to merge its expanded liberal wing with its conservative and moderate elements in 1972. The McGovern candidacy was considered to be extreme not only by the Republicans, but by many Democrats as well, who crossed party lines to vote for incumbent President Richard M. Nixon.

The McGovern debacle left the national Democratic party in shambles. As a leaderless party began to feel its way toward the 1976 elections, the new party rules and the growth of the presidential preference primary system of nomination created a free-for-all among candidates hoping to head the 1976 ticket. Dark horse candidate Jimmy Carter began preparing for his race soon after McGovern's defeat. Carter took a leaf from the McGovern campaign strategy notebooks and began to cultivate grassroots support among Democratic voters throughout the nation who would be the decisive factor in the primaries of 1976. Carter campaign aide, Hamilton Jordan, copied the successful techniques of McGovern's campaign strategist, Gary Hart. But Carter and Jordan went beyond the McGovern strategy in reaching out to Democratic power brokers. Carter not only won the 1976 nomination handily, but was instrumental in shaping the platform even before the convention met. As the convention opened at Madison Square Garden in New York City, the party seemed to be uncharacteristically harmonious, as both Carter and his choice for vice-president, Walter Mondale, were chosen by an overwhelming vote of the delegates. The acrimony of past conventions was not present. The platform was as bland as the convention itself, differing little from the rhetoric of past platforms in its support of civil rights, equal employment opportunity, and federal aid for welfare, the elderly, veterans, education, the arts and humanities, and agriculture. Some platform planks, however, did diverge from the past and reflected the Carter stance. There was a new emphasis upon the need to restore integrity in government, reorganize the bureaucracy, and generally improve governmental efficiency. The platform announced new "rights" of the people to competent and responsive government, to integrity in and fair dealing by government. In an almost religious spirit, reflecting Carter's orientation, the business community was lectured on the need for accountability. The relatively new issues of environmental quality, natural resources, and energy were addressed, and an active federal role in each of these policy spheres advocated. The 1976 Democratic platform left no doubt that the party continued to be rooted in the philosophy and programs of the New Deal, with an expanded role for the national government in shaping economic and social policy. Emphasis on redistributive and subsidy policies continued. Although a move had begun by both Republicans and Democrats during the Ford administration toward deregulation of some industries, such as transportation, no mention was made of this in the 1976 Democratic platform.

While the Democratic party was changing its base, if not its policy, in the decades between 1960 and 1980, the Republicans too were involved in a process of change from a more liberal and moderate orientation to a highly conservative one. In the early 1960s, Governor Nelson Rockefeller of New York, Senator Barry Goldwater, and Richard M. Nixon were prominent Republican figures representing, respectively, the liberal, conservative, and moderate wings of the party. Ronald Reagan, who was to become governor of California in 1966, was slowly emerging as a new conservative voice. Reagan, first a Democrat (who had become a Democrat for Nixon in 1960), did not change his party registration to Republican until 1962. The battles within the Republican party in the early 1960s did not include Reagan, but by 1968 he and his followers had become the conservative wing of the party. The struggle to control the national party apparatus and become the party nominee in 1968 was a bitter one that would determine the policy orientation of the party for years to come. Richard Nixon barely won the nomination on the first ballot, but easily outdistanced Rockefeller and Reagan, both of whom had been backed for the nomination. Nixon had carefully cultivated Republican support throughout the nation after his defeat for the presidency in 1960 and for the governorship of California in 1962. Nixon was to prove that experienced politicians neither die nor fade away when they have an overriding ambition to be president. The Republican platform of 1968 concentrated upon the issue of Vietnam, accusing the Johnson administration of failing militarily, politically, and diplomatically in its conduct of the war. The Republicans promised peace in 1968, as they had in 1952, and the existence of a "Democratic war" at both times helped them to capture the presidency. Although the usual Republican promises of balanced budgets and reduced taxes and federal expenditures were made during the Nixon era, the

Republican president focused in a major way upon foreign policy. Perhaps the major achievement of his administration was to pave the way for the opening of relations with the People's Republic of China, even though the 1968 platform on which Nixon ran declared that relations with Communist nations would only be improved "when they cease to endanger the other states by force or threat. Under existing conditions, we cannot favor recognition of Communist China, or its admission to the United Nations."

Nixon's presidency was, to say the least, an unusual one for a Republican. He became an active conservative, attempting to use the powers of the presidency to implement social and economic change and, even more importantly, to restructure international relations. Nixon's activism was in sharp contrast to the general passivity of Republican presidents in the twentieth century—with the one notable exception of Theodore Roosevelt. Nixon was more interested in power than in policy. He opened relations with China in the face of a specific pledge not to do so. He imposed wage and price controls, an anathema to most Republicans. He expanded the presidential bureaucracy more than any president had done before or after him, adding agency after agency to help him deal with the regular bureaucracy, which was largely controlled by Democrats appointed in previous administrations. He used the power of impoundment to prevent the expenditure of money approved by the Democratic Congress for scores of programs. He was an active president in the best tradition of Franklin D. Roosevelt and the Democratic party, but with a distinctly different emphasis in some areas.

The Republican party barely survived the constitutional crisis of Watergate, which became its Vietnam. Gerald Ford took over the reins of the party after Nixon's resignation in 1974, but was barely able to achieve the nomination in 1976 over Ronald Reagan. The disenchantment of the Reagan forces after their 1976 convention defeat contributed to Ford's defeat at the hands of Jimmy Carter.

The Ford-Reagan conflict in 1976 did not reflect the kind of division within the Republican party between liberals and conservatives that had occurred in 1964, for example, when

Barry Goldwater was the nominee over the opposition of New York Governor Nelson Rockefeller. Both Ford and Reagan were conservatives, and the major differences between them arose on issues of foreign policy, Reagan taking a harder stand against the Soviet Union and proposals to relinquish control of the Panama Canal than did Ford. Both agreed that there should be a reduced federal role in the social and economic life of the country, and both supported the long accepted Republican policies of balancing the budget and reducing taxes and federal expenditures. The real conflict that took place between the two candidates at the convention was not over substantive policy but over procedures, with Reagan fighting for changes in the rules that would benefit him and put Ford at a disadvantage.[9]

The Republican platform in 1976 continued Republican policy preferences of the past, and became the precursor of the future. The Republicans regarded inflation as the "main destroyer of jobs," but rejected wage and price controls as the answer to rising prices. In contrast to the Democrats, the Republicans stressed the importance of bolstering the private sector to increase employment, rather than having the federal government stimulate new jobs. The Republicans favored an independent Federal Reserve with the authority to control the money supply and interest rates in accordance with its view of the economy, whereas the Democrats proposed merging the Federal Reserve into a unified system of national economic planning.

On other economic and social issues the 1976 Republican platform favored a limited role for the federal government, which would cover only catastrophic illness, in any national health plan. The Democrats supported broad national health insurance. The Republicans favored block grants to state and local governments to deal with problems of housing, in contrast to the Democratic policy of direct federal housing subsidies and low interest loans.

On important issues of civil rights, the 1976 Republicans supported a constitutional amendment to prohibit abortions. New Jersey representative Millicent Fenwick led an unsuccessful move to have all references to abortion in the platform

[9] For example, Reagan proposed a rule that would require the candidates to divulge the names of their running mates before the presidential balloting. The rule lost by only twelve votes, 1168–1180, on the convention floor.

deleted. The Democrats specifically opposed an antiabortion constitutional amendment. Both parties endorsed the Equal Rights Amendment.

Parties and Policies in the 1980s

Both the Republican and Democratic parties emerged after the 1980 nominating conventions with sharply contrasting social, economic, and civil rights policies that reflected the past divergencies between the parties. In 1964, Arizona Senator Barry Goldwater, the Republican nominee, had promised the people "a choice and not an echo." The voters in 1964 overwhelmingly rejected the conservative Republican and elected Lyndon B. Johnson by a landslide of the popular vote that was the greatest achieved by any candidate in the twentieth century. In 1980 Reagan, too, promised a real choice to the American people, and once again the electorate voted decisively for change. Whether or not they were voting for a change of *personalities* or *policies* was not entirely clear. The rhetoric of the campaigns of both candidates did not sharply present the policy differences between the two parties that were reflected in their convention platforms and debates. Many Democrats and Independents voted for Reagan, to give him slightly more than a majority of the popular vote. Some voters who crossed party lines to support the winner were undoubtedly surprised when the new Republican president immediately began to implement to the letter the promises of the Republican platform. "He really means it," was the surprised reaction of many in the Washington establishment who had seen presidents come and go, and party changeovers in Congress, but had never seen a party platform taken so seriously by an incoming administration. Again and again Reagan repeated in response to questions about his program, "We have to do this because we promised it to the American people."

What was promised by the Republicans was budget slashing, large tax decreases, massive increases in defense spending—particularly in Latin America—support of Israel, a peacetime draft, the repeal of gun control laws, mandatory sentences for serious crimes, and the death penalty. Deregulation of the economy and the support of nuclear power were

Political Parties, Elections, and the Electorate

also part of the 1980 Republican platform. Finally, on the issue of civil rights, the Republicans backed an antiabortion amendment, and mandated their candidate to appoint anti-abortion judges to the federal judiciary, a plank that Illinois Republican Senator Charles Percy called "the worst plank I have ever seen in any platform by the Republican Party."[10] The party supported equal rights, but not an equal rights amendment, marking a departure from party platforms of the past.

The Democrats offered a meaningful alternative to the Reagan program in 1980. Generally they supported massive federal expenditures for jobs and housing and opposed cutbacks in existing federal programs to aid the poor, such as food stamps. The Democrats characteristically supported federal aid in other areas, such as education—in sharp contrast to the Republican position in favor of elimination of the Department of Education and the end of most federal regulation and direct funding of education. Finally, the Democrats supported the Equal Rights Amendment and freedom of choice on abortion.

The contrasting positions of the Democrats and Republicans as the decade of the 1980s got under way reflected party responsibility on both sides. The parties were indeed offering the electorate a choice on important issues of public policy. But the responsibility of the presidential wings of the parties did not necessarily translate into meaningful party *government* in which electoral choice could become a reality.

[10] *Congressional Quarterly Weekly Report,* 19 July 1980, p. 2005.

ELECTORAL CHOICE AND PARTY PROGRAMS

The national parties that come together every four years for the primary purpose of selecting a presidential nominee and with hopes of capturing the presidency perform a role that largely conforms to the requirements of the liberal-democratic model of government by discussion. The parties formulate programs, offer a choice, aggregate the interests of the electorate, and provide groups representing those interests an incentive to compromise to achieve the goal of the presidency. At the same time, the national parties test leadership qualities of individual candidates in the long campaign processes that precede the nominating conventions, and in the short post-election campaigns as well.

Regardless of the articulation of party programs in platforms that at least during and immediately after the national conventions are widely publicized, government by discussion among the electorate and the final choice of the voters does not focus primarily upon parties as the vehicles of contrasting public policies. The aggregation of interests reflected in the national conventions and party programs begins to break down at other levels of national, state, and local politics. In congressional elections, state and local district politics, candidates, and issues determine the outcome more than party labels. The same holds true for the presidential candidates, who are often judged as much on personalities and appearances as upon the platforms of their parties.

In 1980 the Democratic party seemed to disintegrate under the leadership of Jimmy Carter at the head of the national ticket. While many of the party *programs* were specifically designed to appeal to the minority group constituency of the party, many minority voters did not turn out at all, and some black leaders even endorsed the candidacy of Ronald Reagan. Many Democratic voters clearly did not vote their party, rejecting their own incumbent president for a variety of reasons, including their perception of his weak leadership in failing to deal adequately with the crisis created by the holding of hostages in Iran, and exhibited in the lack of an effective economic program to deal with inflation and unemployment. Many voters apparently selected Reagan over Carter because they liked the personality and style of the self-confident and often humorous Republican in contrast to the bland Carter style and personality.

Public Policy, Public Relations, and Political Candidates

A common theme both of studies by political scientists and popular versions of the electoral process is the irrationality of many voters who can be swayed by clever public relations techniques aimed at their emotions, and not designed to persuade voters that the policy orientations of the candidates make a difference. "Politics, in a sense, has always been a con game," wrote Joe McGinniss in describing the successful Nixon campaign for the presidency in 1968.[11] McGinniss echoes the views of political public relations advisers, who try desperately to shape the images of their candidates to suit what they consider to be the tastes of the American public—tastes which do not concern policy preferences, but psychological needs for leadership and security provided by men who are bigger than life. The public relations industry has spawned consulting firms that specialize in selling political candidates as if they were products. The presence of television sets in nearly every American home challenges the manipulative ingenuity of political public relations consultants. Generally they accept the view that television "seems particularly useful to the politician who can be charming but lacks ideas. Print is for ideas."[12] Personality is what counts on television, the medium is the message, and most advisers urge their politicians to deal only superficially with a few issues that will be of appeal to a broad cross section of the public.

The entry of professional public relations firms into political marketing began with the television age. In 1952, the campaign advisers to Dwight Eisenhower hired a large Madison Avenue advertising agency to shape Republican "spots" on television, thirty-second or one-minute political commercials designed to sell Eisenhower. Issues were pushed to the background. Eisenhower was portrayed as the military hero, the sincere and trustworthy fatherly figure, the person who could lead the nation out of the morass of the Korean War. On the advice of his aides Eisenhower told the American people, "I will go to Korea," but did not tell them what he would do there or what his policy was concerning the Korean War. The remark raised the hopes of the electorate, however, and is given credit by some for Eisenhower's sweeping victory. Eisenhower's opponent in 1952 and 1956, Adlai Stevenson, conducted a campaign that stressed the differences between the Republicans and Democrats on major issues of public policy. Eisenhower buried Stevenson.

By the end of the Eisenhower era, political public relations had become a major force in presidential and most other campaigns for public office. John Kennedy's "appearance" during the celebrated television debates of the 1960 campaign

[11] *The Selling of the President, 1968* (New York: Simon and Schuster, 1969). The quote is from the Trident Press paperback edition, p. 26.

[12] Ibid., p. 29.

established his credibility against the better known Richard Nixon, and is widely thought to have given him the necessary edge to defeat Nixon. The format of the 1960 debates, which was copied in the debates of the 1976 and 1980 campaigns, did not provide time for a substantive exchange on important issues of public policy. Kennedy followed the instructions of a specially hired television coach carefully, giving a three-point answer to each question to give the viewing audience the impression he knew what he was talking about. In contrast to the cool, confident Kennedy, Nixon appeared nervous, perspired heavily, and often seemed overly defensive in response to Kennedy's thrusts. Nixon later accused the Kennedy forces of having infiltrated his make up staff, who had failed to hide his five o'clock shadow from the more than fifty million viewers.

Kennedy's "victory" in the 1960 television debates convinced all future politicians of the necessity of using professional public relations advisers to cultivate an effective image. While the national presidential parties worked long hours to hammer out their platforms, the candidates and their public relations consultants devised campaigns that used psychological warfare rather than a careful presentation of the issues separating the parties. In 1964 the differences between Republicans and Democrats were the sharpest they had been in decades. Arizona Senator Barry Goldwater had temporarily taken over the presidential wing of the Republican party, much to the delight of incumbent President Johnson, who felt the Arizona senator would be an easy political target in a national election. Goldwater was an uncompromising conservative, who told an accepting convention but a startled American public that "Extremism in the defense of liberty is no vice." The 1964 Republican platform represented extreme conservative views on issues ranging from national defense to the economy, civil rights, obscenity, school prayer, and even reapportionment (the Republicans advocated a constitutional amendment to enable states to apportion one house of their legislatures according to factors other than population). The Goldwater platform and the Great Society program of Lyndon Johnson were at opposite ends of the political spectrum. Goldwater's campaign emphasized his conservative views while attacking the extreme liberalism of the Democratic party and its candidate. Johnson, for his part, focused upon the alleged extremism of Barry Goldwater, particularly in foreign affairs. A prominent feature of the Johnson campaign was a television spot that showed the explosion of a hydrogen bomb in the background while a little girl was picking daisies in the foreground, with an accompanying spoken message implying that the election of Barry Goldwater would result in World War III.

The Nixon campaigns of 1968 and 1972 relied heavily upon staged television appearances to project the image of a self-assured and experienced leader. The Republicans did not hesitate to use clips from the raucous Democratic convention to suggest that McGovern would be a disastrous leader. The Republicans believed that McGovern's image, and that of his followers, were even greater liabilities with the electorate than his policies.

The 1976 campaign again saw a public relations battle between Gerald Ford and Jimmy Carter, with the Georgian conducting one of the cleverest media campaigns that had ever been seen. By the time Carter received the nomination, everyone in the United States knew who he was, for he had become the darling of the press and the television media as well. The dark horse candidate from the deep South had captured the imagination of the country through deft manipulation of the media. Marketing genius made Jimmy Carter Huck Finn writ large. In contrast to Carter's smile and easy appearance on television, President Ford, in the words of Richard Cheney, "freezes on camera." The Ford campaign was built around the slogan, "He's making us proud again."[13] But the public relations advisers to the president were unable to convince the people that he made them proud enough to reelect him.

[13] The quote from Cheney, who was President Ford's chief of staff, appeared in Malcolm D. MacDougall, *We Almost Made It* (New York: Crown Publishers, 1977).

Professional public relations continued to be important in the 1980 presidential campaigns, often submerging the issue differences between the parties. Carter and Reagan together budgeted approximately eighteen million dollars for political advertising that was used for television commercials ranging

The 1980 Presidential Campaign: Images and Issues

from thirty-second spots to half-hour specials. Jerry Rafshoon, whom Carter had brought into the White House to become his public relations adviser, handled Carter's campaign advertising, most of which was directed at displaying Carter as a leader rather than giving the views of the candidate and his party on issues. Moreover, the Carter campaign, echoing that of Lyndon Johnson in 1964, used television commercials to accentuate the "extremism" of Ronald Reagan, particularly on foreign policy and military affairs. The commercials emphasizing Carter's positive characteristics pictured him meeting with foreign leaders, working in the White House, signing legislation in the rose garden, and receiving the acclamation of crowds of people. The commercials attacking Reagan focused on interviews of people in the streets who, in response to questions about Reagan's policies, said that the Republican candidate scared them. "Should we send a man like this to Washington?" asks the wary announcer, and responds, "Figure it out for yourself." As the election date neared, the television commercials for Carter increased, showing him with prominent Democratic leaders such as Edward Kennedy and Mo Udall, and with Lady Bird Johnson. Rank and file Democrats were shown praising the president. Through all of the television commercials of Carter, issues barely raised their heads.

The Reagan advertising campaign concentrated upon his record as governor of California, and brief statements of his stand on mostly economic issues. Carter was attacked by the Republicans as being responsible for runaway inflation, unemployment, and a weak defense, and for a lack of leadership in foreign affairs. Because Reagan was considered to be a good communicator, and his stand on issues attractive to the American public, television spots of his short, catchy phrases on what he would do once elected president became a prominent feature of his television campaign. Reagan's views on many issues of public policy were seen by his political consultants as a kind of potential entertainment for the American electorate that had become bored with Democratic rhetoric that promised little change.

As third-party candidates typically do, John Anderson—who had a minuscule advertising budget in comparison to those of the major candidates—concentrated upon issues. Anderson's television spots did not hesitate to proclaim his opposition to increased defense spending, and support for the ERA and the fifty-cent gasoline tax. Anderson's media campaign was by no means solely concentrated upon issues, however, but stressed the candidate's credibility as a potential leader of the nation, picturing Anderson in his congressional office talking with his staff, and on the telephone with the president.

The desultory and distracting nature of the 1980 presidential campaign caused the Pulitzer Prize–winning editorial writer of the *Wall Street Journal,* Robert Bartley, to admonish the candidates and their parties for failing to treat the voters responsibly. "Increasingly," wrote Bartley, "the most 'modern' and 'sophisticated' campaign seems to be based on the premise that voters are children. On the one hand, the campaign wizards try to manipulate the voters with empty images, especially negative attacks on opposing personalities. On the other hand, the wizards pander to the voters with poll readings. . . . The managers pore over every detail but are deaf to the loudest sound of this campaign: the electorate collective groan for some straight-talking leadership."[14] The Carter campaign, according to Bartley, "has proved its mastery of short-term manipulation." Immediately before the Wisconsin primary, Carter talked of hope for the hostages. Reagan was pictured as a "racist and a warmonger."[15] Bartley did not spare the Reagan campaign, which "was handed ready-made issues," but which displayed "a skittishness, fed by the polls, about trusting the voters to understand the issues." The Reagan campaign "seemed to despair of convincing the voters that high taxes do not cure inflation, or that peace is preserved by preparedness. So it left voters hearing only the other side of the case, and by the time it returned to the issues it found them irreparably clouded."[16] As the final debate of the campaign approached, Bartley called upon the candidates to say *something* about the issues.

Bartley's *Wall Street Journal* editorial called attention to a book by the famed political scientist V. O. Key, Jr., entitled *The Responsible Electorate.*[17] The theme of Key's work was that the electorate is indeed interested in and capable of

[14] *Wall Street Journal,* 28 October 1980.

[15] Ibid.

[16] Ibid.

[17] (Cambridge, Mass.: Harvard University Press, 1966.)

making a rational choice among political candidates, but that the choice is made difficult because the candidates themselves, and particularly their public relations advisers, do not believe voters act rationally. Key concluded:

> . . . [V]oters are not fools. To be sure, many individual voters act in odd ways indeed; yet in the large the electorate behaves about as rationally and responsibly as we should expect, given the clarity of the alternatives presented to it and the character of the information available to it. In American presidential campaigns of recent decades the portrait of the American electorate that develops from the data is not one of an electorate strait-jacketed by social determinants or moved by subconscious urges triggered by devilishly skillful propagandists. It is rather one of an electorate moved by concern about central and relevant questions of public policy, of governmental performance, and of executive personality. Propositions so uncompromisingly stated inevitably represent overstatements. Yet to the extent that they can be shown to resemble the reality, they are propositions of basic importance for both the theory and the practice of democracy.[18]

[18] Ibid., pp. 7–8.

Key suggested that the voters are perhaps more responsible than their leaders. The voters want to make rational policy choices, whereas the candidates concentrate upon the projection of their character, styles, and personalities. The cult of personality tends to have the greatest impact at the national level, where the personal characteristics of candidates are highlighted and emphasized to the public in the mass media. The national parties do offer the voters a meaningful choice, but one which often is obscured by campaign rhetoric and ignored by the party's own candidates for office at the congressional, state, and local levels of politics. In presidential election years, party candidates will follow the leadership of their presidential nominee insofar as they feel they can ride his coattails into office. After the election, the power of the president over members of his own party is not automatically strengthened by party ties, but becomes one of persuasion of party members to follow his leadership. The party cohesiveness of presidential election years tends to disintegrate once the election is past and the business of government begins.

PARTIES IN THE GOVERNMENTAL PROCESS

To what extent are government policies influenced by "party" inputs to the branches of the government, all of which have power to shape public policy in various ways? Does it make any difference in terms of public policy which party has the majority in Congress or occupies the White House?

Certainly, if one looks at the broad policies that have been adopted by the government over the years, the impression is that the different outlooks of Democrats and Republicans on critical policy issues have been translated into action. Since the New Deal, Democratic administrations have been able to enact redistributive policies and a wide range of government subsidies of the private sector, and created a score of regulatory agencies before the party shifted to an emphasis on deregulation in 1976. The most forceful and charismatic presidents have always had to compromise with Congress, but one need only observe the New Deal, the Great Society programs of Lyndon Johnson, or the "New Beginning" of Ronald Reagan to conclude that party labels do make a difference in government policies.

The effects that political parties have upon the policy process differ in the preelection and postelection stages. In the electoral stage the party shapes appeals to the electorate, which may or may not be based upon policy issues, in order to gain public support. At this stage party candidates try to keep closely in tune with public sentiment within their particular constituencies. Congressional, state, and local party candidates will divorce themselves from the national party program if they feel it is necessary to do so for reelection. In 1980, for example, a number of leading Democratic senators were targeted by the National Conservative Political Action Committee and by right-to-life groups because of their liberal stands on abortion, welfare, and national defense. Such political veterans as Idaho Senator Frank Church, chairman of the prestigious Foreign Relations Committee, South Dakota Senator George McGovern, and Indiana Senator Birch Bayh found themselves on the defensive against the conservatives, and in their campaigns deliberately avoided stressing the liberal positions taken by the Democratic platform. These Democratic senators, and other party candidates as well, stressed local causes in the hope of overcoming the rising conservative tide.

Parties and Policymaking

After elections end, party campaigning becomes dormant as victorious candidates concentrate their attention upon the multiplicity of tasks confronting them as elected officials. The national party organizations turn their attention to making up campaign deficits if that is necessary, and begin to plan how to build party strength in the future. The victorious party at the presidential level has a distinct advantage over the defeated party because its focus of leadership is in the White House. After the 1980 elections, the Republicans could build from a position of strength while the Democrats searched for new leadership and programs with a view toward the 1984 election.

While the presidential parties lose cohesiveness in the post-election period, the congressional parties form under the banners of old and new leadership, returning and new committee chairmen, to engage in partisan battle among themselves and with the White House. Presidents may find themselves in conflict with members of their own party on Capitol Hill, as well as with the opposition party. If a new president has been elected, after his honeymoon with Capitol Hill is over he will very likely find that powerful members of his own party on the Hill will give him as much trouble as members of the opposing party if he ignores the interests and protocol of Congress. James Madison could observe, if he were alive in the 1980s, that parties do not bind the president and Congress together.

The role of parties in American government differs markedly from the way parties function in a disciplined party system, where the job of the legislator depends upon his or her acquiescence to the dictates of party leaders. In disciplined party systems such as Great Britain's, the national party leadership determines who will be permitted to run with the party label, and in countries where parties are the core of politics, candidates must have a party affiliation in order to compete effectively in election campaigns. In Great Britain, for example, the Conservative and Labour parties have complete control over whom they will allow to join the parties and run in national elections. The parties provide financial backing for their own candidates. Once elected to Parliament, party members must conform to the dictates of the leaders of the

"Parliamentary party," composed of those members of the party in Parliament, led by the Cabinet in the case of a majority party, and by the "shadow cabinet" in the case of the opposition party.

In the United States, legislators have their own party organizations within states and congressional districts that provide them with the necessary support to run for election and, they hope, to remain in Congress. Congressmen form and control their own party organizations, although in some instances they are selected by powerful local politicians who have control over a party machine. In either case, members of Congress are not responsible to the leadership of the congressional party, or to the president. They are representatives of their state and local constituencies, not of the national party constituency. They can defy the wishes of national leaders as much as they want so long as they keep the support of their primary party organization within the constituency they represent. The first responsibility and incentive of legislators is to represent the *expressed* interests of their constituency in the policy process. For example, Democratic members of Congress from oil-consuming states and districts did not automatically follow President Carter's lead in the decontrol of oil prices, but voted to continue federal regulation of oil pricing, which they felt was in the interests of their constituencies.

Congressional Parties

While congressmen will vote for the interests of their constituencies over contrary party programs where constituency needs are clear, there are broad areas of public policy in which the interests of local constituencies are ambiguous, or are not expressed at all. In such cases congressmen have total discretion to choose the stance they will take on Capitol Hill in accordance with incentives other than reelection. In addition to the obvious reelection incentive, congressmen seek power and status on Capitol Hill. The power incentive within Congress works both for and against cohesive congressional parties. One way to achieve power is by seeking positions of leadership within the congressional party. At the same time, members may strive to increase their reputations for power on Capitol Hill through the committee system, by acquiring prestigious chairmanships that will give them power independent of the congressional leadership.

The politics of Capitol Hill is extremely complex and often subtle, sometimes lending support to party government, but more frequently encouraging the dispersion of power to individual members. In the Ninety-seventh Congress, for example, House Speaker Thomas (Tip) O'Neill, the Democratic leader on the House side, was able to exert a great deal of control over junior members for whom the Speaker's favors were important in gaining preferred committee assignments, and generally smoothing their way as they attempted to master the arcane procedures of the House. The Speaker's power could not as easily be exercised over the chairmen of important committees, such as Dan Rostenkowski, the wily Chicago politician who O'Neill himself chose to be the chairman of the powerful Ways and Means Committee. Rostenkowski was close to the Speaker, but in power was his equal. The power of "the party" in the House depends more on ad hoc arrangements than formal organization.

The Senate, more than the House, is a body of equals. In the Ninety-seventh Congress, Senate Majority Leader Howard Baker of Tennessee corralled his fellow Republicans only through his powers of persuasion—the same powers that in the past were so effectively exercised, for example, by Lyndon Johnson when he was Senate majority leader in the 1950s. To be an effective leader in the Senate requires a high degree of sensitivity to the interests and needs of party colleagues, and an ability to soothe the often overextended egos of fellow senators.

The bicameralism of Capitol Hill, which is not only constitutional but is also strictly followed in the politics of the Hill, separates the party politics of the Senate from that of the House. Leaders of the same parties on opposite sides of Capitol Hill conflict with each other more than they cooperate. They are representatives of their respective sides of the Hill first, and only secondarily members of a national or unifying congressional party. Committee chairmen even more than congressional party leaders represent the House and the Senate more than their parties. Before the Ninety-seventh Congress, when both sides of Capitol Hill were Democratic,

Louisiana Senator Russell Long gained his reputation for power by outwitting and outmaneuvering his Democratic counterpart in the House, Oregon Congressman Al Ullman, chairman of the Ways and Means Committee. Before Ullman became chairman of Ways and Means, Arkansas Congressman Wilbur Mills had chaired the committee, and eclipsed Long when House and Senate conferees met to resolve their differences over money bills. Mills and Ullman on the House side, and Long from the Senate, typically were striving to establish their reputations for power not by adhering to party programs, but by defeating their corresponding committee chairmen from the "other body," as members of the House and Senate refer to each other.

Party leadership in both the House and the Senate reflects the fragmentation and specialization of the legislative process, and perhaps most important of all, the quest for personal power within Congress. The power of party leaders on Capitol Hill depends upon their usefulness in serving the interests of party members. There is no party ideology that automatically binds together party members in Congress. To be effective, party leaders must help individual members achieve their goals of personal power, reelection, and public policy. Similarly, the ability of the president to control the members of his own party on Capitol Hill depends upon his powers of persuasion and upon his usefulness in the realization of members' goals. Presidents, for example, may try to persuade a congressman to vote their way by offering to channel federal funds into the congressman's district, helping his reelection prospects. Presidents may increase the status of members of Congress by inviting them to state dinners and special presidential breakfasts. Immediately upon assuming office, President Reagan carefully began to cultivate relationships with Republican leaders on Capitol Hill. The White House established particularly close liaison with Senate Majority Leader Howard Baker, offering the resources of the presidency to boost Baker's power with his Republican colleagues. Through Baker, the White House gave an attentive ear to the concerns of Republican senators regarding the effects of proposed Reagan policies upon their states.

The chasm between the presidential and congressional par-

[19] James MacGregor Burns, *The Deadlock of Democracy* (Englewood Cliffs, N.J.: Prentice-Hall, 1963).

ties has, in the view of James MacGregor Burns, resulted in a "deadlock of democracy."[19] Burns found that the American system consisted of four-party politics, rather than two-party competition. Each party, he concluded, has two district branches, one reflecting the constituency of the president, and the other that of Congress. At the time Burns wrote, the congressional parties had a distinctively conservative cast because the seniority system, under which the most senior members of the party controlled committee chairmanships and leadership positions, was intact in a Congress that had little turnover. In the 1960s, as in the decades before, incumbency virtually guaranteed reelection to Congress. The senior members of each party tended to be most conservative because they came from safe districts without meaningful two-party competition. Safe districts were primarily to be found in the more conservative rural areas of the country. The deadlock of democracy, according to Burns, resulted from the failure of the parties to unite the president and Congress to construct and implement policies that were responsive to the needs of the nation. The inability of the president and Congress to agree upon many important issues of public policy dangerously stalemated the government.

The deadlock cited by Burns continued in a different form in the decade of the 1970s, which witnessed major changes in Congress. While seniority prevailed, the post-Watergate era saw a turnover among members of Congress that had not been witnessed since the nineteenth century. Fewer than half of the members of the Ninety-seventh Congress elected in 1980 had been on Capitol Hill in the early 1970s. In contrast to the early 1960s, when Burns wrote, there was a far closer identification of party ideologies between Capitol Hill and the White House. The conservative Republicans of the Senate, many of whom were newly elected in 1980, agreed to the letter with most of the Reagan programs. In 1980 the White House and the presidential wing of the Republican party became a conservative bastion. Moreover, in 1976 the election of Jimmy Carter reflected a more conservative Democratic party than had characterized the presidential wing of the Democrats in the past. Insofar as ideological differences existed between the president and Congress, they resulted from a more liberal orientation of many party members on Capitol Hill than was to be found in the White House.

Although President Reagan and the conservative Republican majority in the Senate were ideologically in agreement on broad policy issues, including the need to reduce government expenditures and taxes, increase the defense budget, and adopt a hard line in response to the Soviet Union, the "deadlock of democracy" continued because of underlying differences in presidential and congressional power incentives that were often revealed when broad programs produced concrete narrow proposals.

The inability of party government to bridge the gap between the president and Congress is not caused as much by ideological differences between the presidential and congressional wings of the two parties as by the inevitable political conflict between the two ends of Pennsylvania Avenue over specific policies that reflect the relative power of the president and Congress. Simply because Congress is separate from the president, it has an incentive, so cleverly foreseen by the framers of the Constitution who constructed the separation of powers, to remain independent of the president over the long term. New presidents may have honeymoons with Congress, as Reagan seemed to in the opening months of his administration, but soon the separate constituencies and interests of Capitol Hill diverge from those of the White House. It is conflict over power that separates Congress from the president, as much as contrasting views of issues of public policy. That is why presidents have difficulties with Congress even though the legislature may be controlled by a majority of the same party as the president.

The Opposition Party

One of the important components of the party model of government is an opposition party which constantly criticizes the policy positions of the majority party, helping to sharpen public debate over issues of public policy with a view to possible change. It is the task of the opposition party to keep the public continuously informed about major issues of public policy being debated in the legislature and being considered by the executive, and through criticism to point out to the electorate viewpoints in contrast to the government party. If government could formulate public policy without opposition or publicity, the capacity for arbitrary action would be virtually unlimited and the possibilities of change remote. The concept of an effective opposition party implies that public policy is controlled by the majority party rather than by congressional committees, separate legislative parties, the bureaucracy, pressure groups, or the courts. In order to function effectively, the opposition party must operate collectively under a unified leadership, and have an arena within which it can publicly criticize the party in power.

The fragmentation of the American party system, and the separation of powers between the president and the Congress, makes it virtually impossible for an opposition party to function in a collective and meaningful way. What is the opposition party? After the 1980 elections, for example, the Democrats were the opposition party to the president and the Senate, but controlled the House of Representatives. In the American system, the opposition party is generally defined as the one that does not control the White House; however, where the party which does not have the presidency has a majority of both the House and the Senate, it is just as logical to consider the opposition party to be the one controlling the White House. It is the exalted position of the presidency in the minds of most people that leads to a definition of the "out-party" as the one that is outside of the White House. The presidency is the focal point of power in the political system, and the primary initiator of new public policies. The president is the only elected official chosen by a national constituency. The unity and leadership of the presidency makes it uniquely capable of defining a party program that can become the focus of opposition criticism. The dispersion of power among party members on Capitol Hill makes it virtually impossible to identify a consistent congressional party program; nor, when the president is of the opposite party from the legislature, can Congress effectively initiate a broad set of public policy proposals.

It should be remembered that the neat symmetry of government party versus opposition party missing in United States politics is often absent from parliamentary systems as well. Only where there is a disciplined two-party system, such as in Great Britain, does the opposition party perform in accordance with the liberal-democratic model of party government. In Great Britain, when the opposition party leaders criticize the government they know that they may be called upon to face the electorate and to take over the reins of government. This tempers their criticism and directs it responsibly in relation to the policies of the prime minister and the cabinet. In the American system, the leaders of congressional parties know that they will not be running for the presidency in a collective capacity, and probably not as individuals. Moreover, the chairmen of congressional committees rule their fiefdoms on an individual basis to advance their own power. Criticism of the president by Congress is often self-serving, designed to appeal to different congressional constituencies, and to serve individual power goals.

Debate between the president and Congress over issues of public policy takes place in an ad hoc fashion in a variety of forums. Administration witnesses may be subject to sharp criticism during committee hearings. President Reagan sent David Stockman and members of his cabinet to Capitol Hill to explain his new program, which was attacked by Senator Kennedy and other Hill Democrats. Several members of the Senate Foreign Relations Committee and the House Foreign Affairs Committee, both Democrats and Republicans, expressed concern about administration foreign policy when Secretary of State Alexander Haig appeared before them. Hearings are publicized in newspapers, on the nightly news programs, and in special public affairs programs. It is difficult for the electorate to get a sense of direction concerning party differences over public policy from the multitude of separate forums in which politicians exchange their views. And, since members of the president's own party may, and frequently do, oppose his policies on Capitol Hill, the public is properly confused about who is in fact speaking for the party.

PARTIES AND POLITICAL CHANGE

In the face of a constitutional system that discourages political parties more than it encourages them, and in a highly

ELECTIONS AND POLITICAL CHANGE
Recollection of Elections Past

By Vermont Royster

[*The 1980 presidential election was heralded by Republicans as the beginning of a new political era of conservatism. The verdict, however, is not yet in.*]

Dawn of a new era? Political watershed? Change of the tide?

However phrased, the intriguing question now is whether the 1980 election, like that of 1936, marks a major realignment in the forces that could shape American politics for the next generation.

Many are already saying so in the wake of the election returns, and there is much to give credence to that judgment. Supporting evidence lies not just in Ronald Reagan's sweeping victory, stunning though that was to all the prophets. That view is also buttressed by the Democratic casualty lists in state and local elections.

Among the fallen Senators are veteran warriors in the liberal Democratic cause, many once seeming invulnerable—Church of Idaho, Bayh of Indiana, McGovern of South Dakota, Nelson of Wisconsin, Magnuson of Washington. For the first time since the Eisenhower administration, the Republicans will control the Senate.

Although the Democratic House was not quite so decimated, there too the Republicans made enough gains to foreshadow a more conserva-tive Congress next January than we have seen in years. Everywhere Democrats, especially those of more liberal persuasion, must be wondering what hit them.

For all of that, it seems to me that more is needed than [the 1980] election figures to judge whether they mark a changing tide or merely one more ripple in our political history. One useful thing is a long memory.

A recollection of elections past does suggest the "old politics"—that of the New Deal, Fair Deal or New Frontier—has long been played out. It has been crumbling almost unnoticed for about 40 years. What is equally clear is that, so far, no "new politics" has had the strength to take its place.

Each Majority Smaller

Consider: In 1936 the Roosevelt landslide, still the largest on record in the electoral college, confirmed the end of one era. In 1940 FDR won again as he was to do once more in 1944. But in each of those succeeding elections, one of them while he was a war leader, he won by smaller and smaller majorities both in popular votes and the electoral college.

When Harry Truman won in 1948, everyone was so stunned by the fact that he won at all that the narrowness of his vic-tory went almost unnoticed. In the popular vote he was a minority President. And in retrospect that victory can be attributed as much to his own campaigning prowess and the ineptness of his opponent as to the durability of the fabled Democratic coalition.

In any event, the record shows a declining hold of that coalition on the voters between 1936 and 1948. And then in 1952 Dwight Eisenhower ended the 20-year grip of the Democratic Party.

The orthodox view of that election has been that it was due to Eisenhower's personal appeal as a war hero. Possibly, but it's worth noting that the Republicans that year also carried both houses of Congress, hardly a confirmation of the power of the old Democratic coalition.

Since Eisenhower we have had two election "landslides." One was Lyndon Johnson against Barry Goldwater. The other, lest we forget, was Richard Nixon against George McGovern, and in that 1972 election Nixon carried every state but one, which was more than FDR did in 1936. The Republicans did not, however, carry either house of Congress.

The other elections since 1952 have been decided by very narrow margins. Kennedy's margin over Nixon in

1960 was paper thin, a plurality of 119,000 votes out of 68.8 million and even that margin was disputed. Moreover, because Harry Byrd of Virginia, a very conservative candidate running as an independent, got half a million votes (and 15 electoral ones), John Kennedy like Harry Truman was a minority President.

Then in 1968 it was Nixon's turn to be a minority President. His plurality over Hubert Humphrey was 244,000 but George Wallace polled just short of 10 million votes and won 46 votes in the electoral college.

Watergate then gave us our first nonelected President, Gerald Ford. He lost to Jimmy Carter primarily because of Carter's hold on his native South. All the same, Ford won 240 electoral votes, the largest received by a losing candidate since Charles Evans Hughes in 1916.

Look at it another way: With the exception of Lyndon Johnson no Democratic President until Carter won by a true majority of the votes from 1944 onward. Since that year the presidency has see-sawed between the two major parties. Three of those elected Presidents (Truman, Eisenhower and Nixon) had at least one house of Congress controlled by the opposition party, as will Ronald Reagan next January. Three of them (Truman, Kennedy and Nixon) were minority Presidents, two of them Democratic, one Republican.

What are we to make of all this, and what lessons may it suggest for Ronald Reagan and the Republicans after this year's landslide?

One lesson is that the legend of the unconquerable power of the Democratic, or Roosevelt, coalition is just that—a legend. It lost its firm grip on the national electorate somewhere in the 1940s and hasn't been the controlling force in American politics for more than a generation.

The other lesson is that the Republican Party hasn't thus far been able to evolve an alternative political philosophy capable of inspiring the country. It's fared well only when the people have been disgusted with the Democrats. And not always then. Dewey tried to co-opt the New Deal and blew it. Goldwater rejected all its works, which proved disastrous.

Nothing to Survive

Eisenhower had the best opportunity to build a Republican majority, that Chimera of the hopefuls, because he offered a rational conservatism and gave the country good government of which the people approved. Unfortunately he had little understanding of the importance of party in political affairs. He built nothing to survive him.

Any opportunities Nixon had were lost because of Vietnam, which he inherited, and the mess known as Watergate, which he created. For Gerald Ford time was too short.

Obviously [the 1980] elec-tion turned on many factors, including President Carter's incompetence or misfortunes. But his defeat became a Democratic rout because the Democrats refuse to recognize that the issues of the Thirties and Forties are no longer relevant, the nation being confronted with new problems—many caused by the old liberal policies. The voters were disillusioned by shopworn economics, cynical about stale remedies for mounting ills at home and abroad. They said so in unmistakable terms.

For the rest, they've done no more than put Ronald Reagan and the Republicans on trial. If the policies of the new President—call them conservative, if you will—halt the inflation, revive the nation's economic strength and restore its place in the world, then four years hence the Republicans will have built that long-heralded new majority.

If instead the country is in no better estate by 1984, the Republicans will again be discredited. Then it could be another generation before their next chance. It's as simple as that.

"'Twas a famous victory" [in 1980], no doubt about it. But a political watershed? Dawn of a new era? For the answer to that, the nation must wait.

Source: *Wall Street Journal*, November 12, 1980, p. 34. Reprinted by permission of *The Wall Street Journal*, © Dow Jones & Company, Inc. 1980. All rights reserved.

pluralistic society, American parties have performed an invaluable role in the aggregation of political interests throughout the country. They have provided vehicles for broad public choices, and for peaceful political change. At critical times in American history, parties have formed and re-formed to articulate the interests of the electorate, and to alter significantly the course of government action. "Critical" elections—ones in which there are long-term realignments of voters along party lines—have marked significant turning points in the direction of government. The election of Franklin Roosevelt and the Democratic Party in 1932 was one example of a critical election, and the choice of Ronald Reagan in 1980 may be another. The Republican party, long dominated by a white Protestant elite, attracted a far broader cross section of voters in 1980 than it had in the past. Many white Protestants in the South voted for the Republican candidate, as did Catholic and Jewish voters, possibly to form a new Republican majority. The mood of the nation in the 1980s is distinctly conservative, and the Republican party may have become the choice of an electoral majority. The elections of 1982 and 1984 have to be observed closely, however, to determine whether or not the conservative shift toward Reagan in 1980 was for the long or the short term. The apparent conservative tide may dissipate rapidly if the Reagan programs fail to halt inflation and revive the nation's economy.

Given the nation's tremendous diversity, the parties have done the best that can be expected in bridging the gap between people and government. If the nation ever divides itself into two clearly contrasting camps, these will undoubtedly be reflected in two fairly disciplined political parties. But the American tradition of individualism and character, in combination with the almost inevitable continuation of the diversity of interests in the country, will probably prevent political parties in the future from having more distinctive and contrasting policy orientations than they have had in the past. Moreover, the policy differences between the parties have been sufficiently distinctive to offer a real choice to the electorate. The parties have expressed the feelings, often deeply held, of party supporters on broad issues of public policy, and have helped to set a policy agenda for the nation.

Suggestions for Further Reading

Burnham, Walter Dean. *Critical Elections and the Mainsprings of American Politics.* New York: W. W. Norton and Co., 1970. An analysis of American voting behavior and political trends.

Burns, James MacGregor. *The Deadlock of Democracy: Four-Party Politics in America.* Englewood Cliffs, N.J.: Prentice-Hall, Inc., 1963. A provocative study of the failure of parties to overcome the separation of powers and govern effectively.

Fairlie, Henry. *The Parties: Republicans and Democrats in This Century.* New York: Simon and Schuster/Pocketbooks, 1978. A lively examination of Republican and Democratic politics.

Key, V. O., Jr. *The Responsible Electorate.* Cambridge, Mass.: Belknap Press of Harvard University Press, 1966. The author's theme is that a highly rational electorate is often frustrated by manipulative presidential campaigns.

Ladd, Everett Carll, Jr. With Charles D. Hadley. *Transformations of the American Party System.* New York: W. W. Norton and Co., 1975. Political coalitions from the New Deal to the 1970s.

O'Connor, Edwin. *The Last Hurrah.* Boston: Little, Brown and Co., 1956. A best-selling novel, later made into a movie, about an old-time political boss beloved by the people and hated by the Establishment.

Ralph Nader is one of many lobbyists who testify before congressional committees to influence legislation.

CHAPTER 5

Interest Groups and Political Participation

Interest groups, like political parties, link people with government. Unlike parties, interest groups do not offer candidates to run for public office. In the United States, at least, interest groups reflect far narrower concerns than do political parties. Parties supply the personnel of government at the highest political levels. Interest groups may back particular political candidates, but often seek to avoid identification with one political party to the exclusion of the other. Interest-group leaders want to be able to play both sides of the political fence to achieve their political objectives.

The framers of the Constitution viewed interest groups, like political parties, as undesirable factions that should be controlled by constitutional devices. The separate division of powers, representative government, and federalism, all of which were designed to prevent party government, were also thought to be effective constitutional arrangements to disperse the power of interest groups. At the same time, the First Amendment freedoms of expression and the right to assemble and to petition government for a redress of grievances guaranteed a hospitable environment for the proliferation of interest groups.

The Madisonian view that interest groups are opposed to the national interest became representative of the thinking of a large segment of American society. Ironically, while American citizens created and joined interest groups in ever-increasing numbers from the early days of the Republic, pressure groups were often decried as being "selfish" because they were advancing their own interests at the expense of that of the general public. The second half of the nineteenth century witnessed the passage of lobbying regulation laws by state legislatures, requiring lobbyists to register and report on their activities. National legislation to control interest groups followed in the twentieth century.

While interest groups have always operated to some degree under a cloud of suspicion, the fact remains that in our pluralistic political system, groups are important channels of communication between people and government. Indeed, some political scientists have suggested that interest groups are the lifeblood of the democratic process because they are the most important vehicles of political participation.

THE GROUP THEORY MODEL OF GOVERNMENT

In sharp contrast to the Madisonian view of groups, a political theory has developed which proclaims that interest groups do, collectively, represent the national interest insofar as that interest can be determined. Group theorists support the view that public policy should be grounded in the demands of relevant interest groups which, together with the government, should play a large role in shaping policy that affects them. Group theory is both normative and empirical—that is, an expression of what should be and what in fact exists. Group theorists support the domination of the political process by interest groups which characterizes many spheres of American politics.

Group theorists start with the assumption that in the political process people do not function as individuals, but only through interest groups. Political choice is group choice. Public policy decisions are always made on the basis of the interaction of interest groups with government. An interest group is very broadly defined as an organized or unorganized group of people with a common interest. In the political sphere, an interest group is one which shares common public policy objectives and generally agrees on the means of achieving them. Since, according to group theorists, individuals can

Interest Groups and Political Participation

function only as members of interest groups, group politics becomes an inevitable and desirable part of the democratic process.

Interest groups are involved in government at every turn of the political process. Ronald Reagan immediately raised the opposition of a wide range of interest groups when he proposed far-reaching cuts in federal expenditures and programs that had been enacted in the first place largely in response to group demands. Only weeks after Reagan was inaugurated, coal miners marched in the streets of Washington to protest federal cutbacks in health programs to benefit victims of black lung disease. The dairy farming industry protested cutbacks in dairy supports. Veterans began to mobilize to protect their interests, as did a wide array of other groups that were affected by the sharp budget knife of David Stockman, Reagan's director of the Office of Management and Budget. Interest groups often have close ties with congressional committees and administrative agencies, and it seemed likely that Reagan's sweeping program of budget cuts would be severely modified by Capitol Hill in response to various group demands.

Group theorists have always held that "factions" represent genuine and positive political interests that should be taken into account by government in the policy process. Indeed, one of the main dangers in majority rule is not that factions will control, but rather that the power of the majority will override legitimate minority interests.

This viewpoint was one of many eloquently expressed by John C. Calhoun in *A Disquisition on Government*, published in 1853, shortly after his death. Calhoun wanted to construct a theory of government that would assure that minority interests, such as those represented by the southern states during his time, would not be ignored by the national government. Calhoun suggested that all societies are divided into a number of different interest groups, and that the interests of each group are equally legitimate politically and should not be arbitrarily dealt with by government any more than government should deal arbitrarily with individuals. The political

The Origin of Group Theory: John C. Calhoun's Concept of "Concurrent Majorities" interests of the individual are naturally subsumed within the various interest groups of the community. To Calhoun and modern interest group theorists, democracy means group rather than individual participation in public policy formulation. If every person's interests are represented by groups, their argument runs, then the formulation of public policy by groups automatically represents the interests of individuals.

Calhoun was opposed to the development of majority rule and party government. He felt that the division of the country into two major political parties would inevitably produce a major and a minor party, the former dominating the political process completely. Moreover, as the parties developed he felt that they would become more and more detached from the broad interests of the community, and would essentially reflect the viewpoints of party elites. As he explained this process:

The government would gradually pass from the hands of the majority of the party into those of its leaders, as the struggle became more intense, and the honors and emoluments of the government, the all absorbing objects. At this stage, principle and policy would lose all influence in the elections; and cunning, falsehood, deception, slander, fraud, and gross appeals to the appetites of the lowest and most worthless portions of the community, would take the place of sound reason and wise debate.[1]

As the party leadership becomes farther and farther removed from the true interests of the community, the possibility of revolution inevitably increases.

Calhoun's views of the nature and role of political parties suggest a definite conflict between group theory and that branch of democratic theory based upon the idea that the only way in which effective democracy can be realized is through party rule. Moreover, although the constitutional model is not based upon the idea of party rule, and is in fact designed to limit the potential power of majorities and to control the influence of parties in government, Calhoun was not satisfied that the constitutional policymaking model sufficiently took into account the diverse interests of the community. He felt that the classical model set up a government in which the numerical majority would determine policy. By numerical majority, he did not necessarily mean a majority of individuals, but a majority formed on the basis of compromises

[1] John C. Calhoun, A Disquisition on Government (New York: Political Science Classics, 1947, pp. 41–42.

Interest Groups and Political Participation

among diverse interest groups. This interest group majority could dominate the branches of the national government and force its will upon the rest of the community.

Calhoun proposed as a substitute for the constitutional model a system of "concurrent" majority rule. (See Figure 5.1.) The concurrent majority differs from the numerical majority in that in the former each interest group essentially determines for itself whether to reject or accept a government policy affecting it. Calhoun never worked out the details of this system, but it clearly implied that in their spheres of interests, minority groups would be able to determine government policy. Accepting the premise that all legitimate political interests are represented by groups, the concurrent majority system would bring about the greatest possible freedom for the political interests of the community.

Calhoun was writing at a time when the South was strug-

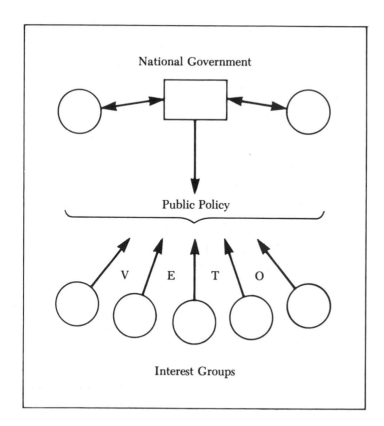

FIGURE 5.1
John C. Calhoun's Theory of Concurrent Majority. *Under Calhoun's concurrent majority theory, each interest group has a veto on national policy affecting it.*

gling to maintain its interests in a government where it was outnumbered by the states of the North and West. The concurrent majority system that was so eloquently expressed by Calhoun was very similar to the doctrine of nullification that had gained favor in the South, although not in the rest of the country. Under that doctrine each state, acting independently, could veto legislation that it did not feel was appropriate to it. The states were considered to be the major political interest groups.

Modern Group Theory

The most important expression of group theory in modern terms is that of David B. Truman, whose book *The Governmental Process,* published in 1953, has had a profound and lasting effect upon the way in which political scientists view the policy process.[2] Drawing upon the works of other group theorists, particularly Arthur F. Bentley's *The Process of Government,* which appeared in 1908,[3] Truman asserted that all policy is the result of group interaction, and that this is the only realistic way that one can view the political process. Although he did not go so far as to suggest that Calhoun's concurrent majority system is in fact in operation, the tenor of Truman's work was in this direction. Moreover, like Calhoun, he suggested that group determination of public policy is the most democratic method of government in channeling legitimate political demands to government.

[2] David B. Truman, *The Governmental Process* (New York: Alfred A. Knopf, 1953).

[3] Arthur F. Bentley, *The Process of Government* (Chicago: University of Chicago Press).

"Potential" Groups

An important part of the group model of policy formation is the concept of the "potential" interest group. This concept is based on the idea that by definition potential political interests always exist, submerged below the surface of society, which can be activated when people sharing those interests are made aware of the need to take action. It might be possible, for example, to view some of the groups that organized to resist the expansion of the Vietnam War as formerly potential groups whose political awareness had not reached the stage necessary for political activism. Similarly, the consumer and environmental groups that organized in the 1960s and 1970s,

Interest Groups and Political Participation

exerting a strong force on public policy, reflected interests that had been dormant, or potential, in previous decades. As long as interest groups remain potential rather than actual they do not directly influence the political process. The possibility that they might organize, however, must always be taken into account by decision makers. Thus, the group theorists suggest that even potential groups exert some influence upon the policy process.

The theory of potential interest groups conveniently solves the problem that is often raised with regard to the group model, that some interests are always far better represented in government than others. The group theorists do not deny this; however, they state that if one accepts the existence of potential groups then in fact all interests of society are, by definition, taken into account in one form or another by the institutions of government. It is presumably primarily through the electoral process that potential groups are able to exert influence, since politicians are constantly seeking the critical mass necessary for their election. There is always a great deal of guesswork among candidates regarding the representative feelings of their constituents. These feelings cannot be determined simply by looking at the positions taken by the leaders of pressure groups, for group leaders do not always reflect the views of the membership. Moreover, the fact that members of one group generally identify with a number of other groups means that the attitudes of individuals toward the official policy positions taken by the groups with which they identify can always shift.

In reality, it is very difficult to accept the views of the group theorists that potential interest groups solve the problem of lack of representation in government for those whose views are not reflected in the positions taken by the leaders of powerful organized interests. For example, it was not until Ralph Nader and others began to represent the interests of consumers and to organize consumer groups that the government took consumer interests seriously. The concern of the government in recent years with environmental matters is also due to the rise of organized pressure groups, such as the Sierra Club, that counterbalance the power of private corporate interests.

Defining the
"National Interest"

Interest group theory requires political pluralism. The group model is premised upon the idea that the "national interest" cannot be clearly identified apart from the interests of the groups in the political community. This is true by definition if one defines groups in such a way that they take into account the political interests of all individuals. No government decision, however, can represent the views of all groups in society, but must compromise among competing interests. Under such circumstances, how are those given the responsibility to make final decisions to determine what is correct and proper, or in the public interest?

Assuming equal access to government among groups whose interests are at stake, it seems reasonable that one can fall back upon the concept of a procedural ethic to produce the national interest. That is, if every relevant interest has its "day in court," the final decision can be considered the closest approximation to the national interest that is possible in any democratic society as long as it takes into account the views that have been expressed by the groups involved. Even the group theorist, however, might not accept this view, because unless the interests of potential groups can also be taken into account in the policymaking process, what emerges cannot be considered the optimum national interest.

The national interest must be more than the sum of the interests of the organized groups of the nation. But by saying that, theorists are really adding such a mystical dimension to their argument that they are allowing for a national interest to be articulated apart from the interests of identifiable groups. Since no one can really know what constitutes a potential interest group, appealing to such a concept in making a public policy decision is tantamount to the invocation of the national interest. When President Nixon stated that the "silent majority" of the American people was supporting his decisions on Vietnam, as well as in certain domestic areas, he was, in the terms of group theory, appealing to a vast potential interest group whose needs had to be taken into account. But in reality no one can know what the "silent majority" is. In fact, the president was embarking upon a course of action that he considered to be in the national interest, regardless of the articulated views to the contrary of many organized groups.

Interest Groups and Political Participation

Nixon's declaration that a silent majority of the American people was supporting his actions was not unique to his administration. In fact, presidents before and after him have voiced the same thoughts. Presidents characteristically believe in what they are doing, and assume that a "silent majority" supports them. As Ronald Reagan embarked upon his controversial budget-cutting program, 24 percent of the American people expressed disapproval of his presidential performance after he had been in office only two months. The disapproval rating was the highest that had ever been recorded for a president at the beginning of his first term. The Reagan White House, however, blithely ignored public opinion polls, and stated that the supportive letters they had received reflected the real views of the American people. Reagan, like most presidents before him, undertook a course of action he considered to be in the national interest regardless of the strong political opposition of organized interests and indications of significant popular disapproval as well. The Reagan White House characteristically counted upon the support of the most important interest group of all, the majority of the American people that had elected the president in November. Electoral choice and group preferences rarely coincide, however, as groups seek to pressure government for policies that advance their own narrow interests. The political clout of organized pressure groups often defeats what presidents proclaim to be the wishes of the people.

Apart from the concept of potential interest groups as a limitation upon excessive power of organized pressure groups, the group model also has developed other concepts that explain why the interaction of groups does not lead to the domination of the policy process by factions. The most important of these is what E. E. Schattschneider once called the "law of the imperfect mobilization of political interests."[4] Based upon the fact that individuals are always members of more than one group, this law states that overlapping group memberships makes it impossible for any one group to claim the total loyalty of its members. (See Figure 5.2.)

For example, a Veterans Administration (VA) doctor has a

Imperfect Mobilization of Political Interests

[4] E. E. Schattschneider, *Party Government* (New York: Holt, Rinehart and Winston, 1942), pp. 32–34.

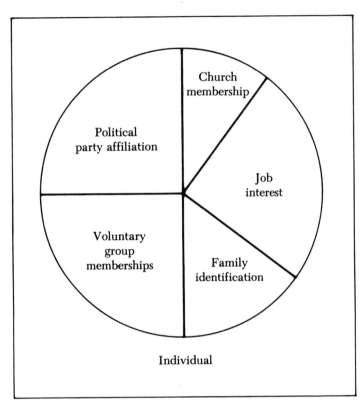

FIGURE 5.2
Imperfect Mobilization of Political
Interests. *Political interests cannot be
perfectly mobilized because each person has multiple group memberships
and identifications.*

group identification with both the American Medical Association (AMA) and with his employer. On the important issue of
socialized medicine, the AMA and the VA are in many significant respects opposed to each other. The former has traditionally favored as much freedom of choice as possible for those
delivering and receiving medical services, and has supported
limited government involvement in medicine. The Veterans
Administration has generally been an example of socialized
medicine in practice, although on a limited scale. Both the
AMA and the VA are interest groups that have vigorously
pursued their viewpoints before Congress, the president, and
throughout the political system. Neither group, however, can
completely claim the loyalty of doctors working for it on this
particular issue, because of the conflicting identifications and
values that they will hold as a result of simultaneous membership in the two groups.

For group theorists, the existence of overlapping group

membership is considered to be the greatest check upon the domination of a particular policy by factions. A strong argument can be made, however, that this check is ineffective because interest groups do not have to claim the total loyalty of their membership in order to be highly effective in the political process. In fact, the official positions of these groups on political issues are shaped primarily by leaders, not by the membership. Interest group leaders are more often than not able to convince policymakers that they reflect the views of their group. This can be a serious limitation upon the effectiveness of the law of the imperfect mobilization of political interests as a check upon group power.

Another concept advanced by group theorists explaining the limited nature of the power of groups is the theory of countervailing power. The essence of this theory is that the power of one group will balance that of another, and throughout the political system groups will tend to check and balance each other. (See Figure 5.3.) For example, the power of industrial

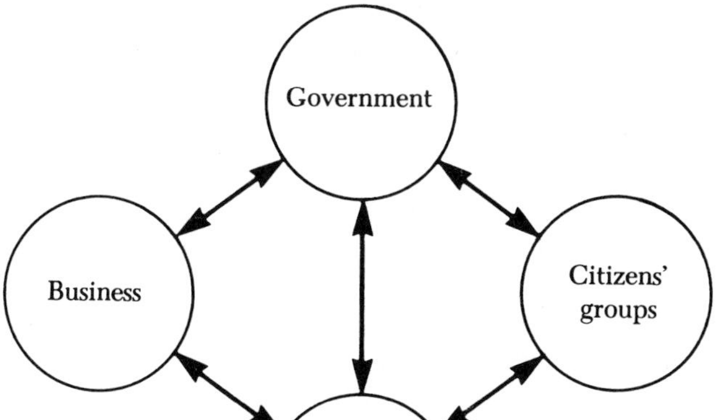

Countervailing Power

Interest Groups

FIGURE 5.3
Countervailing Power. *The theory of countervailing power asserts that interest groups will check and balance each other.*

firms will tend to be balanced by that of labor unions, and this will mean that neither set of groups will be able to get its way in the political system. Originally advanced in the economic realm by John Kenneth Galbraith in the early 1950s,[5] it soon became evident that the theory worked in neither the economic nor the political sphere. The tendency of interest groups is often not to counteract each other, but rather to operate together for mutual benefit. In the economic sphere, for example, the wage demands of labor unions are frequently happily met by business firms which simply pass the burden on to the consumer in the form of higher prices.

In the political sphere, countervailing power is also more myth than reality. Each area of public policy has a set of interest groups concerned with it. This set operates within the framework of a political subsystem, in which the particular interests make demands and give supports to various parts of the government that act as conversion structures for the specialized policy area. In the armaments field, for example, the Defense Department, in conjunction with the armed services and appropriations committees in the House, as well as the presidency, act as the focal points of demands from the armaments industry. Policy is formulated within this system, even though the effects of the policy have a profound impact upon the community as a whole. The interest groups within the subsystem check and balance each other to some extent, but they are mutually agreed upon the need to expand the pie so that their piece can be even larger once it is divided. In terms of the political system as a whole, the interests are in effect in collusion to expand the amount of money appropriated for their sphere relative to other areas. Within their subsystem, however, they are in conflict, but this countervailing power does not effectively limit their operations in terms of the political system as a whole.

Constitutional Checks

Another important way in which interest groups are supposed to be limited is, of course, by the classical constitutional model. Checks and balances, provisions for extraordinary majorities of greater than 50 percent (e.g., treaties, veto overrides, amendments), and the general pluralistic character of the

[5] John Kenneth Galbraith, *American Capitalism* (Boston: Houghton Mifflin, 1952).

Interest Groups and Political Participation

governmental apparatus itself are supposed to make it very difficult for any faction to gain overall control. But in many cases the very structure of government designed to limit and control factions has enhanced their influence, since the Constitution provided so many access points at which interest groups can attempt to influence policy. In the original scheme, these access points were the three branches of the government taken as a whole. Because the policy process was not as highly specialized and delegated to small units of the government as it is now, interest groups could more easily negate public policy in one branch than bring about the agreement of the three branches of the government to make affirmative decisions. At the present time, the highly specialized nature of policy formulation means that the administrative branch, in conjunction with specialized policy committees in Congress, can make both affirmative and negative policy decisions. Pressure groups now bring their influence to bear on these bodies. Regardless of what caused the fragmented nature of our policymaking process, this fragmentation vastly increases pressure group influence over what it would be if our government policy was formulated on the basis of a cohesive majority in Congress led by the president.[6]

On balance, it is difficult to be convinced by the assurances of the group theorists that the pluralism of our system is nothing more than a reflection of a healthy democracy. Perhaps we cannot find the national interest, but it is difficult to believe that it does not ever exist apart from the interests articulated by groups. The concept of potential groups seems excellent in theory, but almost impossible to identify in practice. The groups that are best organized, and that have the most resources and access to government decision makers, exert the most power in the political system. The mystical concept of potential interest groups does not explain this away. Those who go along with Calhoun's theory of a concurrent majority would support the idea that the most powerful interests have the greatest say in policymaking. In fact, Calhoun felt that this was the only way in which a political system could be held together: the more powerful interests should be given a larger voice in public policy formulation simply because of their power and position in the community.

[6] Even where cohesive majorities rule, however, pressure groups may determine public policy. See Harry Eckstein, *Pressure Group Politics* (Stanford: Stanford University Press, 1960).

This does not produce irresponsible government, but rather government responsible to narrow interests.

Another limitation upon the democratic nature of group politics is that pressure groups tend to be run by elites, who are often given very broad boundaries within which they can make decisions. Interest group participation in politics means elite control, rather than the formulation of policies by the memberships of the groups. There is not necessarily anything wrong with such a system, but interest group politics does not overcome the extraordinary difficulties that our system has in bringing about a realization of the democratic ideal.

THE CONTEXT OF GROUP ACTION

The group model of policy formation suggests that interest groups are the focal point of the policy process, subsuming all of the legitimate political interests of the community. An interest group, as defined by group theorists, has shared attitudes concerning the goals it wants to achieve and the methods for reaching its objectives. Interest groups can be public or private. The Defense Department is as much an interest group lobbying other branches of the government for its own purposes as is General Motors Corporation. Most discussions of interest groups exclude the public realm, and thereby eliminate an important dimension. Both public and private groups often seek the same kinds of objectives, focusing upon solidifying their positions and increasing their power within government.

The activities of both public and private pressure groups are affected by a number of factors. The constitutional structure was based upon the premise that factions should be discouraged. The mechanisms of government, especially the separation of powers and the checks and balances system, were designed to make it impossible for any one faction to dominate the policy process. The constitution established a pluralistic structure of government, however, which means that public interest groups, in the form of governmental branches with contrasting objectives, are built into the governmental mechanism. The three branches of government are motivated to

Interest Groups and Political Participation

achieve different goals in response to contrasting constituencies.

Private interest groups are able to exercise influence by gaining access to many parts of the government. The establishment of the bureaucracy with broad policymaking powers leads to the most intense political pressures being focused upon administrative agencies. The first ingredient, then, in the context of pressure group operation, is the pluralism of our governmental structure, reflected in public interest groups, which enables private groups to gain more access to the policymaking process than would be the case in a more unified government.

The Effects of Federalism

Madison argued in *The Federalist* that the federal structure would tend to isolate and reduce the power of pressure groups. But the federal structure can only add to the pluralistic nature of the political process and expand the role of groups. First, it creates a large number of governmental pressure groups at the state and local levels which would not exist in a unitary form of government. State and local governments have their own power bases, and exert strong pressure upon the national political process for particular policy goals. Today, states maintain paid lobbyists in Washington, and many of the larger cities also have lobbyists whose sole responsibility is to look out for legislation and other government activities affecting the interests of the urban areas which they represent.

Federalism tends to increase the power of private groups. In contrast to Madison's argument in *The Federalist,* the fact that state and local governments control many spheres of public policy means that insofar as private groups can exert pressure over them, they can control the policy process. A pressure group may be geographically "isolated" within a state, but this does not mean that its policy power is reduced. In fact, that power will probably be increased, because if the group exerts power over the state government, or over city governments, its influence at the national level may also be felt more than would otherwise be the case. Private groups can use their state power as leverage in the national realm.

**Constitutional Protection
of Interest Groups**

7 United States vs. Harriss, 347 U.S.
612 (1954).

The constitutional system, in addition to expanding and encouraging interest group activity, protects the rights of private groups to organize and petition government for a redress of grievances. These First Amendment rights mean that the government cannot take action which would curb the normal activities of interest groups. The issue was confronted head-on in the case of *United States* v. *Harriss* (1954), when the Court was asked to rule upon the constitutionality of the Federal Regulation of Lobbying Act of 1946.[7] This act required the registration with the clerk of the House and the secretary of the Senate of all persons "attempting to influence the passage or defeat of any legislation by the Congress. . . ." In the registration form the lobbyist was to give his name and address and that of his employer, how long he had been employed, how much was paid, by whom, and for what purposes. He was to list the names of any newspapers and periodicals in which he caused publications to appear in order to influence directly or indirectly the passage or defeat of legislation. The terms of the act were very broad indeed, and vague enough so that on appeal to the courts the plaintiffs argued that it violated the constitutional requirement of definiteness in the criminal realm.

In its opinion, the Supreme Court ruled that the statute could be upheld as long as its provisions were interpreted narrowly to regulate only those directly involved in lobbying for or against pending or proposed legislation before Congress. Chief Justice Earl Warren made it clear that any attempt by Congress to enact broader restrictions upon the activities of pressure groups would be a violation of the First Amendment. Justices Douglas and Black felt that even the Federal Regulation of Lobbying Act, narrowly construed, could "easily ensnare people who have done no more than exercise their constitutional rights of speech, assembly, and press." The majority, however, felt that some limitation upon these rights was justified if Congress was to exercise its legislative function in a rational and deliberative way without undue attention to the demands of pressure groups. In the words of Chief Justice Warren:

Present-day legislative complexities are such that individual members of Congress cannot be expected to explore the myriad pressures to

Interest Groups and Political Participation

which they are regularly subjected. Yet full realization of the American ideal of government by elected representatives depends to no small extent on their ability to properly evaluate such pressures. Otherwise the voice of the people may all too easily be drowned out by the voice of special interest groups seeking favored treatment while masquerading as proponents of the public weal. This is the evil which the Lobbying Act was designed to help prevent.[8]

[8] Ibid.

As long as Congress does not suppress pressure groups, but merely circumscribes them and requires that publicity be given to direct lobbying efforts, the requirements of the Constitution are met.

Aside from requiring the registration of lobbyists, and the public reporting of their sources of funds and expenditures, Congress has prohibited corporations and labor unions from making contributions to or expenditures for the election of any federal official. The corporate spending ban was first enacted in 1907, and became part of the Corrupt Practices Act of 1925. A ban on union spending was first enacted in 1943, and made permanent by the Taft-Hartley Act of 1947. The prohibitions upon corporate and union spending for political campaigns for federal offices was reaffirmed and strengthened in the comprehensive Federal Election Campaign Practices Act, passed in 1971 and amended in 1974 to extend its coverage. In addition to absolutely proscribing corporate and labor union contributions in connection with federal elections, the act limited to a thousand dollars the contributions individuals could make to political campaigns, and placed ceilings upon the amount of money that candidates for federal office could spend in their election campaigns. Rigid reporting requirements were included in the law, and a federal election commission was established to implement it.

The Federal Election Campaign Act was challenged on First Amendment grounds in 1976 by then Senator James Buckley of New York, former presidential candidate and senator from Minnesota Eugene McCarthy, and others who argued that the law impinged upon their First Amendment freedoms of speech and right to associate. The Supreme Court ruled on the case in *Buckley* v. *Valeo* (1976), holding that while the government could control *contributions* to political campaigns, it could not control *spending* on campaigns. Spending, stated the Court, is a form of speech that is protected by the First

Amendment. At the outset of its opinion the Court stressed that the contribution and expenditure limitations of the law "operate in an area of the most fundamental First Amendment activities. Discussion of public issues and debate on the qualifications of candidates are integral to the operation of this system of government established by our Constitution."[9] "The interests served by the Act," continued the Court, "include restricting the voices of people and interest groups who have money to spend and reducing the overall scope of federal election campaigns. Although the Act does not focus on the ideas expressed by persons or groups subjected to its regulations, it is aimed in part at equalizing the relative ability of all

[9] Buckley v. Valeo, 424 U.S. 1, 14 (1976).

LOBBY REGISTRATIONS

[*Under the federal regulations of the Lobbying Act, pressure groups must register their employees and interests.*]

Citizens' Groups

Barrier Islands Coalition, New York, N.Y. Filed for self 1/20/81. Legislative interest— ". . . legislation to protect barrier islands . . . HR 5891 and S 2686. . . ."

Christian Voice Moral Government Fund, Washington, D.C. Filed for self 1/15/81. Legislative interest—"For school prayer. Against IRS attack on private schools. Against national gay rights legislation." Lobbyist—L. Philip Sheldon Jr., Washington, D.C.

Citizens for Tax Justice, Washington, D.C. Filed for self 1/12/81. Legislative interest— "General legislation concerning the Internal Revenue Code and federal tax policy." Lobbyist—Robert S. McIntyre, Washington, D.C.

Five Tribes Confederacy of North Central Okla., Ponca City, Okla. Lobbyist— Abourezk, Shack & Mendenhall, Washington, D.C. Filed 1/29/81. Legislative interest—"Matters relating to Indian Affairs."

National Energy Efficiency Coalition, Washington, D.C. Filed for self 1/19/81. Legislative interest—"Energy efficiency investment incentives, including residential and commercial tax credits, solar and energy conservation bank." Lobbyists—Jerry Brady and David Hurd Moulton, Washington, D.C.

National Legal Aid and Defender Association, Washington, D.C. Filed for self 1/28/81. Legislative interest—"Reauthorization of the Legal Services Corporation . . . establishment of a National Center for Defense Services. . . ." Lobbyist—Julie Clark, Washington, D.C.

National Organization for the Reform of Marijuana Laws, Washington, D.C. Filed for self 1/31/81. Legislative interest—

"NORML favors the elimination of criminal penalties for marijuana smoking under the Controlled Substances Act of 1970." Lobbyists—George L. Farnham, James N. Hall, and Kevin B. Zeese.

National Rifle Association of America, Washington, D.C. Filed for self 1/7/81. Legislative interest— ". . .all aspects of the acquisition, possession, and use of firearms and ammunition, as well as legislation relating to hunting and wildlife conservation." Lobbyist—Susan M. Rogers, Washington, D.C.

Navajo Nation, Window Rock, Ariz. Lobbyist—Hill and Knowlton Inc., New York City. Filed 1/10/81. Legislative interest—unspecified.

Sierra Club, San Francisco, Calif. Filed for self 1/16/81. Legislative interest—"general pollution legislation; specifically reauthorization of the Clean Air Act (PL 95–95)." Lobbyist— David McLane Gardiner, Washington, D.C.

Interest Groups and Political Participation

voters to affect electoral outcomes by placing a ceiling on expenditures for political expression by citizens and groups."[10]

The Court reasoned in *Buckley* v. *Valeo* that the restrictions on contributions could be sustained because they would not diminish effective political advocacy. Contribution limits would merely require political candidates and committees to raise funds from a greater number of persons. The expenditure limitation, however, was an unconstitutional impingement upon freedom of speech and the right to associate freely because it would operate to reduce the scope of political campaigns and advocacy. The Court concluded that restric-

[10] Ibid., p. 17.

Solar Lobby, Washington, D.C. Filed for self 1/23/81. Legislative interest—". . . renewable energy and energy conservation legislation." Lobbyist—Samuel E. Enfield, Washington, D.C.

The Wildlife Legislative Fund of America, Columbus, Ohio. Lobbyist—Stephen S. Boynton, Arlington, Va. Filed 1/12/81. Legislative interest— "Alaska Lands legislation: anti-trapping proposals, RARE II proposals, fur seal treaty."

Corporations and Businesses

Aetna Life and Casualty, Hartford, Conn. Lobbyist—Nossaman, Krueger & Marsh, Washington, D.C. Filed 1/13/81. Legislative interest— "Taxation, fringe benefits, insurance and related areas."

Asarco Inc., New York, N.Y. Filed for self 1/7/81. Legislative interest—"Measures affecting production of nonferrous metals and minerals and associated products. . . ." Lobbyist—Robert J. Muth, New York, N.Y.

Ashland Oil Inc., Ashland, Ky. Filed for self 1/28/81. Legislative interest—"All legislation concerning the petroleum industry, including but not limited to energy, taxes, coal, mining, marine transportation, synthetic fuels, and environment." Lobbyist—Doris J. Dewton, Washington, D.C.

Blue Cross and Blue Shield Associations, Washington, D.C. Filed for self 1/8/81, 1/28/81. Legislative interest—"Health legislation." Lobbyists—James D. Isbister, Stanley B. Jones, Mary Nell Lehnhard, and Molly J. Pierce, Washington, D.C.

Bulova Systems and Instruments Corp., Valley Stream, N.Y. Lobbyist—Cook, Purcell, Hanson & Henderson, Washington, D.C. Filed 1/15/81. Legislative interest—". . . Appropriations for military equipment and procurement."

Burlington Industries Inc., Washington, D.C. Filed for self 1/8/81. Legislative interest— "Legislation affecting, or of

interest to, the textile industry. . . ." Lobbyist—Donna Lee McGee, Washington, D.C.

Chevron U.S.A. Inc., Washington, D.C. Filed for self 1/10/81. Legislative interest— "Legislation affecting Chevron U.S.A. Inc.; its parent, Standard Oil Company of California; and other subsidiaries of Standard Oil Company of California." Lobbyist—Phil M. Bitter, Washington, D.C.

Eli Lilly Inc., Indianapolis, Ind. Lobbyist—Crowell & Moring, Washington, D.C. Filed 1/16/81. Legislative interest— "Legislation affecting product liability tort rules and product liability insurance."

Ford Motor Co., Dearborn, Mich. Filed for self 1/13/81. Legislative interest—". . .federal laws, policies and trends and proposed legislation and regulations in relation to the interests of the Company. . . ." Lobbyist—J. Barry Coughlin, Washington, D.C.

Source: *Congressional Quarterly Weekly Report,* March 7, 1981, p. 431. By permission.

tions "on the amount of money a person or group can spend on political communication during a campaign necessarily reduces the quantity of expression by restricting the number of issues discussed, the depths of their exploration, and the size of the audience reached."[11]

While the decision of the Court in *Buckley* v. *Valeo* did not free interest groups to use money as they wished in political campaigns, it did significantly expand the permissible boundaries within which they could function to influence the electoral process. The Court had left no doubt that there were important constitutional limits upon the authority of Congress to control the freedom of expression of interest groups and their First Amendment right to associate.

The Court continued to expand the constitutional protection of the political advocacy of interest groups by holding that a state public service commission could not forbid a utility to send out with its bills leaflets that advocated particular public policies the utility considered favorable to its interests. The Consolidated Edison Company of New York had sent out with its bills material entitled "Independence Is Still a Goal, and Nuclear Power Is Needed to Win the Battle." The material discussed the benefits of nuclear power, which "far outweigh any potential risk," and assured the reader that nuclear power plants are safe, economical, and clean. The message concluded that only through nuclear power could the energy dependence of the United States be significantly reduced.

The nuclear power advocacy of the Consolidated Edison Company was highly controversial, and was immediately challenged by the Natural Resources Defense Council, an antinuclear group. The Council requested the opportunity to enclose a rebuttal in the next billing, and when Consolidated Edison refused, the Natural Resources Defense Council went to the Public Service Commission of New York to request that the utility make its billing envelopes available to groups with contrasting views. The Commission responded by prohibiting utilities from using bill inserts to discuss political matters, on the grounds that the customers of regulated utilities who receive bills are a captive audience with diverse views, who should not be forcibly subjected to the utility's beliefs. The

---

[11] Ibid., p. 19.

Supreme Court on appeal concluded that, "The Commission's suppression of bill inserts that discuss controversial issues of public policy directly infringes the freedom of speech protected by the First and Fourteenth Amendments."[12] The Court found that the state had not demonstrated, as it was required to, a compelling interest to justify the restriction imposed by the Commission. On the same day the Consolidated Edison case was decided, the Court held that the Public Service Commission could not bar promotional advertising by utilities even if the material advocated a course of action that the state had concluded was against the public interest.[13]

[12] Consolidated Edison Co. v. Public Service Commission of New York, 447 U.S. 530, 544 (1980).

[13] Central Hudson Gas and Electric Corp. v. Public Service Commission of New York, 447 U.S. 557 (1980).

Lack of Disciplined Parties

Another key part of the context within which interest groups operate is the general lack of disciplined political parties in the United States. In many countries, political parties represent very narrow interests, just as pressure groups do. Under such circumstances, they are factions in the Madisonian sense. In our political system, the lack of disciplined parties is a reflection of the diversity of political forces in the nation. There is no way that disciplined parties can develop out of political pluralism and the fragmentation of power in the constitutional system. The lack of disciplined parties is not so much a cause of the increased importance of interest groups, as an effect of interest group pluralism.

Laissez-faire Capitalism

Although the Constitution, in one strand of the folklore of American democracy, discourages a reliance upon interest groups as the best inputs to shape public policy, the dominant attributes of economic, political, and social development have fostered pluralism. The philosophy of laissez-faire capitalism is analogous to political group theory. The belief that if individuals or groups pursue their own interests and thereby produce what is economically in the public interest is directly equivalent to the interest group theory that the interaction of pressure groups will bring about the closest approximation of the public interest that is possible in a free society.

The capitalistic ethic was never fully believed or carried out. It was often used merely for propaganda purposes and as a support for the aggressive and often ruthless activities of private enterprise. Nevertheless, the theory of capitalism seeped into the crevices of the political system at many points by osmosis. It has had a strong impact in both the economic and political realms. As groups transferred their practices in the economic sphere to the area of political action, it was only natural to think that the best policy would be produced through group competition.

The ethic of capitalism lends strong support to the idea that pressure group competition should be the primary procedure for the formulation of public policy. This ethic is different from group theory in several important respects. It does not recognize the counterbalancing role of government against the forces of the private community. It suggests, rather, that the only legitimate interests are those in the private realm, and that government should be no more than a reflection of the powerful groups of society. Minimal government was the capitalistic ideal. Government was to intervene only to maintain the rules of the game and to provide minimum needs such as national defense.

Today, parts of the government are the captives of private interest groups, making government in those areas (for example, the "military-industrial complex") clearly subservient to the private sector. Although government dominated by private power might seem to conform to the capitalistic ethic, in fact this development creates serious dilemmas. Laissez-faire did not mean that government was to be controlled by private enterprise, but rather that government itself was to be virtually nonexistent. When any particular sector of the private economy controls government for its own purposes it clearly can upset the balance of competition and make the concept of the invisible hand a farce. Many industry groups do not want laissez-faire at all, but wish to use the instruments of governmental power to curb competition. Large enterprises seek to become even larger and gain monopolistic control if possible. When government acts as a countervailing force to these monopolistic tendencies, as when it enforces the antitrust laws, it is helping to preserve competition. Thus, we have the seeming paradox that the only way in which the capitalistic ethic can be maintained in practice is through a violation of one of the premises of the theory underlying the capitalistic system—namely that government should not be involved in regulating the competitive interaction of economic groups.

Pluralism is shaped not only by the way in which economic groups interact with each other and relate to government, but also by the tendency of individuals in other spheres to organize associations to represent noneconomic interests. Alexis de Tocqueville wrote in *Democracy in America* that the tendency of Americans to form associations for virtually every conceivable purpose was one of the most notable characteristics of our society:

Rise of Voluntary Associations

In no country in the world has the principle of association been more successfully used or applied to a greater multitude of objects than in America. . . .

A citizen of the United States is taught from infancy to rely upon his own exertions in order to resist the evils and the difficulties of life; he looks upon the social authority with an eye of mistrust and anxiety, and he claims its assistance only when he is unable to do without it. This habit may be traced even in the schools, where the children in their games are wont to submit to rules which they have themselves established, and to punish misdemeanors which they have themselves defined. The same spirit pervades every act of social life. If a stoppage occurs in a thoroughfare and the circulation of vehicles is hindered, the neighbors immediately form themselves into a deliberative body; and this extemporaneous assembly gives rise to an executive power which remedies the inconvenience before anybody has thought of recurring to a preexisting authority superior to that of the persons immediately concerned. . . . In the United States associations are established to promote the public safety, commerce, industry, morality, and religion. There is no end which the human will despairs of obtaining through the combined power of individuals united into a society.[14]

[14] Alexis de Tocqueville, *Democracy in America*, vol. 1 (New York: Vintage Books, 1954), pp. 198–99.

De Tocqueville was emphasizing the proclivity of Americans to organize their activities through groups. In many cases these groups perform functions similar to that of government today. Self-reliance and individualism did not mean that individuals stood by themselves, but rather that they organized with their fellows to meet whatever challenges they faced. As it became increasingly evident that voluntary associations could not by themselves handle the complex problems that were arising in nineteenth century industrial America and that government would have to be expanded, the vast array of private groups formed the reservoir for the major inputs of an expanded political process. In de Tocqueville's terms, both interest groups and political parties were examples of voluntary associations in the society that he studied.

Voluntary associations had obvious limits in attempting to deal with political problems. They could not exercise the authority of the state unless it was delegated to them, and therefore had no legal power of compulsion. The problems of society required an expansion of the apparatus and workload of governments at all levels. Only government could bring a common approach to problems within its jurisdiction. Only government could deal with the increasing demands on the part of interest groups and the public for new services, and regulation of various parts of the private sector. The expansion of government necessarily meant increasing specialization and diversity, reflected in the committee system in the legislatures, and in the expansion of national, state, and local bureaucracies.

The growth of the bureaucracy, in particular, added an important new dimension to the context in which interest groups had to function. Generally, the bureaucracy expanded the representation of various political interests in government as administrative agencies sought to reflect the views of the dominant groups within their constituencies. Many parts of the bureaucracy were established for the sole purpose of representing private interests, as in the case of the Departments of Agriculture, Commerce, and Labor. Insofar as these kinds of departments were delegated responsibility to formulate public policy, their outputs directly reflected the inputs of private interest groups. The "public interest" was identified by administrative departments and agencies with the promotional needs of private economic interests. For this reason, the expansion of government did not always establish a countervailing force to private interest, but rather reinforced the power of the larger interests, usually at the expense of smaller and less influential groups.

Development of Procedures for Decision Making

In the absence of disciplined parties, and a rational issue-oriented electorate, a procedural ethic was devised to deal with the problem of how to formulate a public policy that was different from the concept of majority rule and party government. It also differed from the mechanism of concurrent majority, which would give each group a veto over legislation affecting its interests. The basic procedural ethic employed was drawn from the Anglo-American legal tradition, and involved giving those parties affected by government policy decisions some kind of hearing before a decision was made. The effects of the legal profession upon the American government have been profound. From the beginning, lawyers have tended to be the most well represented profession in Congress, and this, in turn, has not only shaped the nature of the legislative process, but has also affected key points within the bureaucracy through legislation. Just as congressmen consider certain parts of the judicial procedural ethic appropriate to their own deliberations, they also feel that the agents of Congress, those in administrative agencies exercising quasi-legislative and quasi-judicial functions, should employ such procedures if feasible.

The judicial procedural ethic uses selected ingredients of the judicial process. As is done in court proceedings, the first stage of decision making involves holding a hearing in which those parties directly affected by the decision are given the opportunity to testify and present their views. These views may be recorded formally in a written record of the proceedings. The judicial decision-making model requires that the decision of the judge (and jury, if a jury is used) be based upon the record. This strict requirement, however, is not followed in the legislature or by the bureaucracy. The record that is compiled may or may not form the basis for the conclusions made by legislators. The fact that this procedural ethic is followed enhances the access of pressure groups in both Congress and the bureaucracy. The pressure groups are the ones that have the expertise, the time, and the money to testify on behalf of their own interests. Their voices are the ones that are most loudly and frequently heard. To the extent that both congressional and administrative procedures are of a judicial nature, the public interest is defined in terms of narrow rather than broad inputs.

In line with preceding considerations, it should also be

pointed out that the courts make their important policy decisions on the basis of judicial procedure which emphasizes relatively limited group inputs. Courts are far more limited than Congress or the bureaucracy in the procedures they can employ. They cannot initiate cases, but must wait for legitimate cases and controversies to be brought to them. Their rulings must be written, and based upon the record of the proceedings and the relevant issues of statutory or constitutional law that are involved. Limitation of procedure does not prevent the courts, particularly the Supreme Court, from making far-reaching policy decisions. These decisions, however, do not flow from cases brought by individuals, but rather by groups. The groups may, like the NAACP or the American Civil Liberties Union, represent individuals in the judicial process. But individuals by themselves rarely have the necessary resources to gain access to the courts and to exhaust the judicial process, which is often necessary before a final policy decision can be made.

Although the procedural ethic of the judiciary requires expertise on the part of decision makers in the area of procedure only, in the policy process outside of the courts decisions are often made by experts in the area of policy under consideration. This expertise is gained through specialization. Specialization occurs in congressional committees, their staffs, and administrative agencies, buttressed by specialized inputs from pressure groups.

The nature of the policy process means a diminished role for electoral politics as an influence upon policymakers. The average person, whether he or she is aware or not of issues of public policy, cannot register his or her views meaningfully at the ballot box. In the broadest sense, elected politicians can gain an awareness of the public pulse by observing electoral behavior, but the nature of the political process excludes voting as a major input of government. If this is true, what influence do average voters have? They do not get to testify before congressional committees, or to make their views known before administrative agencies. They do not involve themselves in the judicial process. Often they do not even bother to go to the polls to register their preferences at election time. Politicians are well aware that they can be defeated if they do not meet the expectations of those in their electoral constituencies who do vote. But there is simply no way for the elected politician to know what voters are thinking, or what motivates them to vote one way or the other. The entire electoral process becomes guesswork, on the part of both candidates and voters. Neither knows the policy preferences of the other, or how the other is really going to act regardless of statements that are so often made setting forth policy positions of the candidates on the one hand, and public opinion on the other. In this atmosphere of electoral uncertainty, the real decisions and channels of influence flow from constituencies to elected officials through the elites of powerful groups.

In general, the most accurate statement that can be made to summarize the nature of the policy process is that it involves the reconciliation of group interests at all levels and in every branch of government. Under certain circumstances, the operation of the presidency is an exception to this rule. In the foreign policy area, decisions are often made on the basis of a very narrow range of inputs that do not include private pressure groups.

INTEREST GROUPS IN OPERATION

There is a constant circulation between those occupying positions in government and those in the private sector. It is very difficult to describe the world of private pressure groups as being separate from government. Virtually all private groups have their "representatives" located at some point within the political process. Legislators may have direct interests in private corporations. For example, throughout recent history many legislators have had direct interests in the oil industry, and have sponsored legislation favorable to oil interests. The late Senator Robert S. Kerr was an oil and gas millionaire, and president of the Kerr-McGee Oil Industries. More recently, Louisiana Senator Russell Long's family was revealed to have extensive oil interests, which, added to the fact that Louisiana is the second biggest oil producing state, gave the senator unusual incentives to represent the oil industry, which he has done effectively. He used his positions as chairman of the Senate Finance Committee and as ranking minority member in the Ninety-seventh Congress (1981–82) to support legislation to increase profits for the oil industry. In the past, he fought for the oil depletion allowance which gave particularly favorable tax treatment to the oil industry. In the Ninety-sixth Congress (1979–80), he successfully led the fight for decontrol of oil and natural gas prices. Legislation was passed that provided for phasing out the regulation of the oil and natural gas industries, an objective that was finally accomplished in the first year of the Reagan administration.

Influencing Government Appointments

Apart from having direct representatives in the legislature, private pressure groups seek to place their own representatives in administrative agencies that regulate them. By exerting pressure on the president and the Senate, which must give advice and consent to presidential appointments, powerful pressure groups can often control the appointment process. A particularly famous case in this regard was the senatorial rejection of the Truman appointment of Leland Olds for a third term on the Federal Power Commission.

Olds had a reputation as a diligent public servant, one who did not bend readily to the pressures of the oil industry under the jurisdiction of the FPC. He was in favor of federal regulation of the price of natural gas, and at the time of his reappointment nomination the Congress was involved in a heated controversy over what was termed the Kerr Bill, which would have removed certain powers of the FPC over the natural gas industry. Olds was chairman of the FPC, and he had vigorously opposed the weakening of the powers of the commission in testimony before the Senate Committee on Interstate and Foreign Commerce. Partially for this reason the bill had never been reported out of committee in the Senate, although it had been passed in the House in 1948 and 1949 by substantial majorities. The oil industry, with the help of certain key senators, including Lyndon B. Johnson of Texas, set out to smear Olds's record, accusing him of everything from incompetence to being a tool of the Communists. They succeeded in securing his defeat by a large majority in the Senate.[15] During

[15] For the story of Leland Olds see Joseph P. Harris, "The Senatorial Rejection of Leland Olds: A Case Study," *The American Political Science Review* 45 (1951): 674–92.

the Senate debate, Senator Johnson argued that one of Olds's major deficiencies was that "never once in his long career has Leland Olds experienced, firsthand, the industries' side of the regulatory picture."[16] The implication was that the best regulators are drawn from the ranks of the regulated. This gives private groups direct representation of their interests in government. In virtually all administrative agencies exercising regulatory functions, the most intense efforts are made by private groups to insure that appointees have a sympathetic understanding of their needs.

The Leland Olds case is a particularly good illustration of the way in which powerful interest groups can control administrative appointments even in the face of strong presidential opposition. Rarely do presidents make cabinet and high level administrative appointments that will antagonize the powerful interest groups within the constituencies of the departments and agencies involved. Informal consultations always take place between the White House and interest group leaders to assess the acceptability of proposed presidential appointments to the groups. While few presidential appointments are universally acclaimed, the men and women who fill top level positions in the executive branch more often than not have been informally cleared by powerful interests.

Reagan's cabinet appointments, for example, for the most part received the support of important group interests within the jurisdiction of the different agencies. The secretary of the interior, James G. Watt, had direct ties to corporations seeking access to public lands. Although the appointment was opposed by conservationist groups such as the Sierra Club, Watt received strong endorsement from Joseph Coors, the beer magnate, and former Republican Senator Clifford P. Hansen of Wyoming, who advocated an orderly but timely development of public lands. Reagan's secretary of agriculture, John R. Block, was an Illinois farmer and former director of the Illinois Department of Agriculture who was known to be a strong advocate of agricultural interests. Block was endorsed by a wide array of agricultural interest groups and farm-bloc senators. For the secretary of housing and urban development, a department that administers programs in which the black community has a strong interest, Reagan

16 Ibid.

appointed his only black cabinet member, Samuel R. Pierce, Jr. Pierce had served in previous Republican administrations and had a distinguished record as a judge and lawyer. Reagan's secretary of defense, Caspar Weinberger, promised to increase defense spending and sounded like a superhawk in his confirmation hearings. For secretary of the treasury, Reagan chose a Wall Street investment banker, Donald T. Regan, who became known among the wags in Washington as "Reagan's Regan." Among Regan's accomplishments was the building of the Wall Street firm of Merrill Lynch into the largest and most diversified investment banking and brokerage firm in the country. Like all Republican presidents, Reagan

LOBBYING TAKES MANY FORMS
Donovan Roast: Dishing Up Davis-Bacon At a Down-Home Feast

By Leslie Berger

[The Washington social scene provides an important setting for informal contacts between lobbyists, government officials and legislators.]

The symbolic attraction of a country pig roast at the home of Secretary of Labor Raymond J. Donovan was irresistible, with the seasoned presence of Cabinet and Labor Department members, some union leaders, wafts of Davis-Bacon permeating the air—and Strom Thurmond riding a mechanical bull.

"Well, I grew up on a farm," the 78-year-old senator from South Carolina said. "I'm accustomed to riding bull calves."

Thurmond drew a hearty round of applause when, in his pin-stripe pants and open-collared, white button-down, he mounted the steer like the one made famous in the film "Urban Cowboy" and rode slowly, but surely.

The mechanical ride wasn't the only attraction at the Donovans' Saturday night. "The prospect of free pig," as presidential assistant Lyn Nofziger put it, seemed to be another prime motivation for attending the lavish lawn party for about 300 guests—complete with two country and western bands, round tables with centerpieces of yellow and white daisies, a bountiful spread of salad and fruit, liquor flowing as steadily as the Potomac behind the Donovans' McLean home, and several open pits with large slabs of both pork and beef dripping fat.

"I know nothing about the Labor Department," Nofziger said. "We came to eat some of the Davis-Bacon."

And, though the evening was primarily one of "relaxation and fun," as Donovan's wife, Cathy, said they hoped it would be, the Davis-Bacon Act of 1931, which requires construction workers to be paid the "local prevailing wages"—frequently top union scale—on federally funded work, provided some political fat to be sociably chewed.

"I personally think it should be repealed," said Sen. Paul Laxalt (R-Nev.). "It's a throwback to the old days that isn't relevant any longer."

But some of the labor leaders present expressed different opinions. "He [Donovan] knows we're for the Davis-Bacon," said Thomas McGuire, of the New York Operating Engineers.

Robert A. Georgine, president of the AFL-CIO building trades department, said, "I think the Secretary's a decent human being." But he continued, "The administration is misguided . . . it seems like they've already made their policy decision" on repealing

had difficulty in finding a suitable Republican that could work with the major labor unions to appoint as secretary of labor. In the controversial Raymond J. Donovan, however, a New Jersey contractor with working class roots, he found a man whose negotiating abilities were respected by labor union leaders, and who had the backing of some, including the president of the Teamsters Union. Whether or not Reagan's cabinet appointments would always be sensitive to the interests of the clientele of their respective departments remained to be seen, particularly since the president's initial recommendations called for large cutbacks in many departmental programs.

Davis-Bacon. Georgine remarked that not many national labor leaders were present at the party, but said since he didn't know who had been invited, he couldn't explain their absence.

Among the labor leaders who did attend was Capt. John O'Donnell of the Airline Pilots Association ("I thought it would be totally out of character for me to wear a white hat," he said, in reference to the prevalent western dress); Jesse Calhoon, of the Marine Engineers Beneficial Association, and Joe O'Donaghue, head of the Operating Engineers in Philadelphia. "Donovan has a heck of a reputation in construction," O'Donaghue said. "I mean a good reputation—he's a good union contractor. We know he's familiar with our industry and the problems in it. We're counting on the secretary" to protect Davis-Bacon.

Donovan, who wore a cowboy hat, jeans and a western shirt that matched his wife's, said, "I invited the labor lead-

ers who are my friends."

Conversation was spurred on by the bull, surrounded by mattresses to protect those amateur cowpersons daring enough to ride.

Most weren't.

"Riding the bull might be harder than throwing it," presidential counselor Edwin Meese III said. "Since George Bush is from Texas, I'm waiting for him to ride, and then I'll ride."

But the vice president, dressed in a beige Cuban shirt, had previously declined similar offers. "It's not hard, anyone can do it," his wife, Barbara, said. "But I don't see why the vice president should climb up on a machine."

"I'm smart enough not to ride the bull," Secretary of the Interior James Watt said.

David Stockman, OMB director, on riding the bull: "I have another drink to go."

The business community was represented by a number of leaders, including Roger C. Sonnemann, vice president of labor relations for Amax Inc.;

John Post, executive director of the Business Roundtable; Richard Lesher of the U.S. Chamber of Commerce; George A. Moore Jr., vice president of Industrial Relations for Bethlehem Steel, who said, "I think it's a very good idea to get these people together informally to talk"; and Malcolm Lovell, president of the Rubber Manufacturers' Association and a former assistant secretary of labor. Robert Bonitati, White House liaison for labor relations, also came.

What actress Valerie Perrine was doing among this mixed group was a question many guests were asking, to which her escort, Morgan Mason, responded: "We're looking for some pig." Radio talk show host Larry King came because "Ray was on my show."

Long after the sun had set, speaking as a leader of operating engineers, McGuire said, "If the secretary of labor invites me, I don't care who he is, I'm coming."

Source: *Washington Post,* July 13, 1981, p. C1–3. By permission.

While cabinet secretaries are usually beholden to the president who appoints them, and sensitive to the concerns of the White House in their initial months in office, they soon go their own ways as the zeal of a new presidential administration begins to diminish. Cabinet secretaries often attempt to build their own power bases, and naturally turn to the powerful interest groups within their constituencies for support in their quest for independence from the White House. Within weeks of his appointment by President Reagan, Secretary of State Alexander Haig was fighting with the secretary of defense over who would determine foreign policy, and engaged the White House as well in a battle for supremacy. Although Haig did not have a domestic constituency to mobilize, he did cultivate the support of foreign leaders and prominent members of the foreign policy establishment to strengthen his cause.

Influencing the Electoral Process

Just as interest groups seek to control the appointment process for key positions in government, they also make every effort to involve themselves in electoral campaigns to secure the defeat of candidates they consider unfavorable to their interests, as well as to the election of proponents of their viewpoints. Contributions flow freely to candidates who are rated high on the list of supporters of particular groups.

Interests groups "rate" incumbents running for reelection on the basis of their past voting records. The National Farmers Union published its first evaluation of members of Congress in 1919, and the rating game has been played by a host of interest groups ever since. The AFL-CIO is one of the more prominent groups that judge incumbents on the extent to which they support prolabor positions. The conservative Americans for Constitutional Action began the publication of its index in 1958, rating congressmen on the basis of their conservative votes. In the 1980 national election, right-to-life groups and the National Conservative Coalition channeled funds to candidates supporting their positions and were highly effective in defeating targeted candidates such as Senators Frank Church of Idaho, Birch Bayh of Indiana, and George McGovern of South Dakota.

Although corporations and labor unions cannot easily make direct contributions from corporate or union funds to political candidates, and the direct contributions of all groups are limited to $5,000 for any political candidate, there are no restrictions upon expenditures in behalf of candidates. Groups can spend unlimited sums to elect candidates of their choice, provided the money does not go directly into the campaign chests of the office-seekers.[17] In the 1980 elections, for example, the National Conservative Political Action Committee disbursed $1.2 million in independent expenditures in six senatorial races to defeat incumbent Democrats, and won four of those races. The Committee gave $128,169 to congressional candidates, 92.3 percent of whom were Republican, helping 39 percent of its candidates to win. A variety of political action committees copied NCPAC's strategy in attempting to influence elections through indirect expenditures supporting particular candidates. The technique of indirect support had been used before 1980. In 1978, for example, the political action committee of the American Medical Association spent over $42,000 for magazine advertisements backing the reelection of Georgia Democratic Senator Sam Nunn, whose conservative views appealed to AMA leaders.

Congressional attempts to limit campaign contributions have challenged the ingenuity of interest groups and their attorneys. Since the campaign law prohibits unions and corporations from using their own funds for political giving, they have established political action committees that are funded by voluntary contributions solicited from members and employees. (See Figure 5.4.) Each PAC is permitted to give $5,000 to a political candidate in any given election. In the 1980 election, approximately seventeen hundred PACs contributed over $32 million to House and Senate candidates, an unprecedented amount. Political action committees representing the United Auto Workers, National Association of Realtors, National Automobile Dealers Association, the American Medical Association, and the AFL-CIO were among the largest contributors to congressional candidates. For the most part, these groups strictly favored one party over another. For example, the AFL-CIO political action committee called COPE channeled 96.6 percent of its contributions to Demo-

[17] The Supreme Court's decision in *Buckley* v. *Valeo* (1976), discussed above, declared unconstitutional the expenditure ceilings imposed by the Campaign Practices Act upon individuals and groups.

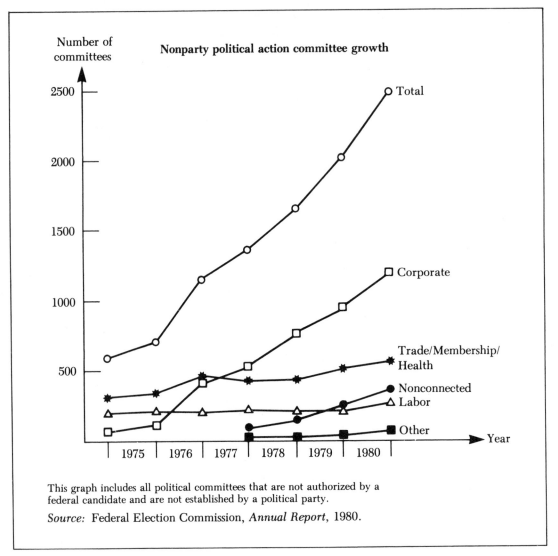

Nonparty political action committee growth

This graph includes all political committees that are not authorized by a federal candidate and are not established by a political party.

Source: Federal Election Commission, *Annual Report*, 1980.

FIGURE 5.4
Nonparty political action committee growth. *Political action committees have become an important political force.*

cratic candidates, while the AMA gave 72.2 percent of its money to Republicans.

Rarely do corporations go so far as IT&T did in 1972, when the company's president promised $400,000 to under-

Interest Groups and Political Participation

write the Republican National Convention in San Diego (the convention was later shifted to Miami). Although it seems to be a custom for hotel owners to raise substantial funds for conventions in their cities, the proposed gift by IT&T raised many eyebrows. This was particularly true because the sequence of events seemed to reveal that the contribution was made in return for a favorable Justice Department ruling on an IT&T merger case. After the contribution was promised by the company, the Justice Department terminated several important antitrust suits that it had filed against IT&T. The major evidence of improper company influence was an internal IT&T memo from Mrs. Dita Beard, an IT&T Washington lobbyist, to the chief of the IT&T Washington office. In part the memo stated:

I just had a long talk with E.J.G. [E. J. Gerrity, IT&T's Public Relations Chief]. I'm sorry we got that call from the White House. I thought you and I had agreed very thoroughly that under no circumstance would anyone in this office discuss with anyone our participation in the convention, including me. Other than permitting John Mitchell, [California Lt. Gov.] Ed Reinecke, Bob Haldeman, and Nixon (besides Wilson of course) *no one* has known from whom the $400,000 commitment had come. . . . Now I understand from Ned that both he and you are upset about the decision to make it $400,000 in *services*. Believe me, this is not what Hal [Harold Geneen, IT&T President] said. Just after I talked with Ned, [Rep. Bob] Wilson called me, to report on his meeting with Hal. Hal at no time told Wilson that our donation would be in services *only*. In fact, quite the contrary. There would be very little cash involved, but certainly some. I am convinced, because of several conversations with Louie [former Kentucky Gov. Nunn] re Mitchell, that our noble commitment had gone a long way towards our negotiations on the mergers eventually coming out as Hal wants them. Certainly the president has told Mitchell to see that things are worked out fairly. It is still only [Antitrust Chief Richard] McLaren's Mickey-Mouse we are suffering. . . .
    I hope, dear Bill, that all of this can be reconciled—between Hal and Wilson—if all of us in this office remain totally ignorant of any commitment IT&T has made to anyone. If it gets too much publicity, you can believe our negotiations with Justice will wind up shot down. Mitchell is definitely helping us, but cannot let it be known. Please destroy this, huh?[18]

[18] *Congressional Quarterly Weekly Report*, 11 March 1972, p. 524.

In extensive hearings held on the propriety and legality of the action by the Justice Department as well as the contribution by IT&T, only Jack Anderson, the syndicated Washington newspaper columnist who originally brought all of the details of the IT&T case to light, clearly stated the facts concerning the proposed IT&T contribution to the Republican party. The immediate issue of the hearing was whether or not Richard Kleindienst, who was deputy attorney general at the time of the IT&T case, had the proper qualifications to become attorney general. He had been appointed to this post by President Nixon. In testimony before the Senate Judiciary Committee on the nomination of Kleindienst and related matters concerning IT&T, Anderson pointed out that:

> . . . Mr. Kleindienst is a man who has trouble recognizing a crime when he sees one. Let us make no mistake about it. The contribution of $400,000 by a corporation to support a political convention is crime. It directly and clearly violates the Corrupt Practices Act, which specifies that it is "unlawful for . . . any corporation . . . to make a contribution or expenditure in connection with any . . . political convention." Yet when questioned about this, Mr. Kleindienst said he didn't have an opinion. He protested that it was "customary" for political conventions to receive such donations.[19]

The IT&T case illustrates that corporations have in the past become financially involved in one way or another in political campaigns, regardless of the provisions of the Corrupt Practices Act specifically prohibiting such contributions. Special Prosecutor Archibald Cox, before being fired by President Nixon in 1973, revealed extensive contributions to CREEP (Committee to Reelect the President) by private corporations.

Controlling Campaign Financing. In part because of the ineffectiveness of the Corrupt Practices Act, and widespread circumvention of other legal restrictions on campaign financing, Congress passed a far stricter campaign finance law which went into effect in 1972. The main purpose of the new Federal Election Campaign Practices Act, as of its predecessors, was to reveal the sources of and place limitations on campaign contributions. The premise of such a law is that there is a direct correlation between campaign contributions and the ability to control the actions of candidates. This was certainly the implication in the IT&T case, where it was alleged that even the president of the United States could be influenced by a substantial contribution to his political party. Legislation controlling campaign finances before and after the Watergate period was severely curtailed by the decision of the Supreme Court in *Buckley* v. *Valeo* in 1976, and has not significantly

[19] Ibid., p. 567.

reduced the influence of money in elections—as the experience of 1980 illustrates. (See Table 5.1.)

Controlling Elected Government Officials. The involvement of pressure groups in political campaigns again illustrates that these groups do not seek only to control policy from the outside, but attempt to determine who will be placed into positions of power in government. Elected as well as appointed officials are fair game. A distinction that is usually made between political parties and interest groups is that the former are geared to supplying the personnel of government, whereas the latter seek only to influence political decision makers from the outside. This distinction breaks down in those cases where pressure groups make definite commitments to one party or the other and to different party candidates. Interest group leaders know very well that the best way to guarantee control over the policy process is to determine who will have the final decision-making authority.

The fact that pressure groups are successful in their endeavors to control elected government officials is illustrated in a field such as oil policy, where it has been stated that

. . . certainly it is difficult to find a congressman from an oil or gas state who will not vote "wrong" on oil or gas legislation. The delegations from Kansas, Oklahoma, Arkansas, Texas, and Louisiana voted unanimously in favor of the Harris-Fulbright Bill to free gas producers from federal control. Many frankly refer to themselves as oil congressmen, in the same sense that others call themselves cotton or farm congressmen. They know what their attitudes on such matters as depletion ought to be. "We oil congressmen represent our people," explained Tom Steed of Oklahoma. "It is my duty to represent their views. I would be replaced otherwise and would deserve to be."[20]

[20] Robert Engler, *The Politics of Oil* (Chicago: University of Chicago Press, 1967), p. 397.

Where particular economic interests dominate the constituencies of congressmen or entire states (for example, oil interests in Oklahoma), they effectively control the electoral process, making it impossible for candidates to get elected without their support. It would be a rare congressman indeed who would not see the public interest in terms of the economic interests of his or her constituency. Similarly, administrators who wish to hold their jobs pay close attention to the demands of the most powerful groups within their constituencies. Administrative constituencies are different from the elec-

Table 5.1
Party and Political Action Committee Campaign Expenditures. *Money is the lifeblood of the political process and is closely connected with power and influence.*

	Total filers existing in 1980	Filers terminated as of 12/31/80	Filers waived as of 12/31/80	Continuing filers as of 12/31/80	Number of reports and statements in 1980	Gross receipts in 1980	Gross expenditures in 1980
Presidential					3,205	$162,289,030	$155,821,594
Candidates	307	230	9	68			
Committees	248	68	0	180			
Senate					6,209	$ 85,238,712	$ 93,190,978
Candidates	643	273	6	364			
Committees	691	220	0	471			
House					26,099	$120,443,620	$118,616,360
Candidates	2,923	1,154	56	1,713			
Committees	2,678	828	0	1,850			
Party	834	243	0	591	6,681	$197,075,615	$205,803,531
National Level Committees	81	17	0	64			
State Level Committees	247	52	0	195			
Local Level Committees	454	153	0	301			
Convention Committees	6	0	0	6			
Delegates	46	21	0	25			
Nonparty (Political Action Committees)	2,777	226	0	2,551	37,646	$ 84,548,985	$ 97,956,149
Labor Committees	343	46	0	297			
Corporate Committees	1,256	52	0	1,204			
Membership, Trade and Other Committees	1,178	128	0	1,050			
Communication Cost Filers	42	0	0	42	107	N/A	$ 1,599,450
Independent Expenditures by Persons Other Than Political Committees	355	139	0	216	1,537	N/A	$ 11,235,247

Source: Federal Election Commission, *Annual Report,* 1980.

Interest Groups and Political Participation

toral constituencies of Congress, but nevertheless, in terms of the way our system operates, they function in the same way. Groups within administrative constituencies do not "elect" administrators, but they do influence administrators through the power that they exercise over the appointment process and their ability to harass bureaucrats through Congress and the presidency.

As one looks at all of the major domestic policy areas, it is clear that the primary shape of public policy is frequently determined by the interest groups concerned in conjunction with those parts of the government that are their "captives." No way has yet been devised to counterbalance the influence of dominant economic groups; however, these groups do not exercise significant power outside of their own economic sphere. For example, Exxon, Mobil, and other large oil companies employ skillful lobbyists in Washington and contribute to the campaigns of sympathetic members of Congress to help shape government oil policy. The incentive of the oil industry, which itself is not monolithic, is to foster policies that benefit company profits. The power of oil does not reach into the agricultural sphere, where entirely different pressure groups operate to sway government decision makers in their favor. Nor are oil and agricultural interests concerned with labor policies, which are the domain of the AFL-CIO, the Teamsters Union, and other powerful labor groups. Powerful economic groups tend to dominate their own policy spheres because of the lack of interest and understanding on the part of the general electorate and outside pressure groups.

When public awareness expands to what were once exclusive concerns of specialized interests, then these interests no longer have the degree of control over public policy they possessed in the past. The rise of environmental and consumer groups in the 1960s, for example, a movement that expanded in the 1970s, checked the power of corporations to deal with the environment and the consumer as they wished. Ralph Nader mobilized citizens to bring pressure upon Congress to enact automobile safety legislation in 1966, and to establish stricter health and safety standards governing unsanitary meat, natural gas pipeline safety, radiation, coal mines, and chemicals. Environmental interests pressured Congress to enact air and water pollution control laws. Labor interests were instrumental in the creation of the Occupational Safety and Health Administration (OSHA), which became the gadfly of large and small businesses throughout the country, constantly tightening safety regulations in the workplace.

Industry groups did not take the attacks of the environmentalists and consumer groups lying down, however, but fought back to elect officials sympathetic to industry views. By the mid-1970s, Congress was awash with members who attacked OSHA as an overbearing and unnecessary government agency reflecting the worst aspects of bureaucratic despotism. The anti-OSHA forces on Capitol Hill received generous support from the business community. In addition to OSHA, conservative members of Congress targeted the Federal Trade Commission and the Environmental Protection Agency as examples of an excessively burdensome bureaucracy. The election of Reagan in 1980, along with a Republican Senate and a House far more conservative than it had been in the past, reflected the victory of private sector economic groups over environmental and consumer interests. Reagan immediately set out to limit both the programs and the agencies, such as OSHA and the EPA, which had been supported by labor and the self-styled "public interest" pressure groups, such as the Nader organization and the environmentalists.

Interest Group Action on Selected Policy Issues

Regardless of which presidential administration is in power, there are clusters of interest groups that surround particular issues of public policy and exert a strong influence on the final government action that is taken. In each policy sphere, sets of interest groups represent one of the points in what has been called the "iron triangle," which connects powerful congressional committees, administrative agencies, and interest groups. (See Figure 5.5.) The components of the iron triangles in different areas of public policy often exert more power than the White House in determining government action. The chairmen of congressional committees have generally had more continuity than presidents, and have developed close relationships with powerful lobbyists and tenured top level administrators in career civil service.

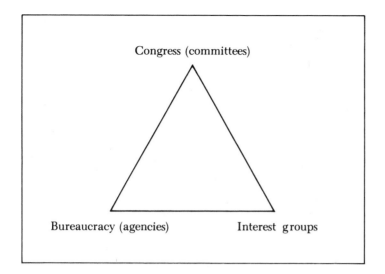

Congress (committees)

Bureaucracy (agencies)   Interest groups

FIGURE 5.5
The Iron Triangles of Politics. *The "iron triangles" of politics connect congressional committees, administrative agencies, and interest groups in mutually supportive arrangements.*

The forces in the battle over public policy are often the president and his allies on one side and the iron triangle on the other. Congressional chairmen, lobbyists, and bureaucrats represent the permanent Washington establishment that knows what it wants and how to get it.

Several examples of interest group politics will serve to illustrate the way in which specialized interests may control government.

Regulation of Toxic Substances. In the second session of the Ninety-sixth Congress (1980), legislation was introduced to regulate the disposal of toxic substances. Toxic wastes were a hidden time bomb, polluting underground water and agricultural products, and posing a major threat to the environment. The tragedy of Love Canal in Niagara Falls, New York, where toxic wastes have severely affected nearby residents, dramatically illustrated the problem. Mike Wallace and his colleagues on the popular television show *Sixty Minutes* alerted the public to the dangers of chemical and nuclear wastes which were produced in the normal course of plant operations throughout the country. Industrial accidents have even more dramatically made the public aware of the problem of environmental contamination. The nuclear accident at Three Mile Island in Pennsylvania in 1979 almost had tragic consequences. The same year, poultry and egg products were contaminated in nineteen states when an electrical transformer blew up and leaked cancer-causing PCBs into the animal feed produced by a Montana company.

While the problem of environmental contamination was widely known to the public, consumer and environmental interest groups, the president, and Capitol Hill, the opposition of the chemical and oil industries to government regulation of their activities prevented the passage of stringent legislation to control industrial contaminants. Differences between House and Senate legislation, and conflicts within both bodies over control of legislation, aided industry efforts to divide and conquer Capitol Hill.

The major focus of industry concern was the Senate bill, reported by the Environment and Public Works Committee chaired by West Virginia Senator Jennings Randolph. Randolph had used his position to build his Senate power and constituency base by doling out pork-barrel projects to his colleagues. When the Public Works Committee was given jurisdiction over environmental legislation, Maine Senator Edmund Muskie became the chairman of the Environmental Pollution Subcommittee, from which he built his reputation in the Senate as the leading advocate of air and water pollution control legislation. Randolph had deferred to Muskie on environmental policy, and after Muskie left the Senate to become secretary of state in the waning months of the Carter administration, the legacy of the Maine senator, particularly his subcommittee staff, remained an important force behind the effort to pass legislation that would increase the role of the government in regulating industrial wastes and impose liabilities upon companies found to have contaminated the environment.

At the outset of the debate over the regulation of industrial wastes, nuclear materials and by-products were exempted, since the regulation of the nuclear industry was covered by other legislation. The spills or releases of oil or petroleum derivatives were also exempted from the legislation, reflecting in part the concern of the sponsors that an attempt by the government to deal extensively with the problem of oil spills and wastes would jeopardize the entire legislation because of

Interest Groups and Political Participation

the opposition of the oil industry. Because oil companies were extensively involved in the production of chemicals, however, the oil industry joined the chemical lobbyists to mount a major campaign to kill efforts that would increase their liability and make them pay for cleaning up wastes found by the government to be hazardous.

As the so-called "superfund" legislation under which a large government fund paid for by the industry would be established to clean up industrial wastes began to move through the committee rooms, offices, and corridors of power on Capitol Hill, the chemical and oil industries set out to kill the legislation. Although the public was generally aware of the problem of industrial pollution, its voice was only faintly heard on Capitol Hill. A staff member of the Senate Environment Committee lamented, "There's been no groundswell of public support . . . to offset the massive campaign being waged by the chemical industry. Unless people are sitting near a chemical dump, they won't write. The lobbying is very lopsided right now."[21]

[21] *Congressional Quarterly Weekly Report,* 6 September 1980, p. 2643.

To offset the intense lobbying by the chemical and oil industries against the legislation, congressional sponsors of the bill attempted to mobilize both organized and potential interest group support for their cause. Staff members of the Senate Environment and Public Works Committee attempted to mobilize the support of sport hunting, fishing, and recreational groups. "Those groups usually carry a lot of weight with senators, because they could suffer economic and job losses in a chemical incident," said one staffer. "We're trying to get them to come forward."[22]

[22] Ibid.

Backers of the legislation also sought out the support of the Sierra Club and other environmental groups. In the end, however, the Senate sponsors of stringent legislation admitted that it was impossible to overcome the effects of industry lobbying, which used the most sophisticated techniques to alert shareholders to the threat to their pocketbooks posed by government regulation, and in addition marshalled the support of a wide range of impressive experts who contacted members of Congress to plead for the industry position.

In the waning days of the Ninety-sixth Congress, a much watered down version of the original waste cleanup legislation was cleared and sent to the president for his signature. Industry liability was substantially reduced from the original Senate proposal, as was the size of the superfund supported by industry contributions. Oil spills were not covered by the legislation, to the disappointment of President Carter and many members of Congress. The oil spill issue almost sank the bill because it reflected a power struggle between the Senate and the House. The House Public Works and Merchant Marine Committees had reported legislation that covered both oil and chemical spills, while the Senate Committee on Environment and Public Works omitted oil spills. The Senate insisted on its version of the bill, which it passed before House action. Senate sponsors of the legislation delivered an ultimatum to the House admonishing House members that if they did not adopt the Senate version of the bill, the legislation would not be called up again in the Senate chamber. Many members of the House considered the position of the Senate to be an insult to the House side. Ohio Republican William H. Harsha expressed the views of many of his House colleagues when he angrily asked, "Are we a coequal branch of the legislative process, or patsies?"[23] Finally accepting the view of New York Democrat Thomas J. Downey that the uncompromising Senate stand put the House in the position of having the "proverbial bird in the hand," the House passed the legislation 274–94 on 3 December 1980.[24] Although the president was unhappy with the legislation, he finally signed it into law.

The fate of the toxic waste bill illustrates several important aspects of the operation of pressure groups in the political system. First, Congress can and does initiate legislation that does not at first have wide outside backing. The initiation of legislation on Capitol Hill often results from the quest for personal power and recognition on the part of committee chairmen and, sometimes even more importantly, the committee and personal staffs of members. While legislation may not at first have outside support, it is necessary for congressional sponsors of bills to marshall the backing of the powerful interest groups that are directly concerned with the effects of the proposed policy if it is to be enacted. The role of the chemical and oil industries in the toxic waste legislation was

[23] *Congressional Quarterly Weekly Report,* 6 December 1980, p. 3509.

[24] Ibid.

Interest Groups and Political Participation

instrumental in shaping its final contents. John C. Calhoun's concurrent majority system was in operation: the pressure groups that would be most affected, at least in economic terms, exercised a veto over many of the provisions of the legislation.

Another important lesson that can be learned from the fate of the toxic waste bill is that the bicameralism of Congress and the decentralization of power on Capitol Hill may work to the advantage of powerful interest groups by giving them more points of access to decision makers. Squabbles among powerful lawmakers to protect their committee turfs delay and disrupt the legislative process, enhancing the influence of cohesive pressure groups that know exactly what they want.

No hard and fast rule can be given on the nature of private group influence in public policymaking. The diversity of groups makes it very difficult to pinpoint whether or not a "concurrent majority" system is in operation in particular areas. To determine this it would be necessary to find out what the dominant groups are for each policy field and whether or not they have a veto on legislation and administrative action affecting their interests. The rise of consumer groups in various areas, from those interested in automobile safety to those concerned with the protection of the environment, has injected an important new ingredient into the balance of power between pressure groups and government. Environmental groups were not able to mobilize to get their way on the toxic waste disposal legislation, but in the past they have been instrumental in securing the passage of wide-ranging environmental legislation. The environmental movement was responsible for the creation of the Environmental Protection Agency, which was given a broad mandate to regulate industrial and automobile pollution. Economic interests have mobilized against the EPA in the 1980s; however, environmental groups continue to be an important underpinning of the agency. The broadening of the base of interest group participation in the political process has reduced the virtually complete power that economic groups once had to determine the content of public policy.

Extent of Group Power in Policymaking

The power of different interest groups depends upon a number of factors, including the skillfullness of their leadership, the nature of political opposition to their policies, the extent of their memberships, and their vote-getting abilities. Power ebbs and flows among interest groups within different policy spheres. For example, until the passage of Medicare, the AMA, along with numerous private economic interests in the health field, such as hospitals and pharmaceutical companies, were generally able to negate government actions they felt were adverse to their interests. But the power of these medical groups is not unlimited. The pharmaceutical industry has been controlled by the passage of food and drug legislation from the first decade of the twentieth century. The Food and Drug Administration has at various times been strengthened by congressional action in response to public pressure and the leadership of key legislators. The American Medical Association's fight against national health insurance failed to prevent the passage of Medicare that covered the health needs of older persons. In the early 1970s Senator Edward Kennedy, chairman of the Health Subcommittee, embarked upon a losing battle to start the nation on the path to comprehensive health care. The AFL-CIO became a powerful counterforce to the AMA in the health care battle, reducing the power of the medical association to veto national legislation it considered detrimental to its interests.

In most major policy spheres an iron triangle can be identified, consisting of congressional committees and administrative agencies in alliance with a discrete set of private interests. The power of pressure groups is felt not only on Capitol Hill, but downtown in the Washington bureaucracy. After legislation is passed, pressure group access to administrative decision making often effectively controls public policy.

Interest Group Use of the Judiciary

In addition to having access to administrative agencies, private groups shape legislation through bringing cases before the judiciary. The courts cannot initiate cases and controversies because of the limitations placed upon them in Article III of the Constitution, but must wait for legitimate cases to be raised before they can act. The power of judicial review makes courts important to private groups in their attempts to control the policy process. This authority, not explicitly detailed in the Constitution, nevertheless gives the Supreme Court and lower courts the power to overturn acts of Congress if they are contrary to the terms of the Constitution. Even more important, executive decisions can be overturned if they are unconstitutional or beyond the intent of Congress. Most legislation delegating authority to the bureaucracy gives the courts the power to review administrative decisions within carefully defined boundaries. Within these limits, when private groups want to challenge an adverse administrative action, they will often go to the courts instead of to Congress or the president.

If administrative decisions are usually in favor of the powerful groups in their constituencies, why do such groups seek judicial review? Within most economic spheres, particular groups are in conflict with each other over how the largesse of government is to be divided among them. For example, when the Federal Communications Commission grants a lucrative television license, those groups that were in competition for the station may decide to challenge the agency's decision in court, provided they can find legal grounds for judicial review.

Judicial Response to Group Inputs

In the past, powerful economic interests have, from time to time, dominated the judiciary. Although it is difficult to generalize, it can be suggested that over the last hundred years the courts have gone through two stages and now are in a third concerning their approach to reviewing the policy decisions of administrative agencies. In the latter part of the nineteenth and the early twentieth centuries, the judiciary took a very conservative stance in relation to the bureaucracy, and frequently overturned any administrative decisions that were considered in the slightest way to be hostile to the interests of corporations. For example, the railroad interests were easily able to use the courts to stymie early efforts by the Interstate Commerce Commission (ICC) to exert control over them.

As the bureaucracy began to grow, particularly during the New Deal era, the courts were faced with both political and practical dilemmas in their quest for a meaningful doctrine of judicial review. Politically, strong demands were being made upon government from a wide range of interests, many of which were not highly organized, to expand the positive role of government in regulation and control of the economy. Any attempt to retreat into conservative doctrines would inevitably lead the courts into political controversy. Aside from political problems, the courts also faced a practical dilemma in attempting to deal with the tremendous number of cases that were beginning to arise before administrative agencies. Any attempt to exercise comprehensive judicial review could only cause a severe breakdown in judicial machinery. Clearly, the best way to avoid both political questions and practical problems was to retreat into the doctrine of judicial self-restraint with respect to both areas.

In the political area, the courts developed a doctrine of restraint suggesting that "political questions" were not appropriate for courts to handle. This meant, in reference to review of administrative action, that policy decisions of the agencies would be allowed to stand provided the proper procedural safeguards had been observed. The doctrine of judicial self-restraint in regard to political questions worked to reduce the practical workload of the judiciary, for by circumscribing their sphere of discretion the courts eliminated most of the policy decisions of administrative agencies from their jurisdiction.

In the second stage of judicial action, then, the courts became passive rather than active instruments of policy determination. There is evidence now that the judiciary is entering upon a third stage, characterized by a new activism that is responding to a broader range of inputs. Public interest law firms and pressure groups are succeeding in getting the courts to intervene more in the administrative process to force careful consideration of consumer interests and the interests of the broader public for formulating public policy. For example, environmental groups have succeeded in delaying administrative action licensing power plants in areas that they consider to be necessary to the preservation of the wilderness, and in delaying pipeline construction and other actions detrimental to the environment. The trans-Alaskan pipeline was delayed for several years by a judicial injunction that came after environmental groups sought to prevent entirely the construction of a pipeline which they felt would have highly adverse environmental effects. The courts are becoming the trustees of the public interest, at least as defined by public interest pressure groups.

GOVERNMENTAL INTEREST GROUPS

Only in recent years has the concept of governmental pressure groups been widely recognized. These groups, at the national level, are essentially composed of government agencies, including the presidency, which are constantly involved in lobbying Congress and other parts of the government to advance their objectives. Congressional committees may also be considered as public pressure groups. Different parts of government become pressure groups because they have separate goals. Although naive observers might feel that the government should work for only one overriding "public interest," there are many public interests.

The diversity of governmental interest groups is fostered by the pluralism of government at the national, state, and local levels. At the national level, the existence of a separation of powers and checks and balances system means that there is no unified focus of power. In each branch of the government, and within the branches, separate groups vie for power among themselves. The greatest source of proliferation of public pressure groups comes from the pluralistic character of the executive branch. Each agency represents a separate constituency, and has organizational goals that differ from those of other parts of the bureaucracy. The goals of administrative agencies tend to tie in very closely with those of the private groups within their constituencies. Some idea of the importance of governmental interest groups can be gained from the fact that rarely is an important piece of legislation passed by Congress without clearance from the administrative agency that will be involved in its implementation. Expert bill drafting is often done by lawyers within administrative agencies, who provide their services to Congress. Private pressure groups also often offer drafts of proposed legislation to congressmen, but such inputs are not considered to be quite as legitimate as those that come from the administrative branch. One reason for this is that the administrative branch is part of the government, and is supposed to reflect broad rather than narrow interests.

Administrative Agencies and the President as Interest Groups

Administrative agencies are not supposed to be involved in lobbying activities, and indeed many administrators and legislators alike would not call the constant interaction between the bureaucracy and Congress "lobbying." The failure of Congress to recognize that public lobbying poses a problem is reflected in the Federal Regulation of Lobbying Act of 1946, which circumscribes only the activities of private lobbyists. There are laws, however, that specifically prohibit the use of public funds for the purposes of public relations activities on the part of administrative agencies. Regardless of such legislative proscriptions, many agencies engage in more extensive public relations campaigns than virtually any private group.

For example, the Defense Department for decades has undertaken skillful propaganda programs to aid in recruitment, and to indoctrinate the public on the importance of the military. Even the individual branches of the Defense Department—the army, air force, and navy—have their own full-time public relations divisions involved in trying to convince Congress and the public, as well as the president, of the unique importance of their particular approach to warfare. Constant pressure is being exerted upon the legislature, for example, to embark upon new shipbuilding programs to support the navy, or to supply funds for the development of new types of aircraft and missiles for the air force and the army.

Although the Defense Department is probably more extensively involved in public relations activity than any other part of the bureaucracy, other agencies as well have undertaken important propaganda programs to advance their own goals. The Department of Agriculture puts out vast amounts of literature not only to inform its constituency of the nature and importance of the programs that it is involved in, but also to make constituents and legislators aware of the key role the department plays in the maintenance and development of American agriculture. The department lobbies vigorously to shape agricultural legislation before Congress, and is often the determining force in agricultural policy as it emanates from Congress.

When agencies embark upon legislative programs in Congress, they are supposed to go through the Office of Management and the Budget (OMB), which is within the Executive Office of the President. The clearance of all legislative proposals from the administrative branch is an important requirement that has been established by the OMB. A forceful presidency can be an extraordinarily powerful pressure group in relation to Congress, as well as to administrative agencies. But since the president does not have automatic control over the administrative branch, he is often placed in the same position as other groups in attempting to get administrative agencies to heed his requests. The president's power and influence are greatest where he has set forth a clear policy position. Under such circumstances he can exert strong influence upon the bureaucracy to fall into line behind his leadership, and this gives him tremendous leverage with Congress. Where the president has not articulated a program, however, the process of clearance of proposals through the OMB does not enhance the power of the presidency, but merely gives the OMB the opportunity to coordinate different requests from within the administrative branch. If it is known that the president does not have a position on the proposals of administrative agencies, they are more likely to ignore the OMB and go directly to Congress, making their desires known informally. They may even go to the president in an attempt to secure his backing. All of this interaction among different parts of the government in the policy process should be considered as pressure group activity.

The superior position of the president and the bureaucracy as lobbyists before Congress is derived not only from the fact that they are legitimate parts of the government, but also from the delegation of specific legislative responsibility to the president in Article II, and to both the president and the administrative branch by Congress. The regulatory agencies are given the specific responsibility to recommend proposals to Congress. They are considered the agents of Congress, and in the regulatory field are supposed to be the primary inputs for legislative change. Congress will often wait for recommendations from these agencies before considering any new legislation dealing with regulatory matters. This is not to suggest that regulatory agencies are necessarily more powerful than other parts of the bureaucracy in lobbying Congress, but only that they are considered by Congress itself to be an integral part of the legislative process. This puts them in a better formal position to exert influence. However, informal factors often determine the power of the agencies. Such factors include the degree of constituency support for agency proposals, the level of expertise of the agencies as opposed to that of Congress, and whether an agency has the backing of OMB and the president. The same factors which shape the power of regulatory agencies in the legislative process also pertain to other parts of the bureaucracy which do not have the same relationship to Congress.

CONTROLLING INTEREST GROUP ACTIVITY

The Federal Regulation of Lobbying Act requires that the receipts and expenditures of private pressure groups be reported. Campaign practices legislation, following the tradition of the Federal Corrupt Practices Act of 1925, limits the political activities of unions and business corporations, and prohibits them from making direct financial contributions to candidates. Pressure groups can no longer extend unlimited credit to political candidates. Public pressure groups are controlled in part by laws preventing the expenditure of public funds for public relations purposes and lobbying activity. Laws aimed at private group activity seek to publicize expenditures and lobbying activities, while only controlling expenditures to political campaigns.

There are numerous difficulties associated with attempting to control pressure group activity through legal devices. Political power and influence depend upon money, access to decision makers, expertise, and control over the channels of communication, among other things. These ingredients of power cannot be readily controlled by legislation. The laws regulating the activities of administrative agencies are so vague and nebulous that they are totally ignored even in the limited area—public relations—they are supposed to control.

Assuming that one could proscribe the public relations activities of administrative agencies, this would only partially reduce their influence in the policy process. They would continue to provide expert advice to Congress and to draft legislation pertaining to their areas of responsibility, and they would also retain rule-making and adjudicative functions that are key ingredients in shaping public policy. All of the constitutional and statutory mechanisms designed to limit and control the authority of government relate to the control of public pressure groups. The constitutional separation of powers was nothing more than a device to control the "interest groups" of Congress, the presidency, and the judiciary. The doctrine of delegation of legislative authority is supposed to keep the discretion of administrative agencies within the boundaries of congressional intent, and thereby control administrative power. Insofar as these governmental arrangements work, the activities of public pressure groups are limited in accordance with constitutional and democratic criteria. The problem of controlling public pressure groups is one of political theory and practice.

As long as our system has no unified source of power, and does not operate on the basis of majority rule and party government, the activities of public pressure groups will continue to expand. Different administrative agencies will press for their own goals, just as Congress through congressional committees and the president will seek the realization of separate policy objectives, which may or may not be in accordance with those of the bureaucracy. The independence and powers of the federal judiciary guarantee that it will in the future be an important instrument of public policy, which it will often define separately from the other governmental branches.

The theory of the constitutional separation of powers supports the idea of conflict among the branches. Although the Constitution does not take into account the role of the bureaucracy, the way in which agencies function as pressure groups separately from the coordinate branches would fit into

Controlling Governmental Interest Groups

the concept of intragovernmental competition built into the constitutional system. Insofar as public pressure groups remain in competition, then, the criteria of the Constitution are being fulfilled. One of the major obstacles posed by the operation of public pressure groups today to this competitive ethic of the Constitution is the frequent collusion that exists between administrative agencies and congressional committees. Since they often have the same outside constituency making demands and giving supports to them, committees and agencies take similar approaches to what public policies are in the "public interest." The separation of powers system was based upon the idea of contrasting constituencies among the branches of government, with a full recognition that similar constituencies would not produce sufficient motivation within the branches to oppose each other regardless of the fact that they would possess independent constitutional powers. It is this collusion of interests within different policy spheres between the legislature and administration that reduces the range of inputs to the policy process, and creates a condition whereby broader community concerns and interests more likely than not will be ignored.

Government-Private Collusion

Insofar as constitutional and statutory standards limit the operation of public pressure groups, they also to some extent place constraints upon private groups. To get what they want, private groups have to operate through the government. The purposes of the constitutional system were to limit the power of outside factions by making it impossible for them to gain unified control over the policy process. Public pressure groups never have interests that are entirely separate from the private sphere. If an agency such as the ICC, for example, is able to operate without significant constraints from other parts of the government, this means that those private groups having access to the agency are able to get what they want. Therefore, the first and most important consideration in approaches designed to limit the power of private groups in government is to recognize that government must first limit itself; however, this has generally not been recognized.

If the power and influence of the armaments industry are to

be curtailed, then it is necessary to curb the Department of Defense and its close arrangements with the Armed Services and Appropriations Committee and the House and Senate. To control the power of pressure groups in regulated industries, such as airlines, railroads, broadcasting, telephone and telegraph, drug manufacturers, and agriculture, the administrative agencies and other parts of the government having jurisdiction over these industries must be limited. So far no way has been devised to prevent the collusion of private interests with government. The main idea behind the constitutional mechanism for controlling factions was that the different constituencies of the policymaking branches of the government would guarantee a balance of power. But the specialization of the governmental process has made it impossible to implement such a system. Today the primary constituencies of government are composed of interests that have specialized policy concerns. Both the constituencies and those parts of the government formulating policy cut across the formal lines that are supposed to divide the branches of government.

Attempting to control pressure group activity through the enactment of legislation only touches the surface of the problems that arise in connection with interest group inputs of the policy process. Requiring the registration of the lobbyist, and reporting of receipts and expenditures for lobbying activities in connection with legislation pending before Congress, at best deals with a tiny fragment of pressure group operation. It may provide information for such journalists as Jack Anderson, but even this is unlikely, for those lobbying Congress are careful to keep up good appearances in public. Lobbying legislation does not touch upon the activities of pressure groups in connection with administrative agencies and the presidency. And with regard to Congress, groups have to register and report only if they are attempting to influence "directly" legislation pending before Congress. This is a matter of interpretation. There is no effective enforcement machinery for the lobbying law, and in recent years no one has been charged with a violation. Even if the law were rigidly enforced, it would not change in any way the nature of the

Ineffectiveness of Legislative Controls

demands made by groups in the policy process, or their impact.

There is little doubt that our system is very close to operating on the basis of concurrent majorities in many key areas of public policy. This means that in many cases minorities have vetoes over government actions, and are often able to shape the content of public policy. Whether or not one calls this system a democracy, it is a fact. The best advice for those who feel that they are being left out of important policy decisions is to encourage them to participate through groups in the policy process. But there is no way that those without influence can be given power unless they possess the tools of power. Simply becoming a member of a group does not guarantee anything in the way of exerting influence upon the political process. Most groups are managed by skillful elites which themselves possess the necessary skill to gain and retain positions of leadership within the group. Pressure group policy does not necessarily reflect the views of the membership, although insofar as the membership is made aware of what the group leaders are doing, some control can be exerted, provided the group follows democratic selection procedures of its leaders. This is not always the case, and elections within groups can be as easily manipulated as those within the political system. Moreover, in some groups, such as labor unions, where the leadership serves the economic interests of the membership, leaders are left relatively free to pursue political goals in other areas. Of course, all issues are interconnected, but some are seemingly of greater relevance to particular individuals than others. The AFL-CIO, for example, can and does take positions on a wide range of political issues which are not always clearly connected either favorably or adversely to the economic interests of its membership. For instance, in 1971, the AFL-CIO vigorously opposed the nomination of William H. Rehnquist to the Supreme Court. The nominee was allegedly a conservative and "strict constructionist." It is dubious that union members would care about such an issue one way or the other, and if they were knowledgeable they very well might support a more conservative justice on the Supreme Court. The AFL-CIO also opposed the admission of the People's Republic of China to the United Nations. This is certainly not an issue connected with the economic problems of workers. Admittedly, the AFL-CIO ranges more widely than most pressure groups in taking policy stands, but there are other examples of groups whose leaders delve into policy areas that are not necessarily supported by or of concern to their memberships. The AMA, although primarily concerned with issues of medical care, occasionally will take a stand, usually conservative, on broader public policy issues. During the McCarthy era in the early 1950s, the AMA was vigorously involved in attempting to root out what it considered to be Communist influences in government. Of course, one could say that communism and health care are intimately connected, in that socialized medicine is part of a Communist state. But, realistically speaking, the issue of communism in the '50s should not have been related to the economic problems of medicine. The leadership of the AMA knew that there was no possibility of a Communist takeover.

The elites of pressure groups, both public and private, will continue to exercise pervasive influence in the policy process in the future. To some extent the rise of "public interest" pressure groups will modify the degree of control over public policy exercised by specialized interests. A trend in this direction has already been seen in such areas as environmental policy, and in legislation protecting the rights of consumers, including requirements for product safety. Without the pressure that has been exerted by public interest pressure groups, laws in these areas would not have been passed. Moreover, these public interest groups are putting continual pressure upon administrative agencies to adhere to the letter of the law. They are also beginning to use the courts as effective instruments for forcing administrative agencies to take effective action against private economic groups in these policy areas. Those who have organized public interest pressure groups recognize the legitimacy of our political system and its underlying pluralistic character.

Common Cause, for example, is attempting to change the character of the men who occupy the elected positions of government. From its beginning, the hope of Common Cause was that by changing the character of elected officials, particularly members of Congress, democratic responsibility could be strengthened and public policy made more responsive to the interests and wishes of the people. Common Cause has consistently lobbied for federal funding of election campaigns, stricter lobbying control legislation, and open decision-making procedures which are commonly referred to as "government in the sunshine."

Common Cause is not the only organization that lobbies Congress in the public interest. Ralph Nader, a Princeton and Harvard Law School graduate, stepped to the forefront of public interest lobbyists after he published *Unsafe at Any Speed* in 1965. The book attacked the safety record of the automobile industry, causing General Motors to put private detectives on his trail in the hope that they could destroy his personal credibility. When the General Motors scheme became public, the corporation, highly embarrassed, abruptly dismissed the detectives. Ralph Nader went on to organize and lead a highly effective consumer movement.

Nader, both individually and through his organization, achieved more than any other public interest lobbyist in the late 1960s and early 1970s. The publicity Nader had given to the problem of automobile safety was largely responsible for the passage of the Motor Vehicle Safety Act in 1966, which mandated vehicle safety standards. Not content with helping to solve the problem of automobile safety, Nader expanded his organization, hiring young law school graduates and students, who became known as "Nader's Raiders."

Nader assigned his Raiders to investigate the Federal Trade Commission (FTC) in 1968. They found an agency in disarray. Ironically, it was Nixon who, as a result of Nader's investigation, began the reinvigoration of the FTC, which in the late 1970s became a highly active and effective agency.

Nader's public interest efforts reached into many other areas. His Raiders found that the Food and Drug Administration (FDA) had approved the use of dangerous chemicals—cyclamates and monosodium glutamate—in the food supply. The resulting publicity brought an end to their use. Nader's legislative victories resulted in stricter controls over natural gas pipeline safety, radiation, coal mines, and air pollution.

As Nader expanded his public interest organization, he created Public Citizen, Inc., and became its executive director.

The citizens' interest group engages in wide-ranging activities to support its view of the public interest. Congress Watch constantly monitors Capitol Hill while other parts of Public Citizen are involved in energy, health, and tax reform policy.

Common Cause, Ralph Nader, and other public interest pressure groups have added an important new dimension to the group process. But whether or not that process alone can effectively reflect the public interest has been questioned.

This is the public interest as Ralph Nader sees it. His group has made progress toward the realization of many of these public interest goals, but there is intense disagreement over some of them. Is it sufficient to accept the argument that the public interest will probably emerge from the conflicting viewpoints in those areas where there is no common agreement?

One of the most important indictments of the group process of politics in recent years is that made by Theodore J. Lowi.[25] In summing up his arguments against group theory, he states first that the practice of the group process of politics runs against the grain of democratic theory and practice. It does not allow for majority rule, or for the establishment of a hierarchy of values within the political system. The values and demands of all interest groups are considered to be of equal merit. This means that "liberal leaders do not wield the authority of democratic government with the resoluteness of men certain of the legitimacy of their positions, the integrity of their institutions, or the justness of the programs they serve."[26] Government cannot plan on the basis of a scale of values different from those of dominant pressure groups. Congress, in the delegation of authority to administrative agencies, frequently gives up its responsibilities and asks the bureaucracy to make rules on the basis of vaguely worded statutory standards.

The practice of delegation of legislative authority supports interest group liberalism because the legislature does not establish adequate standards to guide administrative action. The courts, because of vaguely worded statutes, find it difficult to intervene in the process of bureaucratic decision making to force adherence to statutory principles. In Lowi's terms, most of the rules that guide the development of policy by the administrative branch should be developed by the

[25] Theodore J. Lowi, *The End of Liberalism* (New York: W. W. Norton, 1969).

[26] Ibid., p. 288.

legislature. The Constitution also establishes certain principles, but the reluctance of the judiciary to intervene in the administrative process makes even the Constitution an instrument of dubious value in controlling interest group determination of policy. Past doctrines of judicial review which are based upon the concept of judicial self-restraint have made it difficult for courts to establish principles to guide administrative action. As a result of the lack of formal rules and procedures, public policy is formulated on the basis of informal bargaining. Lowi suggests that: "there is inevitably a separation in the real world between the forms and the realities, and this kind of separation gives rise to cynicism, for informality means that some will escape their collective fate better than others."[27] The expectations of many people about how government should function, in contrast to the way in which it does, have caused grave discontent—especially in the last decade, when higher levels of education for a broader segment of the public in combination with an expanded mass media have made it very difficult to hide the realities of politics.

Lowi indicts the theory as well as the practice of interest group politics. He points out that group theory has falsely propagated a faith that "a system built primarily upon groups and bargaining is perfectly self-corrected."[28] Supposed self-correcting mechanisms, such as overlapping membership, potential groups, countervailing power, and so on, do not in fact operate perfectly, if at all. Moreover, Lowi feels that we would be better off if we leaned toward Madison's concept of groups as expressed in *The Federalist,* rather than toward the more sanguine view of the interest group theorists. Citing Madison's distrust of groups, Lowi concludes that a "feeling of distrust towards interests and groups would not destroy pluralist theory but would only prevent its remaining a servant of a completely outmoded system of public endeavor. Once sentimentality toward the group is destroyed, it will be possible to see how group interactions might fall short of creating that ideal equilibrium."[29] In short, the notion that all is right in the political world as long as interest groups are allowed to function freely should be discarded.

Although Lowi's thesis is well argued and logical, it does not solve the question of how to replace interest group theory

[27] Ibid., p. 291.

[28] Ibid., p. 294.

[29] Ibid., pp. 296–297.

Interest Groups and Political Participation

and practice. One can assert what we should be doing, but this is only a small step in helping to bring about those fundamental changes that are necessary to alter the way in which the system now operates. As Madison acknowledged in *The Federalist,* interest groups or "factions" will remain an important part of the political system. Pluralism is an inevitable consequence of freedom. Pluralism itself is not bad, but it must always be recognized that control over public policy by concurrent majorities of affected interest groups means by definition that a numerical majority of the people do not shape many of the policies that affect their interests. The national interest is more than the sum of group interests and, as Lowi suggests, should be articulated by the president and members of Congress who have been elected to serve the people. To what degree can the major institutions of government, the presidency, Congress, the courts, and the bureaucracy be structured in such a way that their policy outputs will not be a simple reflection of pressure group inputs? We will treat these questions in the following chapters.

Suggestions for Further Reading

Davies, J. Clarence, III. *The Politics of Pollution.* New York: Pegasus, 1970. A case study of the way in which interest groups influence federal pollution control legislation.

Fritschler, A. Lee. *Smoking and Politics: Policymaking and the Federal Bureaucracy.* 2nd ed. Englewood Cliffs, N.J.: Prentice-Hall, Inc., 1975. One of the best studies of the interaction of Congress, the bureaucracy, and pressure groups in the policy making process.

Krasnow, Erwin G., and Longley, Lawrence D. *The Politics of Broadcast Regulation.* 2nd ed. New York: St. Martin's Press, 1978. Governmental and private interest groups attempt to influence an agency's determinations of the public interest.

Lowi, Theodore J. *The End of Liberalism.* 2nd ed. New York: W. W. Norton and Co., 1979. Updates the author's views which criticize the acceptance of interest group power in American politics.

McFarland, Andrew S. *Public Interest Lobbies: Decision Making on Energy.* Washington, D.C.: American Enterprise Institute, 1976. Examines the rise of public interest groups and their role in energy policy.

Truman, David B. *The Governmental Process.* 2nd ed. New York: Alfred A. Knopf, 1971. First published in 1951, Truman's study supports the central role of interest groups in policymaking.

Part III

The Governmental Process

The Constitution requires the president to sign bills before they become law.

CHAPTER 6

The Presidency

Even more than parties and interest groups, the presidency is thought by most citizens to be the focal point of policy making. Witness the tremendous interest in presidential election campaigns, and the relatively large voter turnout compared to that in state and local elections or in elections for congressmen and senators. In our folklore, the president is at the same time king and prime minister. Although the *office* is often held in higher repute than the incumbent, the occupant of the White House usually gains from the stature of his position; people tend to forget that the president is always involved in the realities of exercising political power, meaning compromise and deals undertaken in the capacity of a politician, not a king.

Presidential power depends upon political skill, upon the incumbent's ability to persuade others that it is in their interest to follow the lead of the White House. There is no automatic assurance that presidents can have a major influence upon the course of public policy. To reach their policy goals, presidents must not only surmount congressional hurdles, but often bureaucratic intransigence as well.

Presidential power is generally aided by having a majority of the same party that occupies the White House in Congress; but there is no automatic bridge between the two ends of Pennsylvania Avenue based upon party loyalty. A Republican Congress helped President Dwight Eisenhower enact close to 90 percent of his legislative proposals in the first two years of his administration. The election of a Democratic Congress in 1954 saw Eisenhower's success rate on Capitol Hill drop markedly. Presidents Kennedy and Johnson were highly successful in persuading a Democratic Congress to support their policies. Republican Presidents Nixon and Ford, however, had difficulty with Congress because it was controlled by the Democrats. A Democratic Congress, however, did not help President Jimmy Carter to achieve anything more than a mediocre record on Capitol Hill. President Reagan, on the other hand, displayed an unusual ability to retain the loyalty of Capitol Hill Republicans while persuading many Democrats to his point of view during the first year of his administration. Reagan had only a slim Republican majority in the Senate and a House controlled by Democrats to work with. Nevertheless, he secured the passage of major reductions in the federal budget and taxes largely through his extraordinary ability to persuade both Congress and the people to follow his lead.

The dazzling success of Reagan during the initial stage of his administration caused Washington political reporters to compare him with such charismatic leaders as Franklin D. Roosevelt and John F. Kennedy. But even the most charismatic presidents eventually have difficulty in exercising power within the often byzantine world of Washington politics. Popular expectations about what presidents can do usually far exceed the actual powers of the office. Astute inside observers of the White House continually stress its limits more than its powers. The constitutional and political context of the presidency both restricts and enhances presidential power. The Madisonian model of government emphasizes the limits of the presidency, while the Hamiltonian presidency is imperial in character. Presidents can and have used the prerogative powers of the office, delineated in Article II of the Constitution, to act independently to overcome the constraints of the checks and balances system that Madison stressed would prevent the arbitrary exercise of political power.

THE CONTEXT OF THE PRESIDENCY

Effects of the Separation of Powers

The imperial presidency has developed because of the separation of the executive from Congress, and the establishment of independent prerogative powers in the presidency under the Constitution. (See Figure 6.1.) An executive dependent upon

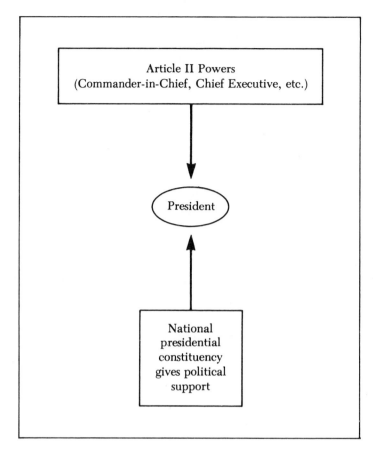

FIGURE 6.1
The Independent, Unified Presidency. *The power of the president is buttressed by independent constitutional authority under Article II and by a nationwide political constituency.*

the legislature is weakened unless he can consistently control a majority of legislators. Such executive control can only result from a disciplined two-party system, such as that in Great Britain. The multiplicity of interests and the lack of a disciplined two-party system in the United States mean that dependency of the executive upon the legislature decreases presidential power.

The independent powers and separate constituency given to the office of the president in Article II of the Constitution have formed the basis for a vast expansion in presidential prerogatives as the responsibilities of the office have increased. Without having to rely upon legislative ratification, presidents from Washington to Reagan have taken bold initiatives in both foreign and domestic policy. Like the courts and parts of the bureaucracy, the White House is capable of making decisions without going through the tedious deliberations of the legislative process. Under the Constitution, the presidency is the only political office under the domination of one man.

Clerk or King?

One should not overemphasize the powers given to the presidency in the Constitution, however, because without the necessary political support and acquiescence on the part of other branches of the government, vigorous presidential action can be and has been nullified. Richard Neustadt claims that the Constitution makes the president more of a "clerk" than a king. He is a clerk not in a sense that he is powerless, but rather because the Constitution establishes no clear hierarchical lines of power and responsibility in government; therefore, all other parts of the governmental process look to the president for leadership, guidance, and help in performing the tasks that they themselves are incapable of carrying out because of the fragmentation of the system. As Neustadt states:

> In form all presidents are leaders, nowadays. In fact this guarantees no more than that they will be clerks. Everybody now expects the man inside the White House to do something about everything. Laws and customs now reflect acceptance of him as a great initiator, an acceptance quite as widespread at the Capitol as at his end of Pennsylvania Avenue. But such acceptance does not signify that all the rest of the government is at his feet. It merely signifies that other men have found it practically impossible to do *their* jobs without assurance of initiatives from him. Service for themselves, not power for the president, has brought them to accept his leadership in form. They find his actions useful in their business. But transformation of his routine obligations testifies to their dependence on an active White House. A president, these days, is an invaluable clerk. His services are in demand all over Washington. His influence, however, is a very different matter. Laws and customs tell us little about leadership in fact.[1]

[1] Richard E. Neustadt, *Presidential Power* (New York: John Wiley & Sons, 1960), p. 6.

Just as in many areas the other branches of government need the president in order to take effective action, the president in turn relies upon his governmental "constituents" to carry out his orders.

The history of the presidency reveals numerous examples of recalcitrance at heeding presidential demands not only on the part of the coordinate legislative and judicial branches, but even in the case of those parts of the bureaucracy that are supposed to be directly under his supervision. Even in foreign and military policy areas, the president cannot automatically control policies that he initiates. For example, he can begin "police actions," which is in reality the same as a declaration of war, but he cannot necessarily control the actions of the military commanders in the field. President Truman had to fire General MacArthur for insubordination because MacArthur was taking actions that threatened to widen the Korean War far beyond what the president wanted. In recent years, examples of independent military action in Vietnam without presidential knowledge have been brought to light, particularly in regard to the selection of bombing targets in North Vietnam during 1972. Air Force General John D. Lavelle had ordered his pilots to undertake twenty-eight missions to strike unauthorized targets in North Vietnam. In testimony before Congress, after he had been demoted and retired from the air force, General Lavelle pointed out that:

The rules of engagement [in the air war], although being fairly specific, also require some interpretation or judgment factor added. . . . I chose to make a very liberal interpretation of these rules of engagement. In certain instances, against high priority military targets, I made interpretations that were probably beyond the liberal intention of the rules. I did this since the crews were operating in an environment of optimum enemy defense. It was isolated instances reported as protective reaction strikes that resulted in General Ryan recalling me and questioning me on what we were doing. From his viewpoint in Washington, I had exceeded my authority. I can sit here now and understand his position, but at that time as the Commander on the spot concerned with the safety of the crews, and, at the same time, trying to stop the buildup that was going on, I felt that these were justifiable actions.[2]

[2] *Congressional Quarterly Weekly Report,* 17 June 1972, p. 1494.

This incident illustrates that even where there is a tight chain of command, the president cannot foresee and control all of the events which occur as a result of general policy decisions he makes.

The constitutional context in which the presidency operates provides for policymaking responsibilities in several ways. The president is given the charge in Article II to recommend legislation to Congress, and the president's legislative pro-

Policymaking Powers of the President

gram forms an important starting point for congressional action. The president can veto congressional legislation, and although Congress has the authority to pass legislation over the veto by a two-thirds vote, it does so rarely because of internal divisions within the legislature itself.

Another important way in which the president affects policy under the Constitution is through his appointments to the Supreme Court. Although he cannot control the actions of judges once they are appointed—sometimes presidents are surprised to find that their Supreme Court appointments do not act in a predictable way—nevertheless, a determined president can go a long way toward giving a liberal or conservative cast to the Court. President Nixon set out to appoint "strict constructionists," by which he meant conservatives, to the Court, and he succeeded in shifting the balance of power on the Court in a conservative direction. Since the Court is one of the most important policymaking instruments in government, the presidential appointment power is a strong policy force. Constitutional appointments made by the president to the Supreme Court must be approved by the Senate. Sometimes there is strong opposition to presidential decisions on particular appointments, such as occurred during the Nixon administration with respects to his first two appointees to fill a vacancy on the Supreme Court. Historically, however, the Senate has rarely interfered significantly with the presidential appointment process. The initiative clearly lies with the Chief Executive.

It is commonly assumed that one of the most important constitutional powers of the president is that of "Chief Executive." Article II states that the president is to see that the laws are faithfully executed. He is given the power to appoint "public ministers," and "officers of the United States," by and with the advice and consent of the Senate. He also may "require the opinion in writing of the principal officer in each of the executive departments, upon any subject relating to the duties of their respective offices." These legal powers are hardly sufficient to enable the president to control the policymaking activities of the bureaucracy. The key to potential presidential control over the administrative branch lies with Congress, for the Constitution delegates to the legislature the most significant authority over the bureaucracy. Administrative agencies cannot be set up in the first place without congressional approval, and Congress outlines what the agencies are to do. Whether or not an agency is placed under the legal control of the president is entirely at the discretion of the legislature.

Congress, the bureaucracy, and the Supreme Court all become independent forces in the president's constituency because of the way in which the Constitution has structured the system. The positions that these branches of the government take with regard to various issues of public policy cannot help but influence the policy stance of the White House. Legislation cannot be enacted without the consent of Congress; this is complicated because the legislature is a bicameral body, split internally with different constituencies for the House and the Senate. Moreover, within Congress power is decentralized among three hundred committees and subcommittees, each striving to make its mark in the legislative process. Often legislation is within the jurisdiction of six or seven committees on each side of Capitol Hill, and in some cases far more. Fifty-six congressional committees have some jurisdiction over energy legislation. The president, then, must deal not only with the broader bodies of the House and the Senate, but with the little legislatures, the committees that exercise the real power on Capitol Hill.

Assuming that the president is able to get one of his legislative proposals passed, he next must deal with the bureaucracy, which is delegated responsibility to implement congressional laws. Whether or not the bureaucracy follows presidential wishes will depend upon the relative power of the presidency within the constituencies of administrative agencies. Finally, legislation and executive actions may come under the scrutiny of the Supreme Court, which will not hesitate to overrule the president if it feels that he has acted *ultra vires* (beyond authority) in terms of constitutional or statutory law.

Just as presidential policy outputs are shaped by a variety of governmental institutions, the policy inputs to the White House are often complex and conflicting. These inputs include

The Policy Constituency of the President

demands from Congress, the bureaucracy, party and pressure group leaders, public opinion, and leaders of other nations. Clear mandates for presidential action rarely exist. The president must balance a variety of demands from many sources before he makes a policy decision. Public opinion may constrain presidential actions; however, the president usually leads rather than follows public opinion on most policy issues. Although he must depend upon broad public support at election time to remain in office, the public is far too fragmented itself to be able to speak with one voice to the White House. (See Figure 6.2.)

As one observes the variety and contrasting nature of the inputs upon the presidency, it becomes difficult to make generalizations about how particular presidents arrive at policy decisions. This will depend to a considerable extent upon the nature of the man who occupies the office, and the way in which he assesses the different forces affecting him.

Presidential style differs markedly from one person to another. Presidents Franklin Roosevelt, Harry Truman, and John Kennedy brought to the White House personal self-assurance and political skills that enabled them to be decisive and effective leaders. Dwight Eisenhower adopted a more passive approach to the White House, and although he was a highly popular president who gave the nation perhaps a much needed period of rest, he did not make a broad impact upon the institution of the presidency. Lyndon Johnson and Richard Nixon were both consummate politicians who had a dramatic impact upon public policy. Johnson was the major force behind the Civil Rights Act of 1964 and the Voting Rights Act of 1965 that vastly expanded civil rights protections for minority groups. Johnson's Great Society program extended the earlier New Deal philosophy. Richard Nixon paved the way for the opening of relations with the People's Republic of China, an extraordinary feat by any political measure. Neither Johnson nor Nixon could extricate himself from the major crises of his respective administrations, Vietnam and Watergate. The style of presidents is as much remembered as their impact upon public policy. Each president must deal with the same constituency forces, but each brings a unique style to the White House.

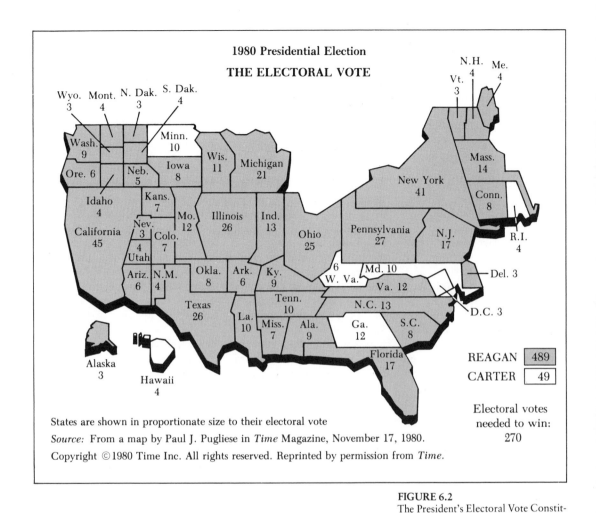

1980 Presidential Election

THE ELECTORAL VOTE

Wyo. 3 Mont. 4 N. Dak. 3 S. Dak. 4 N.H. 4 Me. 4 Vt. 3

Wash. 9 Minn. 10 Wis. 11 Michigan 21 Mass. 14

Ore. 6 Neb. 5 Iowa 8 New York 41 Conn. 8

Idaho 4 Kans. 7 Illinois 26 Ind. 13 Ohio 25 Pennsylvania 27 N.J. 17 R.I. 4

California 45 Nev. 3 Colo. 7 Mo. 12

Utah

Ariz. 6 N.M. 4 Okla. 8 Ark. 6 Ky. 9 W. Va. 6 Md. 10 Va. 12 Del. 3

Texas 26 Tenn. 10 N.C. 13 D.C. 3

La. 10 Miss. 7 Ala. 9 Ga. 12 S.C. 8

Alaska 3

Hawaii 4

Florida 17

REAGAN 489
CARTER 49

Electoral votes
needed to win:
270

States are shown in proportionate size to their electoral vote

Source: From a map by Paul J. Pugliese in *Time* Magazine, November 17, 1980.

Copyright © 1980 Time Inc. All rights reserved. Reprinted by permission from *Time.*

FIGURE 6.2
The President's Electoral Vote Constituency. *The electoral vote often does
not reflect the popular vote. In 1980
Reagan received only 51 percent of the
popular vote, but won the electoral
college vote by a landslide.*

An important part of the constitutional and legal context within which the president formulates policy arises from the legal definition of his constitutional prerogatives based upon Article II, and on the extent to which Congress by statute can delegate him discretionary authority. There is little doubt that if both the Supreme Court and Congress want to control the president, his legal discretion will be severely limited. Rarely,

**Limits Upon Presidential
Policymaking Discretion.**

PRESIDENTIAL STYLE

Hail the Conquering Hero

[*Ronald Reagan displayed the style his presidency would adopt on his first visit to Washington as president-elect. Despite predictions by savvy insiders that the new president would not be able to bring the Washington political establishment under control, Reagan was remarkably successful in achieving his goals during the first year of his administration.*]

For the first time since America cast him as its 40th President, Ronald Wilson Reagan played Washington last week —and won. His vehicle was a tightly booked five-day tour in which he shook hands and made up with Jimmy Carter, massaged the barons of both parties in both houses of Congress, sipped white wine with the Justices of the Supreme Court, and swept the city's civic and cultural glitterati off their feet simply by paying attention to them. At every stop, his I'm-OK-you're-OK bonhomie seemed to dispel the anxieties of a capital once disposed to view him as Rome must have viewed Alaric at its gates. "He's playing this town

like a bass fiddle," a Carter campaign higher-up said enviously—and Reagan's single insistent theme was that, notwithstanding his anti-Washington rhetoric, he belongs.

The price of admission was not being Jimmy Carter, and Reagan was effusively willing to pay it. Carter made a similar (though shorter) visit to Washington during *his* interregnum in 1976, to similarly warm notices. But his stubborn outsiderliness thereafter shortened his honeymoon, undermined his programs and provided Reagan his working model of how not to do business in an insider's city. Reagan accordingly radiated signals that he will be different—that he will happily visit Capitol Hill, whose leaders Carter dragged to the White House and then billed for breakfast; that he will mix with the lords and ladies of Washington society, toward whom Carter was standoffish; that he means to ride in his Inaugural parade, where Carter ostentatiously walked. "The Presidency as people know it will return," said his man Mike Deaver.

"We'll have a return to normalcy."

'Spectacular'

Reagan's . . . sallies forth from his borrowed government town house on Jackson Place . . . first led up Pennsylvania Avenue to the Hill—an earnest of his intent to work with Congress where Carter too often seemed to work against it. "Government is a partnership," his chief of staff James Baker said. "That's something Jimmy Carter never understood." Reagan swirled through both houses, paid court to the leaders of both parties, lunched with 180 Republicans from both chambers, dined with the new GOP majority in the Senate and granted even Teddy Kennedy an audience. At every stop, he promised to stay in touch, avoid surprises, perhaps to repossess the dusty President's Room in the Senate and "come up and see you folks once in a while." He said he would involve George Bush heavily in dealings with the Hill, but nothing so flatters a Congressional ego as a Presidential

however, is there such agreement between the legislative and judicial bodies. The Supreme Court has not placed strict limits upon the legal authority of the president in either the domestic or the international spheres. It has stated that there is a greater presumption of the validity of discretionary presidential decisions in foreign than in domestic policy. That is, the president has a great deal more leeway to act without consult-

promise to come courting them himself. "That," said Howard Baker, the Senate Majority Leader-in-waiting, "would be spectacular."

Reagan's *gemütlich* way with a wink, a smile and a story sat equally well after Carter's remorselessly serious Square Deal. He set a caucus roomful of Republicans howling with the one about how Nancy called him out of the shower to the phone on election night—and how he stood "dripping wet, with a towel wrapped around me," listening to the President of the United States concede defeat. It has been years since the Hill heard a President laugh at himself; Tip O'Neill misremembered his name soon after their visit, calling him "Nixon," but even he confessed liking Reagan across their continental divide in politics and style. "Don't let all the smiles around here this week kid you," a House Democrat said. "There's going to be some tough hardball played around here next session. But at least he's being a gentleman and shaking hands first—and that is appreciated."

The Smart Set

Reagan was at least as assiduous—and as winning—at paying court to Washington's other regnant power elites. His visit to the Supreme Court was, so far as its historians could determine, the first by any President-elect since Monroe; he sipped a glass of *blanc* with Chief Justice Warren Burger and swapped sporting reminiscences with Justice Byron (Whizzer) White, once a football All-American. And, where Carter and the Capital's smart set had held one another in mutual dislike, Reagan reached out for its friendship at a party of his own at the tony F Street Club and a dinner thrown for him by columnist George F. Will. The combined guest lists exposed him to a mix of dozens of BP's and VIP's from politics and business, the arts and the media, the churches and the local pro sports teams. Most were surprised to be asked—the Democrats to the point of guessing the invitations were a joke. They weren't. "There is only one letter separating 'President' from 'resident,'" Reagan said, toasting Washington on F Street, "and I intend to be both." . . .

Reagan floated through Washington serenely above the hum of rumor; he owed his success there in part precisely to the fact that he has not yet had to decide anything serious or offend anyone important. A guest at one of his hey-look-me-over dinners last week listened to his tales of how he made Sacramento work and was struck by his innocence—by his resemblance, that is, to all the other fledgling presidents who have blown into town promising to work with Congress, tame the bureaucracy, revivify Cabinet government and change the world. "I'm afraid he's in for some surprises," the guest said. "He doesn't realize what kind of bricks he's going to get hit with." But Reagan could hardly be faulted for believing his notices—or their unanimous verdict that he had conquered the capital he ran so long and hard against.

Source: Peter Goldman with Gerald C. Lubenow, Thomas M. DeFrank, Eleanor Clift, Gloria Berger, and Martin Kasindorf, *Newsweek,* December 1, 1980, pp. 30–35. Copyright 1980, by Newsweek, Inc. All rights reserved. Reprinted by permission.

ing Congress when he is engaged in foreign policymaking. This is the formal context within which the president operates. Informal forces may expand or curtail his policymaking discretion.

It is an unusual president, especially in modern times, who will embark upon bold foreign policy actions without attempting to secure a base of political support in the legislature, even though this may not be strictly needed under the terms of the Constitution. President Johnson was proud of the fact that he was able to attain overwhelming congressional approval of the Gulf of Tonkin Resolution, which he cited as authorizing his initiatives in the Vietnam War. Historic foreign policy decisions have more often than not been presented to Congress. The League of Nations Treaty had to be approved by the Senate, which failed to ratify President Woodrow Wilson's dream. It would have been unthinkable at that time, even if it had been possible in terms of international politics, to bypass the Senate by negotiating some form of executive agreement that would have involved the United States in the League of Nations. Of course, where appropriations are necessary to carry out a foreign policy, congressional assent is required, as in the case of the Marshall Plan after World War II.

The Curtiss-Wright Case. Where Congress delegates authority to the president to act as its agent in foreign policymaking, it does not need to place the same kinds of boundaries upon presidential discretion as when it delegates authority for domestic policymaking. The key case here is *United States* v. *Curtiss-Wright Export Corp.* (1936), in which congressional law was challenged on the basis that it delegated to the president power to "legislate" which should properly have been retained by Congress. Under the doctrine of delegation of legislative power, Congress cannot transfer to the executive its lawmaking function. It cannot, presumably, say to the president "go forth and make policy," when this is constitutionally reserved to the legislature itself.

In the *Curtiss-Wright* case, Congress had transferred to the president the authority to establish an embargo on the sale of arms and ammunitions by American companies to countries that were at war in Paraguay and Bolivia. By granting the authority to put an embargo into effect, Congress was really giving the president a legislative function. This is constitutionally proper, provided that Congress retains control over the policy that is finally implemented by the agent (the president in this case) to which it delegates authority. Theoretically this is done by establishing strict legislative "standards" to guide the agent in decision making. The agent cannot go beyond the boundaries set by Congress, which means that the "primary" authority still resides in Congress even though power to shape and implement the policy has been delegated.

In fact, it is virtually impossible for Congress to establish definite enough standards to control the authority which it delegates. In the *Curtiss-Wright* case, the president could proclaim an embargo if he found that such action "may contribute to the reestablishment of peace between those countries." This was to be the guiding standard that would assure that control would remain in the hands of Congress. But in reality its vagueness left complete discretion in the hands of the president. The Court recognized this, but nevertheless held that since foreign policymaking was involved, it was constitutionally proper for the president to be able to exercise such discretion.

In its opinion, the Court cited favorably a report of the Senate Committee on Foreign Relations issued in 1816, which stated in part:

The president is the constitutional representative of the United States with regard to foreign nations. He manages our concerns with foreign nations and must necessarily be most competent to determine when, how, and upon what subjects negotiation may be urged with the greatest prospect of success. For his conduct he is responsible to the Constitution. The Committee considers this responsibility the surest pledge for the faithful discharge of his duty. They think the interference of the Senate in the direction of foreign negotiations is calculated to diminish that responsibility and thereby to impair the best security for the national safety. The nature of transactions with foreign nations, moreover, requires caution and unity of design and their success frequently depends on secrecy and dispatch.[3]

[3] United States v. Curtiss-Wright Export Corp., 299 U.S. 304, 319 (1936).

In upholding the broad grant of authority to the president in the *Curtiss-Wright* case, the Court held that congressional legislation "must often accord to the president a degree of discretion and freedom from statutory restriction which would not be admissible where domestic affairs alone are involved."[4]

[4] Ibid., p. 320.

Interestingly enough, the same Court held that in domestic affairs, strict standards should be established by the legislature to assure that the president would not be able to act in an arbitrary fashion, and beyond the intent of Congress. This Court held key New Deal legislation unconstitutional on this basis, the only time in our history that legislative delegations of authority have been declared unconstitutional. This was done in the cases of *Panama Refining Company* v. *Ryan,* and *Schechter Poultry Corp.* v. *United States,* decided by the Supreme Court in 1935.

The Panama *and* Schechter *Cases.* At issue in both cases was the National Industrial Recovery Act of 1933, which contained sections granting broad authority to the president and subordinate administrative officials appointed by him to establish codes of fair competition within industries. The act contained very few standards to guide the president in the formulation of codes, and the plaintiffs claimed that this constituted too broad a delegation of legislative power. In the *Panama* decision, the Court held one section of the act unconstitutional for its overly broad delegation of legislative authority. In the *Schechter* case, the Court finally declared the entire act unconstitutional, not only on the basis of unwarranted delegation of legislative authority, but also because Congress did not have the power to enact such legislation under the provisions of Article I of the Constitution.

In that portion of the *Schechter* decision concerning the delegation of power, the Court noted:

> . . . Section III of the Recovery Act is without precedent. . . . Instead of prescribing rules of conduct, it authorizes the making of codes to prescribe them. For that legislative undertaking, Section III sets up no standards, aside from the statement of the general aims of rehabilitation, correction, and expansion described in Section I. In view of the scope of that broad declaration, and of the nature of the few restrictions that are imposed, the discretion of the president in approving or prescribing codes, and thus, enacting laws for the government of trade and industry throughout the country, is virtually unfettered. We think that the code-making authority thus conferred is an unconstitutional delegation of power. . . .[5]

[5] Schechter Poultry Corp. v. United States, 295 U.S. 495, 541–42 (1935).

Although *Schechter* established the principle that the president is limited by the Constitution in his capacity to exercise the lawmaking function, which is properly reserved to Congress, the fact that neither before nor after that decision did the Court ever hold another delegation of presidential power to be unconstitutional because of vague standards makes the issue seem academic. During World War II in particular the president was granted extraordinary discretion to "legislate" in the domestic arena to meet emergency conditions.

The Steel Seizure Case. Just as the president is theoretically limited by congressional laws where these have granted jurisdiction to him, where no such statutory delegations exist, he is bound by the Constitution. To what extent does Article II limit his prerogatives? The key case here is the *Steel Seizure* case of 1952.[6] During the Korean War, President Truman, threatened by steel workers with a crippling strike that had not been settled by the Federal Wage Stabilization Board to which the dispute had been referred, issued an executive order directing Secretary of Commerce Sawyer to seize most of the steel mills and operate them. As authority for doing this, President Truman cited his Article II powers as Commander-in-Chief and Chief Executive.

Although Congress had previously passed the Taft-Hartley Act, which established procedures for such emergencies, the president did not invoke its provisions. At that time the Taft-Hartley Act was the major *bête noire* of the Democratic party, and repeal of it was a key plank in the party platforms during the Truman and Eisenhower administrations. While ignoring the Taft-Hartley Act, President Truman, after seizing the mills, did send a message to Congress telling what he had done, and requested supporting legislation or some other proposal to settle the dispute.

After the seizure order was issued, the companies involved immediately sought an injunction in the district court of the District of Columbia. The court issued a preliminary injunction, which, however, was stayed on the same day by the Court of Appeals. On May 3 the Supreme Court, bypassing the Court of Appeals, granted a *writ of certiorari* (a writ to review the record of the lower court), heard oral argument on May 12, and decided the case on June 2—an unusually short period of time for deciding a case. In brief, the Court had to decide whether or not the president was acting within his constitutional power when he seized the steel mills. Since the president did not act on the basis of a statute, the question before the Court was whether or not such authority could be inferred from the Commander-in-Chief and Chief Executive

[6] Youngstown Sheet and Tube Company v. Sawyer, 343 U.S. 579 (1952).

clauses of Article II. The majority of the Court found no such inherent authority in the Constitution, and declared the presidential action to be *ultra vires*. It found that the order to seize the mills was essentially legislative in character and therefore within the jurisdiction of Congress. The Court implied that if a real emergency had existed, perhaps presidential prerogatives would have extended to taking possession of private property if necessary for national defense. But the Court could find no such emergency at the time President Truman took over the steel mills.

Is the Court's decision in the *Steel Seizure* case an isolated example of curtailment of presidential policymaking discretion in the domestic arena, or has it created an important precedent? The four dissenting justices, led by Chief Justice Vinson, pointed out that the decision was not based upon precedent. The dissenters noted that numerous actions similar in implications to the *Steel Seizure* case were taken by Presidents Lincoln, Wilson, and Franklin Roosevelt. For example, in referring to Lincoln, the dissenting opinion stated:

Without declaration of war, President Lincoln took energetic action with the outbreak of the war between the States. He summoned troops and paid them out of the Treasury without appropriation therefor. He proclaimed a naval blockade of the Confederacy and seized the ships violating that blockade. Congress, far from denying the validity of these acts, gave them express approval. The most striking action of President Lincoln was the Emancipation Proclamation, issued in aid of the successful prosecution of the war between the States, but wholly without statutory authority.
. . . President Lincoln without statutory authority directed the seizure of rail and telegraph lines leading to Washington.[7]

Although later affirmed by Congress, these actions of President Lincoln, as well as other actions in later years of Presidents Wilson and Roosevelt, were *faits accomplis* in every case. Presidential actions before the *Steel Seizure* case suggest that there is no constitutional impediment to the exercise of arbitrary presidential power during times of recognized crisis.

It has been argued that presidential actions in times of emergency require public and congressional approval to be upheld. John P. Roche, writing shortly after the *Steel Seizure* case, sanguinely stated that:

---

[7] Ibid., p. 685.

The danger of unconstitutional presidential dictatorship, based on vigorous exercise of domestic prerogative, seems virtually nonexistent. In real terms, Congress and the public must agree with presidential emergency actions if they are to be effective. The silences of American constitutional history lend strong support to this proposition for, with the exception of the seizure of the steel industry, there has not been one single instance of the president actually taking prerogative action in a domestic crisis against the wishes of Congress.[8]

[8] John P. Roche, "Executive Power in Domestic Emergency: The Quest for Prerogative," *Western Political Science Quarterly* 5 (December 1952): 592–618.

Endorsement by Congress does not necessarily mean that the wishes of the legislature are being followed, but only that a majority of legislators recognize the impracticality and undesirability of overruling the president once he has made his decision in a crisis situation. An entirely different legislative action might occur if the president sought congressional approval in advance. Presidential decisions carry their own momentum, difficult to overcome once put into motion.

Political Checks on the President. If Congress and the electorate are stirred up enough to oppose the president in an important decision-making area, then ultimately they may act together as a check upon the course of presidential decisions. The difficulties of obtaining congressional majorities and marshalling meaningful public opinion make it very unlikely that such a check would be invoked except under the most extreme circumstances. For example, the adverse public reaction to U.S. involvement in Vietnam, once the true import of the war was brought home to the American people, played an important role in President Johnson's decision to step down in 1968. Ultimately, public opinion forced the decision of President Nixon to withdraw our armed forces from Vietnam.

But adverse reaction did not occur in the early stages of escalation, when President Johnson was left with a virtually free hand to embark upon what turned out to be a disastrous policy. The Gulf of Tonkin Resolution, passed by an overwhelming vote in Congress in 1964 after North Vietnamese had attacked American destroyers off the coast of North Vietnam, reflected congressional acquiescence in at least retaliatory strikes against the North Vietnamese. At that time Congress and the people were fully behind President Johnson, not realizing that major plans for escalation were being laid.

Nor was Congress aware that its Gulf of Tonkin Resolution would be used later as a justification for a full-scale war.

Every political system must have a mechanism that provides for rapid policymaking to meet crisis situations. The presidency is the best vehicle for this in our system, although both the bureaucracy and the Supreme Court as well as Congress have been known in extreme situations to act with dispatch to meet crises. It took Congress only a few hours to declare war upon the recommendation of the president in 1941 after the attack on Pearl Harbor. But such situations are rare for Congress, which is bogged down in cumbersome parliamentary maneuvers and a disjointed committee system.

Administrative agencies often play it safe rather than take decisive action, rendering the bureaucracy less efficient than the president in providing for the necessary decisions in emergencies. The president might also wish to avoid difficult situations arising from bold crisis decisions, but as President Truman remarked: "The buck stops here." The president has no alternative but to face up to the responsibilities that inevitably are placed upon his shoulders. Every other branch of the government can more readily avoid responsibility for immediate action.

In a constitutional democracy the necessity for strong executive leadership at times poses dilemmas for the maintenance of the principles of the constitutional system. Our government is supposed to be limited, and based upon popular representation in the policymaking process. Insofar as the president is able to take independent action, without consultation of Congress and outside of the jurisdiction of the Supreme Court, limited and democratic government is diminished. Clinton Rossiter pointed out in 1948:

That constitutional dictatorship does have a future in the United States is hardly a matter for discussion. Dismal and distressing as the prospect may be, it seems probable that in the years to come, the American people will be faced with more rather than fewer national emergencies. . . . [T]he continuing tensions of a world of sovereign nations and the irrepressible economic convulsions of the twentieth century . . . have made it plain that the Second World War was not to be the last but only the latest of the American Republic's great national crises. . . .

That this nation's present-day institutions and procedures of emergency government present considerable room for improvement seems equally beyond dispute.[9]

Rossiter felt that the instruments of "constitutional dictatorship," particularly the broad delegation of powers from Congress to the presidency and administrative agencies, should be constructed to render the system politically responsible. Dates should be set in advance for the termination of delegated power. Moreover, every possible measure should be taken to make certain that the legislature and not the president determines the extent of authority to be exercised during the crisis. Rossiter particularly emphasized that: "the decision to institute a constitutional dictatorship should never be in the hands of the man or men who will constitute the dictator."[10]

The difficulty in the American constitutional system is that although presidents can be checked after they exercise their independent constitutional prerogatives under Article II, the prerogative decisions that they make initially can set the course of future events. Virtual automatic approval by Congress and the Supreme Court for prerogative actions is often assured. When Rossiter speaks of constitutional dictatorships he is referring to relatively long time spans, during which governmental authority is centralized in the hands of the Chief Executive and the bureaucracy. But single presidential prerogative actions can have drastic consequences for the political system, particularly when they lead to involvement in a major war. The residual powers of the constitutional dictatorship reside in many important areas in the hands of the president, and at any given time he can make an independent decision having far-reaching consequences. The political checks upon the president under such circumstances are not sufficient to curb his constitutional powers.

Although the president may sometimes become for a while a "constitutional dictator," there is little possibility that such a condition will last for long, or that the political system in itself could ever become a dictatorship. This would require the elimination of all other bases of independent political power, which is clearly an impossibility. The diverse forces within the nation, the structured conflict designed by the framers of the Constitution among the branches of the government, and the

[9] Clinton Rossiter, *Constitutional Dictatorship* (New York: Harcourt Brace Jovanovich, 1963), pp. 306–7. This book was first published by the Princeton University Press in 1948.

[10] Ibid., p. 299.

limitation of the president's term all work together to prevent any permanent coalescence of power in the hands of the president. Ironically, these factors make it all the more imperative to have a presidency capable of taking vigorous and direct action in crisis situations.

Some of the most disturbing aspects of political power within our system do not stem from the constitutional prerogatives of the president, but from coalitions of administrative agencies, congressional committees and other parts of the government with private interest groups which form closed policy subsystems, or what were described in Chapter 5 as "iron triangles." The "military-industrial complex" is one example of such a policy sphere. President Eisenhower warned against the domination of military and industrial elites in the policy process, and during his administration he stood firmly against overzealous impingement of military leaders on the formulation of public policy.

There are many policy subsystems apart from the military-industrial complex. In such areas as agriculture, business regulation, and health, policy is outside of the purview of the president and within the hands of a relatively narrow set of interests, both governmental and private. A strong presidency is a countervailing force to these interest group clusters. But the president is anything but a "constitutional dictator" when he confronts the almost impossible task of curbing the power of the groups within these specialized subsystems. There are those who, far from decrying the arbitrary powers of the president, feel that the office should be strengthened to bring some unity and overall planning to the amorphous forces of policymaking. Presidents from Theodore Roosevelt and William Howard Taft in the first decade of the twentieth century to Carter and Reagan have sought to establish a more efficient and accountable bureaucracy under the direct control of the White House. But the bureaucracy is a kingpin in the iron triangle, which has made presidential efforts to control it less than successful.

Statutory Limits on the President

Just as the Constitution grants and limits powers to the president, Congress by statute may grant broad delegations of authority to the president, or it may decide to limit him strictly. One of the major limitations upon the legal authority of the president comes from congressional restrictions in statutory law. Frequently Congress grants independent authority to administrative agencies to formulate policy, and at the same time limits presidential supervision over the agencies. In some cases Congress establishes agencies on an independent basis, outside of the president's jurisdiction. These independent agencies have limited accountability to the White House. The independent regulatory commissions, for example, are not accountable to the president for their day to day operations, or for their decisions. One exception is the awarding of international air routes by the Civil Aeronautics Board which, because of the international implications, is subject by statute to presidential veto. Although the president appoints the commissioners of the independent regulatory agencies, by and with the advice and consent of the Senate, it is difficult for him to remove them during their fixed terms of office. Conditions of removal are established by statute, and generally require a demonstration of malfeasance in office before removal can be upheld. The president's appointment power to these agencies, however, is significant in that he can stack them with men favoring his point of view. Moreover, he does have the power to appoint the chairmen of all regulatory agencies except the Interstate Commerce Commission.

Outside of the area of independent regulatory agencies, Congress frequently grants independent powers to parts of the executive departments, which in the conduct of their broader activities are under presidential supervision. Those who feel that a strong presidency is vital to the preservation of the Republic seek to eliminate such congressional undermining of presidential authority within the bureaucracy. The President's Committee on Administrative Management in 1937 and the Hoover Commission of 1949 strongly recommended that Congress remove the numerous legal limits upon the president's authority over the administrative branch.

Whether the president is the recipient of broad congressional and constitutional delegations of authority, or whether his powers are legally curtailed, his real power does not depend solely upon these formal definitions of the office.

It is determined by a number of informal factors that affect his power of persuasion over others. For instance, the president has complete legal authority over the Army Corps of Engineers, but traditionally because of the independent political constituency of the Corps, and its power base in Congress, the president has not been able to turn his legal authority into political power.

The president can get others to move for him when he holds the balance of political power within the constituency of the persons involved. His party in Congress will heed his requests if the disparate membership of the legislative party considers it to be in their collective interest to support the White House. Bureaucrats will heed the president if he is important to them for present or future trade-offs.

Theodore C. Sorensen has pointed out that the president is free to make a decision only:

1. within the limits of permissibility; 2. within the limits of available resources; 3. within the limits of available time; 4. within the limits of previous commitments; and 5. within the limits of available information.[11]

[11] Theodore C. Sorensen, *Decision Making in the White House* (New York: Columbia University Press, 1963), p. 23.

The "limits of permissibility" refer to legal and constitutional restraints upon the president, and in the foreign area upon the acceptance of other nations where that is required to put a presidential decision into effect. A president, for example, cannot order other nations into war to support the United States unless they agree to become part of a collective effort, as was the case in the Korean War after United Nations involvement.

Although the context of the presidency points up the limitations upon the policymaking powers of the office, these powers pertain to the ability of the president to make effective decisions—what might loosely be called "good" decisions in terms of political realities—rather than the capacity of the office to make decisions at all. That is, the president is perfectly free to make whatever decisions he wants, but he may not see them implemented or, if they are put into effect, achieving the result that he originally intended. President Johnson was perfectly capable of escalating the Vietnam War, since the military went along with him, and he received the initial backing of Congress. He had all the constitutional and statutory authority he needed to wage the war. However, he was unable to control the series of events that occurred as a result of his decision. He could not control the government of South Vietnam, nor did his military policy eliminate the Viet Cong or bring North Vietnam to heel. His policy failed, not for lack of authority, but because he attempted to extend his power beyond his reach.

In the domestic sphere, presidents can and have ordered administrative agencies to implement policies only to see their orders vanish in the bureaucratic maze. The limits upon the presidency pertain not to decision making per se, but to effective and responsible decision making. The responsibilities that have been placed upon the office demand that the president not waste his time tilting at windmills, but that he use whatever resources are at his command to perform adequately.

What is "adequate performance" in the White House? An important part of the context within which the president must function is the expectations that people have concerning the responsibilities of the office. Virtually every group that is within the constituency of the president looks to the White House at one time or another for positive action, but this has not always been true. In the early days of the Republic, many people viewed the potential power of the presidency with caution, and men such as Thomas Jefferson (before he became president) viewed with alarm the possibility of an overly vigorous executive. Although the Constitution emerged as a Hamiltonian document, during the Constitutional Convention serious consideration was given to making the presidency a potentially weaker branch of the government. This would have resulted, for example, from proposals to make the executive dependent upon the election of the legislature.

Originally, the narrow electoral constituency of the president reduced popular expectations concerning the office, and gave to the president far less of a political base upon which to operate. Broadening the base of popular involvement in presidential elections did not immediately increase the prestige of the office; election statistics indicate that voter turnout in early presidential elections was less than half of that in con-

Growth of Presidential Responsibilities

gressional and gubernatorial elections. But the democratization of the office provided an important base for the expansion of presidential prerogatives, as well as inputs for an expanded policymaking role for the White House.

The modern presidency resulted from the culmination of many factors that made it evident that a strong presidency is necessary in order for the political system to survive. Repeated crises, and vigorous presidential responses to them, established precedents for a strong executive. Time and time again it became evident that in certain kinds of crisis situations no other branch of the government was capable of providing the necessary political response. The present day responsibilities of the presidency have grown out of the inadequacies of other parts of the government in certain areas of public policymaking. In particular, the dominant role of the president in foreign and military affairs is based on a general recognition that the dispatch and secrecy necessary for the proper conduct of policymaking in these areas reside only in the president.

The most elaborate list of responsibilities assigned to the presidency is that enumerated by Clinton Rossiter in *The American Presidency*.[12] The jobs that Rossiter attributed to the presidency are truly imposing, and certainly could not possibly be carried out by one man acting alone. Under the Constitution, the president is Chief of State; that is, he must exercise the ceremonial functions of the government. Article II makes the president Chief Legislator and Chief Executive. Also stemming in part from Article II, the president is Chief Diplomat. He is Commander-in-Chief, a provision put into Article II to ensure civilian supremacy over the military.

Apart from these constitutional roles, the presidency has

[12] Clinton Rossiter, *The American Presidency*, 2nd ed. (New York: Harcourt Brace Jovanovich, 1960).

Table 6.1
Presidential Responsibilities

Constitutional	By Custom and Tradition
Chief of state	Chief of party
Chief executive	Manager of prosperity
Commander-in-chief	Voice of the people
Chief diplomat	
May initiate legislation	

The Presidency

assumed a number of other responsibilities that have developed as events have unfolded. For example, he is considered to be responsible for the state of the economy, making him "manager of prosperity." He is the head of his political party, reflecting the deep involvement of the presidency in politics. His party role requires that he hold together the national party organization, and do everything that he can to ensure the election of party members. As a result of the cold war that ensued after World War II, the president has become the leader of the free nations of the world, because of the predominant position of the United States among non-Communist countries. The president is expected to be the voice of the people, to express the feelings of the nation at appropriate times. For example, President Franklin D. Roosevelt voiced the anger of the American people after the attack on Pearl Harbor in 1941. After natural disasters, people look to the president to aid them by declaring a state of emergency and releasing federal funds for reconstruction (Table 6.1).

Although people expect the president to perform these various policymaking roles, he does not necessarily have the power to carry them out. There is often a gap between expectations and reality, which may cause disillusionment with the president and with government itself. The president can perform virtually none of these roles without the cooperation of coordinate branches of the government, particularly the bureaucracy.

Because of the multiple responsibilities of the presidency, the modern conception of the office is that effectiveness requires strength, vigor, and a positive approach on the part of the incumbent. People expect leadership in their president. Good presidents use the office to its fullest capacity and capabilities. They employ the authority of the office in combination with its political power to initiate and advance important legislation, to attempt to control the bureaucracy, and to take necessary action to deal with foreign and domestic problems. People agree now more than at the time it was written with Alexander Hamilton's statement in *The Federalist* (70):

Need for Presidential Leadership

Energy in the executive is a leading character in the definition of good government. It is essential to the protection of the community against foreign attacks; it is not less essential to the study of administration of the laws, to the protection of property against those irregular and high-handed combinations, which sometimes interrupt the ordinary course of justice, to the security of liberty against the enterprises and assaults of ambition, of faction, and of anarchy.

. . . A feeble executive implies a feeble execution of government. A feeble execution is but another phrase for a bad execution; and a government ill-executed, whatever it may be in theory, must be in practice a bad government.

Energy in the executive must be directed for "good," not "bad" ends. A major dilemma of the modern presidency is how to balance the need for independent action with the maintenance of responsible presidential decision making. Perhaps too many policymaking responsibilities have been placed on the shoulders of the president. The great visibility of the White House makes it impossible for presidents to shift the burden of decision making to others, as Congress does when it delegates authority to the White House or the bureaucracy.

Presidents tend to be blamed for those things that go wrong during their administrations. But many of the most important policy decisions that are made in those areas commonly attributed to the presidency are made by parts of the government outside of the White House. Realistic expectations concerning the policy role of the president would not expect him to be able to bring about single-handedly significant shifts in the course of public policy. The limits upon the office are too great. Most people's expectations of what the president is able to accomplish are too high. A reevaluation of what constitutes "proper" performance in the White House should put less emphasis upon the policy roles of the president and more upon his general leadership posture and usefulness to those other parts of the government that are deeply involved in the formulation of policy, particularly the bureaucracy. And where the president is capable of policy leadership, as in foreign and military affairs, the possibility of personal decision making should be avoided at all costs, because this will mean that the nature of the decision will depend upon the character, particularly the emotional makeup, of the man who occupies the office. A rational decision-making process should be used, where various viewpoints are weighed.

The confusing and complex context of the presidency cannot help but befuddle new occupants of the office. The president finds that numerous and often conflicting responsibilities have been placed on his shoulders, but he does not necessarily have the power to meet his obligations successfully. Each man brings with him his own personal equipment, which may or may not make a strong imprint upon the office.

Although the presidency is an institution, composed of numerous staff aides in the Executive Office of the President, including the White House staff and the Office of Management and Budget, there is little doubt that presidential character has a considerable impact upon the performance of the office.[13] Presidential character may have a profound effect not only upon the policies, but also upon the responsibilities of the White House that do not directly pertain to policymaking. Presidential style, the way the president appears to the people, and moral leadership are deeply affected by presidential character. These attributes of the presidency have an important indirect effect on policymaking.

James Barber has listed recurrent themes in American political culture that set the stage for presidential action and deeply influence the way in which presidents perceive their responsibilities.

Americans vastly overrate the president's power—and they are likely to continue to do so. The logic of that feeling is clear enough: the president is at the top and therefore he must be able to dominate those below him. The psychology is even more complicated. The whole popular ethic of struggle, the onward and upward, fight-today-to-win-tomorrow spirit gets played out vicariously as people watch their president. The president should be working, trying, striving forward—living out of his life what makes life meaningful for the citizen at work. Life is tough, life is earnest. A tough, earnest president symbolizes and represents that theme, shows by the thrust of his deeds that the fight is worth it after all. Will he stand up to his—and our—enemies, or will he collapse? Has he the guts to endure the heat in the kitchen? Will he (will he please) play out for us the drama that leads through suffering to salvation?

To a character attuned to power, this popular theme then can

Effects of the Political Culture upon Presidential Policymaking

[13] See James D. Barber, *The Presidential Character* (Englewood Cliffs, N.J.: Prentice-Hall, 1972).

[14] Ibid., p. 446.

convey a heavy message . . . for Wilson, Hoover, Johnson, and Nixon, and for active-negative presidents in the future, the temptation to stand and fight receives wide support from the culture.[14]

Barber defines "active-negative" presidents as those who bring a Protestant ethic attitude to the office and devote a great deal of energy to their tasks, but because of inner struggles demanding perfection a great deal of the energy is misdirected. To these kinds of men the tasks of the presidency are painful, not enjoyable. This belief in the need to do what is right, regardless of how painful it is, is reflected in the following passage from President Johnson's memoirs:

Every president must act on problems as they come to him. He must search out the best information available. He can seek the counsel of men whose wisdom and experience and judgment he values. But in the end, the president must decide, and he must do so on the basis of his judgment of what is best—for his nation and for the world. Throughout these years of crucial decisions I was sustained by the memory of my predecessors who had also borne the most painful duty of a president—to lead our country in a time of war. I recalled often the words of one of these men, Woodrow Wilson, who in the dark days of 1917 said: "it is a fearful thing to lead this great peaceful people into war . . . but the right is more precious than peace."[15]

[15] Lyndon B. Johnson, *The Vantage Point* (New York: Holt, Rinehart and Winston, 1971), p. 531.

Another attribute of the political culture that Barber suggests is important is people's need for affection, and their focus upon politicians and particularly the president as a charismatic and affectionate leader. This constant stroking of the president can bolster his self-image and may lead either to striving for greater and greater power, or simply to passive and pleasant acceptance. The fact that people seek in the presidency both a friend and a charismatic leader affects the style of presidents, who therefore seek to strike the right pose to fulfill the image that the public has of them and they of themselves. This part of the political culture, by concentrating upon presidential style, tends to deemphasize the policy role of the president.

Another important factor in the political culture, according to Barber, is that "in our culture the religious-monarchical focus of the presidency—a tendency to see the office as sort of divine-right kingship—gets emphasized . . . in a quest for legitimacy."[16] To operate in a legitimate fashion, presidents

[16] Barber, *The Presidential Character*, pp. 450–51.

must not go too far in attempting to change the rules of the game of the political system. Legitimacy can also be sullied by any demeaning of the "image of the president as dignified, episcopal, plain and clean in character. Part of the public mind always realizes that the president is only a man, with all man's normal ability to moral error; part wants to deny that, to foist on the president a priestliness setting him above the congregation."[17]

[17] Ibid., p. 451.

After the Democratic Convention of 1972, when vice-presidential candidate Thomas Eagleton of Missouri revealed that between 1960 and 1966 he had been hospitalized three times for nervous exhaustion and fatigue, pressure was immediately put upon him by politicians and influential newspapers to step down because of what they felt would inevitably be an adverse public reaction. Actually, public opinion polls revealed a great deal of sympathy for Senator Eagleton, and although a certain amount of voter-switching because of the relevation of his "mental illness" was indicated, there was no immediate strong indication of a large-scale desertion of the party because he was on the ticket. Nevertheless, the reaction of Democratic leaders and influential newspapers reflected the idea that the presidency might be "demeaned" by such a man, and that any person with such a past history might not be capable of fulfilling the responsibilities of the office. The real reason that Senator Eagleton was asked to step down was that he did not fit the classical image of the president as a man invulnerable to ordinary afflictions. The "legitimacy" of the office might be reduced if he were to occupy it.

Presidential policymaking is affected when presidents in office are highly aware of the need to maintain the image of the office as a legitimate, almost nonpolitical institution. Examples of presidents straying from this rule occurred during the New Deal administration, when Franklin Roosevelt attempted to "pack" the Supreme Court by pressing Congress to pass a law that would have given him the authority to appoint a new justice for every justice over seventy years of age. This was widely attacked in the press as being an "unconstitutional" plan, entirely inappropriate for the president. President Truman's seizure of the steel mills in 1952 invoked a similar, if not so intense, response. And, as the Vietnam War pressed on, increasing criticism was directed at Presidents Johnson and Nixon for abusing the authority of the president as Commander-in-Chief by directing our military forces into inappropriate foreign engagements. Finally, perhaps the most widely cited abuse of the presidency in recent decades was President Nixon's attempt to use the powers of the office to cover up the Watergate affair.

The image of the president as High Priest of the political system raises support for the White House among many elements of the population, because of reverence for the institution and the man who occupies it. A king is criticized if he behaves in an un-kingly way, but at the same time, being king, he has greater latitude of behavior than ordinary individuals. One possible result of the Watergate scandals may be to destroy in large part the reverence that Americans have traditionally held for the presidency. Clearly the priestly character of the office did not rub off on President Nixon, when, after firing special Watergate prosecutor Archibald Cox, approximately 50 percent of the electorate favored impeaching him. It may take many years for the sullied image that Watergate has given to the White House to wear off. President Ford did help to make the nation, as his campaign slogan proclaimed, "proud again." Jimmy Carter restored integrity to the White House. Ronald Reagan revived the dignity of the office, and brought to it a sense of humor that had been so sadly lacking in the administrations following John Kennedy's.

THE PRESIDENCY IN OPERATION

What should be the role of the president in policymaking? Clearly the office cannot be expected to meet single-handedly all of the responsibilities that have been given to it. As long as the political system remains highly fragmented, the presidency is going to stand out symbolically as the focal point of action. There seems to be little question of whether or not the president should be powerful, at least in the domestic realm. From the President's Committee on Administrative Management in 1937 to the present, presidential commissions and task forces have recommended that the White House be given vastly increased staff assistance to meet presidential responsibilities. "The president needs help" has been the repeated theme of these commissions.

On the basis of recommendations of the president's Committee on Administrative Management, the Executive Office of the President was created in 1939 to assist the president in developing policy, and in dealing with his multiple administrative responsibilities. (See Figure 6.3.) The Office of Management and Budget, originally the Bureau of the Budget, is the key component in the Executive Office. It is responsible for sifting the numerous legislative and budgetary proposals that come from administrative agencies before they go to Congress.

Before the Bureau of the Budget was originally given this responsibility, it was common practice for administrative agencies to go directly to Congress to recommend legislation and budgets dealing with matters under their jurisdiction. Today, OMB not only carefully reviews the legislative proposals coming from the bureaucracy, but also holds tight reins on the budgetary proposals of the agencies. No agency can legally submit a budget proposal to the legislature without first going through OMB.

It is difficult to say to what extent OMB really dominates the bureaucracy. Administrative agencies are often more capable of dominating the president and OMB than vice-versa, due to the agencies' political power and expertise in the policymaking areas with which they deal. Specialization and political power are characteristics of administrative agencies. To deal with the bureaucracy, the president and his staff must be able to counterbalance these forces by developing independent political power and expert knowledge. This is a very difficult task, because expert knowledge in many policymaking areas is virtually monopolized by specialists in the bureaucracy and outside interests groups. To get advice that is "independent" of experts in the field is impossible by definition.

Regardless of the existence of procedural formalities requiring the channeling of legislative and budgetary proposals

Presidential Staff and the Executive Office

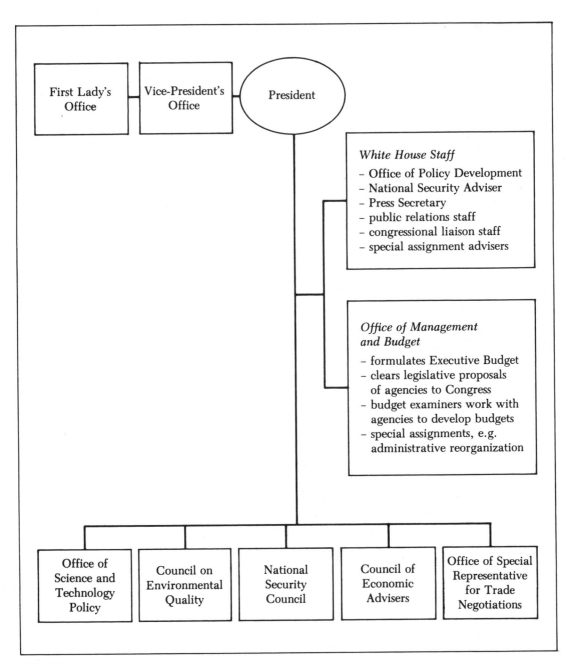

FIGURE 6.3
The Executive Office of the President.

through OMB, the major source of OMB inputs remains the bureaucracy. OMB is often able to do nothing more than coordinate the many complex proposals coming to it. Where the president knows his own mind, and has a definite policy that he wishes to see carried out, OMB can be his agent; but in the absence of clear presidential viewpoints, OMB is left alone in its confrontations with the bureaucracy.

It is vitally important for the president to be able to exercise some measure of control over the bureaucracy if he is to have any effect upon public policy, because it is within administrative agencies that policies are formulated and carried out. Merely coordinating the policymaking activities of agencies does not put the president in an ascendant position. In practice, the president is only one part of the governmental system, and must enter what is often unequal combat in attempting to persuade other branches, including the bureaucracy, to follow his wishes.

The president's staff contains several other agencies besides OMB. The White House office consists of the personal staff of the president, upon whom the president can rely to any degree that he sees fit, just as he can use any components of the Executive Office as he wishes. Presidents from Eisenhower to Reagan have relied a great deal upon their personal staff, in some cases to the exclusion of other parts of the Executive Office as well as the cabinet. President Nixon not only relied upon his personal staff, but delegated substantial decision-making powers to them. Former White House aides John Ehrlichman and H. R. Haldeman ruthlessly wielded power in the name of the president. Watergate was partially a result of the president's failure to oversee his personal staff operation.

In the foreign policy area, Henry Kissinger totally dominated foreign policymaking in his capacity as advisor to the president. Again, President Nixon was using Kissinger not solely as an advisor but as a person to whom he delegated considerable policymaking responsibilities. After Kissinger became secretary of state, he continued to be foreign policy advisor to the president, resulting in a great deal more coordination between State and the White House than had previously existed.

Kissinger operated in conjunction with the National Security Council, created by the National Security Act of 1947. This Council, consisting of the president, vice-president, secretary of state, secretary of defense, and director of the Office of Emergency Preparedness is convened by the president when he feels that it can give him useful advice concerning foreign and military policy matters. In fact, during critical foreign policy crises the president convenes whatever group of advisors he feels most appropriate, which may or may not include all of the members of the National Security Council. In other words, he does not rely upon the formal mechanism of the National Security Council for foreign policy advice.

The Council of Economic Advisors was established in 1946 to aid the president in planning economic policy. This three-member council issues a yearly economic report to the president and the Congress assessing the state of the economy. The Joint Economic Committee of Congress works with the council to coordinate White House and Capitol Hill efforts in economic planning. The placement of the council in the Executive office of the president reflected a recognition of the important presidential responsibility to be "manager of prosperity." That presidential role was assumed by the White House during Franklin Roosevelt's administration. Roosevelt and his brain trust accepted Keynesian economics, which proclaimed that the government should have a central role in managing prosperity. While the supply-side economics of the Reagan administration rejects the Keynesian view, and emphasizes the role of free enterprise and individual initiative in bringing about economic prosperity, there is little doubt that it is the White House and not the private sector that is blamed if unemployment, inflation, and low productivity continue to plague the economy.[18]

Other agencies with the Executive Office that assist the president include the Office of Science and Technology Policy, the Council on Environmental Quality, the Intelligence Oversight Board, and the Office of the Special Representative for Trade Negotiations. These components of the Executive Office reflect presidential responsibilities for the policy areas they cover. The Office of Science and Technology Policy, for example, advises the president on science policy, and has direct ties to the scientific community which is largely responsible

[18] Supply-side economics reflects the assumption that individual and corporate tax reductions will stimulate the supply of goods by providing an incentive for investment and productivity. The Keynesian school, on the other hand, supports tax reduction when an increase in demand is deemed desirable to raise the level of economic activity. Keynesians, in contrast to advocates of supply-side economics, support a far greater role for the government in the stimulation of economic activity through government expenditures.

for its existence. The Council on Environmental Quality, created by the National Environmental Policy Act of 1969, gives the president direct responsibilities in environmental policymaking. The president's pivotal role in trade negotiations is performed with the assistance of his special representative in that area.

Since the creation of the Executive Office in 1939, the White House staff and OMB (formerly the Bureau of the Budget) have remained its most important components. The White House staff in particular has grown to become one of the largest and most important parts of the office. Presidential promises to reduce the size of the federal bureaucracy, a goal that has never been achieved, have never been seriously applied to the presidential bureaucracy—the Executive Office. Republican as well as Democratic presidents have seen in their personal staff and agencies of the Executive Office a necessary and important underpinning of the power of the White House. In the political battles of the Capitol, the presidential bureacracy is often pitted against the regular bureaucracy and the narrow iron triangles of congressional committees, agencies, and pressure groups.

The White House staff is considered by the president to be his most loyal coterie of advisors. He personally appoints many members of the staff, and they represent him directly in dealing with other parts of the presidential bureaucracy, the cabinet, administrative agencies, and Capitol Hill. Presidents organize their White House staffs differently, but the functions performed by the staff have remained generally the same from one administration to another. The White House staff consists of a press office that handles daily negotiations with an often aggressive, cynical, and always probing White House press corps. The daily press briefings supply much of the material on the White House for the nightly news programs and the front pages of newspapers throughout the country. While presidents often view the press with suspicion, they know that good press relations are an absolutely essential ingredient of successful politics.

The White House staff always contains one or two persons who are particularly close to the president, giving him political advice and sometimes acting in his name in relations with other parts of the government and the private sector. During the Carter administration, White House Chief of Staff Hamilton Jordan was the president's closest advisor in domestic policy. The personal friendship between the two men buttressed Jordan's power within and without the presidential bureaucracy. In the Reagan administration, presidential counsel Edwin Meese III, aided by White House Chief of Staff James A. Baker III, emerged in the first year of the administration as the president's spokesmen.

In addition to the press secretary and the president's close personal advisors, the White House staff consists of a national security advisor (who may or may not be close to the president) and a domestic policy group. Moreover, there is an extensive staff to deal with congressional liaison.

Regardless of how the White House staff is organized, it has clearly become the dominant force in the Executive Office. President Carter, who ran on a promise that he would reduce the size of the federal bureaucracy and the Executive Office as well, actually increased his staff from that of Presidents Nixon and Ford. Regardless of presidential proclamations—usually before or immediately after the election and during the first months of new administrations—that "cabinet government" will be practiced, it is the presidential bureaucracy and especially the White House staff that overshadows the cabinet. As presidential administrations progress, the cabinet tends to split into individual fiefdoms, with cabinet secretaries striving to strengthen and solidify their own power, sometimes *against* the White House. Presidents tend to view the federal bureaucracy with suspicion and often distrust, causing them to buttress the numbers and the powers of their own personal bureaucracy. Republican Presidents especially have a difficult time with the largely Democratic career bureaucracy. President Nixon expanded the Executive Office more than any president had before him. President Ford added to the number of aides in the White House, and although President Reagan again promised cabinet government, it seems likely that he too will go the way of his predecessors in relying increasingly upon the support of the White House staff and other components of the Executive Office.

The presidency has become institutionalized in the Executive Office. Members of both the president's personal staff and the regular agencies of the Executive Office often act in the president's name to become in effect an invisible presidency—one that may not always act in the best interests of the president or the country. Although the press keeps an eagle eye on what goes on within the confines of the White House and the presidential bureaucracy, it is not always possible to assure accountability of the men and women who work for the president, who often can and do act on their own initiatives.

The White House staff in particular is an arena of power in which the players sometimes go to any lengths to elevate their personal status. The atmosphere of the White House tends to breed, as one notorious former aide wrote, "blind ambition."[19] George Reedy, a particularly astute political observer with long Washington experience on Capitol Hill and in the Johnson White House, has written: "Below the President is a mass of intrigue, posturing, strutting, cringing, and pious 'commitment' to irrelevant windbaggery. It is designed as the perfect setting for the conspiracy of mediocrity—that all too frequently successful collection of the untalented, the unpassionate, and the insincere seeking to convince the public that it is brilliant, compassionate, and dedicated."[20] Reedy concluded that the White House is and has always been "an ideal cloak for intrigue, pomposity, and ambition."[21]

While members of the president's staff can exercise a great deal of power on their own, ultimately they are responsible to the president when he makes his wishes clear. Perhaps the greatest problem of the institutionalized and bureaucratic presidency is not the exercise of independent power by staff members, but their sycophancy in relation to the president himself. The president needs good and independent advice, which means staff members that will tell him if in their view he is embarking upon the wrong course of action. But whether presidential staffs are the "best and the brightest," or merely mediocre, they consistently seem unable in the environment of the White House to criticize a president who is bent upon a particular course of action. "For a thousand days I would serve as counsel to the President," wrote John Dean about the Nixon administration, and "I soon learned that to make my

[19] For an account of an admittedly extreme situation, but one which is nevertheless highly instructive, see John Dean, *Blind Ambition* (New York: Simon and Schuster, 1976).

[20] George E. Reedy, *The Twilight of the Presidency* (New York: New American Library, 1971), p. xiv.

[21] Ibid.

way upward, into a position of confidence and influence, I had to travel downward through factional power plays, corruption, and finally outright crimes. Although I would be rewarded for diligence, true advancement would come from doing those things which built a common bond of trust—or guilt—between me and my superiors. In the Nixon White House, these upward and downward paths diverged, yet joined, like prongs of a tuning fork pitched to a note of expediency. Slowly, steadily, I would climb toward the moral abyss of the president's inner circle until I finally fell into it, thinking I had made it to the top just as I began to realize I had actually touched bottom."[22] Thomas E. Cronin writes, "Can a lieutenant vigorously engaged in implementing the presidential will admit to the possibility that what the president wants is wrong or not working? Yet a president is increasingly dependent on the judgment of these same staff members, since he seldom sees some of his cabinet members."[23] Cabinet secretaries, too, if they are close to the president, may find it difficult to challenge what they consider to be a wrong course of action. It was not until the waning days of the Johnson administration that Secretary of Defense Robert McNamara began to dissent from the president's stubborn pursuit of the Vietnam War, only to find himself suddenly appointed head of the World Bank. Johnson appointed Clark Clifford to become secretary of defense in the expectation that he would support the Vietnam War, only to find Clifford telling him that the war could not be won. The government needs more men like Clark Clifford, but regrettably they are rarely to be found in the political arena.

[22] John Dean, *Blind Ambition,* p. 21.

[23] Thomas E. Cronin, "The Swelling of the Presidency: Can Anyone Reverse the Tide?" reprinted in *American Government: Readings and Cases,* ed. Peter Woll (Boston: Little, Brown and Co., 1981), p. 355.

The Presidency as an Instrument of Policy Innovation

In most areas of public policy the president cannot significantly innovate unless there is substantial support both within and without the government for such action. Broadly based forces of change focus upon the presidency. This is what led to the election of President Roosevelt in 1932. It is when the presidency is riding the crest of a wave of change, such as occurs after critical elections in which major shifts take place in voter alignments from one party to the other, that the White House can be the catalyst for new directions in public policy. Critical elections do not occur because large parts of the public have specific ideas of policies they want to see put into effect, but because voters feel that something has to be done which is different from the policies the party in power has supported.

The electorate was discontented, to say the least, in 1932 because of the Depression, and naturally blamed the inaction of President Hoover. A variety of proposals were made to Hoover by experts inside and outside government as to how he might meet the crisis of the Depression, but those who were unemployed and marching in the streets did not know of these, nor did they have specific policy recommendations of their own. They only wanted to see Hoover out, and someone—anyone—in to replace him. At such times the president must offer leadership to shape new programs, although this is no guarantee that they will be accepted by Congress, the Supreme Court, or the bureaucracy.

President Franklin Roosevelt was the major force behind the New Deal, but it took a long time before New Deal legislation was acceptable to Congress and not declared unconstitutional by the Supreme Court. Once Roosevelt's "honeymoon" with Congress was over in 1933, he met increasing resistance to his proposals in the legislature. Although a large majority of the voters supported the president, as revealed in his landslide election in 1936, they were supporting the man more than the specific content of his policy proposals. Regardless of Roosevelt's continuing frustrations on the domestic front in policy innovation, there is little doubt that it was his tenacity in the pursuit of his goals that brought the New Deal from the realm of ideas to reality.

The New Deal program continued even after the election of Dwight Eisenhower in 1952. Eisenhower's election did not mark a long-term shift to the Republican party, nor did Eisenhower represent a major ideological contrast to many New Deal programs. Public policy, particularly monetary and fiscal policy, took a more conservative turn during the Eisenhower years, but it was not Eisenhower's intent to use the White House to make radical changes in government policy.

After the relative cautious Eisenhower administration, the

Kennedy and Johnson years produced significant White House initiatives in domestic and foreign policy that changed the political face of the nation. The Great Society programs of Lyndon B. Johnson, in particular, put the federal government in a dominant position over the states in controlling economic and social policy. Presidential initiatives in civil rights, which admittedly sprang from the nationwide civil rights movement of the 1960s, changed the political face of the nation. It was President Johnson, for example, who issued an executive order based upon Title VI of the 1964 Civil Rights Act that established affirmative action programs throughout the federal government and in private institutions receiving federal funds. While Johnson declared that his order was based on Title VI, in fact the language of title VI which bars discrimination in federally funded programs in no way explicitly provides for "reverse discrimination," which affirmative action requires.

Johnson's initiatives in domestic policy were more than matched by his foreign policy, which was concentrated almost solely upon the pursuit of the Vietnam War. No president in history has had a greater impact upon foreign relations.

In the decade following the Johnson administration, perhaps the most significant presidential policy innovation was that of Richard Nixon in opening relations with the People's Republic of China. President Jimmy Carter carried the Nixon initiative to its logical conclusion in recognizing the government of mainland China, but it was Nixon who, with the help of his astute and politically skillful secretary of state, Henry Kissinger, made history by reversing the policy of nonrecognition that had prevailed for over two decades.

Ronald Reagan's victory in the 1980 presidential election promised major White House initiatives to alter drastically the course of domestic policy. The conservative tone of the Reagan administration was at the opposite end of the political spectrum from the Democratic New Deal policies that had governed the nation since the 1930s. Reagan's "new beginning" represents an effort to end the dominant role of the federal government in economic and social policy. Reagan is the first Republican elected since the New Deal who has seriously undertaken to carry out a program that will drastically reduce federal expenditures, taxes, and government regulation of the economic and social life of the country. Reagan has found, however, like presidents before him, that presidential prerogatives in domestic affairs are extremely limited. Major policy innovation cannot be carried out without the cooperation of Congress, the bureaucracy, and the courts.

Today the president, while continuing to be frustrated in many of his domestic pursuits, nevertheless possesses the power of life and death over the nation. This is a true paradox, because with relative ease a president can involve the United States in a major war that might mean the destruction not only of this country, but of all mankind; however, he often cannot secure the passage in Congress of the most trivial legislation, nor necessarily receive the support of the bureaucracy for the implementation of his own policy initiatives.

The Exercise of
Presidential Prerogatives

These far-reaching prerogative life and death decisions reflect a distinctly personal attribute of presidential power, for they are often dependent solely on the man, his perceptions of the world, and his character. Perhaps the most important current issue in relation to presidential power and policy-making pertains to this area where the president acts in a personal capacity to shape the course of the nation.

Presidential discretion in the military and foreign policy spheres is generally accepted, but this general compliance has been punctuated from time to time with complaints that the president has too much power. During the twentieth century, the actions of all presidents that have involved the United States in wars have been attacked by various groups. Woodrow Wilson was subject to criticism for leading the country into World War I, and the initiatives taken by Franklin D. Roosevelt to aid our allies against Germany before World War II were criticized by various isolationist groups as inappropriate and exceeding the constitutional authority of the office. One of the main campaign issues in 1952 was the Korean War; the Republicans implied that once again the Democratic "war party" had improperly led the United States into a foreign involvement.

The Korean Decision. President Truman's decision to send

troops to Korea without consulting the United Nations or Congress was at first generally accepted by congressional leaders. But as the war dragged on, and American commitments and casualties in Asia began to mount, so did criticism of the president's discretionary authority. On 5 January 1951, Senator Robert Taft, in a major Senate speech, accused the administration of formulating defense policy since the end of World War II without consulting either Congress or the people. Taft asserted that without authority the president had "involved us in the Korean War and without authority he apparently has now adopted a similar policy in Europe." A few days after Taft's speech Republicans in the Senate introduced a resolution that expressed the sense of the Senate that American ground forces should not be sent to Europe in the absence of a congressional policy relating to the issue.

In characteristic style, President Truman contended that he could and would send troops wherever he wanted without consultation with the legislature. During 1951, hearings were held by Senate committees on alleged plans of the secretary of defense to send more troops to Europe. Resolutions were reported out of these committees asking that the president not take action on troop deployments abroad without first consulting the Senate and House Foreign Relations, Affairs, and Armed Services Committees. Intensive debate ensued and attempts were made by Republicans to amend the resolutions to increase congressional control over the president. The Senate finally passed a resolution which stated that no more than four divisions could be sent to Europe without Senate approval. President Truman hailed the action as an endorsement of his troop plans, and skillfully avoided the question of Senate approval. The controversy over the scope of presidential authority and discretion in military and foreign policymaking was a precursor to Vietnam. President Johnson's decisions were based on clear historical precedents, as was the political feedback.

The Vietnam Decision. The Vietnam War once again gave rise to extensive discussion within Congress about the proper role of the legislature in the exercise of the war power. Quick to give President Johnson his Gulf of Tonkin Resolution, many congressmen later regretted their vote, for it was widely interpreted as giving Johnson blanket authority to pursue whatever military action he wished in Southeast Asia. The president himself used the resolution as a reminder to legislative critics that he was pursuing the war with the consent of Congress.

The mounting congressional criticism of President Johnson's Vietnam policies continued into the Nixon administration. President Nixon's decisions to invade Cambodia in 1970 and Laos in 1971 provoked particularly heated congressional opposition. After the United States assisted the South Vietnamese invasion of Laos, Senator Edmund S. Muskie of Maine expressed the views of many of his colleagues when he stated: "I think that the use of combat air support . . . goes beyond the spirit of any policies that Congress has endorsed. . . . And, I think before we get involved in that kind of activity in Cambodia and Laos, the president ought to come to Congress to ask for its support, define his proposals, so that we can consider it on its merits."[24]

Prior to President Nixon's unilateral actions in Cambodia and Laos, various resolutions had passed Congress attempting to limit the president's war-making discretion. In June of 1969, the Senate passed a resolution much like that passed during the Korean War, declaring it to be the sense of the Senate that no further military commitments overseas should be undertaken without the consent of Congress. By a vote of 288–38, on 16 November 1970 the House passed a joint resolution stating that, "whenever feasible" the president should consult with Congress before involving the country in an armed conflict. If it is not feasible for him to do so, then, the resolution stated, he should at least promptly report his actions to Congress, which presumably would give legislators a small, if belated, role in the decision-making process.

During 1971, the Senate considered additional ways to curb presidential war-making authority. Characteristic of the various proposals made was a resolution introduced by Senator John C. Stennis (D. Miss., chairman of Senate Armed Services Committee). The Stennis resolution would prevent the president from involving United States forces overseas except: (1) to repel an armed attack on the country or on American troops; (2) to prevent or defend against a nuclear

[24] *Congressional Quarterly Weekly Report,* 12 February 1971, p. 363.

attack if the president had clear and convincing evidence that such an attack was imminent; (3) finally, to evacuate United States citizens from a foreign country if the government of that country would no longer protect them.

In those categories where the president would be authorized to use troops without consulting Congress first, he would, under the terms of the resolution, have been required to give a "detailed account of the reasons of so using the Armed Forces" to Congress, which in turn would be given thirty days to decide whether or not to extend or terminate the president's authority. Therefore, specific congressional authorization would be required for the continuation of any war beyond thirty days. The introduction of this "resolution by Senator Stennis prompted Senator Jacob Javits (R. N.Y.) to remark, "I say we are witnessing a miracle. . . . it is both a miracle of the human personality and a miracle of this Chamber."[25] For his part, Senator Stennis noted that the resolution did not reflect his views on the Vietnam conflict, for it expressly did not apply to that war. But, he said, "the war power should be reasserted by Congress, for . . . the decision to make wars is too big a decision for one mind to make and too awesome a responsibility for one man to bear. There must be a collective judgment given and collective responsibility shared."[26]

Responding to the Stennis resolution and other similar proposals, Secretary of State William P. Rogers testified before the Senate Foreign Relations Committee in 1971 that the proposals went too far in limiting the discretion of the president to deploy armed forces. The president, Rogers stated, should be able to take immediate action without consulting Congress, and without necessarily having to report to Congress afterwards. Early attempts to curb presidential authority were unsuccessful, as their predecessors had been; however, in 1972 the Senate finally passed by a margin of only two votes (49–47) a resolution calling for the withdrawal of all troops from Vietnam within four months, provided the North Vietnamese released American prisoners. If the House of Representatives had gone along with the Senate (which it did not) in this resolution, great pressure would have been exerted upon President Nixon to conform to congressional wishes;

[25] *Congressional Quarterly Weekly Report,* 21 May 1971, p. 1103.

[26] Ibid.

however, it is doubtful if Nixon would have changed his course of action in Vietnam, claiming presidential prerogatives as Commander-in-Chief for ignoring congressional legislation in this area. In 1973 Nixon was forced to stop bombing Cambodia on August 15, a deadline set by both houses of Congress, but only after Congress threatened to cut off appropriations for the entire federal government if the president continued the bombing.

The most serious congressional incursion upon the war-making authority of the president occurred on 7 November 1973, when Congress overrode a Nixon veto of the War Powers Resolution of 1973, first passed by Congress in October of that year. Under the terms of this resolution, the president "in every possible instance" must consslt with Congress before involving the armed forces in hostilities. The resolution requires regular presidential consultation with Congress during war to keep the legislature informed of presidential actions. Where the president orders troops into the war without a declaration of war from Congress, he must within forty-eight hours submit to the Speaker of the House and to the president pro tem of the Senate a report setting forth:

1. The circumstances necessitating the introduction of United States armed forces;
2. The constitutional and legislative authority under which such introduction took place;
3. The estimated scope and duration of the hostilities or involvement.

After this report is submitted to Congress, the president must terminate within sixty days the use of United States armed forces unless Congress has declared war or given other specific authorization for the use of the armed forces, or has extended by law the sixty-day period or is physically unable to meet as the result of an armed attack upon the country. The initial sixty-day period during which the president can take independent action cannot be extended by Congress under the resolution for more than thirty additional days. President Nixon's veto of the bill was overridden by a vote of 284–135 in the House, and 75–18 in the Senate, indicating strong congressional sentiment to limit the president's war-making powers. The 1973 resolution would have prevented President Truman's unilateral action in sending troops to Korea. It can be argued that the Gulf of Tonkin Resolution met the conditions of the War Powers Resolution. Certainly President Johnson would have interpreted it in that way. Had the War Powers Resolution been in existence, however, Congress might have been far more careful in its terminology, recognizing that there was a possibility that a resolution such as the Gulf of Tonkin could and undoubtedly would be used by the president as a blanket authorization to engage in war in Southeast Asia.

Presidential Policymaking and Public Opinion

History reveals that presidents are least influenced by the public in military and foreign policymaking. This is partially because of the amorphous and ambiguous nature of public attitudes concerning policy issues in this area. Presidents may completely ignore public opinion polls that clearly demonstrate opposition to a particular foreign or military policy, in the belief that under certain circumstances it is the responsibility of the president to do what is "right" regardless of political opposition. President Johnson quoted fondly the words of Woodrow Wilson: "It is a fearful thing to lead this great peaceful people into war. . . . but the right is more precious than peace." President Johnson did not waver, until the very last days of his first full term of office, in his Vietnam policies, and even then there was very little evidence that substantial changes were taking place in his mind regarding what should be done in Vietnam.

Until recently, presidents didn't have the advantage of public opinion polls to tell them what the majority might support in the way of foreign or military actions, making it far easier to justify virtually any policies. When President Lincoln made those critical decisions which provided a spark igniting the Civil War, he was not listening to national public opinion, or even to strong northern opinion opposing the war. Woodrow Wilson knew that much of his popularity would vanish if he led the country into World War I, and he even promised during the election campaign of 1916 to stay out of foreign involvements. Nevertheless, as soon as the election was over he made the decisions that led to American entry into the war.

Major decisions made by Franklin Roosevelt in the 1930s to draw the country away from its isolationist stance and into a posture that would inevitably involve it in World War II were not made on the basis of electoral opinion, nor were they in any way geared to the electoral process. Roosevelt, like Wilson before him, promised in the campaign of 1940 that Americans would not be involved in foreign wars, but he knew that such involvement was inevitable, and the "right" course of action.

President Truman, like his predecessors, made major decisions on military aid and involvement in Greece, Turkey, and Korea. All of these decisions were made on the basis of his own judgment, fortified by inputs of foreign governments, the bureaucracy, and from advisors within the presidency itself. President Truman told President Johnson that "his confrontation of those international challenges—particularly in Korea—had been horrors for him politically, bringing his popularity down from a high of 87 percent to a low of 23 percent."[27]

The Johnson presidency received a wide range of inputs in the domestic arena, from both governmental and private sources. President Johnson never lost sight, however, of his leadership role. He notes in his memoirs that "I saw my primary task as building the consensus throughout the country, so that we could stop bickering and quarreling and get on with the job at hand. Unfortunately, the word consensus came to be profoundly misunderstood."[28] He goes on to say that to him obtaining a consensus did not mean reaching for the lowest common denominator of public opinion by simply attempting to support programs acceptable to the majority of the people. Rather, consensus meant:

. . . First, deciding what needed to be done regardless of the political implications and second, convincing a majority of the Congress and the American people of the necessity of doing those things. I was president of the United States at a crucial point in its history, and if a president does not lead he is abandoning the prime and indispensable obligation of the presidency.[29]

[27] Lyndon B. Johnson, *The Vantage Point* (New York: Holt, Rinehart and Winston, 1971), p. 31.

[28] Ibid., p. 27.

[29] Ibid., p. 28.

Johnson applied his general philosophy of leadership in both
the domestic and international arenas. "Deciding what
needed to be done" involved essentially internal presidential
decision-making processes, and inputs from the executive
branch. After the exhaustion of this procedure, the next step
was to convince Congress of the correctness of the course of
action decided upon or already taken. Although there were
extensive congressional inputs in the formulation of many of
Johnson's programs, he looked upon Congress not as a part-
ner, but as a necessary ally because of its authority over
legislation. If congressional inputs had to be taken into account in order to get a law passed, then they shaped the
drafting of the legislation by the executive branch. In no case,
however, did Johnson allow potentially strong congressional
opposition to deter him in a course that he considered to be
essential and right for the nation. For example, he notes in his
memoirs:

Under our system of government, with its clearly defined separation
of powers, the greatest threat to the Chief Executive's right to "govern" comes traditionally from the Congress. Congress is jealous of its
prerogatives. All too often jealousy turns into a stubborn refusal to
cooperate in any way with the Chief Executive.

The Congress had been in such a mood from the first day that John
Kennedy took office in 1961. . . . An entire program of social
legislation proposed by President Kennedy—from aid to education to
food stamps to civil rights—remained bottled up in committee while
the Congress defiantly refused to budge or act in any way. . . .

We were, in my opinion, facing a real crisis, and it was more than
a crisis of unfulfilled needs throughout the nation. There was also a
crisis of confidence in our system of government. There was a clear
reason for moving forward, and moving with dispatch and energy;
for acting while the sobering influence of national tragedy caused
men in all walks of life to think of the country's interest rather than
their own.[30]

[30] Ibid., pp. 33–34.

Johnson pressed a recalcitrant Congress for a wide range of
legislation that he felt was in the national interest.

While President Johnson could not afford to ignore Congress in the domestic field, in the international arena he had
far greater initiative. Although he proclaimed an interest in
gaining congressional support for his foreign policy actions,
he did not really consider such support a necessary prerequi-
site to the implementation of his decisions.

The history of the Gulf of Tonkin Resolution, passed by Congress in August 1964, reveals the true relationship between president and Congress in the foreign policy area. At 11 A.M. on August 4, 1964, a message was received by the Pentagon that two United States destroyers were being attacked by North Vietnamese torpedo boats. Immediately the Joint Chiefs selected target options for reprisal air strikes, drawn from a list that had been prepared as a contingency plan in May of 1964. A National Security Council meeting had been previously scheduled for 12 o'clock on August 4. The Tonkin Gulf crisis was discussed briefly at that meeting, and according to Johnson's memoirs, after the meeting his principal advisors unanimously recommended retaliation for what had been a second strike against the United States naval vessels off the coast of Vietnam. President Johnson agreed with his advisors, and "we decided on air strikes against North Vietnamese P T boats and their bases plus a strike on one oil depot."[31] According to *The Pentagon Papers*, while President Johnson was at lunch with his advisors (Rusk, McNamara, Vance, McCone, and Bundy), the director of the Joint Chiefs of Staff telephoned McNamara reporting that the Joint Chiefs had unanimously agreed on the nature of the retaliatory action that should be taken. The recommendation of the Joint Chiefs was in fact the decision that was unanimously endorsed by the president's advisors and supported by the president himself.[32]

President Johnson officially ordered the reprisals at a second National Security Council meeting early in the afternoon. After a short delay, due to uncertainties regarding whether or not an attack on the destroyers had actually occurred, the formal execution orders for retaliation were sent to Honolulu at 4:49 P.M., specifying that within approximately two and a half hours United States aircraft carriers were to launch their planes for the attack.[33] At the second National Security Council meeting on August 4, it was decided that a congressional resolution of support should be sought immediately, and with this in mind the president met with sixteen congressional leaders from both parties at approximately 6:45 P.M. By this time, of course, the decision to launch a

[31] Ibid., p. 114.

[32] See Neil Sheehan, "The Covert War in Tonkin Gulf: February–August, 1964," in *The Pentagon Papers* (New York: Bantam Books, 1971), p. 262.

[33] Ibid., pp. 262–63.

retaliatory strike had already been made on the basis of plans drawn up months earlier. According to Johnson's memoirs, at this meeting with congressional leaders:

I told them that I believed a congressional resolution of support for our entire position in Southeast Asia was necessary and would strengthen our hand. I said that we might be forced into further action, and that I did not "want to go in unless Congress goes in with me." At this meeting "McNamara described in detail what had happened in the Gulf of Tonkin and what we proposed to do." I then read a statement that I planned to deliver to the American people later in the evening.[34]

[34] Johnson, *The Vantage Point*, pp. 115–16.

Whether or not the congressmen present were fully aware that the formal order had been issued for the attack, and that the planes were in fact to be airborne while the meeting was taking place, is not fully clear, although it can be inferred that they were apprised that the decision had been made. This is confirmed by *The Pentagon Papers*, which reported that the president "told them that because of the second unprovoked attack on the American destroyers, he had decided to launch reprisal air strikes against the North and to ask for a congressional resolution. . . ."[35] Presented with this *fait accompli*, the congressional leaders had no alternative but to support the president. As President Johnson noted, at the conclusion of the meeting:

[35] *The Pentagon Papers*, p. 263.

I went around the table asking each Senator and Representative for his frank opinion. Each expressed his whole-hearted endorsement of our course of action and of the proposed resolution.
"I think it will be passed overwhelmingly," said Congressman Charles Halleck.
"I will support it," said Senator Fulbright.
At the close of the meeting I felt encouraged by the show of solidarity and support. As Speaker McCormack said near the end of our discussion, we were presenting a "united front to the world."[36]

[36] Johnson, *The Vantage Point*, p. 117.

During the Cuban Missile Crisis, President Kennedy also consulted with congressional leaders after the internal executive decision-making processes had come to the conclusion that a blockade of Cuba was the suitable response to the Soviet Union. At no time during the deliberations leading to this decision did President Kennedy or his staff feel that it was appropriate to extend the discussions to include congressional leaders. The decision was made on the basis of inputs from presidential advisors, the Joint Chiefs of Staff, several members of the cabinet, a few other selected individuals from the executive branch, and Vice-President Johnson.[37] This group reflected the spectrum of views on what action should be taken, from those few who felt no action was required to those who wanted to take the most drastic military reprisals against Cuba.

After settling upon the decision to carry out the blockade, President Kennedy informed those members of the cabinet not present during the deliberations of the crisis and the decision that had been made. After this, and shortly before he was to announce his decision in a nationwide address, the president called in congressional leaders and informed them for the first time of the crisis and what action he was going to take. They reacted sharply, as Robert Kennedy describes:

> Many congressional leaders were sharp in their criticism. They felt that the president should take more forceful action, a military attack or an invasion, and that the blockade was far too weak a response. Senator Richard B. Russell of Georgia said that he could not live with himself if he did not say in the strongest possible terms how important it was that we act with greater strength than the president was contemplating.
> Senator J. William Fulbright of Arkansas also strongly advised military action rather than such a weak step as the blockade. Others said that they were skeptical but would remain publicly silent, only because it was such a dangerous hour for the country.[38]

The president carefully explained to the congressional leaders that military action might have devastating consequences, and therefore he was not willing to take such a gamble until he had exhausted all other possible courses of action. The initial militant reaction of most of the congressional leaders was, according to Robert Kennedy, similar to the first reactions of the executive group upon hearing of the missiles. It is quite possible that if the congressmen had been consulted over a longer period of time, and put into a position where they would have had to bear part of the collective responsibility for the decision that was ultimately made, they would have taken a more judicious approach and weighed the various alternatives carefully. Nevertheless, it is interesting to observe that at the time the response of the congressional leadership, including Senator Fulbright (who was later to lead the doves in an attack on President Johnson's Vietnam policies), was in favor

[37] Robert F. Kennedy, *Thirteen Days* (New York: W. W. Norton, 1969), p. 8.

[38] Ibid., pp. 31–32.

of direct military intervention. Consultation with the leaders of Congress inevitably means consultation with the most conservative parts of the legislature, and at the time of the Cuban missile crisis, these key legislative leaders leaned towards strong military intervention where they felt United States interests were at stake. Many of these same individuals were far more cautious in their attitudes towards military involvement by the latter stages of the Vietnam War, and led congressional efforts to curb the discretionary authority of the president to make war.

Presidents must deal with Congress, of course, not only in the area of foreign and military affairs, in which the White House is always dominant, but in the domestic policy arena as well, where Congress and the bureaucracy in combination with powerful private interests more often than not prevail. Presidents can and have exercised strong initiatives in domestic policy, however. Charismatic Presidents like John Kennedy, and politically brilliant presidents like Lyndon B. Johnson, have been able to garner the support of Congress for most of their major legislative proposals. But presidents do require broad political backing to persuade Congress to their point of view where important domestic legislation is concerned. President Nixon, for example, was unsuccessful in his efforts to impound funds for domestic programs that had important congressional, bureaucratic and interest group support. Presidential authority to impound funds that had been appropriated by Congress, which was first granted to the president by Congress itself at the end of the nineteenth century, was taken away by the Budget and Impoundment Control Act of 1974, in legislation that was a direct rebuke of President Nixon. The resurgence of Congress after the Nixon administration intensified the conflict between the two ends of Pennsylvania Avenue during both the Ford and Carter administrations. President Reagan, whose initiatives have so far been primarily in the domestic policy sphere, carefully courted Congress at the outset of his administration to help insure the success of his program. His early and impressive legislative victories, however important, did not preclude an increase in presidential difficulties with Congress and the entrenched

Washington establishment, which in the past had always been able to modify and often defeat White House initiatives.

Our system of government was originally constructed with a negative orientation, designed to prevent the effective exercise of governmental authority. The intricate intermeshing of the various branches of the government that was required before a policy output could be produced was to limit potentially "evil" influences upon government, emanating from factions and demagogic individuals who were more concerned with their own interests than with the national interest. However, a government primarily designed to work inefficiently, if at all, obviously could not meet the wide range of responsibilities that inevitably were placed upon it, nor could it produce effective government during times of crisis. The bureaucracy developed to take over expanded governmental responsibilities and the powers of the presidency grew to provide leadership and effective decision making in times of crisis.

In the foreign and military affairs areas, the presidency does not conform to traditional constitutional restraints. Although the Constitution did foresee in part that the president would have to have wider discretionary powers in the foreign than in the domestic sphere, nevertheless, the authority to declare war clearly resided with Congress, and the Senate was to advise and consent on treaties and ambassadorial appointments. A major question for the future of the presidency is how to balance the need for power with constitutional requirements of responsibility and constraints. In the domestic arena, without the development of stronger parties which will bring about closer linkage between the White House and Congress, the president will be severely curtailed in his legislative activities. Moreover, the bureaucracy inevitably will place constraints on the ability of the president to shape and implement public policy. Even in parliamentary governments with a strong two-party system, such as Britain's, the administrative branch exercises wide discretion in policymaking.

Although the presidency is usually called an institution, the fact remains that the White House is more a reflection of the man who holds the office than of its bureaucratic components. It is an extension of the president's preferences and inclinations in most critical areas of decision making. Each president shapes the institution more than it shapes him, particularly in the way in which it deals with foreign policy.

As the presidency embarks upon the 1980s, it continues to be the focus of national attention and hope. The widely perceived abuses of presidential power that occurred in the foreign policy sphere during the Johnson administration, and in both domestic and foreign policy areas in the Nixon years, brought the presidency as an institution into temporary disrepute. The resurgence of congressional power in the 1970s as a result of the Watergate affair and Nixon's secret bombing of Cambodia may be only temporary. The same forces that have increased presidential responsibilities and powers in the past will continue to buttress the White House. National crises, both foreign and domestic, have been a major cause of the "imperial" presidency. Americans will continue to expect the president to be the initiator of broad public policy changes. President Reagan's overwhelming electoral victory represented a hope in the hearts of many people that the presidency would once again be able to cope with a crisis—this time inflation, unemployment, high taxes, and an overbearing government.

Suggestions for Further Reading

Cronin, Thomas E. *The State of the Presidency.* 2nd edition. Boston: Little, Brown and Co., 1980. A comprehensive and fresh interpretation of the modern American presidency.

Crouse, Timothy. *The Boys on the Bus.* New York: Random House, 1973. A superb book on the activities and antics of the press during a presidential campaign.

Hess, Stephen. *Organizing the Presidency.* Washington, D.C.: The Brookings Institution, 1976. A detailed analysis of the institutional presidency, the way in which the White House has been organized from Franklin D. Roosevelt to Richard M. Nixon.

Neustadt, Richard E. *Presidential Power: The Politics of Leadership.* Rev. ed. New York: John Wiley, 1976. The presidency viewed by an insider who argues that presidential power does not extend beyond the ability to persuade.

Rossiter, Clinton. *The American Presidency.* New York: Harcourt, Brace and Co., 1956. A classic work on the powers and responsibilities of the presidency.

Schlesinger, Arthur M., Jr. *The Imperial Presidency.* Boston: Houghton Mifflin, 1973. Against the backdrop of the Nixon administration, the author criticizes the escalation of presidential power.

House Speaker Thomas P. (Tip) O'Neill administers the oath of office to the House of Representatives at the opening of the Ninety-seventh Congress. Members are often accompanied by their families on such occasions.

CHAPTER 7

Congress

Every two years, after elections are held for the House of Representatives and the Senate, those who have been elected to Congress for the first time often take with them a high sense of mission. They hope to influence new directions in public policy. Not only do they hold the institution of Congress in high regard, and consider it to be the primary influence upon public policy in government, but they also feel that their individual roles can be significant within the framework of the legislature. After all, doesn't the Constitution designate Congress to be the primary legislative body? And doesn't legislation mean public policy? No other branch of the government is given direct legislative authority by the Constitution.

At least one "public interest" pressure group, Common Cause, feels that if new directions are to be made in public policy, the electoral process should be the primary channel through which demands for change are made. In the early 1970s John Gardner, the head of Common Cause, mounted an extensive effort to elect congressmen he considered to be sympathetic to the policy interests of his organization. A central premise of this effort was that changes in the makeup of Congress could have a major impact upon public policy.

At times during the Johnson and Nixon administrations, groups of students traveled to Washington hoping to convince their congressmen to vote against the Vietnam War. In some cases, classes were recessed at election time so that students could work for peace candidates. Nationwide appeals were made to support senatorial doves threatened with the possibility of defeat in 1968. And, in many districts and states, representatives and senators were elected primarily on the basis of their stand against the war. The primary effect of these efforts was not reflected in legislative proposals opposing the war, but in making the White House aware of national sentiment on the war issue. It was not until 1973 that Congress was able to agree on policies to limit the president's war-making prerogatives, by establishing the August 15 deadline for stopping the bombing of Cambodia and in the War Powers Resolution (see Chapter 6).

The experience of the Nixon administration with a Democratic Congress, and the seeming inability of Republicans to elect a majority of either the House of Representatives or the Senate, convinced Republican leaders in the late 1970s to make a major effort to aid Republican incumbents and challengers with money and expertise in the 1980 election. The House Republican Congressional Campaign Committee, for example, spent five times as much money as their Democratic counterparts to elect Republicans to the House in 1980. On the Senate side, the Republicans outspent the Democrats by an even greater margin.[1] The Republican National Committee also outspent its Democratic rival on congressional races. (See Table 7.1.) The increased efforts of the Republicans combined with the help of important pressure group support for conservative candidates, particularly those opposing abortion, paid off. The Republicans took control of the Senate for the first time since 1953, and the Democratic margin in the House was sharply reduced, raising the distinct possibility of Republican control after the 1982 elections. Republicans recognized that control of Congress should be a top priority of the party because Congress is the keystone of the Washington power establishment.

[1] The House Republican Congressional Campaign Committee spent approximately $3 million in 1980, compared to the $750,000 expenditure of the Democratic Committee. In the Senate, the Republican Campaign Committee disbursed 5.5 million dollars, in contrast to $800,000 provided by the Democratic Committee to their candidates.

CHARACTERISTICS OF CONGRESS

The most important characteristic of Congress is that it is an amorphous body. It is not a collective force. "The Congress" simply does not exist in reality.

Fragmentation

Congress is composed of numerous subgroups, particularly committees, which exert power in the policy process. If the legislature were dominated by one party, then Congress

Table 7.1
Political Party Fund Raising to Control Congress. *The Republicans made a major effort to control Congress as the decade of the 1980s began.*

The Democrats Have a Long Way to Go to Catch the GOP

Reports filed with the Federal Election Commission document the dramatic difference between Democratic and Republican Party fund raising. Listed below are the receipts, contributions to candidates and expenditures on their behalf made by the principal party committees in 1979–80. The final two columns, based on interviews with party officials, include estimates of their expected receipts for 1981–82 and the number of active direct-mail contributors, typically defined as those who have donated money during the past year.

	1979–80			1981–82	Current active contributors
	Receipts	Contributions to candidates	Expenditures for candidates	Receipts goal	
Democratic National Committee	$15,112,775	$24,600	$555,733	$18,000,000	60,000
Democratic Congressional Campaign Committee	2,094,109	614,097	34,686	6,000,000	15,000
Democratic Senatorial Campaign Committee	1,653,849	481,500	589,316	6,000,000	—
Democratic total	$18,860,733	$1,120,197	$1,179,735	$30,000,000	75,000
Republican National Committee	63,231,442	852,125	848,109	30,000,000*	870,000
National Republican Congressional Committee	27,231,333	1,790,961	927,467	40,000,000	750,000
National Republican Senatorial Committee	20,603,452	414,234	5,052,823	25,000,000	350,000
Republican total	$111,066,227	$3,057,320	$6,828,399	$95,000,000*	1,970,000

*The Republican National Committee goal is for 1981 only.
Source: *National Journal,* May 23, 1981, p. 923. By permission.

would cease to be amorphous and would become identified with a majority party. In Britain, Parliament speaks with one voice through the majority party, and although there are a few powerful standing committees, they do not control the flow of legislation as is the case in the Congress.

While delegating legislative business to committees diminishes the meaning of Congress as a collective force, the combined legislative power of the committees makes Congress anything but a rubber stamp. In his dealings with Congress, the president cannot count on a majority of his own party to enact proposals that he submits. Relative to most other democratic legislatures in the world, Congress is a powerful countervailing force to the executive.

The fragmentation of the legislative process makes it difficult for Congress to be responsive to broad forces for change in the community. It usually acts on a specialized basis, with its individual committees being responsive to narrow sets of interests that are concerned with particular policy spheres. The narrow and localized constituencies of Congress are in sharp contrast to the national constituency of the presidency. This is not to suggest that the president always takes into account "the national interest" while Congress represents something else. It is merely to point out that congressional committees tend to be more specialized and to reflect narrower interests than does the presidency.

The broader policy perspective of the president in contrast to Capitol Hill can be observed in the frequent presidential vetoes of pork-barrel legislation, which Congress passes each year to give direct benefits to constituents, hopefully in return for their votes. Pork-barrel projects generally consist of dams and water projects built by the Army Corps of Engineers, and federal buildings. The appropriations for such projects exceed four billion dollars each year, and presidents usually do not agree with members of Congress that such federal largesse is in the broader national interest.

The narrow perspective of Congress can be seen not only in the attempts of members to channel federal funds into their districts, but also in legislation and appropriations that serve special interests. For example, Congress has always been generous in appropriating funds for veterans' benefits and providing special veterans' preferences for jobs in the federal civil service. Much of this legislation has been vetoed by presidents for decades on the grounds that it does not serve a broad national interest. One of President Reagan's first cost-cutting proposals sent up to Capitol Hill was for a drastic reduction in veterans' benefits, a recommendation that immediately met strong opposition from congressmen, veterans' organizations, and the Veterans Administration. The Veterans

Affairs Committees of the House and the Senate immediately began to mobilize the forces of the veterans' "iron triangle" to defeat the president's program. Party lines made little difference in the battle, as Mississippi Democrat G. V. "Sonny" Montgomery, chairman of the House Veterans Affairs Committee, joined Republican Senator Alan K. Simpson of Wyoming, who headed the Senate committee, in opposition to the White House. Congress finally gave the President only half of his proposed cuts in veterans' benefits.

The distinction between legislation and public policy is important to bear in mind. The mere passage of legislation does not always produce public policy. In areas of intense group conflict, Congress frequently resorts to the passage of "skeleton" legislation in order to avoid directly confronting difficult political questions. That is, it purposely passes vague legislation, with statutory language couched in very general terms, requiring interpretation by the president or the administrative agency to which the legislature delegates authority to carry out its intent.

Ambiguous statutory provisions are not only the result of congressmen attempting to avoid taking political stands, but also of the complexity of the problems before the legislature. It is difficult for Congress to write comprehensive laws. Legislative reliance upon the technical expertise of the bureaucracy is common. The technological problems that must be taken into account in most areas of public policy also change rapidly from year to year. Even if a legislative committee has the expertise to deal with such matters, it is cumbersome to pass new legislation as frequently as conditions change. Legislation must be kept flexible, delegating a large amount of discretionary authority to the administrative agencies charged with implementation. Legislative committees may oversee agencies on a fairly continuous basis (although this is rare), and in this way affect the nature of the policy that is being formulated and carried out by the administrative branch. However, this is not the same thing as legislating. The policy outputs of government, then, are often not to be found in the language of statutes, but in interpretations made by legislative commit-

Legislation
and Public Policy

tees, administrative agencies, and sometimes the presidency and the courts, after legislation has been passed.

Except where the president and the Supreme Court are exercising independent constitutional prerogatives, all public policy decisions have a statutory basis, however vague. Through legislation, Congress determines the general areas in which government agencies will have policymaking authority, the boundaries of their authority, and the amount of money needed for particular programs. Complementing statutory law is administrative law—that is, the rules and regulations formulated by administrative agencies. These fill in the details of congressional legislation, and are supposed to follow the intent of Congress. Ambiguity of congressional intent often leads to challenges of administrative actions in the courts, which may overrule agencies if they find that they are acting beyond the authority *(ultra vires)* granted to them by Congress, as interpreted by the judges.

Adjudication is a very important ingredient in the policy process, as carried out by courts and by administrative agencies. It is often through the settlement of individual cases and controversies that policy is clarified and given concrete meaning for individuals. Outside of the areas of constitutional lawmaking by judges and the exercise of independent constitutional powers of the presidency, the policy process goes through three fairly identifiable formal stages: (1) the passage of a statute; (2) the promulgation of regulations based upon that statute by administrative agencies; (3) the adjudication of disputes that arise under statutory and administrative law by administrative agencies, initially, and under certain circumstances by the courts where they exercise their authority to review the decisions of the agencies.

Congressmen as
Policymakers

Individual congressmen and congressional committees are involved in all three stages of the policy process. They initially shape and vote upon legislation. They may informally influence the administrative agencies before the promulgation of regulations. And, they may become involved indirectly in the adjudication of disputes by the agencies. Neither congressmen nor anyone else are supposed to make *ex parte* (for one party only) representations in formal adjudicative decisions, whether in the administrative or the judicial processes. Most administrative adjudication is informal, however, in which there are far fewer restrictions and in most instances congressional intervention is perfectly proper.

The complexities of the policy process, and the numerous access points to those who have power to shape it, mean that many congressional activities besides legislating may affect the course of public policy. This poses an interesting dilemma for constituents; if they are interested in public policy, some judgment must be made about the effectiveness of congressional candidates within government. If the candidate is an incumbent, judgment can be made as to his or her position in Congress, what committees he or she is on, and what rank he or she holds. This in turn will have an important effect upon the candidate's influence in government generally. If a candidate is running for the first time, there is virtually no way to predict his or her performance within Congress in opening avenues to power.

The general policy statements of congressmen on broad issues may in reality be of little importance to their constituents. But a congressman who holds a powerful committee chairmanship may be able to serve his or her constituents very well in shaping the impact of policy to meet their needs. The public works committees, appropriations subcommittees, and commodities subcommittees of the House Agriculture Committee are particularly useful to their chairmen and members in channeling pork-barrel projects to their districts. Other committees as well may be useful in cementing the relationship between congressmen and their districts because they have jurisdiction over subject matter areas of particular concern to constituents. For example, the House Interior and Insular Affairs Committee, chaired by Democrat Morris K. Udall of Arizona, is eagerly sought by many freshmen members from the West because the committee has jurisdiction over public lands, parks, and natural resources.

While all congressional constituents are interested in narrow distributive policies that specifically benefit their districts, they are generally unaware of most of the broader policy-making activities of legislators. Most congressional committees are not engaged in distributing specific benefits to districts or states, but have broad jurisdiction that creates a policy constituency for their members that goes far beyond the geographical boundaries of their districts and states. For example, the powerful Armed Services committees on both sides of Capitol Hill—which admittedly have been used over the years to benefit the constituents of their chairmen, who have directed military installations to their districts and states—have a broader constituency that includes the Defense Department and the armaments industry. Many of the policymaking activities of these committees have little if anything to do with providing benefits to the local districts and states of committee members. Before the Ninety-seventh Congress, for example, Democratic Senator Sam Nunn of Georgia was the chairman of the Manpower subcommittee of the Seante Armed Services Committee, a position he used to develop and demonstrate his expertise in the area of military manpower and general strategic military planning. Nunn's involvement in military policymaking was not designed to get him reelected in Georgia, but to build his reputation as an effective legislator on a committee that he hoped to chair in the future. Much of the legislative activity of Capitol Hill reflects power struggles among members of Congress, between the House and the Senate, and between Congress and the White House. The world of Congress, like the rest of Washington, is often isolated from the broader electorate in the policymaking process.

THE CONSTITUTIONAL CONTEXT OF CONGRESS

Formal Structure of Congress

The formal constitutional provisions governing the operation of Congress shape its approaches to policy tasks. The bicameral nature of the legislature inevitably causes internal conflict between the House and the Senate. Bicameralism is fortified by differing constituencies for the two legislative branches, by contrasting powers, and by different terms of office. (See Figure 2, page 348.) These legislative differences make it impossible to develop a unified legislative policy. It also is a partial cause for the fragmentation of legislative power in the hands of diverse committees.

Originally, the major reason for the bicameral legislature was to secure the representation of differing interests—the states in the Senate, and the people in the House. It was not until 1913, with the adoption of the Seventeenth Amendment, that the Senate was elected directly by the people; previously, senators were selected by state legislatures. The indirect selection of the Senate, in combination with longer tenure and a slightly older age qualification (senators have to be thirty years of age, representatives twenty-five), was to give the Senate a more conservative cast than the House.

In *The Federalist* Hamilton and Madison argued that the House and the Senate were to have different policy orientations and responsibilities. Direct election and a two-year term of office rendered the House continuously dependent upon the interests of local constituents. The Senate, on the other hand, was capable of acting in a more deliberative fashion; it could give greater thought to important issues of public policy, particularly in foreign affairs, and where necessary check rash actions by the House. The most important objects of federal legislation within the purview of the House were to be the regulation of commerce, taxation, and regulation of the militia (No. 56).

Under the terms of the Constitution, all bills for raising revenue must originate in the House; the House thus has powerful initiative that often determines the course of tax policy. The real balance of power between the House and the Senate in tax policy is not determined by the Constitution, however, but by the political skills of the respective chairmen of the Ways and Means Committee of the House on the one hand, and the Senate Finance Committee on the other. By proposing amendments to tax legislation, the Senate can in effect initiate tax policy.[2] Power over tax policy tends to shift from the House to the Senate, depending upon the political astuteness of the tax chairmen. Democratic Ways and Means chairman Wilbur Mills skillfully guided tax legislation through many Congresses. His replacement by the less effective Democratic

Constitutional Division of Power

[2] Article 1, sec. 7 of the Constitution specifically authorizes the Senate to propose amendments: "All bills for raising revenue shall originate in the House of Representatives; but the Senate may propose or concur with amendments as on other bills."

Congressman Al Ullman of Oregon allowed Democratic Senator Russell Long of Louisiana, chairman of the Senate Finance Committee, to become the dominant Capitol Hill power in tax legislation. Beginning in the Ninety-seventh Congress, the House Ways and Means Committee again returned to powerful control under the chairmanship of Chicago Democratic Congressman Dan Rostenkowski, a protégé of House Speaker Thomas (Tip) O'Neill, who is a powerful politician in his own right. Rostenkowski seemed likely to restore the dominance of the House. On the Senate side, the elections of 1980 dethroned Russell Long and put in his place Kansas Republican Robert Dole, an often acerbic but nevertheless able senator. Although Dole promised to work closely with ranking minority member Long, it seemed unlikely that the Senate Finance Committee would command the respect of the House to the same degree that it had under Long's chairmanship.

In addition to providing for House initiation of revenue legislation, the Constitution assigns different tasks to the two sides of Capitol Hill in other areas as well. Most importantly, the Senate is to be the predominant power in foreign policy-making. The Constitution gives the upper body exclusive authority to advise and consent to treaties made by the president, and to approve ambassadorial appointments. The prestige of the Senate Foreign Relations Committee is tied directly to the constitutional role of the Senate in foreign policy. The power of the committee ebbs and flows in response to the need for and effectiveness of presidential power in foreign affairs. During times of crisis, the president tends to dominate foreign policy. Since World War II the leading position of the United States in world affairs has generally increased presidential power relative to that of the Senate in foreign policy-making. The foreign policy arena seems to be one of constant crisis—cold war, hot wars, and continuing world instability. Because the Constitution allows the president greater prerogative authority in foreign affairs, the White House has been able to overshadow Congress in foreign policymaking far more than in the domestic sphere.

Other constitutional differences in the roles assigned to the House and the Senate give the House the authority to impeach presidents and other civil officers, while the Senate is to try impeachments, which require a two-thirds vote for conviction. The Senate has the important authority to advise and consent on presidential appointments not only of ambassadors, but of Supreme Court justices, "public ministers"—which means cabinet appointments—"and all other officers of the United States, whose appointments are not herein otherwise provided for, and which shall be established by law: but the Congress may by law vest the appointment of such inferior officers, as they think proper, in the President alone, in the court of law, or in the heads of departments."[3] The constitutional power of the Senate to advise and consent on appointments has given it an important role in shaping the executive branch. Congressional legislation has extended the requirement of senatorial approval of appointments far beyond those designated in the Constitution to include hundreds of top-level bureaucratic officials.

[3] Constitution of the United States, Article II, sec. 2.

Judicial Interpretation of Policymaking Authority under Article I

The Constitution can be interpreted as both a negative and a positive document. That is, powers enumerated for the national government can be conceived of as limiting or extending its authority. With few exceptions, the course of American constitutional interpretation by the Supreme Court was set by Chief Justice John Marshall in the early nineteenth century. In such famous cases as *McCulloch* v. *Maryland* (1819) and *Gibbons* v. *Ogden* (1824), a "loose" rather than "strict" constructionist view was taken of the Constitution, and particularly of the implied powers clause, which gives the legislature all authority that is "necessary and proper" to implement its enumerated powers.[4] Although from time to time in American history the Supreme Court has limited the authority of Congress, the major trend of judicial decisions has been toward permitting Congress to do whatever it wishes, provided that there is not a clear violation of the Bill of Rights.

[4] McCulloch v. Maryland, 4 Wheaton 316 (1819); Gibbons v. Ogden, 9 Wheaton 1 (1824).

It was during the New Deal era that the most serious challenge to congressional authority occurred, when the Supreme Court ruled several important pieces of New Deal legislation unconstitutional for exceeding the enumerated powers of Congress. The era of the New Deal was not the only time when the Supreme Court struck down legislation because it was beyond congressional authority, but it was the most serious judicial threat to the actions of the political branches of government—Congress and the presidency—based upon the idea of constitutional restraints.

After the elections of 1936, and Roosevelt's attempt to change the composition of the Supreme Court, the more liberal Court interpreted the Constitution more loosely, thus upholding New Deal legislation. What is or is not unconstitutional is a matter of subjective opinion on the part of the Court, and proponents of the New Deal had argued vigorously that their standards of constitutionality were as valid as those of the justices. The latter, they held, were rewriting the Constitution in line with their conservative orientation.

During the early New Deal, such important legislation as the Agriculture Adjustment Act of 1933 and the National Industrial Recovery Act of 1933 were invalidated as having gone beyond the authority of Congress. However, in the historic case of *NLRB* v. *Jones and Laughlin Steel* (1937), Chief Justice Charles Evans Hughes and Justice Owen J. Roberts switched to the liberal side of the Court, thus giving the New Deal a victory.[5] At issue in the case was the Wagner Act (National Labor Relations Act) of 1935, which, on the basis of the commerce clause, extended federal regulatory power to deal with labor disputes that burdened or obstructed interstate commerce. The National Labor Relations Board (NLRB) was created with the authority to issue cease and desist orders that would be enforced through the courts against business firms that were found guilty of engaging in "unfair labor practices." The terms of the act did not extend merely to businesses involved in transporting goods across state lines, but also included manufacturing firms that were antecedent to and separate from the process of transportation of goods.

In cases previous to *NLRB* v. *Jones and Laughlin Steel,* the Court had held that such extensions of federal regulatory power were beyond the authority of Congress under the commerce clause. After upholding the extension of regulatory power in labor relations, the Court went on to support New Deal legislation in agriculture on the basis of the commerce

[5] NLRB v. Jones and Laughlin Steel, 301 U.S. 1 (1937). For an extensive discussion of this case, see Chapter 9, pp. 439–440.

clause. Early New Deal legislation in this field had been declared unconstitutional because Congress had attempted to base it upon its authority to tax and to provide for the general welfare.

The New Deal settled once and for all the controversy over whether the boundaries of congressional authority in domestic legislation were to be narrow or broad. It also revealed that in reality this is a political, not a constitutional, question, decided not by the Supreme Court operating in a vacuum, but by the ebb and flow of political forces. Roosevelt's unrelenting pressure upon the Supreme Court, backed by his enormous popular support, caused it to reverse its position.

A month before the *Jones and Laughlin* decision, the Court had indicated a more liberal stance in *West Coast Co.* v. *Parrish.* Harold L. Ickes noted the case in his diary:

The Supreme Court yesterday did a complete somersault on the question of minimum wages for women. It reversed itself on the *Adkins* case decided in 1923, in which the Court declared unconstitutional a law establishing minimum wages for women. . . .

. . . I do not know just what the effect on public opinion will be, or on the Court fight, but it seems to me that it is an admission on the part of the Supreme Court of charges that we have made to the effect that it hasn't been following the Constitution, but has been establishing as the law of the land, through Supreme Court decisions, the economic and social beliefs of the judges of the Court. It seems to me that on the whole, the effect will be to weaken the prestige of the Court in public estimation because when it was under fire, the Court ran to cover. For my part, I would have had more respect for the Court if it had gone down fighting and smiling after the manner of Justice McReynolds [who wrote a vigorous dissenting opinion]. Hughes and Roberts ought to realize that the mob is always ready to tear and rend at any sign of weakness.[6]

[6] Harold L. Ickes, *The Inside Struggle* (New York: Simon and Schuster, 1954), pp. 106–7.

Policymaking Based Upon Treaties. Another, and rather esoteric, area in which the authority of Congress has been challenged is in relation to its powers to implement treaty provisions. Congress, in addition to having the authority to carry out its enumerated powers, may "make all laws which shall be necessary and proper for carrying into execution . . . all other powers vested by the Constitution in the government of the United States, or in any department or office thereof." The treaty-making power is an example of a power vested by the Constitution "in the government of the United States, or in any department or office thereof," on the basis of which Congress can enact laws. Article VI of the Constitution provides in part:

> This Constitution and the laws of the United States which shall be made in pursuance thereof; and all treaties made, or which shall be made, under the authority of the United States, shall be the supreme law of the land. . . .

Since treaties and the Constitution are equally legitimate sources of authority, can Congress in pursuance of the treaty pass laws that would be unconstitutional solely on the basis of its enumerated powers?

[7] Missouri v. Holland, 252 U.S. 416 (1920).

In *Missouri* v. *Holland* (1920),[7] the Supreme Court held that Congress can make a law to put into effect the provisions of a treaty that would be unconstitutional in the absence of the treaty, because it could not be implied simply from its enumerated powers. However, the law in the *Missouri* case did not violate a specific provision of the Constitution. The Court has held that Congress cannot use a treaty or an executive agreement (treated as a treaty by the Supreme Court) as authority to pass a law that violates an explicit provision of the Constitution.

In *Reid* v. *Covert* (1957), the Court, after citing the language of Article VI making treaties the supreme law of the land along with the Constitution, pointed out that:

> There is nothing in this language which intimates that treaties and laws enacted pursuant to them do not have to comply with the provisions of the Constitution. Nor is there anything in the debates which accompanied the drafting and ratifications of the Constitution which even suggests such a result. . . . It would be manifestly contrary to the objective of those who created the Constitution, as well as those who are responsible for the Bill of Rights—let alone alien to our own entire constitutional history and tradition—to construe Article VI as permitting the United States to exercise power under an international agreement without observing constitutional prohibitions. In effect, such construction would permit amendment of that document in a manner not sanctioned by Article V. The prohibitions of the Constitution were designed to apply to all branches of the national government and they cannot be nullified by the Executive or by the Executive and the Senate combined. . . .[8]

[8] Reid v. Covert, 354 U.S. 1, 21 (1957).

The *Reid* case involved an executive agreement between the

United States and Great Britain which provided that United States military courts would have exclusive jurisdiction over criminal offenses committed in Great Britain by American servicemen and their dependents. Violations of British laws by Americans would be tried by court martial. The case involved a court martial trial that had convicted the wife of a serviceman of murdering her husband. Court martial trials do not provide the full protections of the Bill of Rights, and on this basis the Supreme Court upheld a lower district court judgment that Mrs. Covert (the wife) should be released from custody. Provisions for court martial trials, established by Congress, cannot be extended to civilians on the basis of executive agreements because such action would violate the Bill of Rights.

Effects of Judicial Interpretation of Article I. Today, the issue of constitutional limitations upon Congress is dormant. In the past, such limitations have always resulted from political rather than legal factors, that is, from the conservative orientation of the Court which led to a desire to curb what it considered too liberal policies of Congress. Certainly from the standpoint of the Constitution itself it is difficult to visualize how Congress might be limited in the future. Except for clear violations of the Bill of Rights, constitutional restraints upon the legislature are largely irrelevant. Congress has been able to use the war power, the power to tax and to provide for the general welfare, and the commerce clause to justify virtually any legislation expanding the role of the federal government.

Although the Court has not, since the New Deal, interpreted the Constitution to restrict congressional authority beyond the constraints of the Bill of Rights, the Madisonian model of the separation of powers frequently limits the ability of Congress to act. The legislature is checked not only by the president, but also by the internal checks and balances of bicameralism, the separate constituencies and powers of the House and the Senate.

While the Constitution formally determines the powers and structure of Congress, informal forces have profoundly shaped the politics of Capitol Hill.

Congress is generally viewed as an institution accessible and responsive to outside forces, such as public—and particularly constituent—opinion, pressure groups, the presidency, the bureaucracy, and, less directly, the courts. The external world is important to Congress, but to a considerable extent Capitol Hill is a world unto itself, with its own norms and patterns of behavior that in many important respects are not directly connected to the world beyond the community of Capitol Hill. Above all, it is a mistake to assume that members of Congress are simply rubber stamps for their voting constituents. Legislators usually strive for reelection, of course, but their Washington careers are not necessarily directly responsive to electoral needs and forces.

The President and Congress

Presidential powers and responsibilities profoundly affect the legislature. Under the Constitution, the president is "chief legislator," based upon his responsibility to recommend legislation and to provide Congress with a State of the Union message each year, and his veto power. Presidents, especially in the initial stages of new administrations, set the agenda for Capitol Hill. Where presidents take strong stands on legislative proposals there is a very good chance of their passage. Effective presidents have been able to achieve an 80–90 percent success ratio on Capitol Hill; less politically persuasive presidents have barely been able to secure the passage of a majority of their proposals.

The president's program, particularly in the initial stages of a new administration, sets the agenda for Capitol Hill. The legislative recommendations of President Ronald Reagan, for example, dominated Congress's agenda in 1981. The focus of legislative debate was upon the president's proposals, and a Republican Senate, along with a conservative coalition of Republicans and Democrats in the House, were favorably disposed toward the White House and initially supported the key budget and tax reduction plans of the president.

The president works with Congress through an extensive legislative liaison staff in the White House, and through the

Office of Management and Budget. The White House liaison team courts the party leaders on Capitol Hill and the powerful committee chairmen. Knowledgeable presidents do not try to push Congress farther than it is inclined to go, withdrawing proposals that have little chance of passage. The president's reputation for power on Capitol Hill can only remain intact if he has a creditable success in securing the passage of legislation.

When the president takes a stand on legislation, his powers are imposing. The OMB performs a clearance function for all legislative recommendations of administrative agencies, requiring agency proposals to be in conformity with the president's program. Administrators cannot testify before congressional committees without first having their testimony cleared by OMB. They cannot formally transmit any legislation to Capitol Hill without OMB approval. The budgets of the agencies are shaped by OMB into a comprehensive executive budget that is always the first item on the legislative agenda.

While the president has enormous powers to deal with Congress, it would be a mistake to conclude that the White House is the dominant force on Capitol Hill. Congress has interests and powers of its own that easily counterbalance those of the president. Ironically, it is the executive branch itself, apart from the presidential bureaucracy, that often effectively represents and implements legislative views that contrast with those of the White House. The president formally controls much of the operation of the bureaucracy, but informally, agencies develop their own patterns of political support and avenues of communication with Congress that conflict with and bypass the president.

From the vantage point of Capitol Hill, the regular bureaucracy—that is, those agencies outside of the Executive Office of the president— is an agent of Congress. It is a congressional creation, mandated to carry out congressional programs. Congressional committees are assigned specific oversight functions to review the way in which agencies are doing their job and determine if they are acting in accordance

Congress, the Bureaucracy, and Policy Formulation

with congressional wishes. The supervisory function may not always be effectively carried out because congressmen frequently find it is in their interest to engage in other activities more directly related to their principal incentives of reelection and building power within Congress. However, the symbolic recognition of the importance of supervision is a reflection of a strongly held congressional belief that the agencies are adjuncts of the legislative and not the executive branch. Washington's iron triangles, formed by congressional committees, agencies, and pressure groups, represent collusive interests that exclude the president.

The bureaucracy is a major input in congressional policy formulation. The close cooperation that exists between many parts of Congress and the bureaucracy is a vital component of the context of congressional policymaking. Such cooperation gives administrative agencies special access to Congress to influence the legislative process. And, at the same time, it gives congressional committees special avenues of influence to the bureaucracy so that they can influence administrative decision making and thereby shape public policy that is often in its final form determined by administrators rather than legislators. Admittedly, the scope of governmental activities and the necessary specialization tend to reduce the influence of Congress as a whole in administrative policymaking. Even specialized legislative committees and congressmen of long tenure and great skill in particular areas cannot begin to keep up with the rapidly moving activities of the bureaucracy and the complexities of administrative policymaking. Often the bureaucracy acts in secret, and is responsible to Congress only after the fact.

The extent to which administrators consult congressmen depends upon a variety of political factors and personalities. Sometimes very close ties exist, and administrative action is not taken without prior knowledge on the part of key congressmen. In some instances congressional authorization is sought in advance. Insofar as Congress does operate through the bureaucracy, it is because of the knowledge and power of a small group of senior members who control appropriations committees and committeees that oversee particular administrative agencies.

An important aspect of the relationship between the bureaucracy and Congress is that the agencies are often instrumental in shaping the technical details of legislation that they must administer. As early as 1937, the report of the president's Committee on Administrative Management recognized that well over two-thirds of all legislation emanating from Congress originates in and is often drafted by the bureaucracy. This does not mean, of course, that the agencies stand apart as a separate political force dictating the contents of congressional bills.

Special interests within the constituencies of the agencies often help to shape the agencies' positions, but administrative agencies are not simply pipelines between private interests and Congress. Congress itself hears the views of private interests in the legislative process. Moreover, it is a gross oversimplification to suggest that administrative agencies are always completely dominated by private interests. All agencies must maintain a balance of political support in order to survive, but this does not mean that they must consistently heed the requests of a particular segment of the community that comes under their jurisdiction. Within administrative constituencies there is often conflict and ambiguity, just as in the electoral constituencies of members of Congress. And there are many areas of legislation where special interests are so diffuse and conflicting that the judgment of a powerful department or agency will determine Congress's course of action.

The direct influence of administrative agencies in the legislative process stems from their political clout and expertise. Administrative agencies have more expertise than the average congressman because of long specialization by the staffs of the agencies—although not necessarily at higher levels, where political appointees have more frequent turnover. The only approximation of this kind of expertise in Congress is to be found in the senior members who have dealt for considerable periods of time with limited policy spheres. In the give and take between the executive and legislative branches, the expert views of bureaucrats are often determinative in shaping the content of final legislation.

Unlike most congressmen, agencies deal with policy matters under their jurisdiction continually on a day-to-day basis.

They have a chance to develop programs and policy positions from the constant inputs of private groups with which they deal and from the settlement of cases and controversies arising within their jurisdiction. Congress is often at a disadvantage in the policy process because it does not receive the constant flow of information available to administrative agencies.

Faced with the ambiguity of constituent attitudes, and the lack of consistent and meaningful party guidance in many areas of public policy, it is natural for key congressmen to pay particularly close attention to the inputs from the agencies in the legislative process. Many agencies, such as the independent regulatory commissions, are formally assigned the responsibility in their enabling statutes to advise Congress on appropriate legislative changes in their respective regulatory fields. These agencies are considered to be "arms of Congress," and they have been given quasi-legislative tasks within the framework of delegated legislation. At the same time, they have continual legitimate access to congressional committees to recommend whatever changes they consider necessary in the formal statutory framework under which they operate.

Formally, all bills originating within the bureaucracy must be channeled through the Office of Management and Budget for clearance before going to Capitol Hill. In reality, however, this process is often short-circuited through informal contacts that administrators make with congressional allies. Moreover, OMB is often swayed by the positions of agencies in many legislative areas where the president cannot possibly have a well-defined program. If new legislation does not involve the expenditure of additional funds, OMB is naturally more likely to approve it, provided it does not intrude upon and contradict a presidential policy position.

Historically, the important role of the administrative branch in recommending legislative proposals to Congress is relatively new, dating from the middle New Deal era. The vast expansion of the bureaucracy during the Roosevelt administration, and the increasing responsibilities assumed by the federal government, necessitated the injection of large amounts of expertise and man-hours into the process of formulating legislation for Congress. Congress itself, operating under antiquated rules and without adequate staff, naturally turned to the executive branch as the only source of available help outside of private interest groups. The latter were then, as they are now, only too willing to supply Congress with information that backed their policy stances; however, most legislators recognized that the bureaucracy was a far more legitimate source of direct influence than private interests since it was, like Congress, part of government and presumably representative of broad interests. This belief remains true today, and gives bureaucrats far easier access to the offices and committee rooms of Congress than is available to the paid lobbyists for private interests.

Congressmen generally recognize that private interests often dominate the agencies, and that the proposals emanating from the administrative branch are in many cases nothing more than a reflection of private concerns. Rarely, however, do agencies simply represent one group; rather, they attempt to balance the needs of the large number of organizations under their jurisdiction. On an industry-wide basis certain common demands may show up in Congress as a result of a proposal of an administrative agency. However, an agency is highly unlikely to transfer directly to Congress a bill that would benefit only one firm. Since many agencies are delegated responsibilities to foster industry-wide interests, it cannot be claimed that legislative proposals which they make to further this purpose reflect illicit pleading in behalf of private interests.

One of the more paradoxical aspects of our governmental system is that while agencies are continually involved in lobbying Congress, they are proscribed by law from doing this. Various acts prohibit the use of public funds for public relations purposes, which presumably includes attempts to influence legislation pending before Congress. Administrative agencies don't have to register, as do private groups, under the Federal Regulation of Lobbying Act of 1946. On the unlikely chance that some conscientious administrator might suggest that this is appropriate, given the fact that agencies are powerful lobbies, the proposal would undoubtedly be dismissed on the basis that such activities simply do not exist by definition. "Lobbying" is an activity that can only be undertaken by private interests.

It is important to emphasize that while administrative agencies shape a great deal of legislation (the standard current estimate given by congressmen is that 80 percent of the bills coming from Congress are initiated and in large part drafted by the executive branch), the communications that exist between Congress and the agencies inevitably open up a two-way street of influence. Congressmen have far better access to the agencies because of the lack of separation between the administrative branch and the legislature than would be the case if barriers were erected between these two branches. One such barrier is OMB. Legislative and executive proposals of the executive branch now have to be approved by OMB, which reduces the direct influence of congressmen on the agencies while at the same time increasing the power of the Executive Office. It is more difficult for congressmen to get agencies to develop positions which they favor because of the possibility of a veto from OMB. As long as the legislature is fragmented and operates through specialized committees, power over the bureaucracy will be diminished to the extent that the administrative branch is centralized under the control of the Executive Office of the President.

It is difficult to calculate the extent to which congressional autonomy has been reduced with the growth in the powers of the presidency and the administrative branch. Although administrative agencies may initiate most of the legislation before Congress, congressional inputs upon the legislative process are still important. As a minimum, Congress has the power and more often than not the inclination to negate legislative recommendations coming from the White House and the bureaucracy. It is a foolish president indeed who underestimates the irascibility of Congress. While the complexities of the modern policy process may frequently give legislators the feeling that their understanding of most policy issues is very thin, the same is true for bureaucrats, presidents, and judges. Only through specialization, whether within or without the legislature, can knowledge in depth of policy spheres be gained.

Interest Groups and the Congress

Interest groups complete the iron triangle in the Washington power establishment. Private groups and associations of all kinds have always been a prominent feature of the Washington landscape; however, the decade between 1970 and 1980 witnessed an extraordinary increase in the presence of groups in Washington. The landscape of the city changed from a relatively sleepy southern town to a bustling metropolis crowded with office buildings, restaurants, and sparkling new hotels, all of which were supported by pressure groups and trade associations that had decided a permanent presence in Washington was necessary to protect their interests. High-paid lobbyists and high-powered Washington lawyers benefitted from the largesse of groups that found it necessary to hire people with specialized skills to find their way through the maze of Washington politics. Retired and defeated members of Congress are an important part of the core of Washington lobbyists. "A former U.S. Congressman, no matter how capable, is worth more in Washington than any place else—considerably more," declared one representative.[9] Connections and inside knowledge can be sold for a great deal of money in Washington. The fact that many former members of Congress are highly paid lobbyists only serves to make the iron triangles of the city more closely connected and more effective bastions of political power.

[9] *Congressional Quarterly Weekly Report,* 27 December 1980, p. 3647.

Interest groups, like the bureaucracy, do not simply exert pressure on Congress, but are frequently an integral part of the legislative process itself. Just as administrative agencies detail employees to work for congressional committees, interest groups put their staffs at the disposal of legislators who may call upon them to supply information, draft legislation, testify at hearings, and provide needed political advocacy for the passage of legislation. Many former staff members of Congress, themselves captivated by Potomac fever and under the gun of high mortgage payments for their Washington condominiums and townhouses, work for interest groups and continue to supply expertise to Congress although they are not directly employed on Capitol Hill. Members of Congress find comfort in dealing with former colleagues and staffers who understand the needs of elected officeholders.

In addition to supplying staff assistance to Congress, pressure groups through their political action committees provide much of the money that supports the campaigns of incumbents seeking reelection. Money and politics are closely connected, and the support given to congressmen by interest groups is another strong link in the iron triangles of Washington politics.

Electoral and Policy Constituencies

While most members of Congress, in order to get reelected, must have close ties with their constituents, their constituency relationships are frequently based upon activities that have little to do with their Washington careers. On Capitol Hill, congressmen are primarily interested in demonstrating their power and status within the House and the Senate. To do this they may seek prestigious committee assignments, and chairmanships of important committees with large staffs. Other ways of gaining a reputation for power are through effective legislative work, investigations, and the achievement of party leadership positions such as majority or minority leader, chairman of the Democratic Caucus or Republican Conference in the House, or their counterparts in the Senate. While Washington careers are oriented to the achievement of internal power, constituency careers pursue the goal of reelection.

The large gaps that frequently exist between Washington and constituency careers do not mean that legislators do not spend a great deal of their time in Washington engaged in activities relating to reelection. They use the emoluments of their offices, particularly their staffs, to remain in contact with voters in their districts and states. Political scientist David Mayhew has written that congressmen advertise, claim credit, and take positions to strengthen constituency relationships and ensure reelection.[10] Mayhew stresses that congressmen "must constantly engage in activities related to reelection."[11]

Advertising by members of Congress involves efforts to "disseminate one's name among constituents in such a fashion as to create a favorable image, but in messages having little or no issue content. A successful congressman builds what amounts to a brand name, which may have a generalized electoral value for other politicians in the same family."[12] Advertising is particularly necessary for House members, who generally have far less visibility among constituents than do senators. Congressmen advertise through newsletters, opin-

---

[10] David Mayhew, *Congress: The Electoral Connection* (New Haven: Yale University Press, 1974).

[11] Ibid., p. 49.

[12] Ibid.

ion columns of newspapers, radio and television reports to constituents, and questionnaires. Members also seek to heighten their name recognition by attending social events, such as marriages and bar mitzvahs, in their districts.

The goal of reelection is also pursued by credit-claiming, which is taking credit for particularized benefits to constituents. Pork-barrel projects and casework are the primary credit-claiming activities of congressmen. Members distribute "pork" to their constituents in the form of dams and buildings.[13] Casework concerns the handling of specific constituent requests and complaints, largely related to the rulings and activities of bureaucrats who for one reason or another displease voters.

Finally, congressmen pursue reelection by taking positions on issues which they feel will be appealing to their constituents. Rarely, however, do legislators want to take strong stands on issues because of the likelihood of alienating some voters. The "best position-taking strategy for most congressmen at most times is to be conservative—to cling to their own positions of the past where possible and to reach for new ones with great caution where necessary."[14] Safe position-taking would include such statements as, "I will support Poland if it is invaded by the Soviet Union," "I will support the president," "I'm in favor of a balanced budget to reduce inflation," or "The government must take action to reduce unemployment."

Because of the importance of advertising, credit-claiming, and position-taking, it would seem likely that most congressmen and senators would build their Capitol Hill careers to facilitate their performance of these activities. Indeed, Mayhew argues that congressmen do just that—for example, choosing their committees and pursuing legislative goals that will enhance their prospects for reelection. As much as members may be worried about reelection, however, there is little doubt that much of what goes on in Congress does not directly relate to reelection. While freshmen and more junior members of Congress must pay strict attention to building constituency organizations that are capable of returning them to Capitol Hill, even they do not always seek assignments to committees that will facilitate their reelection—such as

[13] William Safire traces the term "pork-barrel" to "the pre–Civil War practice of distributing salt pork to the slaves from huge barrels. C. C. Maxey wrote in the *National Municipal Review* in 1919: 'Oftentimes the eagerness of the slaves would result in a rush upon the pork barrel, in which each would strive to grab as much as possible for himself. Members of Congress in the stampede to get their local appropriation items into the omnibus river and harbor bills behaved so much like Negro slaves rushing the pork barrel, that these bills were facetiously styled "pork barrel" bills, and the system which originated them has become known as the "pork-barrel system." ' " *Safire's Political Dictionary* (New York: Random House, 1978), p. 553.

[14] Mayhew, *The Electoral Connection*, p. 67.

the Public Works committees in charge of pork-barrel legislation—nor do they always pursue legislative goals that are directly related to pleasing constituents. Astute freshmen, wishing to build their power within Congress, are more interested in pleasing the leadership of their congressional party and the chairmen of powerful committees than they are concerned with shaping their congressional careers primarily in terms of reelection needs.

Richard Fenno, Jr., has pointed out that congressmen pursue reelection goals by building effective constituency organizations and an appealing home style, achievements which have little relationship to what members do in Washington.[15] Even David Mayhew would admit that, with the important exception of credit-claiming, much of the advertising and position-taking done by congressmen is external to what members do to build their power on Capitol Hill. Particularly as members gain seniority, based upon an effective constituency organization and style, they are freer to pursue a Washington career oriented towards power and, in Fenno's terms, "good public policy."[16]

The freedom of individual congressmen to pursue power and good public policy in Washington without having to worry about the reactions of voters in their constituencies is primarily due to the electorate's lack of knowledge about or interest in the details of what goes on in Congress. While most of the activities of congressmen are a matter of public record, the public rarely takes the time to examine the record. Relatively few individuals and interest groups within electoral districts are interested in the fine points of most of the policy issues with which congressmen deal, or in the byplay of power on Capitol Hill.

Warren E. Miller and Donald E. Stokes have pointed out in one study of constituency influence in Congress that less than 20 percent of the electorate had even read or heard anything about candidates running in their district.[17] Ignorance of representatives' policy positions means that the electorate is not concerned with what policy preferences candidates or incumbents have. As a result:

. . . The communication most congressmen have with their districts inevitably puts them in touch with organized groups and with indi-

---

[15] Richard F. Fenno, Jr., *Home Style* (Boston: Little, Brown, 1978).

[16] Richard Fenno lists three primary goals of members of Congress: reelection, power and influence on Capitol Hill, and good public policy. See Richard Fenno, Jr., *Congressmen in Committees* (Boston: Little, Brown, 1973).

[17] Warren E. Miller and Donald E. Stokes, "Constituency Influence in Congress," *The American Political Science Review* 57 (March 1963): 45–56.

viduals who are relatively well informed about politics. The representative knows his constituents mostly from dealing with people *who do* write letters, *who will* attend meetings, *who have* an interest in his legislative stance. As a result, his sample of contacts with a constituency of several hundred thousand people is heavily biased; even the contacts he apparently makes at random are likely to be with people who grossly overrepresent the degree of political information and interest in the constituency as a whole.[18]

Constituency influence, then, may help congressmen with respect to a narrow set of issues, but it does not provide them with a well-charted guide for legislative actions. In many of

[18] Ibid., pp. 54–55.

their votes on legislation they will have to act as Burkean trustees for the interests of their constituencies. They will vote in accordance with their perceptions of the needs of the district they represent.

Charles O. Jones has developed the concept of a "policy constituency" to explain how congressmen behave in the policy process.[19] This consists of substantial interests within the legislator's constituency that have knowledge of and are concerned with particular issues of public policy. Jones found in one case study of the House Agriculture Committee that legislators having clearly defined policy interests in their dis-

[19] Charles O. Jones, "Representation in Congress: The Case of the House Agricultural Committee," *The American Political Science Review* 55 (June 1961): 358–67.

LETTER FROM A CONGRESSMAN TO HIS CONSTITUENTS

[*The late Congressman Clem Miller of California gave an insider's view of Congress in a series of letters to his constituents. Here, he describes the committee process—one that has changed little since Miller's writing.*]

Dear Friend:

While action on the Floor of the House is the "moment of truth"—when you must say "yea" or "nay"—this is only the climax of years of patient work. Most of this time is consumed in the committee to which the bill was originally assigned. Here is where Congress does its job. Here is where congressmen work on each other endless, endless hours. Here is the heart of Congress, at least of the House of Representatives.

These committee rooms can be very imposing, and the semicircle of benches quite magisterial. The Appropriations Committee Room of the new Senate Office Building must be seen to be believed. There are sheets of green marble and huge bronze fixtures. Marks of ancient Rome are immediately at hand. Other rooms are friendly and warm, with a colonial patina that is very reassuring.

Members range about the chairman according to strict seniority, Republicans on the left, Democrats on the right. Everyone has a nameplate and status is faithfully guarded.

Should the chairman of our full committee enter the hearing room during subcommittee proceedings, the sitting chairman will immediately invite him to assume the chair. It is done in a gracious, natural, and spontaneous manner that speaks respect for the authority of our senior chairman. His quiet refusal to assume the chair is equally gracious. One can see in this sort of exchange the deepest loyalties of the House to tradition and seniority. Observing these forms, it may be difficult to recall the bitter debates that have raged down through the years.

Committees are variously run, depending on the temperament of the chairman. He has the widest latitude, and he may play the Caesar role or not, as he sees fit. Most committees are run with some attention to junior members. According to seniority, they are given the privilege of questioning witnesses. This privilege is vastly appreciated when granted, resented when not. Of course, in the large committee, the pickings may be a little lean when they get down to the freshman. But, being a politician, he will extract some advantage from the most meager bones.

Congressional hearings may serve many purposes. The principal one is to build the recorded base of knowledge upon which legislation can be constructed. Even where this is the honest desire of the committee, its crabbed way must often seem strange to the untutored bystander. Many of the

tricts sought and usually succeeded in getting assignments to committees having jurisdiction over those interests. For example, a representative who had substantial interests in tobacco would be assigned to the Tobacco Subcommittee of the House Agriculture Committee. At the committee stage the representative would work hard to take into account the demands of pressure groups in his or her district. Since most legislation is given final shape within committees, representatives who are on the relevant policy committee or committees for their district are in a good position to serve private interests within their constituencies.

---

issues before Congress have been around for years. The chairman may be excused if he leaves holes in his investigation. Why develop a long line of inquiry when it was fully covered by Report umpty-ump of the 84th Congress?

Many times, the hearings seem to be *pro forma*, just going through the motions, with the key decisions already made. They resemble a large verbal orchestration, as a "record" is carefully shaped under the vigilant gavel of the chairman. A standard parade of witnesses files by from the national organizations—AF of L, U.S. Chamber of Commerce, National Association of Manufacturers—then a seasoning of university professors, and so on. The witnesses are carved up or blown up, or tailored to the need. Some are dismissed peremptorily, others are drawn out solicitously.

Committee members engage in pages of fulsome, politically-laden flattery. And they

engage in almost unbearable cross-examination, only an eyelash from irreparable rudeness. There may be interminable irrelevance while a member chases down his own local, quirky byway to squeeze some personal advantage from a witness.

Sometimes the committee room is almost somnambulant as the hearing drifts on to arrive at its predetermined destination. Two members may be dwarfed in the large room, the lone witness below, with the court reporter puffing happily on a big cigar as he punches out the responses on his stenotype.

Other times there is excitement and novelty as, for example, listening to a tape recording of West Virginia miners out of work for two and three years—graphic testimony on the Depressed Areas Bill. Flat, soft voices, filling the room with an almost unbearable pathos. And then the blunt voice of the chairman: "That's

enough of that. We get the idea."

Or there is contrast: The very large executive testifying for the National Association of Manufacturers on the same bill. A long statement, an impenetrable reading of every ponderous word. Not a single solitary sentence in the entire statement to admit that there is a depressed area problem. Accompanying him, exquisitely groomed in *haute couture*, a woman sitting behind him precisely and erectly, her mind a thousand miles away, her head turning slowly, idly, by degrees, around the room. An unforgettable scene.

Very sincerely,
Clem Miller

Source: Clem Miller, *Member of the House: Letters of a Congressman*, Edited by John M. Baker. Copyright © 1962 by Charles Scribner's Sons (New York: Charles Scribner's Sons, 1962). Reprinted with the permission of Charles Scribner's Sons.

The internal political world of Capitol Hill shapes the character of Congress as much as the external political context within which the legislature functions. Members reach out to the president, the bureaucracy, interest groups, and constituents to achieve internal congressional goals of power and good public policy. They also seek these goals through committee assignments, party leadership positions, and the leadership of special caucuses in Congress, such as the Black Caucus.

Committees— the "Little Legislatures" of Congress

Congress, like most legislative bodies, has organized itself into committees in order to provide the requisite division of labor and specialization to meet the political demands made on it. Legislative efficiency and responsiveness, however, are not the only reasons for the decentralization of Congress into over three hundred committees and subcommittees. These goals would be accomplished far better through an integrated and coordinated system of a limited number of major committees. The real reason behind the dispersion of committees on Capitol Hill is the personal quest for power by both members and staffers, a goal that is often reached by both members and congressional aides through committees.

Power on Capitol Hill, which is in large part the reputation for power, is acquired by members when they become chairmen of standing or subcommittees. Staffers, too, who become the chief counsel or chief of staff for committees are thereby placed above their peers in power and status. The staff chiefs of committees often have as much power as their chairmen. Over the years, top congressional aides have gained power through greater continuity and expertise than their bosses. "The chairmen's representatives," a Senate group of top staffers that met each week for breakfast when the Senate was under democratic control in the 1970s, was carefully courted by the legislative liaison staff of the White House, which believed that the approval of the group was necessary to the passage of presidential programs.

There is a hierarchy of committees on Capitol Hill. The standing committees, which are the permanent committees that do not formally "rise" at the end of a legislative session, but continue from one session to another, have final power over all legislation. The standing committees are divided into subcommittees, many of which have in effect become little different from standing committees themselves in terms of their permanency and power. (See Tables 7.2 and 7.3.) The legislative jurisdiction of the fifteen standing committees of

Table 7.2

Ninety-seventh Congress (1981–1982), U.S. House of Representatives

Standing and select committees	Number of subcommittees
Agriculture	8
Appropriations	13
Armed Services	7
Banking, Finance and Urban Affairs	8
Budget	0; 9 task forces
District of Columbia	3
Education and Labor	8
Energy and Commerce	6
Foreign Affairs	8
Government Operations	7
House Administration	6; 1 task force
Interior and Insular Affairs	6
Judiciary	7
Merchant Marine and Fisheries	5
Post Office and Civil Service	7
Public Works and Transportation	6
Rules	2
Science and Technology	7
Select Aging	4
Select Intelligence	3
Select Narcotics Abuse and Control	0
Small Business	6
Standards of Office Conduct	0
Veterans' Affairs	5
Ways and Means	6
Total: 25	Total: 138

Table 7.3

Ninety-seventh Congress (1981–1982), U.S. Senate

Standing and select committees	Number of subcommittees
Agriculture, Nutrition and Forestry	8
Appropriations	13
Armed Services	6
Banking, Housing and Urban Affairs	7
Budget	0
Commerce, Science and Transportation	7
Energy and Natural Resources	6
Environment and Public Works	6
Finance	9
Foreign Relations	7
Governmental Affairs	8
Judiciary	9
Labor and Human Resources	7
Rules and Administration	0
Select Ethics	0
Select Intelligence	4
Select Small Business	8
Special Aging	0
Veterans' Affairs	0
Total: 20	Total: 105

the Senate and nineteen standing committees of the House are determined by the rules of each body. Subcommittees and their jurisdiction are created and determined by the standing committees. Additionally, both the House and the Senate have select or special committees that have been created to do specific tasks. Generally, select committees are investigative in nature and do not have the authority to report legislation, but some are little different from regular standing committees. For example, the select intelligence committees of the Senate and the House have legislative and budgetary authority over the Central Intelligence Agency, the Federal Bureau of Investigation, and other parts of the intelligence community.

New members of Congress seeking committee assignments make their requests known to the appropriate party committees. In the Senate, the Democratic Steering Committee, chaired in the Ninety-seventh Congress by Minority Leader Robert C. Byrd of West Virginia, determines the assignment of new members as well as transfers from one committee to another. In addition to Byrd, there are twenty-one Democratic senators on the Steering Committee, making it directly representative of close to half of all the Democratic senators. Senate committee assignments by Republicans are made by the party's Committee on Committees, chaired in the Ninety-seventh Congress by Indiana Senator Richard G. Lugar, who ran the committee with the help of fifteen Republican colleagues.

On the House side, assignments to the standing committees are made by the Democratic Steering and Policy Committee, and by the Republican Committee on Committees. The Speaker appoints members of select committees in the House, but in the Senate they are appointed in the same manner as standing committees.

The standing committees of Congress have jurisdiction over major spheres of public policy and the administrative departments and agencies that implement policy. The most prestigious committees—the House Appropriations and Ways and Means committees, the Senate Foreign Relations and Judiciary committees, and the predecessors of the Armed Services committees of both parties—date to the early days of the Republic. The most important responsibilities given to Congress by the Constitution have been delegated to these committees. Members seeking to build their Washington careers around the goal of personal power ardently strive to join committees such as Appropriations and Ways and Means because they represent the constitutional role of the House in the broader political system. On the Senate side, the unique powers of the Judiciary and Foreign Relations committees make them choice assignments for senators who want to achieve power and status in the body.

There is always a committee that serves the goals of members, whether they be striving for reelection, power, or good public policy. House members who have been unsuccessful in their attempts to join the Appropriations or Ways and Means committees may turn to the House Administration Committee, which has the authority to rule the budgets of each and

[20] Marguerite Michaels, "The Biggest Bully on Capitol Hill," *New York Magazine*, March 8, 1976, p. 39.

every committee of the House, including travel expenses for the much sought after foreign junkets, with an iron hand. The House Administration Committee came into its own under the chairmanship of Ohio Democrat Wayne Hays, who was proud of his reputation as the "meanest son-of-a-bitch on the hill."[20] Hays used the committee's power over office allowances, travel vouchers, telephone service, and office space to reward his friends and punish his enemies. From 1971 to 1976, when he was forced to resign when it was revealed that he kept his mistress, Elizabeth Ray, on the public payroll, Hays thoroughly enjoyed his reputation for power in the House.

Members of Congress who have reelection as their primary goal—mostly freshmen congressmen—seek pork-barrel committees from which they can claim credit for particularized benefits to constituents. Agriculture, Interior and Insular Affairs, Merchant Marine and Fisheries, Post Office and Civil Service, and Public Works and Transportation are good reelection committees. Appropriations subcommittees, too, have been used by members to channel public funds to their districts. And, in the House particularly, the Armed Services Committee was used effectively by its former chairman, South Carolina Democrat L. Mendel Rivers, who funnelled so much military money into his Charleston district that 35 percent of the employment payroll in the district came from military installations or defense industries. At the same time, Rivers was considered one of the most powerful members of the House, virtually equivalent to the secretary of defense. The Rivers example illustrates that both reelection and power may be achieved in one stroke by ingenious members who have chosen their committees and built their congressional careers carefully.

The passage of the Budget and Impoundment Control Act of 1974 created two potentially powerful new budget committees on each side of Capitol Hill. The Budget Committee of the House, however, was hobbled by the stipulation that its twenty-five members could not serve for more than four years out of any ten-year period, preventing members from developing a vested interest in the committee through long seniority. Moreover, ten of the twenty-five members of the Budget Committee come from the Appropriations and Ways and

Means committees, giving these traditional institutional committees what amounts to control over Budget Committee decisions. Although the Budget Committee has tried to claim increased powers to force the budgetary proposals coming from authorization and appropriations committees to conform with the budget resolutions passed by the House, members seeking influence still prefer the traditionally most powerful committees of Appropriations and Ways and Means.

The Budget Committee in the Senate is potentially more powerful than that in the House because its membership is not restricted, nor controlled by outside committees. The first chairman of the Senate Budget Committee, Democrat Edmund Muskie of Maine, spent years attempting to use the position to bolster his power within the Senate. Muskie won some battles, but generally found that he was outmaneuvered by Finance Committee chairman Russell Long of Louisiana, who saw the Budget Committee as a distinct threat to his turf. Long consistently undermined the authority of the Budget Committee through skillful parliamentary tactics and political persuasion, to the point where Muskie seriously considered resigning as chairman.

The prominence of budgetary problems in the Ninety-seventh Congress, in response to the new Reagan program, focused attention once again upon the congressional Budget Committees. Their new chairman, Oklahoma Democrat Jim Jones in the House and New Mexico Republican Pete Domenici in the Senate, immediately began to seize the reins of budgetary power, and prepared to dominate the budgetary process rather than merely act as mediators between powerful committees.[21]

[21] The congressional budget process is discussed in more detail below.

The establishment of the Budget Committees in 1974 introduced a new dimension to the balance of power that had prevailed among congressional committees in the budgetary process. Before that, the Appropriations Committees of both bodies had been the dominant force in making final determinations regarding the amounts of money that actually could be spent for particular programs.

Appropriations and Subject Matter Committees. There are two types of committees in Congress—appropriations and subject matter—that have different kinds of authority over the policy process. Appropriations committees, as the name implies, have the responsibility of actually designating how much money will be spent to implement legislation that has been passed by the subject matter committees. Subject matter committees have jurisdiction over particular areas of policy, such as agriculture, defense, and veterans' affairs. (See Figure 7.1.) They may *authorize* money to be spent in the areas over which they have jurisdiction, but they cannot in any way guarantee that the levels of authorization will be the same as the budgets finally approved by the appropriations committees.

The appropriations committees can stymie the implementation of any legislation simply by refusing to appropriate adequate funds for administration. Of what use is it for Congress to pass a law that guarantees equality in voting rights and hiring practices if insufficient funding is given to administrative agencies to enforce such policies? There is little doubt that the vigor with which administrative agencies are capable of developing and implementing policies is profoundly affected by their financial resources. The appropriations committees of both the House and the Senate have a large say in the way in which the revenues flowing to government will be distributed among the various components of the executive branch, and therefore among different policy objectives.

The prestige of the Appropriations Committees of both the House and the Senate is indicated by the fact that the most senior members of both bodies serve on those committees. The chairmanships of the Appropriations Committees are the most sought after in Congress. The second-ranking members of the committees always move up to the chairmanships when vacancies occur, unhesitatingly relinquishing their chairmanships of other committees. For example, when the senior Arkansas Democrat John McClellan, chairman of the Appropriations Committee, died in the second session of the Ninety-fifth Congress (1978), the second-ranking member, Warren Magnuson of Washington, gave up his chairmanship of the Commerce Committee, which he had used so effectively to build popularity and power, in order to take over the Appropriations Committee. Magnuson knew that the Commerce Committee had been important to his career and his

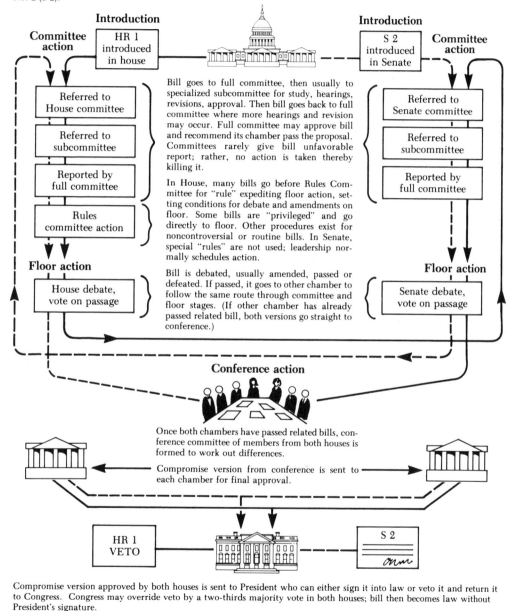

This graphic shows the most typical way in which proposed legislation is enacted into law. There are more complicated, as well as simpler, routes and most bills fall by the wayside and never become law. The process is illustrated with two hypothetical bills, House bill No. 1 (HR 1) and Senate bill No. 2 (S 2).

Each bill must be passed by both houses of Congress in identical form before it can become law. The path of HR 1 is traced by a solid line, that of S 2 by a broken line. However, in practice most legislation begins as similar proposals in both houses.

Introduction
Committee action

HR 1 introduced in house

Referred to House committee

Referred to subcommittee

Reported by full committee

Rules committee action

Floor action

House debate, vote on passage

Introduction
Committee action

S 2 introduced in Senate

Referred to Senate committee

Referred to subcommittee

Reported by full committee

Floor action

Senate debate, vote on passage

Bill goes to full committee, then usually to specialized subcommittee for study, hearings, revisions, approval. Then bill goes back to full committee where more hearings and revision may occur. Full committee may approve bill and recommend its chamber pass the proposal. Committees rarely give bill unfavorable report; rather, no action is taken thereby killing it.

In House, many bills go before Rules Committee for "rule" expediting floor action, setting conditions for debate and amendments on floor. Some bills are "privileged" and go directly to floor. Other procedures exist for noncontroversial or routine bills. In Senate, special "rules" are not used; leadership normally schedules action.

Bill is debated, usually amended, passed or defeated. If passed, it goes to other chamber to follow the same route through committee and floor stages. (If other chamber has already passed related bill, both versions go straight to conference.)

Conference action

Once both chambers have passed related bills, conference committee of members from both houses is formed to work out differences.

Compromise version from conference is sent to each chamber for final approval.

HR 1 VETO

S 2

Compromise version approved by both houses is sent to President who can either sign it into law or veto it and return it to Congress. Congress may override veto by a two-thirds majority vote in both houses; bill then becomes law without President's signature.

Source: Guide to Congress, November 1976 (Washington, D.C.: Congressional Quarterly, Inc.) p. 345. By permission.

FIGURE 7.1
How a Bill Becomes a Law. *Committees play a dominant role in the legislative process.*

reelection prospects, but chose the Appropriations Committee instead because of its even greater prestige within the body. What impresses Senate colleagues, however, does not necessarily sway voters. The Republican sweep cost Magnuson his seat in the 1980 elections.

Congressional Parties

The parties of Congress, while not disciplined, represent an integrative force that often is in direct conflict with the dispersed and individualistic committees. The effective exercise of power by the party leaders requires that headstrong committee chairmen be kept in line, a task that even the most skillful congressional leaders have been unable to accomplish consistently.

While it is clear that it is difficult to maintain party discipline in Congress, members of both parties vote along party lines more than 65 percent of the time. This indicates that party ideologies do mean something, and that the leaderships of the congressional parties have a higher degree of success than is generally attributed to them in marshalling their forces to vote along party lines.

Party rule in Congress, particularly in the House, has been made more difficult by important changes that began to occur in the 1960s and culminated in the decade of the 1970s. "Reforms" were enacted to disperse greater power to rank and file party members in the House, and, most importantly, to increase the number and power of subcommittees so that more members could get a piece of the action.

Ironically, the decentralization of power within the House as well as within the Senate in the 1970s resulted from a feeling among party members that powerful committee chairmen were unrepresentative of a cross section of party views. Many party members felt that party responsibility would be increased if it became more difficult for a small clique of party leaders to rule Capitol Hill. During the 1950s and early 1960s the Democratic parties on both sides of Capitol Hill were largely controlled by conservative southern congressmen and senators who did not reflect the views of a majority of the congressional Democratic party, nor of the national presidential Democratic party. The Democratic

Study Group, composed of liberal members of the House, was formed in 1965 to work on a strategy to break the control of the conservative Democrats, but it was not until 1973 that the Democratic Study Group began to see the fruits of its efforts.

One of the major bastions of conservative strength in the House had been the Rules Committee, traditionally chaired by conservative Southern Democrats. The power of the Rules Committee was formidable, for it essentially had a veto over what legislation would reach the floor, and the terms of the debate that would be allowed on legislation. Although there were ways to bypass the Rules Committee, through a suspension of the rules by a two-thirds vote or a discharge petition that required a majority vote, they were rarely used.[22] Even the most powerful Speakers, such as Texas Congressman Sam Rayburn, who led the House between 1940 and 1961, with the exception of four years of Republican rule (the Eightieth Congress, 1947–48; and the Eighty-third Congress, 1953–54), found the Rules Committee to be an important obstacle to his leadership. Rayburn did succeed in weakening the committee somewhat by enlarging it, but it was not until 1973 that the Democratic Speaker was given the power to select the Democratic members of the Rules Committee.

The weakening of the Rules Committee in 1973 marked the beginning of a major trend towards decentralization of party power in the House. A "subcommittee bill of rights" was passed that prevented the chairmen of standing committees from arbitrarily controlling the budgets and staffs of subcommittees. Moreover, the parent standing committees could not arbitrarily remove jurisdiction over important legislation from subcommittees. As the reforms of the Ninety-third Congress (1973–74) continued, the Democrats removed the power of appointment of all committee members from the Democratic members of the Ways and Means committee, where it had been lodged in the past, and gave it to an expanded Democratic Steering and Policy Committee of twenty-four members—three chosen by the caucus, twelve elected by regional groupings of Democrats in the House, and nine appointed by the Speaker. Democratic committee chairmen were first nominated by the Steering Committee, but had to be approved by the larger Democratic Caucus of all Demo-

[22] Another complicated method of bypassing the Rules Committee was the "calendar Wednesday procedure," used successfully only twice, under which committee chairmen could place bills that had been reported from their committees on a special calendar that was called each Wednesday. A bill passing on the Wednesday it was called became law without going through the Rules Committee.

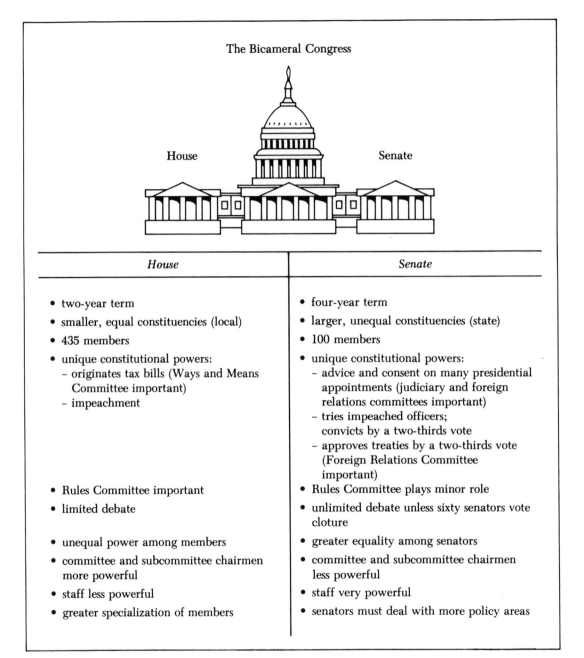

The Bicameral Congress

House   Senate

House	Senate
• two-year term	• four-year term
• smaller, equal constituencies (local)	• larger, unequal constituencies (state)
• 435 members	• 100 members

• unique constitutional powers:
  – originates tax bills (Ways and Means Committee important)
  – impeachment
	• unique constitutional powers:
	  – advice and consent on many presidential appointments (judiciary and foreign relations committees important)
	  – tries impeached officers; convicts by a two-thirds vote
	  – approves treaties by a two-thirds vote (Foreign Relations Committee important)

• Rules Committee important	• Rules Committee plays minor role
• limited debate	• unlimited debate unless sixty senators vote cloture
• unequal power among members	• greater equality among senators
• committee and subcommittee chairmen more powerful	• committee and subcommittee chairmen less powerful
• staff less powerful	• staff very powerful
• greater specialization of members	• senators must deal with more policy areas

FIGURE 7.2
The Bicameral Congress

cratic members of the House. The Caucus flexed its newly acquired muscles at the beginning of the Ninety-fourth Congress in 1975, voting to unseat the powerful senior chairmen of the Agriculture, Armed Services, and Small Business Committees.

Although the Republicans were a persistent minority in the 1960s and 1970s, they too decentralized party power in the House. The Republican Conference was revived, led by Illinois Congressman John Anderson, and adopted the practice of voting by secret ballot on the Republican committee nominees selected by the Republican Committee on Committees. Formerly, seniority was not required to become the ranking member of a committee or, if the Republicans were in a majority, its chairman. Republicans, like Democrats, were not permitted to hold more than one position of party leadership in the House.

The winds of change in the House which led to a decentralization of power swept to the north side of Capitol Hill and modified the Senate as well. The adjustments made by the Senate, however, were more subtle and informal than those of the House. (See Figure 7.2.) Prior to the 1970s the Senate had long been dominated by an "establishment," an inner corps of senators, mostly southerners, who had seniority and who determined the norms of the body. The Senate establishment was a collegial elite, an inner club of senators who liked each other and who had the same values of hard work, reverence for the institution, courtesy, and respect for colleagues. Members of the club did not have to be of any particular ideological persuasion, but they did have to conform to the norms of the Senate that had been developed by its senior members over the years.[23]

The decade of the 1970s saw far greater turnover in the Senate than had occurred in the past. As early as 1970, newly arrived freshmen senators began to demand a greater voice in Senate proceedings, a voice that had traditionally been denied senators until they had served an apprenticeship of at least several years. The Senate freshman class of 1970 formed its own caucus and made it known that new senators would not remain silent while their senior colleagues controlled the institution and received its choice plums in the form of committee chairmanships and staff.

[23] The Senate establishment, or inner club, is described in William S. White, *Citadel: The Story of the United States Senate* (Boston: Houghton Mifflin, 1956); and Donald R. Matthews, *U.S. Senators and Their World* (Chapel Hill: University of North Carolina Press, 1960).

By the mid-1970s, the iron grip that the old Senate establishment had on the body had been loosened to the point where freshmen senators of the majority party were customarily given subcommittee chairmanships and staffs of their own. Moreover, newcomers to the body were not expected to serve a long apprenticeship period before actively participating in Senate proceedings. Many of the norms of the Senate, however, such as hard work, courtesy, and collegiality, remained and were followed by a new group of senators that rapidly were on the way to becoming a new Senate establishment that was more open than the inner club of the past, but which nevertheless required senators to adhere to many of the traditional norms in order to be accepted. A major difference between the new and the old inner clubs was the ability of freshmen senators to become part of the establishment. Democratic Senator John Glenn of Ohio, for example, immediately made his mark in the Senate and was accepted by powerful colleagues as one of their own. Glenn was a Senate insider. During the same period South Dakota Senator James Abourezk took a different path, and became a Senate maverick, which automatically placed him outside of the newly emerging inner club of the 1970s. As Abourezk approached the end of his first term in 1978 he decided not to seek reelection, publicly proclaiming that he had been excluded from the Senate elite and did not feel that he could be effective in the body.

The opening up of the inner club of the Senate reflected a decentralization of power that required Senate leaders to cultivate their party colleagues carefully in order to wield power effectively. No longer could a small group of senators determine the course of Senate action.

The break-up of the old inner club in the Senate was reflected in the passage of Senate Resolution 4 in 1977 that reorganized the committee system and gave junior senators more staff than they had been able to claim before. The 1977 reforms limited the number of committee chairmanships that could be held by any one senator as well as the number of committees on which senators could serve. The result of this "reform" was to spread power more evenly throughout the body. The reforms themselves were initially pushed by more junior senators who were able to garner enough support to defeat strong opposition from such powerful members as Louisiana Senator Russell Long, Mississippi Senator John Stennis, Abraham Ribicoff of Connecticut, and other powerful committee chairmen who saw in the reforms a threat to their internal Senate power.

In the Ninety-seventh Congress, party leaders in both the House and the Senate had to rely upon their powers of persuasion more than ever before to achieve party cohesion in the numerous stages of the legislative process, which extend from committee to floor. A brief review of the apparatus of congressional parties will serve to illustrate their effectiveness.

The Speaker of the House. The Speaker of the House, a constitutional office, is in his own right one of the most powerful politicians in Washington.[24] That power can be greatly enhanced through astute political persuasion. Because the Speaker is chosen by a majority of the House, he is the first-ranking leader of his party. On the Democratic side, the Speaker chairs the Steering and Policy Committee and appoints nine of its twenty-four members. Through the Steering and Policy Committee, which controls the scheduling of legislation as well as Democratic committee assignments, the Speaker has the greatest influence of any member of the House in setting the legislative agenda. Knowing that the Speaker is the key to success in the House, presidents carefully court him to help their legislative programs to survive the complicated legislative maze of Capitol Hill. The Speaker not only determines the scheduling of legislation on the floor, but also controls the Rules Committee through which most legislation must pass, and appoints the House members of conference committees to meet with their Senate counterparts to resolve legislative differences between the two sides of Capitol Hill. Not to be overlooked as an important adjunct of the Speaker's power is his ability to determine Capitol office and parking spaces, and who will travel with him on foreign junkets.

The Speaker of the House has always had seniority, which means that he comes from a safe district. In the twentieth century no Speaker has been defeated at the polls. House

[24] Article I, sec. 2, provides that the House of Representatives "shall choose their speaker and other officers...."

Speaker Thomas O'Neill has represented the Eighth District of Massachusetts, which includes Cambridge and parts of Boston, since 1953. O'Neill, the classic Massachusetts "pol," became Speaker in 1977. Much of the success of President Carter's energy program and other legislative proposals can be credited to O'Neill's political and parliamentary skills, although the Speaker was at first disenchanted with the new president, who knew little about how to deal with the politics of Capitol Hill.

Floor Leaders. Assisting the Speaker is the majority leader, an important position that usually is a stepping-stone to the speakership itself. Both the majority and minority floor leaders have the responsibility to marshall the troops on important party issues. The floor leaders have their own staffs as an adjunct of their offices, an important emolument and symbol of power within the House. The floor leaders are in touch with each other and with the Speaker in guiding the legislative agenda, and communicate regularly with other party members, particularly the chairmen of key committees, to improve the chances for party cohesion. Democrat James Wright of Texas was elected to the House in 1954, and decided in 1976 to run for majority leader, an election he won by the narrowest of margins. The Republican floor leader, Robert Michel of Illinois, was elected in 1956 and rose through the ranks of the party to become the minority leader in the Ninety-seventh Congress. Michel had chaired the congressional campaign committee and served as whip before he replaced Arizona Congressman John Rhodes, who voluntarily stepped down, as minority leader in 1981.

The Senate majority leader informally holds many of the powers of both the Speaker and the majority leader of the House. He does not preside over the Senate, but closely directs parliamentary proceedings on important matters through informal consultation with the presiding officer.[25] The powers of the majority leader extend as far as his ability to persuade his colleagues to support him and his party's position. Effective majority leaders stress the importance of collegiality and lead by consensus, not by command. The majority leader, with the assistance of a parliamentarian and staff aides, as-

[25] The presiding officer of the Senate is the vice-president, the president *pro tempore,* or most commonly an acting president *pro tempore.* Senators rotate as acting presidents *pro tempore* over the Senate.

signs legislation to committees and determines what legislation will be brought to the floor for debate and a vote. Standing opposite the majority leader, the minority leader attempts to bring about as much cohesion as possible among his party colleagues. Both majority and minority leaders are judged by their fairness and efficiency, qualities that are usually necessary to be elected to the leadership positions in the first place.

The opening of the Ninety-seventh Congress in 1981 saw the first Republican majority leader since 1953, Tennessee Senator Howard Baker. Former Majority Leader Robert Byrd of West Virginia, having fought so hard to become majority leader in 1976, found himself as minority leader in a position for which he was totally unprepared and that he had hardly expected. Byrd had originally been chosen by his colleagues because he was a skillful tactician, devoted to the Senate, and always paid meticulous attention to details of running the Senate that made life easier for his colleagues. Baker, elected minority leader in 1977, was, like Byrd, considered fair and efficient, and also charismatic. Baker was far more of a national political figure than Byrd, and once he assumed the position of majority leader his impressive style and political skills resulted in an unusually large measure of party support for President Reagan. The new Republican majority in the Senate, appreciative of their newfound power, were happy to follow Baker's lead.

Party Whips. Assisting the majority and minority leaders in both the House and the Senate are the majority and minority "whips," who monitor the moods of party colleagues in an effort to bring about as much party cohesion as possible. In the House, the majority whip is appointed by the Speaker when the Democrats are in control, and by the majority leader on those rare occasions when the Democrats have been in a minority. The Republicans elect their majority whip in the House. In the Senate, both majority and minority whips are elected by caucuses of the respective parties.

The position of whip in the House has been an important stepping-stone in the Democratic party to the higher party posts of majority leader and Speaker. At the opening of the

Ninety-seventh Congress, Illinois Congressman Dan Rostenkowski, for example, had the choice of becoming chairman of
the Ways and Means Committee or majority whip. Rostenkowski had strong ambitions to become Speaker, and knew
that becoming whip would put him on the right track as it had
others before him, like Speaker Thomas (Tip) O'Neill, whom
the then Speaker Carl Albert had chosen to become whip in
1971. Rostenkowski finally decided to take the Ways and
Means chairmanship, however, after strong persuasion by
O'Neill who wanted the politically astute Illinois congressman to head the most important committee in the House.

On the Republican side, the whip is elected by the party
conference or caucus of its members, and that position is also
a stepping-stone to higher party posts. Illinois Republican
Bob Michel, for example, who became minority leader in
1981, was elected to be the Republican whip in 1974.

Both parties in the House have a number of subordinate
whips that are appointed and elected by the leadership to
assist in bringing about a semblance of party discipline. The
Democrats and Republicans, respectively, have zone and regional whips chosen by state delegations within major geographical areas of the country. The whip organizations in the
Senate are less significant positions of party leadership than
those in the House. Both parties elect their whips in the
Senate, and on occasion party whips have been in sharp
conflict with party leaders. For example, Louisiana Democrat
Russell Long, when he was the party whip from 1965 until
1969, openly challenged the majority leader, Montana Democrat Mike Mansfield. Although the position of whip is not
considered to be a stepping-stone to the majority or minority
leadership posts in the Senate, Robert Byrd, who defeated
Edward Kennedy for the whip position in 1971, used the post
to cultivate party support that would lead to his becoming
majority leader in 1976.

Party Committees, Caucuses, and Conferences. Party organization in both the House and the Senate is assisted by special
party committees and by caucuses or conferences of party
members. The House Democratic Steering and Policy Committee, controlled by the Speaker, selects Democratic commit-

tee members, subject to final approval by the Democratic caucus. The position of chairman of the caucus, held in 1981–82 by Louisiana Congressman Gillis Long, has been important in the party hierarchy since the resurgence of the power of the caucus in the early 1970s. On the Republican side of the House, a party Committee on Committees, chaired by the minority leader, makes Republican committee assignments. The Republican conference, which is the caucus of all Republican members, must approve committee assignments. The position of chairman of the conference, held in 1981–82 by New York Congressman Jack Kemp, is an important party leadership post, although not equivalent in power to the caucus chairman on the Democratic side.

The Senate also has party committees that make committee assignments, the Democratic Steering Committee and the Committee on Committees. The Democratic Steering Committee in the Senate is chaired by the Democratic leader, but the Republican leader does not chair the Committee on Committees.

Other party positions of importance in Congress are the House and the Senate Campaign Committees for each party, policy committees (merged with the Steering Committee in the House Democratic organization), and several minor committees. The party policy committees were an outgrowth of the Legislative Reorganization Act of 1946, and were established to aid the parties in the development and coordination of party programs. The policy committees are most effective as party instruments where they are chaired by party leaders, as in the case of the Democratic Policy Committee in the Senate, under the chairmanship of party leader Robert Byrd. The Republican Senate Policy Committee, however, is chaired by Texas Senator John Tower, and does not include the party's floor leader, Howard Baker. The House Democrats have developed the most effective party policy committee by merging it with the Steering Committee and placing it under the control of the Speaker and majority leader. The Democratic Steering and Policy Committee can provide leadership at the same time it represents a cross section of party views by including ex officio nine of the most important party leaders of the House. In addition to the Speaker and majority leader, the

Steering and Policy Committee includes the party whip, and the chairmen of the Appropriations, Budget, Rules, and Ways and Means Committees. If the Democrats were the minority party, the ranking members of these important committees would be represented on the Steering and Policy Committee.

The committees and party organizations of Capitol Hill are the principal vehicles through which the members of Congress play out the constant and continuous drama of legislative politics. The vast number of committees and subcommittees reflect the forces of decentralization, while the parties strive to bring some cohesion and meaningful ideological debate to Congress. The forces of change on Capitol Hill have favored the fragmentation rather than the integration of power. The iron fist of party leaders has been replaced by kid gloves. Even committee chairmen, especially in the House, have had to relinquish some of their power to subcommittee chairmen as the result of the "subcommittee bill of rights" and other procedural rules.

The dispersion of power on Capitol Hill has resulted not only from rules changes and the explosion of subcommittees, but also from the formation of special groups and "caucuses" that reflect special interests.

The Caucuses and Special Groups of Congress

Special interests exist within Congress as well as outside it. Primarily a phenomenon of the House of Representatives, members have organized caucuses, coalitions, and groups to represent special interests, points of view, and most importantly, to become a basis for exercising power within Congress. Over twenty special groups have been formed in the House, including the Black Caucus, the Congressional Hispanic Caucus, the Congresswomen's Caucus, the Environmental Study Conference, the Textile Caucus, and the Steel Caucus. One of the most interesting groups is the congressional Tourism Caucus, formed in 1979 to promote tourism throughout the United States. Two hundred and fifty members of Congress are part of the Tourism Caucus, making it by far the largest special group within Congress. The Tourism Caucus is the envy of other groups, as it boldly holds fundraisers to fill its treasury. At its first fundraiser, fifty-seven groups contributed the maximum amount of a thousand dollars each for a ticket to a lavish dinner. The fundraiser brought in over two hundred thousand dollars, which members of Congress cannot use directly, but which pays a large staff that is generously given space in House office buildings.

Admittedly, most of the caucuses on Capitol Hill are not as rich or effective in shaping policy touching their interests as is the Tourism Caucus, but all of them employ staff that uses House offices, usually in one of the "annexes" down the street from the Rayburn Building on the south side of Capitol Hill.

Legislators who chair important caucuses receive recognition within and without Congress. The chairman of the Black Caucus, for example, is considered by the president to be a representative of black opinion and is invited to the White House to discuss presidential programs affecting black interests. The chairwoman of the women's caucus has high visibility among women's groups and is considered to be the spokeswoman for the interests of one segment of the women's community on Capitol Hill.

While the caucuses do not directly impinge upon congressional parties, other groups have been formed that do. The Democratic study group became an important component of the Democratic party in the House after it was established in 1956, representing the views of liberal members. Liberal Republicans created the Wednesday Club in the Eighty-eighth Congress (1963–64). Understandably, the Wednesday Club has had little influence in the largely conservative Republican party, a conservatism that was greatly strengthened after the 1980 elections. That conservatism was reflected in the creation of the conservative Democratic Forum after the 1980 elections, composed of conservative Democrats, mostly southerners, who planned to join with House Republicans to form a majority on critical issues. The group, organized by Texas Democrat Charles Stenholm, quickly moved to push the House Democratic leadership to the right. O'Neill responded by appointing more conservatives to the Steering and Policy Committee and supported the appointment of one of their members, Texas Congressman Phil Gramm, to the Budget Committee. As the Reagan budget proposals were sent to Capitol Hill, the forty-four–member

Democratic Forum held the balance of power, a strategic position of strength from which it could effectively negotiate both with the members of its own party and with the Republicans.

The expansion of caucuses and special groups within Congress is consistent with the trend toward decentralization of power that has made it so difficult for party leaders to maintain even a semblance of discipline.

THE CONGRESSIONAL BUDGET PROCESS

Capitol Hill has always reflected a tug-of-war between the forces of decentralization and centralization. The expansion of committees, caucuses, and special groups and coalitions has fragmented the legislative process. Party leaders have struggled against these centrifugal tendencies with only limited success. Party leaders, particularly in the House, strongly supported the new congressional process created by the Budget and Impoundment Control Act of 1974 in the hope that it would make Congress more effective as a collective body in confrontation with what had been the overriding power of the executive in the formulation of the national budget. However, the attempt to integrate and centralize the congressional budget process threatened the power of both appropriations and authorization committees that had always had free rein in determining budgetary allocations.

The Budget and Impoundment Control Act of 1974

The new congressional budget process was created by the Budget Act of 1974. At first sponsored by only a small group of leaders in the House and the Senate, the legislation finally passed overwhelmingly after it had been sufficiently amended to assure committee chairmen that their traditional powers would not be threatened.

Both external and internal politics shaped the Budget Act. The immediate impetus for the legislation was the struggle between the Democratic Congress and the Nixon White House, which saw the president vetoing congressional appropriations bills and impounding funds that Congress had appropriated for a wide range of programs. The president's impoundment authority was based upon a series of anti-deficiency acts that were first passed in the 1880s to allow the president to prevent the expenditure of funds that would lead to deficits in the federal budget. The impoundment authority was first extensively used during the Truman administration, when the president ordered substantial impoundments of defense appropriations. Although previous impoundments had raised the ire of Capitol Hill, the extent of the Nixon impoundments, coupled with the fact that a Republican president was defying a Democratic Congress, precipitated congressional action to end the president's impoundment authority.

The impoundment issue of the Nixon administration was coupled with the congressional budgetary process because one of President Nixon's major rationale for impounding funds was that Congress had acted irresponsibly in authorizing and appropriating expenditures that exceeded government revenues. The argument of the White House was not that a balanced budget was required, but that budgetary planning was necessary that could reasonably determine the revenues and expenditures of the government for upcoming fiscal years. Before the passage of the Budget Act, Congress had little response to the president's challenge, since there was no way to coordinate effectively the congressional committee process that had the final authority to determine government revenues and expenditures.

Presumably, if Congress could engage in effective budgetary planning, assuring that within limits revenues and expenditures would be balanced, there would be no need for a presidential impoundment authority. The Budget Act of 1974 linked the end of the president's impoundment authority with the establishment of the new budget process on Capitol Hill. Under the law, the president can no longer permanently impound funds without congressional approval. At the same time, the act establishes an elaborate procedure to encourage responsible budgeting by Congress.

The Budget Act created new budget committees in both the House and the Senate, and established a congressional Budget

The Budget Committees and Budget Process

Office to assist all congressional committees in assessing the budgetary implications of their recommendations. The Act also introduced a new budget timetable for both the committees and Congress itself in submitting and approving budgetary proposals. (See Table 7.4.)

The budget process focuses upon the formulation of two concurrent budget resolutions, the first scheduled for May 15, and the second for September 15, just before the beginning of the fiscal year on October 1. The budget committees formulate the resolutions after receiving the president's budget and the views of the congressional committees. The first budget resolution represents a target for Congress, one that may be and usually is amended extensively as the budget process continues over the summer months, leading to the passage of the second and final budget resolution in the fall.

On its face, the Budget Act seems to give the Budget Committees power superior to that of the Appropriations and Authorization Committees. However, the politics of Congress have dictated far weaker Budget Committees than the proponents of a centralized congressional budgetary process wanted. In the House, the Budget Committee itself was greatly weakened in relation to other committees when it was made a temporary rather than a permanent committee. Members cannot serve for more than four years in a ten-year period, and the Appropriations and Ways and Means Committees control ten of the twenty-five slots on the committee. As the Budget Act was being considered, the chairmen and powerful members of the Appropriations and Ways and Means Committees were trying to make certain that their power would not be threatened by the new House Budget Committee. The Senate Budget Committee was not formally weakened, like its counterpart in the House, but powerful Senate chairmen—particularly Louisiana Senator Russell Long of the Finance Committee—did not hesitate to undermine the authority of the new Budget Committee when it threatened their turf.

The budget process has reflected the politics of Capitol Hill, the constant power struggles among committees, staff, and party leaders. The formalities of the budget process that were so easily laid out by the Budget Act do not represent the

Table 7.4
Congressional Budget Timetable

Deadline	Action to be completed
15th day after Congress convenes	President submits his budget, along with current services estimates.*
March 15	Committees submit views and estimates to Budget Committees.
April 1	Congressional Budget Office submits report to Budget Committees.†
April 15	Budget Committees report first concurrent resolution on the budget to their Houses.
May 15	Committees report bills authorizing new budget authority.
May 15	Congress adopts first concurrent resolution on the budget.
7th day after Labor Day	Congress completes action on bills providing budget authority and spending authority.
September 15	Congress completes actions on second required concurrent resolution on the budget.
September 25	Congress completes action on reconciliation process implementing second concurrent resolution.
October 1	Fiscal year begins.

Note: Congress has not always adhered to these deadlines. In recent years, Congress has fallen increasingly behind schedule.

* Current service estimates of the dollar levels that would be required next year to support the same level of services in each program as this year's budget. The Budget Act originally required submission of the current services estimates by November 10 of the previous year. Since the president was still in the midst of developing his budget proposals for the next year, Congress later agreed to permit simultaneous submission of the current services and executive budgets in January.

† The Budget Committees and CBO have found April 1 too late in the budget process to be useful; hence CBO submits its report(s) in February, although April 1 remains the date required by law.

realities of the process. The Budget Committees have been unable to control the Appropriations, Ways and Means, Finance, and Authorization Committees. The budgetary process is dictated more by the iron triangles of committees, agencies, and pressure groups than by a rational overview of budgetary needs emanating from the budget committees. The centrifugal forces of Capitol Hill dominated budgeting regardless of the best intentions of the proponents of centralized budgeting procedures.

In the first few Congresses after the Budget Act went into effect, the Budget Committees were little more than rubber stamps for the far more powerful traditional committees on the Hill. Far from dominating the budgeting process, the House Budget Committee essentially shaped the budget resolutions to accommodate the interests of the most powerful committees in the body. On the Senate side, Budget Committee Chairman Edmund Muskie valiantly fought for control, only to find his efforts constantly undermined by Finance Committee Chairman Russell Long and other chairmen as well, including those of Appropriations, Armed Services, Agriculture, and Veterans Affairs. The chairmen of the Budget Committees of the House and the Senate knew that their power could extend only so far as they were supported by the membership of their respective bodies. But that membership was more used to and supportive of the power of the regular committees and their prominent chairmen. Even congressmen and senators who had not yet achieved a committee chairmanship knew that the power they ultimately sought would be less significant if a precedent was established under which the Budget Committees could dominate the other committees and subcommittees of Congress.

The Reagan administration's emphasis on the need for responsible budgeting, and the overriding emphasis upon budgetary problems in the Ninety-seventh Congress, once again put the Budget Committees and the entire congressional budget process in the limelight. The new chairmen of the committees, Democrat James Jones of Oklahoma in the House and New Mexico Republican Pete Domenici in the Senate, basked in the glow. They did not hesitate to use the opportunity to strengthen their power within Congress and visibility outside it. Efforts were made once again to make the Budget Committees a more effective instrument of centralized control. The chairmen wanted more power to deal with specific budget items within the jurisdiction of the Appropriations Committees. For example, Senate Budget Committee Chairman Domenici wanted to amend the Budget Act to permit his committee to set binding spending limits in particular budget areas.

As the House and Senate Budget Committee chairmen and their staffs looked for ways to increase the power of the budget panels, the Appropriations Committees of both bodies, the Ways and Means Committee of the House and the Senate Finance Committee began to marshall forces to oppose legislative changes that would reduce their power by limiting their traditional jurisdiction.

The Budget Act of 1974 contained a potentially important provision that gave Congress the authority to change government expenditures and revenues by using its budget resolutions to force changes in programs already in existence. Under the reconciliation process, a majority of the House or the Senate instructs Appropriations and Authorization Committees to adjust revenues and expenditures under existing law. The Budget Committees recommend reconciliation resolutions subject to the approval of the House or the Senate. Reconciliation was used for the first time in 1980, for the budget resolution for the fiscal year 1981. In the first budget resolution, Congress required committees to trim programs by 4.6 billion dollars and increase revenues by 3.6 billion. President Reagan relied heavily on the process of reconciliation to implement his proposals to bring the federal budget under control. In the Senate, the Budget Committee unanimously supported a reconciliation resolution that instructed fourteen authorizing and appropriations committees to cut $36.4 billion from the fiscal 1982 budget that had been proposed by President Carter in January of 1981. Shortly after the Budget Committee action, on 2 April 1981, the Senate endorsed the reconciliation resolution by a vote of 88–10, indicating that both Republicans and Democrats strongly supported the idea of government savings. Although the reconciliation orders (see Table 7.5) were supported nearly unanimously in the Senate, powerful committee chairmen warned that although they would make the necessary reduc-

Reconciliation

tions, the specific items that would be eliminated from the budget would be within their discretion. The chairmen made this claim even though the Senate in certain cases instructed the committees to make cuts in programs as designated by the Senate.

The House also adopted reconciliation in the first session of the Ninety-seventh Congress in 1981. Unlike the Senate, however, the House incorporated its reconciliation recommendations into its first budget resolution. The Democratic majority in the House, however, while supporting Reagan's proposal for a balanced budget, did not agree with many of his specific recommendations. The reconciliation orders of the House did not cut as deeply into social programs as those passed by the Senate.

Table 7.5
Senate Reconciliation Orders *(fiscal years, in millions of dollars)*

| Committee | 1981 | | 1982 | |
	Budget Authority Cuts	Outlay Cuts	Budget Authority Cuts	Outlay Cuts
Agriculture	$ 645	$ 166	$ 3,717	$ 4,128
Appropriations	13,300	1,500	—	3,200
Armed Services	233	233	966	966
Banking	6,146	133	15,460	958
Commerce	—	—	1,708	1,034
Energy	2,071	106	3,714	3,404
Environment, Public Works	2,350	68	4,935	978
Finance	212	295	4,450	9,466
Foreign Relations	—	—	1,050	301
Governmental Affairs	—	—	4,776	5,203
Judiciary	—	—	116	13
Labor, Human Resources	2,427	463	10,961	8,550
Small Business	97	67	526	390
Veterans	14	14	446	407
*Total Cuts**	$14,667	$2,353	$52,825	$36,945
Reagan Cuts	17,180	2,951	49,736	34,091

Source: *Congressional Quarterly Weekly Report*, 4 April 1981, p. 603.
* *Totals have been adjusted to eliminate double counting for programs affected by cuts in both authorizations and appropriations.*

The future of the budget process of Capitot Hill depends upon the trend of congressional politics. While those politics have occasionally dictated the need for collective action and a strengthening of congressional procedures, as in the passage of the Budget Act itself, more commonly the politics of Capitol Hill support the decentralization and dispersion of power. The strong Senate action taken at the outset of the Reagan administration to pass the president's budgetary proposals and force the reconciliation of existing programs with the recommendations of the White House was an unusual occurrence. It came about because of the astute leadership of Howard Baker and a temporarily disciplined Republican majority that was able to overcome the normally disintegrative forces of powerful committees linked in the iron triangles of Washington politics.

Even on those rare occasions when the House and the Senate can act effectively by themselves as collective bodies, they must contend with each other before legislation can be completed and passed. The budget process requires passage of two concurrent resolutions reflecting the often sharply contrasting views of the House and the Senate. Differing economic assumptions of the two sides of Capitol Hill can be a major obstacle to integrated and centralized congressional budgeting. Senate and House conferees must reconcile the opposing views of their respective bodies.

CONGRESS AND POLICYMAKING

The Budget Act of 1974 was an attempt to improve the policymaking machinery of Congress by providing effective budgetary leadership on Capitol Hill; centralization and integration were its themes. Other efforts have been made in this direction as well, particularly the Legislative Reorganization Act of 1946, which attempted to make the committee system more centralized and integrated than it had been in the past, and provide Congress with expert staff. Today Congress has staff assistance in the form of the Congressional Research Service, an outgrowth of the Legislative Reference Service created by the 1946 law, and thousands of aides have been

THE BUDGET CONFERENCE COMMITTEES AT WORK
Conferees by the Hundred Trade Millions at Capitol

By Marjorie Hunter

Special to the New York Times

[*The annual meetings of the budget conference committees reconcile the often-contrasting proposals of the Senate and the House.*]

WASHINGTON, July 25 — "How about $800 million?"

"No way. How about $700 million?"

"Well, let's split the difference. $750 million."

"Sold!"

That's the way it's gone in recent days as senators and representatives have engaged in a concentrated, high-stakes round of horse trading in their attempts to reach agreement on the budget before the August recess. The trading is continuing in small informal gatherings through the weekend.

Meeting in cavernous hearing rooms and in small hideaways, the 72 senators and 183 representatives assigned to 58 separate budget conference committees have doffed coats and even neckties as they attack the awesome job of agreeing on $37 billion in cuts from programs that affect millions of Americans.

With frequent votes on other legislation being held on the floors of both chambers, the conferees have sought to place themselves as close as possible to their respective chambers.

Action in 58 Rings

This has resulted in an almost frantic vying for meeting space in the Capitol, whose builders never anticipated such a 58-ring circus. So most conferences have met in small rooms that some members say they never knew existed.

In S-206, for example, conferees from the two Agriculture Committees sought to reconcile their differences over funds for food stamps and farm programs.

S-206 is so small that staff members had to engage in a game of musical chairs, taking turns at squeezing into the room to offer advice on their areas of expertise.

For a while, staff members not on call in the meeting room relaxed on the sofas that had been moved into the corridor to make room for another set of conferees meeting nearby. But when janitors moved the sofas back to their usual home, the aides were left standing.

Under Mansfield's Gaze

Less cramped but still not spacious enough for the dozens of lobbyists who tried to get in is S-207, the Mike Mansfield Room, just a few yards from the Senate chamber. There, as a portrait of former Senator Mansfield peered down benevolently on the gathering, Senate and House conferees sought to thresh out sharp differences over aid to elementary and secondary schools.

"Where is this $50 million in loose change coming from?" asked Representative George Miller, Democrat of California, momentarily breaking the tension as he and his colleagues argued over billions of dollars.

At another conference, Senator Edward M. Kennedy, Democrat of Massachusetts, sought to earmark $2 million for national adoption centers. "We're talking about nickels and dimes," he said. Senator Orrin G. Hatch, a conservative Republican from Utah, winced visibly.

The most sought-after room is EF-100, exactly halfway between the Senate and House chambers and thus within sprinting distance for floor votes.

added to the statutory staff created by the act. When regular congressional staff work with detailed expertise from administrative agencies and advice from interest groups, there is no lack of information flowing to members of Congress seeking to make "correct" judgments concerning public policy.

Regardless of the sporadic attempts that have been made to strengthen Congress as a collective force in the policy making process, there is no doubt that Congress continues to reflect the pluralism of American politics. Legislators often act on their own to influence public policy, using their positions of power on Capitol Hill to achieve their goals.

The influence of legislators upon the policy process is not limited to the passage of legislation. Indeed, it can be argued that Congress influences policy most effectively outside of the legislative process. Remember that most legislation is vaguely stated, leaving the power to fill in the details to administrative agencies. It is in the continuous interaction between congressional committees and agencies that policy decisions are often made. Committees, particularly the appropriations committees in the House and Senate, use various formal and informal means of communication between themselves and administrative policymakers to make sure that the latter do not have total discretion in policymaking.[26] As Michael Kirst has reported:

> . . . the appropriations committees use their reports and hearings to advance suggestions on policy that they would hesitate to legislate. Or, take the case where the appropriations committees wish to expand programs but are unable to translate their desires into specific money terms. Here they can employ nonstatutory directives that urge expansion at as fast a rate as the administrator feels is optimal. In these and many other situations nonstatutory techniques enhance the scope and depth of appropriations control over broad policy and thereby better enable the appropriations committees to fulfill one facet of their proper role.[27]

Through "nonstatutory" techniques, legislative committees can control the policy process without submitting their actions to the scrutiny of Congress as a whole. This continuous interaction between agencies and committees partially limits the authority of the bureaucracy to fill up the details of vague

Policymaking
Without Legislation

[26] For a provocative study of "nonstatutory" techniques influencing policymaking by Congress, see Michael W. Kirst, *Government Without Passing Laws* (Chapel Hill: University of North Carolina Press, 1969).

[27] Ibid., p. 153.

statutes. Kirst points out that "nonstatutory devices provide an important supplement to statutory regulation of executive implementation. Numerous details of personnel, procedure, procurement, and organizations not suited to statutory control are regulated through hearings and reports. Also, the committees frequently earmark money for specific purposes in the reports rather than the statutes."[28]

A partial indication of the way in which nonstatutory techniques work can be seen by observing the comments of congressmen in reports and hearings. Legislators on the appropriations committees will frequently let it be known to administrators by their questions and comments how they want money to be spent, how particular programs should be carried out, and generally how policy should be shaped and implemented by the agencies. Subject matter committees use the same techniques, although since they do not have the same clout as the appropriations committees they are not as effective in controlling administrative policy.

"Congressional Intent"

Since Congress is divided into what amounts to feudal fiefdoms, it is difficult to develop a meaningful definition of "congressional intent" that goes beyond the intent of committees and powerful congressmen. This is why administrative agencies and courts, in attempting to assess the intent of Congress, are forced to concentrate more upon the hearings and reports of committees than on debate on the floor of the House. The "debates" that take place over particular pieces of legislation are so unstructured and ambiguous that they are useless as evidence of the nature of the pulse of Congress. Obtaining a majority of the House and Senate requires a broad consensus of the membership, which reflects diverse constituencies. The necessity of division of labor means that the legislation emanating from committees is respected, and congressmen will vote either for or against it without making any serious attempts to change it on the floor.

In the House of Representatives, much of the legislation is not subject to floor amendments under the rules. The extent to which legislation will specifically spell out the terms of policies to be implemented depends upon the drafting of the bill

---

[28] Ibid., p. 155.

by committee. Legislation is more often than not expressed in terms that leave wide discretion in the implementation of programs to administrative agencies. A cursory reading of legislation may seem to indicate that it is fairly specific, but upon careful analysis the exact meaning of the legislation is not revealed by the text. For example, regulatory agencies that have rate-making authority are directed to act in the "public interest, convenience, and necessity," and to establish "just and reasonable" rates. But these legislative standards are anything but exact, and must be defined further by those who have the responsibility of carrying out the programs. The real definition of policy, then, is made by both legislators and administrators outside of the formal legislative process itself.

Since congressional committees receive specific inputs from private interest groups and government agencies, and are themselves composed of legislators who often have had long contact with the policy field under their jurisdiction, why is it a common practice to use what amounts to vague generalities in writing legislative standards to guide administrators charged with carrying out legislative intent? One reason is that sometimes legislators pass the burden of reconciling group conflict on to the bureaucracy by drafting legislation with vague standards, thus getting themselves off the hook and placing the final decision-making responsibilities upon outside administrative agents. For example, everyone may agree that regulation of railroads is in the "public interest," but there may be intense differences between consumer-oriented groups and railroads concerning what constitutes appropriate kinds of regulation. Should railroad mergers be encouraged or discouraged? Should the railroads be allowed to drop passenger train service simply because it is unprofitable, or should some effort be made to force the railroads to accept a public responsibility to carry passengers even if this activity is not as profitable as the freight business? Should railroad rates be structured to eliminate or to foster competition within the industry, and with competing modes of transportation? These are important issues of public policy, and their resolution is required. It is impossible, however, to satisfy all of the competing interests with any single decision on such complex matters.

Congressmen may feel that they should avoid getting involved in the actual decision-making process, which they can safely do simply by creating a regulatory agency to deal with such controversial issues. But it is far too simple to suggest that the ambiguity of legislative standards is due solely to the desire on the part of congressmen to avoid unnecessary political conflict. The need for continuity and specialization in the policymaking process is also required if issues are to be understood and dealt with adequately. No congressional committee can devote as much time to specific areas of public policy as can an administrative agency, whose sole responsibility may be established within a fairly limited policy sphere. The agencies supply the continuity and expertise that Congress necessarily lacks.

A Sample Congressional Policy— Water Pollution Control

Although legislation does not determine the final shape of public policy, it is certainly a central component of the policy process. Without congressional authorization, no administrative agency would have the authority to act. The major function that legislation fulfills is to authorize administrative agencies to enter particular policy spheres. The boundaries within which agencies can formulate public policy are set by Congress, although these boundaries are very broad. Consider, for example, the water pollution control bill which was passed by Congress on October 4, 1972, vetoed by the president, and subsequently passed over his veto in a congressional act of defiance on October 18. The bill provided for the establishment of a comprehensive water pollution program, to be created by the administrator of the Environmental Protection Agency (EPA), who was given the responsibility to develop regulations under the terms of the statute.

In almost every respect, the guiding standards of the Water Pollution Control Act, to be followed by the administrator, were expressed in such vague terms that virtually total discretion resided in the hands of the agency. The objective of the Act was "to restore and maintain the chemical, physical, and biological integrity of the nation's waters."[29] To accomplish this purpose, the statute directed the administrator to develop research programs relating to the problems of water pollu-

[29] *Congressional Quarterly Weekly Report,* 14 October 1972, p. 2692.

tion. Construction grants were to be authorized by the administrator, at his discretion, to state and local agencies for treatment works, with the federal government picking up a maximum of 75 percent of the cost. Title III of the statute defined the "standards" to be followed by the EPA and how the act was to be enforced. This section clearly illustrates the nature of a typical delegation of legislative authority to an administrative agency. The standards and enforcement provisions of the Water Pollution Control statute include the following:

1. Required by 1 July 1977, effluent limitations for point sources (mostly factories) which used the "best practicable control technology currently available" *as defined by the EPA administrator.*
2. Required by 1 July 1983, effluent limitations based on the "best available technology economically achievable" *as determined by the administrator.*
3. *Authorized the administrator* to set water quality related effluent limitations, after holding public hearings.
4. *Directed the administrator* to develop and publish detailed water quality information and guidelines.
5. *Directed the administrator* to list categories of industrial pollution sources and set national performance standards for each new source. States were authorized to take over enforcement if their laws were as strict as the federal standards.
6. *Directed the administrator* to list toxic pollutants and prohibit their discharge and to set effluent limitations providing "an ample margin of safety."
7. *Required the administrator* to set pretreatment standards for discharges into publicly owned treatment plants.
8. Gave the EPA the right of entry to pollution sources and the right to inspect records and monitoring equipment, and to make the data public (except trade secrets).
9. *Authorized the administrator* to hold public hearings and take other necessary action to stop international pollution originating in the United States if requested by the secretary of state.
10. *Directed the administrator* to set federal performance standards for marine sanitation equipment.

11. *Required the administrator* to set effluent limitations for thermal discharges that would ensure a balanced population of fish, shellfish, and wild life.[30]

[30] Ibid., pp. 2693–94. (Emphasis added.)

The EPA administrator was authorized to issue federal discharge permits if they met the requirements of the act. He was authorized to suspend state programs that did not meet federal guidelines. Although the amount of discretion this statute conferred upon the administrator of the Environmental Protection Agency may seem excessive, it is actually a typical statute establishing a federal regulatory program. Aside from providing for certain procedural checks upon the administrator, as in its requirement for public hearings before certain administrative actions could be taken, the content of the rules and regulations that will "fill in the details" of the statute will be entirely at the discretion of the administrator, as will be the enforcement of the act. The "discretionary enforcement" provisions of the bill drew strong objections from some environmental groups and Ralph Nader's Task Force on Water Pollution Control. A joint statement of the Environmental Policy Center and the Nader Task Force stated in part that "Congress has failed to repair the most serious loophole in the old [water pollution control] law— discretionary enforcement. By leaving the government free not to prosecute politically powerful polluters, the bill virtually guarantees abusive underenforcement."[31]

[31] Ibid., p. 2692.

One can see that Congress affects regulatory policymaking through legislation by determining the boundaries of administrative action rather than by the specific content of policy outputs. Although legislation does not determine the final shape of public policy, it is a central component of the policy process. Except where the presidency and the courts can take action under the Constitution and thereby shape policy, no part of the government can formulate policy without congressional authorization. Congressional action is a necessary first step in the policy process. The failure of Congress to be responsive to demands for new policies has always been a major roadblock in the path of policy innovation. Of course both the president and the bureaucracy are capable of initiating new policies under the broad delegations of authority

Congress

usually given to them by the legislature. Major changes in public policy, however, must be approved by Congress, for without legislative ratification not only would the executive branch be liable to accusations of usurpation of power, but it would also be unlikely to receive the funds necessary for continuous support of new programs.

While regulatory legislation is characteristically vague, Congress often passes very specific legislation that does not allow for administrative discretion to change legislative intent. For example, subsidies for agricultural products are given to farmers who meet specific conditions set forth in statutory law. Social security and food stamp programs are available to all persons "entitled" to receive such benefits under the law. Although there is a certain amount of administrative discretion in determining the eligibility of claimants under such programs, the discretion is minimal. Tax laws, too, allow little administrative discretion, although the complex rules of the Internal Revenue Service sometimes do constitute new tax legislation. Even where legislation is relatively specific, Congress cannot always rest assured that its intent will be carried out.

CONCLUSION

It is clear that both legislation and the nonstatutory communications between Congress and the bureaucracy shape the nature of policy outputs of government. In the case of the water pollution legislation mentioned above, the real details of water pollution policy will be shaped by the administrator of the Environmental Protection Agency. It is only through the exertion of influence after the passage of legislation that Congress can determine the details of public policy. This raises a very important dilemma, because insofar as Congress exerts influence over policy through nonstatutory means it is reflecting highly specialized inputs. At least the entire membership of the legislature has a chance to vote when legislation is brought before Congress, whereas the interaction between legislative committees and administrative agencies excludes even the possibility of majority control over the nature of the legislative outputs.

Congress is supposed to be representative of the people, and when it does act in a collective capacity it is supposed to reflect, even in a disorganized way, a loose consensus of popular opinion that is concerned with the policy issues at stake. Legislation is a matter of public record, which can be judged by the electorate in deciding whether or not to vote for a particular congressman. A broader sense of accountability, therefore, exists with respect to congressional legislation than prevails in the dialogue between powerful congressmen and particular policymakers in the executive branch. Where nonstatutory influence is exerted through formal communications, as in congressional hearings, voters who are aware of the hearings can make a judgment. However, except in the case of congressmen who wish to acquire national publicity by holding spectacular hearings investigating such areas as crime, drug abuse, and the Watergate affair, most hearings escape the scrutiny of a majority of voters. In essence, much of what Congress does to influence public policy is hidden from the public, although not from relevant interest groups.

Those who have the authority and power to make public policy within our system must not have uncontrolled discretion. Because of the way Congress functions, there is little evidence that it acts more responsibly and within tighter boundaries than the other branches of the government. Because of the constant publicity surrounding the presidency, presidential actions are far more likely to be scrutinized by the press and revealed to the public. The electorate is far more conscious of who occupies the White House and what policies are being formulated there than in the legislature. Since the public rarely knows how its own congressmen vote on particular public policy issues, it is even less aware of what actions outside of voting are taken by congressmen to affect the course of policy. Congress is checked not so much by the people as by the president, the bureaucracy, interest groups, and the courts. In the bureaucracy, however, it has found an ally as frequently as it confronts an enemy.

Suggestions for Further Reading

Fenno, Richard F., Jr. *Homestyle: House Members in Their Districts.* Boston: Little, Brown and Co., 1978. An important theme of the book is that the way in which members of Congress win reelection is often different from the way in which they build their Washington careers.

Fiorina, Morris P. *Congress: Keystone of the Washington Establishment.* New Haven: Yale University Press, 1977. Members of Congress, their growing number of aides, bureaucrats, and lobbyists have become an important Washington establishment that is, in some respects, manipulative and uncontrolled.

Jones, Rochelle, and Woll, Peter. *The Private World of Congress.* New York: The Free Press, 1979. The principal goals of members of Congress and their aides on Capitol Hill are internal power and status.

Mann, Thomas E., and Ornstein, Norman J., eds. *The New Congress.* Washington, D.C.: American Enterprise Institute, 1981. Eleven scholars examine important changes that have occurred in Congress, and the consequences of those changes for the policy process.

Mayhew, David R. *Congress: The Electoral Connection.* New Haven: Yale University Press, 1974. The organization, procedures, and norms of Congress are designed to assure the reelection of its members.

Redman, Eric. *The Dance of Legislation.* New York: Simon & Schuster, 1973. A lively case study by a former Senate staffer of how a bill becomes a law.

The downtown Washington landscape is crowded with department and agency buildings, reflecting the vast bureaucracy that has become an important fourth branch of the government.

CHAPTER 8

The Bureaucracy

The bureaucracy is a critical link in the chain of power for both the president and Congress. In the twentieth century, presidents have viewed the bureaucracy as an integral part of the executive branch, properly subject to their control. At the same time, Congress considers the bureaucracy to be its agent, and considers most administrative agencies as logical extensions of the legislature. Presidents stress that agencies exercise "executive" functions, while Congress properly points out that the bureaucracy performs legislative tasks in addition to exercising executive responsibilities. And, while the president and Congress battle for power over the bureaucracy, the courts, noting the widespread exercise of judicial powers by the bureaucracy, intervene directly in administrative proceedings through judicial review.

Presidents and politically ambitious congressmen know that the support of the bureaucracy is essential to their power. Presidents from William Howard Taft at the beginning of the century to Jimmy Carter and Ronald Reagan have unsuccessfully attempted to make the bureaucracy an arm of the White House. The lack of presidential success in bringing the bureaucracy to heel is the direct result of a Washington politics that makes administrative agencies a central component of a permanent political establishment consisting of powerful members of Congress and a vast array of interest groups. The impenetrable linkage of congressional committees, agencies, and pressure groups—Washington's iron triangles—have consistently frustrated presidential attempts to dominate the executive branch.

These iron triangles have existed for a long time. Presidential frustrations in the face of general administrative rigidity, intransigence, and obstreperousness, can be explosive. Talking to one of his top aides, Franklin Roosevelt said:

". . . When I woke up this morning, the first thing I saw was a headline in the *New York Times* to the effect that our navy was going to spend two billion dollars on a shipbuilding program. Here I am, the Commander-in-Chief of the Navy, having to read about that for the first time in the press. Do you know what I said to that?"
"No, Mr. President."
"I said, 'Jesus Chr—rist!'"

Roosevelt continued:

"The Treasury . . . is so large and far-flung and ingrained in its practices that I find it is almost impossible to get the action and results I want—even with Henry [Morgenthau] there. But the Treasury is not to be compared with the State Department. You should go through the experience of trying to get any changes in the thinking, policy, and action of the career diplomats and then you'd know what a real problem was. But the Treasury and the State Department put together are nothing as compared with the Na—a—vy.[1]"

The bureaucracy is a critical link in Washington's politics and policies. In most policy areas the burden of refining and enforcing public policy rests upon the bureaucracy. Administrative agencies are the delegates of both Congress and the president to fulfill the broad policy purposes of the legislative and executive branches. Since much of the legislation passed by Congress sets policy guidelines only in very broad terms, it is the bureaucracy that must fill in the details of legislation and make the concrete decisions that give meaning to government policy.

The scope of activities of administrative agencies, their generally large size, and the complexity of issues with which they deal often restrict administrative accountability to any of the original three branches of the government. Although created by Congress, and unable to act without congressional authority, agencies often tend to dominate the legislative process that gave them birth. The expertise of Congress is often no match for that of the bureaucracy, and most of the subject matter with which modern legislation deals is highly technical and requires specialized skills for proper formulation. The inputs of the bureaucracy to Congress often determine congressional output. Moreover, through its rulemaking powers the bureaucracy legislates independently of Congress, al-

[1] Marriner F. Eccles, *Beckoning Frontiers* (New York: Alfred A. Knopf, 1951), p. 336.

The Bureaucracy

though of course always within the framework of congressional delegations of authority. The content of our laws is often determined more by administrative legislation than by statutory law.

The Constitution makes no specific provision for the bureaucracy, although the administrative branch is a central component of our government. The framers of the Constitution envisioned that the functions of government would be neatly divided into three categories—legislative, executive, and judicial. These functions were to be exercised, respectively, by Congress, the president, and the judiciary. No one branch of the government was to have exclusive control over public policy. Implicit in the constitutional system was the idea that public policy was not to be solely identified with legislation, execution, or adjudication. It involved the merger of all three functions of government. That is, the framers of the Constitution fully recognized that once Congress announced its intentions, the concurrence of both the executive and the Supreme Court would be necessary to implement the intent of Congress.

The administrative branch exercises, under delegations of authority from Congress, the functions of each of the original branches. In its performance of legislative, executive, and judicial responsibilities it should be accountable to some degree to the original branches having primary responsibility in these areas. In the legislative sphere, the bureaucracy can be considered an agent of Congress; in the executive and judicial spheres, it is accountable to the president and the judiciary.

Under the separation of powers system, however, each of the branches of government was to exercise to some degree the functions of coordinate branches. Congress was given the ability to interfere in the operation of the executive branch, and the president is given legislative responsibilities under Article II, which grants him authority to veto legislation and to recommend proposals to Congress. This means that Congress can and does interfere in the exercise of executive functions by the bureaucracy, just as the president in the performance of his legislative responsibilities seeks to supervise the legislative functions of administrative agencies. The constitutional picture is far from clear regarding control over the administrative branch.

Even though the Constitution does not explicitly provide for the bureaucracy, the system it sets up has a profound impact upon the structure, functions, and general place that the administrative branch occupies in the scheme of government. At the time of the framing of the Constitution there was no discussion of the administrative process as we know it today. Rather, the concept of "administration" was incorporated under the heading of "the executive branch." Executive agencies were to be adjuncts of the presidency, and were to be involved in the "mere execution" of "executive details," in the words of Alexander Hamilton in *The Federalist*.

The Hamiltonian view, which admittedly favored a stronger presidency, was simply that the president as Chief Executive would have the responsibility and power to control the small executive branch that would be established. Hamilton himself foresaw a vigorous and independent role for the president and the executive branch, and was not adverse to having the executive dominate the legislature, a practice he later encouraged when he became secretary of the treasury. Nevertheless, in *The Federalist* Hamilton advanced the theory that the executive branch would not exercise independent political power, but would be politically neutral under the domination of the president, and the executive branch acting as a unit would carry out the mandates of the legislature. In *The Federalist* (No. 72), Hamilton clearly stated what was to be the relationship between the president and the administrative branch:

. . . The persons, therefore, to whose immediate management the different administrative matters are committed ought to be considered as assistants or deputies of the Chief Magistrate, and on this account, they ought to derive their offices from his appointment, at least from his nomination, and ought to be subject to his superintendence.

The Bureaucracy

Since Hamilton did not foresee the role of the administrative branch in legislation and adjudication, he felt it should properly be under the control of the president. In the classical constitutional model, the bureaucracy was not to be a primary policymaking branch.

Although Hamiltonian theory suggested that the administrative branch should be incorporated into the presidency, the constitutional system itself in many ways supported an independent bureaucracy. Comparing the powers of Congress and the president over the administrative branch, it becomes clear that both have important constitutional responsibilities. (See Figure 8.1.) Congress retains primary control over administrative organization. It alone creates and destroys agencies and determines whether they are to be located within the executive branch and responsible to the president, or outside of it and independent. Congress has created a large number of independent agencies and placed many of their operations outside of presidential control. Presidential powers to reorganize the executive are delegated to him by Congress.

Presidential
vs. Congressional Control
of the Bureaucracy

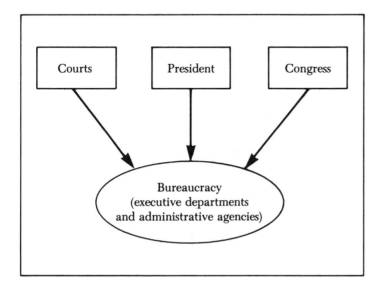

FIGURE 8.1
The Constitutional Context of the Bureaucracy. *Each of the constitutional branches exercises important powers over the bureaucracy.*

Originally Congress was to have the authority to control appropriations, and the power of the purse was critical in exercising control over administrative agencies. Today the Office of Management and Budget and the president have assumed the initiative in this area, although the centralization of the budgetary process within Congress may restore legislative initiative.

Other ways in which Congress controls the bureaucracy include setting forth the "intent of Congress" to be followed by agencies in exercising policymaking powers. Moreover, Congress can and does interfere in the appointment and removal process for top-level officials. Ministerial appointments are to be "by and with the advice and consent of the Senate" under the terms of the Constitution, and this stipulation has been extended by Congress to include a large number of administrators. Congress also may establish conditions for removal, granting administrators such as those on the independent regulatory commissions "tenure" for specified periods of time during which they cannot be removed except for specific causes stated in legislation. In such cases, Congress excludes "political" reasons as a justifiable basis for removal, and usually provides that removal may only be for "malfeasance" or "moral turpitude."

The antagonism between Congress and the president often results in the legislature placing numerous roadblocks in the path of presidential domination of the administrative branch. This counters a strong trend in public administration circles to have the president assume more and more power over administrative agencies to produce greater efficiency through coordination and planning from a central point. The President's Committee on Administrative Management in 1937, and later the Hoover Commissions of 1949 and 1954, called upon Congress to initiate a series of reforms to increase presidential authority over the bureaucracy. These groups particularly did not like the independent authority that Congress often grants to administrative agencies, which gives them the means to defy presidential wishes.

It is in the independent agencies of government, particularly the regulatory commissions, that one finds congressional attempts to insure agencies are capable of acting in some respects, if not in all, independently of the White House. For example, Congress has delegated to the Interstate Commerce Commission (ICC) final authority to approve or disapprove railroad mergers. The president has no power to veto a decision of the ICC. Should the president and the Commission disagree, the ICC has the legal authority to ignore presidential wishes. Under such circumstances the president must rely upon his political clout to dissuade the agency from contradicting his wishes.

The exercise of judicial functions by the bureaucracy means that the courts have constitutional responsibilities to review administrative action in this sphere. The rule of law is a central component of our constitutional system. If the separation of powers were accepted in its purest form, judicial functions could not be performed outside of the realm of the ordinary court system. Of necessity, however, Congress has delegated judicial functions to administrative agencies, which may or may not be subject to review in the courts. This has been done because of the vast expansion of the regulatory functions of government, which require not only the establishment of rules and regulations governing various private groups, but also the ability to adjudicate individual cases and controversies arising under such rules.

Rise of
Administrative Law

Why were the courts not given the responsibility to adjudicate these newly created cases that arose as governmental regulation expanded? Would it have been profitable to create a series of new courts and many more judges to absorb the increased workload? Certainly this would have been possible in theory. A number of special reasons, however, some rational and some not so rational, led to the establishment of specialized administrative agencies that combined all three functions of government.

First, administrative agencies were given what effectively amounted to legislative power because Congress was both unable, and on many occasions unwilling, to bear the burden of passing concrete legislation to deal with the myriad problems that began to confront government in the late nineteenth century. A mere glance at the Code of Federal Regulations, which is the law developed by administrative agencies on the basis of broad congressional delegations of authority, illustrates the magnitude of the legislative tasks that confront government. Particularly in recent decades, commencing with the rapid increase in governmental activities during the New Deal, Congress scarcely has been able to deal even with major problems confronting it. A fragmented and dispersed body without powerful presidential leadership, it finds the passage of legislation a very tedious and time-consuming task indeed. On a purely technical basis, Congress must rely upon outside agencies to fill in the details of the legislation that Congress passes in broad outline. Congress can still be specific in legislation; but it does not have the time today, for example, to write the regulations that are formulated by departments such as Health and Human Services, which employs over 120,000 bureaucrats, or agencies such as the Occupational Safety and Health Administration (OSHA), the Environmental Protection Agency (EPA), and the numerous other regulatory bodies.

Another important reason that administrative agencies are given such extensive legislative responsibilities is that in politically sensitive areas Congress is motivated to transfer the burden of reconciling intensive group conflict onto the shoulders of bureaucrats, thus relieving congressmen from having to take stands on controversial issues. Until the advent of Ralph Nader and the consumer movement, Congress was more responsive to the influence of powerful private pressure groups in formulating legislation. At the same time, it was buffeted by a certain amount of public pressure which often came to it under the auspices of the president as a representative of the nation at large. During the New Deal period, administrative agencies were created largely from recommendations of President Roosevelt and his staff. Many of these agencies were created to regulate business enterprises. In such cases, recognizing that crisis conditions, presidential demands, and public pressure necessitated the extension of the regulatory authority of government, Congress nevertheless did not have to get into the even more tricky political and technical issues of the content of such regulatory policies. It avoided this simply by delegating legislative authority to administrative agencies under very broad standards. It mandates the agencies, for example, to act in the "public interest, convenience, and necessity," or to establish "just and reasonable rates." This essentially gives the agencies carte blanche in the legislative field. Under such circumstances, the agencies become the centers of political controversy, subject to the most intense pressure from regulated groups to secure policies favorable to their interests.

Since administrative legislation is generally highly complex and technical in nature, the adjudication of disputes arising under it requires expertise and a specialized knowledge of the subject for proper resolution. This is an important reason that Congress has assigned judicial responsibilities to administrative agencies to decide cases and controversies arising under their jurisdiction, rather than giving the courts original jurisdiction. However, Congress has provided for judicial review after agency decisions are rendered in many areas, and this does provide a judicial check upon administrative discretion.

In the early twentieth century, a major reason agencies were given adjudicative responsibilities in regulatory and welfare fields was that the courts were not sympathetic toward the purposes of federal and state legislation. The courts, generally conservative in nature, were essentially nullifying regulatory statutes by their decisions. For example, when the ICC was originally created in 1887, the courts had to act affirmatively before ICC decisions could go into effect. The commission was given no independent judicial powers. A conservative judiciary rendered the ICC a totally ineffective regulatory body during the first decade of its existence, until Congress recognized its plight and granted it judicial power subject only to later court review.

In the workmen's compensation area, it was common practice for the courts to nullify workmen's compensation laws in states where the legislatures had failed to provide for independent workmen's compensation commissions. The courts simply applied old common law rules to workmen's compensation cases, essentially substituting substantive common law standards for those contained in legislation that was in fact passed for the sole purpose of granting more extensive rights to workmen than had prevailed under the common law. The only way to get around the courts in such instances was to grant independent judicial authority to the workmen's compensation commissions; this violated traditional concepts of the rule of law that required all adjudication to be handled by regular (common law) courts.

Although conservative legal scholars considered the development of administrative adjudication to be unconstitutional, the courts, faced with the responsibility of having to confront political necessities, eventually invented easy rationalizations for the exercise of both legislative and judicial functions by administrative agencies. This occurred despite the fact that there was no constitutional provision for an administrative branch with such powers. Basically, the courts found that as long as the "primary" legislative and judicial powers remained in the hands of the Congress and the judiciary, respectively, the exercise of "quasi-legislative" and "quasi-judicial" functions by administrative agencies would not undermine the constitutional separation of powers. In the legislative field, as long as Congress clearly states its intent, it is the responsibility of agencies to follow legislative mandates. Filling in the details of legislation is not the same as formulating the legislation in the first place.

Rationalizing the placement of judicial functions in the hands of administrators was somewhat more difficult than justifying administrative exercise of legislative functions. The courts essentially solved this problem rhetorically. They held that "real" judicial power is exercised only by constitutional courts, which must conform to the conditions stated in Article III. In reality, of course, although administrative agencies do not meet the various requirements of Article III, they are extensively involved in adjudication.

THE POLITICAL CONTEXT OF THE BUREAUCRACY

Agency Response to Political Support

Agencies often develop distinguishable characteristics that shape their orientation toward public policy. Most important is the primary basis of their political support. "Clientele" agencies, such as Agriculture, Labor, and Commerce, were originally created to serve special interests, not the public interest. It is the job of the Department of Agriculture to protect farmers, not to lower food prices in the cities. The Department of Labor was established as an organization to represent the interests of workers directly, as the Department of Commerce was established to give business interests a voice in government. The public policy outputs of such departments tend to reflect clientele inputs. Moreover, even agencies that were not originally established on a clientele basis tend to develop in such a manner as to serve a narrow set of interests from which they draw political support. Independent regulatory agencies are often characterized as being captives of the groups that they regulate. There is little doubt that the railroad industry found a strong voice in government in the Interstate Commerce Commission, and similarly the securities industry in the Securities and Exchange Commission (SEC), labor unions in the National Labor Relations Board (NLRB), and broadcasters in the Federal Communications Commission (FCC). Regulatory agencies were not originally to be representatives of clientele interests, but were to serve the public interest in implementing regulatory policies.

The Politics of Administrative Reorganization. The close ties that have developed between most agencies and private groups within their jurisdiction have made it virtually impossible to make major reorganizations of the federal bureaucracy. The impetus for reorganization always comes from the White House as presidents try to expand their authority over an executive branch that from the vantage point of the Oval Office often seems to operate on the principle of anarchy. In reality, the agencies are closely attuned to the interests they regulate or benefit, and to members and staffers on Capitol Hill who have the ultimate authority to determine their fate.

While Congress jealously guards its administrative preserve, it has been willing to grant the president the authority to reorganize the bureaucracy subject to a congressional veto. The first reorganization act was passed in 1939, permitting presidential reorganization plans to go into effect unless they were vetoed by a simple majority in both houses of Congress. Reorganization acts generally have two-year time limits, after which they must be renewed by Congress. After the 1939 act lapsed (during World War II President Roosevelt was given absolute authority to reorganize the executive branch under a special War Powers Act), Congress did not renew it until 1949, when it adopted the single house veto provision for presidential reorganization plans. Congress continued to renew the reorganization acts until Eisenhower's second term, when the authority was again allowed to lapse. In 1961 Congress restored the reorganization power for President Kennedy, only to become angered at his attempt to use it to create a new Department of Urban Affairs in 1962, rather than submitting legislation to Congress. The House vetoed the proposed Department of Urban Affairs, and Congress again allowed the reorganization authority to lapse. It was not renewed until 1964, and then only for one year. The 1964 law prohibited the president from using a reorganization plan to create a new executive department. This provision has been continued in all subsequent reorganization acts. President Johnson requested permanent reorganization authority in 1965, but the Senate rejected the proposal.

The history of the reorganization acts reveals that Congress is willing to give presidents temporary reorganization authority to accomplish limited changes in the bureaucracy, but has often allowed the reorganization authority to lapse.

While Congress does not like to see major changes carried out by reorganization orders, preferring instead legislation requiring affirmative congressional action, determined presidents have unilaterally made important changes in administrative organization without suffering a congressional veto. President Nixon used the reorganization power that Congress had reluctantly given him to abolish the Bureau of the Budget and create in its place a new Office of Management and Budget completely under presidential domination. Nixon used an executive order to create the Environmental Protection Agency, and made major changes in the Executive Office of the president. Congress allowed Nixon's authority to reorganize to lapse in 1973, and did not pass a new reorganization bill until President Carter requested it in 1977.

President Carter set out to reorganize the bureaucracy with a vengeance. He had promised the electorate a major reduction in federal agencies and in the Executive Office of the president. In the end, Carter found that he could not make most of the major reorganizations he wanted because of the opposition of Washington's iron triangles. His proposal for a unified Department of Energy under White House control was drastically altered on Capitol Hill by powerful members of the Senate Governmental Affairs Committee, who were suspicious of excessive presidential power over the bureaucracy. In addition, powerful oil and natural gas interests supported the continued independence of the judicial arm of the new department which would hear cases involving their interests. The new department was a hodgepodge of bureaus and agencies whose relationship to each other was determined by political compromises on Capitol Hill rather than by careful planning in the White House.

President Reagan, unlike Carter and many previous presidents, wisely avoided a frontal assault on the *structure* of the bureaucracy in the initial stages of his administration. Not only had the reorganization authority once again lapsed, but Reagan knew that the politics of reorganization often exhausted the reserves of the White House that could be better spent on achieving major domestic and foreign policy objectives. (See Figure 8.2.) Although Reagan had made a campaign pledge to abolish the Departments of Energy and Education, he immediately began to hedge his promise after the election. Even if the reorganization authority were renewed, the abolition of major departments would require congressional legislation. Reagan decided to fight his major battles on Capitol Hill—those involving his budgetary recommendations—first, perhaps leaving for the second session of the Ninety-seventh Congress recommendations to abolish the departments.

Reagan knew that it is far more difficult to abolish agencies than it is to reorganize them. The Carter administration, in combination with powerful committee chairmen on Capitol Hill, had succeeded in completing the deregulation of the airlines industry that was begun during the Ford administration. Carter's appointee as chairman of the Civil Aeronautics Board aided the president and Congress in their efforts to bring an end to the agency's responsibilities—the CAB is scheduled to go out of existence in 1985. Congress also passed legislation to deregulate the trucking and railroad industries,

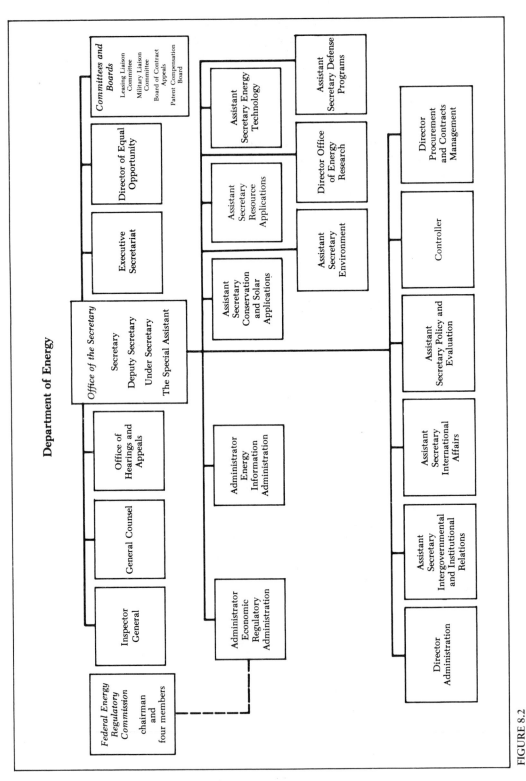

Department of Energy

Office of the Secretary
Secretary
Deputy Secretary
Under Secretary
The Special Assistant

Inspector General

General Counsel

Office of Hearings and Appeals

Executive Secretariat

Director of Equal Opportunity

Committees and Boards
Leasing Liaison Committee
Military Liaison Committee
Board of Contract Appeals
Patent Compensation Board

Federal Energy Regulatory Commission chairman and four members

Administrator Economic Regulatory Administration

Administrator Energy Information Administration

Assistant Secretary Conservation and Solar Applications

Assistant Secretary Resource Applications

Assistant Secretary Energy Technology

Assistant Secretary Environment

Director Office of Energy Research

Assistant Secretary Defense Programs

Director Administration

Assistant Secretary Intergovernmental and Institutional Relations

Assistant Secretary International Affairs

Assistant Secretary Policy and Evaluation

Controller

Director Procurement and Contracts Management

FIGURE 8.2
Department of Justice. *Bureaucratic organization is highly complex and difficult to change.*

significantly reducing the powers of the Interstate Commerce Commission. The success of deregulation legislation during the Carter administration resulted from an unusual combination of liberal and conservative forces on Capitol Hill. These forces were headed by particularly astute committee chairmen—especially Edward Kennedy of Massachusetts and Howard Cannon of Nevada, of the Judiciary and Commerce Committees, respectively, who, with the help of effective staff, mobilized an outside constituency of economic interests that would benefit from deregulation. Many airline executives were at first opposed to giving up the shield of protection the CAB had given them in the past, and which was particularly beneficial to marginal carriers. Sufficient airline support was finally mustered, however, to buttress congressional action supporting deregulation. Large rail carriers favored deregulation that would give them flexibility in setting rates. Trucking deregulation, at first strongly opposed by the American Trucking Association and the Teamsters Union, was finally passed after these groups reluctantly gave their support for congressional action in the hope that it would be more protective of their interests than deregulation orders that were starting to come from the Interstate Commerce Commission.

The government's move toward deregulation of the powerful airline, railroad, and trucking industries seemed in many respects to defy the laws of political gravity. Powerful groups in all three industries concerned had long enjoyed a virtual monopoly protected by the government. The economic interests concerned had powerful allies, or so they thought, in the CAB and the ICC. The iron triangles of policy seemed to be working perfectly until outside forces, the White House, and Senator Edward Kennedy committed themselves to breaking the triangles that had supported the airline and the trucking industries since the New Deal, when the CAB was created and the ICC was given the power to regulate the trucking industry. Deregulation of the railroads was another matter, for many carriers supported the congressional plan of deregulation, which they helped to shape and which they considered to be a last-ditch effort to make them economically viable. In the end, it was the persistence and skill of White House and congressional proponents of deregulation that resulted in breaking the seemingly impenetrable iron triangles of agencies, pressure groups, and committees involved in transportation.

THE POLICY PROCESS IN ADMINISTRATION

Administrative agencies affect public policy not only by helping to write legislation, but also through rule making and the adjudication of cases and controversies arising under their jurisdiction.

Administrative Rule Making

Administrative rule making is the establishment of prospective rules. Under the requirements of the Federal Administrative Procedure Act (APA), general notice of proposed rule making must be published in the *Federal Register.* The notice must indicate clearly where the proceedings are to be held, under what legal authority rules are being proposed, and the substance of the proposed rules. After such notice is given, interested parties are to be provided with the opportunity to participate in the rule-making proceedings through the presentation of written data. At the discretion of the agency, oral presentation may be permitted. Unless notice or hearing is required by the statutes governing the agency's operation, notice of rule making can be withheld if the agency considers it to be "impracticable, unnecessary, or contrary to the public interest." This exemption potentially excludes a large body of rule-making proceedings from any possibility of public participation; however, in practice, agencies do attempt to conform to the general requirements of the APA, which are designed to allow public participation in rule making.

Agency flexibility in rule-making procedures is far greater than in formal administrative adjudication. Formal hearings are not held in rule making unless required by statute. Administrators are free to consult informally with interested parties, and are not bound by the more rigid requirements of adjudicative hearings. The number of parties that may participate is also potentially far greater than in adjudicative proceedings, where only those directly and immediately affected by an administrative order have standing—although the strict definitions of standing that prevailed in the past have been loosened up in recent years to allow for a greater range of parties to intervene in administrative adjudication.

Most of the voluminous code of federal regulations is composed of the substantive rules of administrative agencies. Collectively these rules constitute a large part of the formal public policy of the federal government. The Internal Revenue Code, for example, is part of this compendium of regulations. It consists of a seemingly endless number of rules interpreting the internal revenue statutes passed by Congress. Regulatory agencies, both those that are independent and those that reside within formal departments of government, state many of their regulatory policies through rule making. The Food and Drug Administration similarly determines policies governing the labeling, availability and safety of drugs by rule making. Rate-making proceedings of regulatory bodies are considered to be rule making. Outside of the regulatory realm, departments such as Health and Human Services, Transportation, Interior, and Defense are constantly stating their general policies through the issuance of rules. In the past, the selective service policy of the United States was given final form by the interpretations of statutory law on the part of the selective service system.

Although administrative agencies have been engaged in rule making for almost a century, since the creation of the Interstate Commerce Commission in 1887, it was not until the decade of the 1970s that the full implications of administrative rule-making power seemed to sink in on Capitol Hill. The New Deal agencies, such as the SEC and the NLRB, and departments such as HEW, had been going along for years issuing rules that determined the rights and obligations of individuals and groups within their jurisdictions. Conservative groups had attacked the New Deal generally, and isolated scholars had referred to the "new despotism" of the burgeoning administrative process, but it was more the adjudicative than the rule-making activities of the bureaucracy that attracted the concern of groups that sought to control it, such as the American Bar Association. The Administrative Procedure

Act of 1946 had far fewer general restrictions upon administrative rule making than it did on administrative ajudication.

The expansion of the role of the federal government under the Great Society programs of Lyndon Johnson in the 1960s and the creation of important new agencies in the 1970s brought about an exponential increase in administrative rule making that raised the ire of a wide range of private groups—particularly small businesses—and caught the attention of Capitol Hill. Under the Civil Rights Act of 1964 and the Voting Rights Act of 1965, HEW (now Health and Human Services) used both the legislation and executive orders to issue regulations requiring affirmative action and the elimination of racial and gender discrimination throughout the country. The department even went so far as to prohibit public school authorities from requiring different dress codes for male and female students. HEW rules required the integration of athletic facilities and team sports, prompting some cynics to proclaim that the day of the gender-integrated locker room was at hand. The department was serious, however, in its intention to eliminate discrimination, even if it had to take the law into its own hands.

While HEW, its civil rights office, and adjunct agencies such as the Equal Employment Opportunity Commission were issuing voluminous affirmative action regulations and rules requiring nondiscrimination in the private sector, new agencies such as the Environmental Protection Agency and the Occupational Safety and Health Administration, both created in 1970, began to flood the nation with new rules of their own. The EPA was given vast jurisdiction over air and water pollution, hazardous waste disposal, and toxic substances programs, and OSHA was charged with protecting workers in their places of work. OSHA regulations in particular seemed to attract the attention of Capitol Hill because of the flood of complaints from small businesses throughout the country, who suddenly found themselves being visited by OSHA inspectors to determine whether or not they were in conformity with the extensive new safety regulations of the agencies that ranged from the proper construction of wood ladders to required safeguards for heavy machinery. Yet another new agency, the Consumer Product Safety Commission, added its output to the volume of administrative rule making that for all agencies was filling up 68,000 pages of small print in the *Federal Register* by the middle of the 1970s.

The seemingly endless volume of administrative rule making appeared to many legislators on Capitol Hill to represent a replacement of Congress by the bureaucracy. President Carter embarked upon a major effort to reduce the volume of administrative rule making and put rules into language comprehensible to those affected. A special White House monitoring team was set up to review administrative regulation; in reality, however, the president had little control over what the agencies could do because they had been given independent rule-making authority by Congress. For its part, Congress responded to the problem by proposing legislation that would allow either the House or the Senate to veto administrative regulations. The constitutional balance of power now seemed to have come full circle, with the agencies making laws subject to congressional vetoes. Provisions for the congressional veto of the regulations of various agencies became law, but they were constitutionally questionable on separation of powers grounds. Some constitutional scholars saw the congressional veto as an unwarranted legislative interference in the affairs of the executive branch. Nevertheless, the Ninety-sixth Congress (1979–80) expanded the use of the congressional veto, although it was unable to pass a major regulatory reform bill that would have enabled Congress to veto any regulation of an administration agency. Moreover, squabbling between the House and the Senate prevented legislation that would have enabled Congress to veto the regulations of independent regulatory bodies such as the Federal Trade Commission.

As the Ninety-sixth Congress came to an end, the FTC became a battleground between the House and the Senate over the legislative veto. The FTC had become embroiled in political controversy because of its aggressive stance, largely due to President Carter's appointment of former Senate Commerce Committee staffer Michael Pertschuk to chair the agency in 1977. Business groups subject to the agency's jurisdiction charged it with overstepping its mandate, and demanded congressional action to curb the agency's powers. The House insisted upon the inclusion of a congressional veto provision in the agency's funding legislation. The Senate opposed the veto, and the agency was funded through regular channels as the debate was carried over into the Ninety-seventh Congress in 1981–82, where a more conservative House and a Republican Senate raised the distinct possibility that a legislative veto law would be passed pertaining to the FTC as well as many other agencies.

The Reagan administration inherited the "problem" of excessive administrative rule making which, in spite of the efforts of the Carter White House to control it, had almost doubled in volume since Carter took office. The president immediately appointed a regulatory relief task force, chaired by Vice-President George Bush, to review administrative regulations with a view toward suspending as many of them as possible. The White House task force at once suspended new regulations that had been established by the EPA, OSHA, and other agencies and were scheduled to go into effect. The approach of the Reagan administration was a general regulatory freeze, to be supervised by the Office of Management and Budget. The freeze could not last indefinitely, however, because of the lack of presidential authority to suspend administrative rules permanently. Ultimately Reagan would have to rely upon his administrative appointees to lead their agencies and departments toward a less aggressive rule-making stance than had generally prevailed under previous administrations, including the Republican presidencies of Nixon and Ford. Agency rules, however, like congressional legislation, are not passed in the abstract, but generally have political backing from outside the agencies. Rules without political support, like agencies without political underpinnings, cannot be sustained for a long period of time. The political advocates of both rules and rule-making powers have prevented Congress from taking strong action to limit the administrative rule-making process. The same political problems may reduce the ability of even such a determined president as Reagan and his conservative aides to make significant inroads on the substance and the process of administrative rule making.

Just as significant, and perhaps more important than rule making as a component of administrative policymaking, is the authority of agencies to adjudicate cases and controversies within their jurisdiction—subject to judicial review under certain circumstances. Administrative adjudication differs from rule making in several important respects. First, while rule making is *general* in effect, adjudication pertains only to a few specific parties. Second, rule making determines what the law is within the boundaries of congressional authority, while administrative adjudication applies congressional statutes and rules to the individual cases. Third, administrative rule making is prospective in effect, while adjudication is retrospective, applying to action that has already taken place and which must be judged in accordance with prevailing standards. Fourth, rule making is based upon the subjective judgment of administrators concerning appropriate policies in the public interest, as that interest has been defined by Congress. Rule making is similar to the legislative process that forces members of Congress to make judgments about what policies can best serve the public in the future. Adjudication, on the other hand, applies the law to a situation that has already occurred, and is supposed to apply the law objectively to the facts of the case. Administrative adjudication, like adjudication by the courts, is intended to determine accurately factual matters that pertain to and are derived from the parties directly involved in the case.

While adjudication is supposed to apply law that has already been formulated, often policy is in fact made through specific adjudicative decisions. The licensing of television stations by the Federal Communications Commission, for example, is essentially an instance of adjudication. When television licenses are renewed, or new television channels opened, the FCC must frequently decide who shall be the licensee among several competing applicants. What "policy" or law does the FCC apply in its licensing cases? First, it refers to the Federal Communications Act of 1934, which provides little guidance since its only standard is that the agency must serve the "public interest, convenience, and necessity" in the licensing process. On the basis of the statute, the Commission could

Administrative
Adjudication and
Policy Making

engage in rule making to set more specific standards for awarding licenses. The Commission, however, has never engaged in full-fledged rule making to determine the appropriate standards for licensees, although it has issued general policy statements concerning some licensing requirements. When licensing cases are decided, the administrative law judges attached to the agency who first hear the case, and subsequently the agency itself, must make ad hoc determinations regarding what criteria they will apply in judging the facts presented. Much administrative adjudication produces, in the generic sense, a common law that becomes the substantive policies of the agencies. Unfortunately, administrative common law is not always consistent, leading to conflicting administrative decision making from one administration to another. For example, conservative Reagan appointees to the regulatory agencies will view the implications of the "facts" presented to them in individual cases far differently than did the more liberal appointees of the Carter administration. Whether or not the rules of the agencies are suspended, administrators can readily interpret existing law to meet their own policy objectives.

| Substantive and Procedural Guidelines for Administrative Action | Very little of the voluminous writing in administrative law or court opinions concentrates upon the need to develop consistent *substantive* as well as procedural law. In the decades preceding the passage of the Administrative Procedure Act of 1946, the American Bar Association and administrative law scholars emphasized the need to pass a statute that would control the *procedures* used by administrative agencies in adjudication and rule making. The APA says nothing about substantive law. Nor can a general statute really go beyond establishing the general procedures that agencies are to use in adjudication and rule making. The APA reflects the faith of the legal profession that proper procedures will produce good substantive policy outputs. Through a stretch of the imagination, one might liken the APA to the Constitution, the APA establishing a broad outline of procedures to be followed by administrative agencies while the Constitution does the same for the government as a whole. Insofar as Congress can deal |

with substantive policy, it must do so through the specific statutes establishing and controlling the agencies, rather than through a general instrument such as the APA.

A major change resulting from the passage of the APA was the expansion of judicial review of agency decisions. Although subject to varying interpretations, and in some cases severely limited by judicial decisions, the intent of section 10 of the APA was to give to any party "aggrieved" by an agency action the right to judicial review, and to provide that when courts go to the merits of individual cases they are to weigh all the evidence on each side rather than uphold an agency decision that is supported only by adequate evidence on the affirmative side. Before the passage of the APA, it was common practice for the courts simply to weigh the evidence in favor of an agency's decisions and overlook or ignore evidence on the other side. If the agency had substantial supporting evidence, the courts would not overturn it. The APA made the courts a potentially stronger force in administrative policy making, which they have become since the era of the 1960s, with its strong civil rights, consumer, and environmental movements making demands upon the judiciary which the courts could not resist. Judicial activism replaced past judicial self-restraint in relation to administrative agencies as the courts forced the agencies to open up their processes to participation by a wide range of "public interest" groups. The courts did not become directly involved in shaping the substantive policies of the agencies, but they indirectly helped to determine those policies by strictly overseeing agency procedures, requiring hearings and other standards of due process to be followed before agency action could be taken. While agencies could still act arbitrarily, their capacity to do so was reduced.

Another major accomplishment of the Administrative Procedure Act was the establishment of a separate class of hearing officers, now called administrative law judges, who were not dependent upon the agencies for their salaries or jobs. Administrative law judges are technically employed by the Office of Personnel Management (OPM), which replaced the Civil Service Commission in 1977. The OPM maintains a list of administrative law judges (ALJs), and upon agency request assigns judges to hear their cases. The ALJs generally work in the same office buildings as the agencies, but since they are not dependent upon them for the emoluments of their offices, they have no fear of rendering independent decisions that may run counter to the policies of the agencies. The Administrative Procedure Act does permit agency heads to overrule administrative law judges, and the courts have interpreted this provision to grant the agencies wide discretion to overturn the decisions of their judges. The courts will not challenge agency reversals of ALJ decisions if the agency overturns the ALJ on the ground that his or her decision ran counter to the agency's stated policies governing the case under consideration. While agencies can readily overrule their ALJs, the administrative judges do have a great deal of independent authority, and most private practitioners dealing with the agencies feel that the independence of the ALJs gives them an adequate opportunity to present their side of a case and have it fairly judged before the agency.

Finally, the Administrative Procedure Act has been extended to increase public access to agency proceedings and to protect individual privacy. The Freedom of Information Act, passed in 1966 and strengthened in 1974, requires agencies to disclose records requested by the public. The request may be made for any reason whatsoever, but the act does allow agencies to exempt from public disclosure certain internal materials and information that would invade the privacy of any individual or reveal commercial secrets. The Freedom of Information Act has made administrative agencies vulnerable to a wide range of requests for information. Many of the requests have been denied, leading to a large number of lawsuits challenging agency decisions not to disclose information.

Controlling Administrative Discretion

Whether exercising legislative, judicial, or executive functions, or some combination of the three, administrators are constantly involved in the formulation of policy. Administrative discretion is a fact of life. Administrators can negate the policies established by legislatures, the directives of chief executives, and even the dictates of the judiciary. This can be done by administrative action or inaction. As the bureaucracy began to expand and flourish under the administration of Franklin Roosevelt, conservative critics stated that the central problem of administrative expansion was the delegation of too much power to the agencies. In Britain, the Lord Chief Justice referred to the powers of the burgeoning British bureaucracy as "the new despotism." In the United States, this cry was echoed by Herbert Hoover, Roscoe Pound, and numerous other conservative thinkers.

More recently, liberals and conservatives in both of the major parties have united to support legislation to curb administrative discretion. Liberal Democrat Edward Kennedy led the fight for the Freedom of Information Act, and for legislation that would expand the ability of the public to participate directly in agency proceedings. Liberals and conservatives joined to pass the privacy act that curbs administrative invasions of personal privacy. While the legislative veto is more strongly advocated by conservatives, liberals, too, have joined in the fight to establish machinery for congressional overrides of administrative rule making. Finally, the significant deregulation of the transportation industry reduces administrative discretion simply by abolishing many administrative powers. Proponents of deregulation, like advocates of other legislation to curtail administrative discretion, represent views along the entire spectrum of political opinion.

In another context, activists like Ralph Nader worry not that the bureaucracy possesses too much power, but that it has too little; and, that where it does possess power it often refuses to exercise it, making the bureaucracy inadequate as an effective instrument of regulation and policy making.

What should be the proper role of the administrative branch in the formulation and execution of public policy? How does it fit into our system of constitutional democracy? If it can negate the will of the other branches of the government, can it make the democratic process a sham? Where does the responsibility of the bureaucracy lie?

THE PROBLEM OF ADMINISTRATIVE RESPONSIBILITY AND POLICYMAKING

"Administrative responsibility" means adhering to standards that are considered to be legitimate within the political sys-

Definition of Responsibility

tem. Administrators who act responsibly are, by definition, acting in conformity with certain criteria. Administrative discretion, and the power of agencies in the policymaking process, complicates administrative responsibility immensely. For example, if administrators exercise discretion, then the only meaningful checks are self-imposed. For decades, since the growth of the bureaucracy as a significant political force, political scientists, politicians, and lawyers have attempted to devise ways of ensuring that the administrative branch is made accountable to standards developed by branches outside of the bureaucracy itself. The myth that Congress does not delegate primary legislative authority to the agencies, but only creates agencies to act as agents of the legislature, conforms to the folklore of our constitutional system. In this way the problem of administrative responsibility is solved rhetorically.

Those who feel that the essence of responsibility lies in establishing administrative accountability for each of the original three branches of the government in their respective spheres want to eliminate administrative discretion. Administrators are not to create their own standards of responsibility. Herman Finer, the classic spokesman for creating administrative accountability to legislatures, states the problem as follows:

> Are the servants of the public to decide their own course, or is their course of action to be decided by a body outside themselves? My answer is that the servants of the public are not to decide their own course; they are to be responsible to the elected representatives of the public, and these are to determine the course of action of the public servants to the most minute degree that is technically feasible. . . . This kind of responsibility is what democracy means; and though there may be other devices which provide "good" government, I cannot yield on the cardinal issue of democratic government. In the ensuing discussion I have in mind that there is the dual problem of securing the responsibility of officials, (a) through the courts and disciplinary controls within the hierarchy of the administrative departments, and also (b) through the authority exercised over officials by responsible ministers based on sanctions exercised by the representative assembly.[2]

[2] Herman Finer, "Administrative Responsibility in Democratic Government," *Public Administration Review* 1, no. 4 (1941): 335–50, at 336.

Accountability to Congress

Administrative accountability to the legislature can be maintained through continuing legislative surveillance of administrative activity. Such legislative surveillance can be through close committee supervision of administrative actions, budgetary controls, and the development of sources of expertise for the legislature outside of the bureaucracy. In varying degrees, Congress has formally attempted to strengthen itself in all of these ways in the hopes that it can better control the administrative branch. The Legislative Reorganization Act of 1946, and that of 1970, were designed to increase the technical proficiency of the legislature and to establish a more streamlined committee network to supervise administrative activities. If Congress is to control the bureaucracy, it must have its own independent sources of information and, what is even more important, independent motivation to check and balance the power of the bureaucracy.

One of the principal devices in the checks and balances system of the Constitution was the establishment of separate constituencies for the three branches of the government, so that they would be motivated to act in opposition to each other. If the bureaucracy is to be checked within this system, the branches of government that are to control it must also have contrasting interests to those of the agencies. With regard to Congress, administrative agencies and congressional committees are often in close alliance rather than in opposition. The same inputs that affect the committees operate as well upon the agencies. In order for legislative oversight to be meaningful, congressional committees must be able to oversee administrative action on an independent basis. Accountability to the legislature must mean accountability to an independent organization. Congress must reflect a public interest that goes beyond the spheres of specialized interest groups.

Another way in which the legislature can insure administrative accountability is to write strict laws, in which the delegations of authority are clear-cut and provide guidelines for administrative action. This has been recommended by Theodore Lowi in *The End of Liberalism*.[3] He advocates that we return to the *Schechter* rule, which prohibits broad delegations of legislative authority to the president or administrative agencies. Such a solution is impossible, however, because the *raison d'être* of the administrative process is the need for agencies to fill in the details of legislation passed by Congress,

[3] Theodore Lowi, *The End of Liberalism* (New York: W. W. Norton and Co., 1969, 1979).

applying their expertise and professional skills to areas where Congress does not have the necessary resources to develop public policy.

The bureaucracy and administrative discretion go together. Of course Congress should strive to make its intent as clear as possible, and both the president and administrators can be kept within the boundaries of this intent through judicial review. But responsibility to Congress can never realistically be achieved by the clearer expression of statutory language. Not only has Congress generally been unwilling to be specific in the enabling statutes of administrative agencies, but once they have been passed, it is difficult to get the legislature to amend these statutes to deal with new problems that may arise.

The independent regulatory agencies are considered to be statutory arms of Congress, with responsibilities to recommend legislative proposals to meet regulatory needs in their respective areas. Marver Bernstein and others have pointed out, however, that congressional committees rarely respond to the legislative recommendations of these agencies.[4] Judge Henry J. Friendly amusingly cites the writings of the French writer Dean Rippert in explaining why legislators, regardless of their nationality, prefer not to legislate:

> ... What Dean Rippert has written of the Palais Bourbon could have been written of the Capitol just as well. I commend the entire discussion; here I can extract only a few plums: every man with a privileged position tries to keep it; "when the legislator is asked to legislate, he knows the benefits he will be conferring on some will be matched by burdens on others; he will have his eye fixed on the relative number of his constituents on one side or the other." Moreover, he realizes that "the benefit accorded to some will bring less ingratitude than the loss suffered by others will in resentment"; the optimum is thus to do nothing, since failure will be understood by those desiring the legislation whereas success will not be forgiven by those opposing it. If legislation there must be, the very necessity of a test arouses further opposition, hence the tendency to soften it in the sense of compromise or even of unintelligibility.[5]

[4] Marver H. Bernstein, *Regulating Business by Independent Commission* (Princeton: Princeton University Press, 1955).

[5] Henry J. Friendly, *The Federal Administrative Agencies* (Cambridge, Mass.: Harvard University Press, 1962), p. 167.

Accountability to the President

In public administration circles, the most frequently heard recommendation for curtailing administrative discretion is to place the executive branch under the control of the president. Since the development of the scientific management school in the early part of the twentieth century, "principles of public administration" have been fostered in varying forms, one of the most tenacious being that administrative efficiency requires hierarchical control, with one person (in the case of the federal bureaucracy, the president) at the top capable of commanding those below him, and therefore accepting responsibility for what is done. A classic statement of the scientific management position is that by W. F. Willoughby in his *Principles of Public Administration* (1927):

> It can be stated without any hesitation that a prime requisite of any proper administrative system is that . . . the Chief Executive shall be given all the duties and powers of a general manager and be made in fact, as well as in theory, the head of the administration.[6]

Why does it go without saying that the president is to be, to use Clinton Rossiter's term, "chief administrator"? As Willoughby states, certain advantages flow from this arrangement:

> Fundamentally these advantages consist in making of the administrative branch, both as regards its organization and its practical operations, a single, integrated piece of administrative machinery, one in which its several parts, instead of being disjointed and unrelated, will be brought into adjustment with each other and together make a harmonious whole; one that possesses the capacity of formulating a general program and of subsequently seeing that such program as is formulated is properly carried out; one in which means are provided by which duplication of organization, plant, personnel, or operations may be eliminated, conflicts of jurisdiction avoided or promptly settled, and standardization of methods of procedure secured; and finally, one in which responsibility is definitely located and means for enforcing this responsibility provided.[7]

The recommendations of Willoughby and the scientific management school were directly translated into the proposals of the President's Committee on Administrative Management in 1937, and later in the recommendations of the Hoover Commission of 1949.

Many of the same factors that limit the control of Congress over the bureaucracy also serve to prevent presidential domination. The size, complexity, and scope of activities of the agencies preclude control by the president, even with the assistance of the staff of the Executive Office, which was specifically created in 1939 to aid White House supervision of the bureaucracy.

[6] W. F. Willoughby, *Principles of Public Administration* (Baltimore: Johns Hopkins University Press, 1927), p. 36.

[7] Ibid., p. 51.

Scientific management theorists supported the idea of presidential control of the bureaucracy for the purposes of administrative efficiency. During the New Deal, liberal Democrats supported the same idea in order to ensure that the programs of President Roosevelt would be carried out. This gave a political coloration to the concept of presidential control. The same liberal supporters of the New Deal, and later Democratic presidents who endlessly sought increased presidential power over the bureaucracy and a general strengthening of the presidency, were not overly concerned to see the legacy of their efforts pass to President Eisenhower, who

---

THE PRESIDENCY AND THE BUREAUCRACY
The Survivors—How to Stay in Office Despite a Change in Administrations

By William J. Lanouette

[Most political appointees are purged routinely whenever the White House changes hands. Those who survive do so because their talents appear to be indispensable.]

A hostile foreign power, bent on creating chaos within the U.S. government, couldn't do much better than any new Administration does by purging almost all incumbent political appointees.

"It's ludicrous," said Alan L. Dean, chairman of the National Academy of Public Administration and a former federal bureaucrat. "No other functioning democracy in the world turns out such a large per cent of competent people when there's a change of Administration."

That purge is now in full swing, in a process that screens appointees for ideological zeal as well as competence and experience. But among the flurry of pink slips, there remain a handful of survivors: senior officials who by their skill, expertise and perseverance serve one Administration after another in important policy-making posts.

These survivors temper their experience in government with a flexible loyalty to whoever is in power. Their personal styles and professional techniques are very different; some succeed by their flamboyance, others by creative anonymity. But their roles are always the same: to provide perspective and continuity in a world where

memories often reach only to the last election.

The survivors' broad experience is both a strength and a weakness. By remaining in power when their political rulers change, they are unavoidably identified with Presidents and policies of the past. But for reasons that vary with each person, they offer talents that are indispensable to incoming Administrations.

"The more you do a variety of things, the better able you are to do a lot of other things," said Donald Rumsfeld, Defense Secretary in the Ford Administration, former House Member from Illinois and now president of G. D. Searle & Co., a pharmaceutical manufacturer.

He had in mind his college pal and former Washington

they considered a responsible if somewhat ineffective president. Before Eisenhower came into office, President Truman had been careful to "blanket" the New Deal–Fair Deal bureaucrats under civil service regulations, so that they could not be removed by any incoming president. This was a common practice of presidents before presidential elections, to prevent the possibility of the opposition party firing unsympathetic administrators.

The Nixon presidency shed a new and disturbing light upon the role of the president as Chief Administrator. More than any other president before him, President Nixon attempted to

colleague, Frank C. Carlucci, who is now deputy Defense secretary—his eighth presidential appointment since 1969. But Rumsfeld's comment applies equally to the other high-level survivors.

Political purges aren't the only reason survivors are so rare. Turnover is normally high among presidential appointees: they stay an average of two years, according to Dean. And pay ceilings keep their federal salaries at a fraction of what they usually are offered by the corporate world. It sometimes takes considerable sacrifice to stay in government service very long. . . .

There might be more survivors than there are if incoming Administrations took more time learning their way around, said a former agency official under two Republican Presidents.

"It's natural, having gone through a campaign, but they don't realize how complex the federal structure has become," he said. "You must know how the system works to become effective in the first six months; and those first months are most important. It doesn't take long for a new Administration to realize it's in up to its armpits. But by that time, the people who could help them have all been fired."

Joseph Laitin, a celebrated survivor in Washington who was recently fired as assistant Treasury secretary for public affairs and held similar posts in the Ford Defense Department and Federal Aviation Administration and in the Johnson White House, points out that most of the successful survivors have Cabinet patrons who mollify critics of their political past with arguments about their competence.

"You survive," Laitin said, "because you serve the purposes of the politicians who are elected and the bureaucrats who rule."

Being around for several changes of government, survivors naturally acquire detractors; some critical of their past or flexible loyalties, others angry over specific decisions or policies. But while most critics beg anonymity, those inclined to praise them are usually glad to speak up. . . .

Those who see problems in the steady turnover of experienced administrators are hard-pressed to propose a remedy. To stop this loss of talent would require a fundamental change in the political system.

"Once you start bringing in a large number of people on the basis of their partisan loyalty and their campaign achievements, the next Administration is not going to leave them there," Dean said. "The question, is how do you reverse that practice?"

Source: *National Journal*, May 23, 1981, p. 28. By permission.

centralize power in the White House and dominate the executive branch. He vastly expanded the personnel of the Executive Office, and created a supercabinet in January of 1973—abandoned in May of that year—designed to centralize control over administrative activities in the White House. Administrative agencies were bluntly ordered to impound funds appropriated for programs that did not meet with the approval of the president.

Opposition to the Nixon program led many former supporters of presidential supremacy within the executive branch to reassess their ideas. Because of the Watergate scandals, prospects of total control over the executive branch by a potentially ruthless presidential staff raised the specter of a police state. It was, ironically, the opposition of J. Edgar Hoover and the FBI that prevented President Nixon from carrying out an extensive plan, devised in 1970, of spying upon his political adversaries. The Internal Revenue Service also refused Nixon's request to harass those on his "enemy list" by conducting special audits of their returns. In order to carry out the break-in of Daniel Ellsberg's psychiatrist's office, Nixon's staff had to employ a special group known as the "plumbers" who operated outside of the official bureaucracy. Administrative efficiency under the control of the president can mean carrying out legitimate programs and, in the words of the President's Committee on Administrative Management of 1937, "making democracy work." But, at the same time, such efficiency can give to the president tools to eliminate political opposition, and thereby to undo the carefully woven design of our democratic government.

Administrative Independence

Among other things, the Watergate scandals illustrated that an independent bureaucracy is necessary for the maintenance of a system of governmental responsibility. The powers of the executive branch are far too extensive to be controlled by any one of the primary branches of government without upsetting the delicate balance of powers in the Constitution. The bureaucracy must be maintained as a semiautonomous fourth branch of the government to check any potential excesses on the part of the president or Congress. Administrators are always subject to partial control by coordinate branches. Over the long run, administrative discretion is never absolute, but the fact of discretion will remain with us. Administrative discretion in policymaking cannot be entirely eliminated.

Carl Friedrich forcefully put forward the argument that in a wide area of administrative action the only way to insure responsibility is through autolimitation—that is, administrative adherence to professional standards.[8] Where administrators are faced with no guidance from the legislature, the people, or the president, what are they to do when the task of making public policy has been delegated to them? Friedrich suggests that they are to be responsible to "technical standards" that have been developed in the particular policy-making area. He places a great deal of emphasis upon the scientific community and its development of standards of professional conduct. A major problem with Friedrich's argument is that there is little agreement within any profession on what the best public policy is in novel areas. Current debates over environmental policy reflect sharp splits within the scientific community, for example. When the secretary of the interior is confronted with deciding whether to authorize the trans-Alaskan pipeline, to push for the development of a trans-Canadian pipeline, or to grant offshore oil leases, he cannot refer to clear-cut professional or scientific standards for guidance. The issues are simply too complex, with conservationists arguing vehemently against the trans-Alaskan plan and the leases at the same time that energy specialists, equally reputable within the scientific community, argue for its rapid development. How does an administrator balance the conservation costs of such an energy policy with the benefits to the nation that will accrue from greater energy resources? This is the kind of decision that administrators are again and again forced to make on their own, although not without inputs from all of the other branches of government.

[8] Carl J. Friedrich, "The Nature of Administrative Responsibility," *Public Policy* (1940): 3–24.

CONCLUSION

The most important source of administrative responsibility lies in the acceptance by administrators themselves of those procedural standards that have been developed as an integral part of our system of constitutional democracy. These standards require respect for the rights of individuals and the support of procedural due process as that has been defined with regard to administrative adjudication and rule-making proceedings. It means respect for the mandates of Congress if they have been clearly stated. All points of view should be weighed and carefully considered before policymaking decisions are made. Above all, the bureaucracy must not be politically neutral when it comes to supporting the values of the system. Fortunately these values have been clearly articulated, and there is no excuse for administrative arbitrariness, unreasonableness, or blind obedience to distorted authority, whether in the White House or the legislature.

Suggestions for Further Reading

Dodd, Lawrence C., and Schott, Richard L. *Congress and the Administrative State.* New York: John Wiley and Sons, 1979. Examines the close relationships that exist between Congress and the bureaucracy.

Hummell, Ralph P. *The Bureaucratic Experience.* New York: St. Martin's Press, 1977. A provocative analysis of the causes and effects of bureaucracy.

Lewis, Eugene. *American Politics in a Bureaucratic Age.* Cambridge, Mass.: Winthrop Publishers, Inc., 1977. Traces the implications of the evolving bureaucratic state for democratic values.

Nachmias, David, and Rosenbloom, David H. *Bureaucratic Government U.S.A.* New York: St. Martin's Press, 1980. Analyzes the increasing bureaucracy not only in the executive branch, but also in the presidency, Congress, the judicial branch, political parties, and interest groups.

Seidman, Harold. *Politics, Position, and Power.* New York: Oxford University Press, 1980. Investigates the dynamics of federal organization.

Woll, Peter. *American Bureaucracy.* 2nd ed. New York: W. W. Norton and Co., 1977. The emergence of the federal bureaucracy as a major force in American government and the effect of its role on the constitutional system of checks and balances is covered.

The Supreme Court building stands majestically on Capitol Hill as a symbol of the power and independence of the judiciary.

CHAPTER 9

The Courts

When Chief Justice John Marshall stated in the historic case *Marbury* v. *Madison* (1803) that the last word on interpretation of the Constitution resides in the hands of the Supreme Court, an important precedent was established: The High Court was given the power and responsibility to define constitutional law. The entire federal judiciary as well as the Supreme Court had this power and responsibility, according to Marshall. Throughout American history the judiciary has from time to time rendered decisions that have had a major impact upon the community at large. In this and many other ways, the judiciary has played a central role in defining public policy.

THE JUDICIARY AS A POLICYMAKING INSTRUMENT

Courts are involved in the policymaking process in several ways. The federal courts have the authority to declare both state and federal legislation unconstitutional. The Supreme Court has been far more active in exercising constitutional review over state than over national actions. The Court has held 123 provisions of federal laws to be unconstitutional in whole or in part out of a total of 85,000 public and private laws that have been passed. By contrast, 950 state laws and provisions of state constitutions have been overturned by the Court since 1789, and 850 of these actions came after 1870.[1] These figures illustrate that the Supreme Court has not been an important check upon Congress during most periods of American history. In maintaining the supremacy of the Constitution and federal law, however, the Court has unhesitat-

Judicial Review

---

[1] Henry J. Abraham, *The Judicial Process*, 4th ed. (New York: Oxford University Press, 1980), pp. 296–97.

ingly followed John Marshall's *McCulloch* doctrine in overturning state legislation that it considers to be in direct conflict with national law.

While constitutional review is a vital ingredient of the judicial power to shape public policy, the Courts raise constitutional issues only where they feel it is absolutely necessary to apply the Constitution to resolve cases before them. Over 99 percent of all cases are settled without having to resort to the Constitution. Courts are significantly involved in the policy-making process through interpretations of statutory and administrative law independent of the Constitution. For example, when the courts decide that the attorney general does not have unreviewable discretion to deport aliens, an important policy decision is being made. The issue is not decided on the basis of the Constitution, however, but upon interpretation of legislation and administrative practice, as well as prior judicial precedent.[2] Virtually all judicial review of administrative decision making—deciding, for example, whether or not the challenged action was beyond the authority granted to the agency by Congress—is based upon statutory interpretation. A related question that frequently arises in judicial review of administrative action is whether the agency has followed the intent of Congress. Review of state action as well is more often based upon statutory rather than constitutional interpretation.

Final determinations of constitutional law are made by the Supreme Court. (See Figure 9.1.) Lower courts, by deciding federal constitutional questions, may force the Supreme Court to exercise its appellate authority to either ratify or nullify the action that has already been taken. When the Supreme Court refuses to grant review of a lower court decision, it does not necessarily mean that the Court agrees with the reasoning and decision of the lower body. A primary task of the Supreme Court is to foster consistency of legal interpretation of the Constitution and federal laws. Conflicting judicial opinions of the lower courts are reviewed by the Supreme Court in order to establish uniform legal principles.

One of the most remarkable facts about judicial policy-making in the last several decades is the extent to which it has been innovative, and has exceeded in this respect the outputs

[2] See, for example, Wong Wing Hang v. Immigration and Naturalization Service, 360 F. 2d 715 (1966).

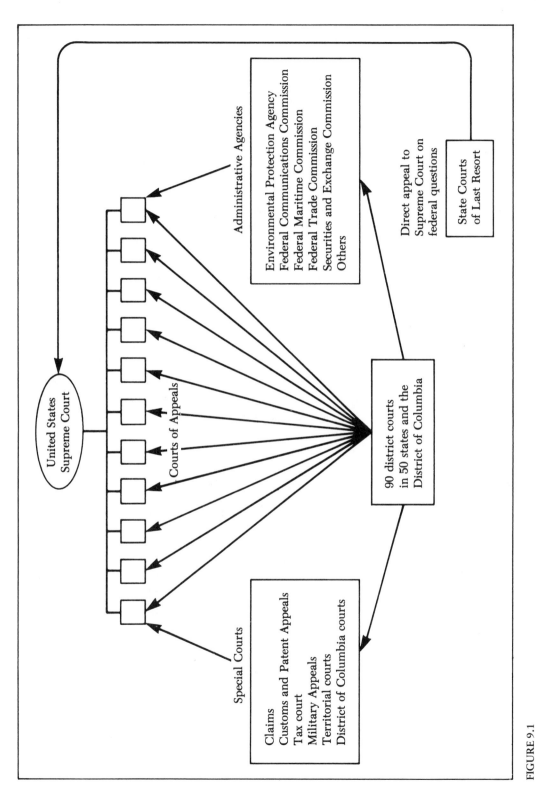

FIGURE 9.1
Organization of the Federal Judiciary.

of the other branches of the government—Congress, the presidency, and the bureaucracy. Whether the outputs of the Supreme Court are "liberal" or "conservative," one fact about its operation stands out in stark contrast to most domestic policymaking by coordinate branches—its independence. Of course, no court is an ivory tower, and judges have been accused of everything from "following the election returns," to being the captives of the dominant economic interests of the nation.

Judicial Self-Restraint

Courts have often exercised judicial self-restraint to avoid becoming embroiled in political controversies that would threaten their independent status. Certainly the Supreme Court of the latter nineteenth century was not a bold innovator, upholding as it did vested property rights and ingeniously inventing the "separate but equal" doctrine to avoid altering the institution of segregation. No one would argue that the Supreme Court was being particularly independent of at least the dominant political interests of society in ruling as it did during this period. The judiciary often seems to have a built-in conservative bias, reflecting the age and training of most judges. A. V. Dicey, that great English scholar of the common law who extolled the virtues of the common law courts and the need for maintaining their independence in opposition to the Parliament and the king, noted that:

> . . . [W]e may, at any rate as regards the nineteenth century, lay it down as a rule that judge-made law has, owing to the training and age of our judges, tended at any given moment to represent the convictions of an earlier era than the ideas represented by parliamentary legislation. If a statute, as already stated, is apt to reproduce the public opinion not so much of today as of yesterday, judge-made law occasionally represents the opinion of the day before yesterday.[3]

One of the major reasons for creating administrative agencies with adjudicative authority was to bypass the conservative biases of the judiciary. Judges all too frequently were nullifying the intent of legislative enactments by interpreting them to conform to conservative common law doctrines.

Judicial Activism

Regardless of what labels are affixed to the decisions of the Supreme Court, whether "liberal" or "conservative," the fact

[3] A. V. Dicey, *Law and Opinion in England,* 2nd ed. (1926), p. 369. Quoted in James M. Landis, *The Administrative Process* (New Haven: Yale University Press, 1938), pp. 96–97.

The Courts

remains that at critical times in our history the Supreme Court has helped to shape our destiny by bold and independent interpretations of constitutional and statutory law. It was the Marshall Court that established such important principles as the supremacy of the authority of the national government over the states, and the doctrine of implied powers permitting Congress to expand its constitutional authority far beyond the strictures of Article I of the Constitution.

The fact that John Marshall succeeded in getting the Supreme Court to uphold the federalist interpretation of the Constitution gave to the new Republic the necessary legal authority to withstand the attacks from proponents of state sovereignty that would have seriously undermined the national government. Marshall's decisions certainly did not demonstrate judicial servility to the president or Congress, from which numerous threats of impeachment issued because of the course of action taken by the Court. With the possible exception of the Warren Court, the Supreme Court has never been as innovative over such an extended period of time as it was during Marshall's tenure.

THE CONTEXT OF JUDICIAL POLICYMAKING

The judiciary operates within much more closely defined procedural limits than the other branches of government. The president can operate secretly, and does not have to give reasons for his actions. Congress can obscure its decision-making processes and avoid placing direct responsibility upon any one part of the legislature. The bureaucracy too is more flexible procedurally than the courts. Judges must adhere to written standards. Initial decisions must be reasoned, and in writing, available to the parties involved, and subject to appeal.

Constitutional Courts and Policymaking

Constitutional courts consist of the Supreme Court and other courts created by Congress under the Supreme Court pursuant to Article III. The stipulations of Article III limit these courts to the consideration of concrete cases and controversies arising under the Constitution, laws, or treaties. Congress cannot delegate "nonjudicial" authority to these courts without violating the Constitution. Historically, judges have been careful to avoid the acceptance of nonjudicial responsibilities, when Congress has, from time to time, attempted to lodge such functions in the judicial branch.

The very first Congress, in 1791, passed a statute that delegated to the circuit courts the responsibility for settling claims of disabled veterans of the Revolutionary War. Circuit judges examined proofs submitted by the veterans regarding the extent of their disabilities, and on the basis of such submissions the judges determined levels of disability and the amount of benefits the veterans would receive. Such judicial determinations under the statute were subject to the supervision of the secretary of war, who could overrule the decisions of the circuit courts. This statute clearly delegated nonjudicial authority to the courts, and in 1792, in *Hayburn*'s case, the act was held to be an unconstitutional delegation of authority to the judiciary. Chief Justice Jay declared the statute unconstitutional because:

> . . . neither the legislative nor the executive branches can constitutionally assign to the judicial [branch] any duties but such as are properly judicial, and to be performed in a judicial manner.
> . . . the duties assigned to the circuit courts by this act are not of that description, and . . . the act itself does not appear to contemplate them as such, inasmuch as it subjects the decisions of these courts, made pursuant to those duties, first to the consideration and suspension of the secretary of war, and then to the revision of the legislature; . . . by the Constitution, neither the secretary of war, nor any other executive officer, nor even the legislature, are authorized to sit as a court of errors on the judicial acts or opinions of this court.[4]

[4] Hayburn's Case, 2 Dallas 409, 410, fn. 2 (1972). *In Re Hayburn's Case* is discussed in Muskrat v. United States, 219 U.S. 346 (1911).

Hayburn's case was the first in which the Supreme Court held an act of Congress to be unconstitutional.

A key attribute of judicial power is that it is final, subject only to review within the judicial system itself. Congress cannot confer authority upon the judiciary which subsequently can be reviewed by an administrative officer or other outside party. Another important restriction upon judicial power is that it can be applied only within the framework of cases and controversies. In *Muskrat* v. *United States* (1911), the Supreme Court refused to accept jurisdiction that Congress had conferred upon it to rule upon the constitutionality

The Courts

of certain congressional statutes in an advisory capacity—that is, in the absence of specific cases and controversies. The congressional statute in question clearly violated the case and controversy requirement of Article III.[5]

[5] Muskrat v. United States, 219 U.S. 346 (1911).

The courts can and often have used the provisions of Article III to limit the reach of their authority and thereby to restrict the realm of questions that can be brought before them for consideration. For example, before the Supreme Court ruled the Connecticut birth control law unconstitutional in 1965 (*Griswold* v. *Connecticut*), it had refused in other challenges to the law to rule on the statute.[6] The Court held that a concrete case and controversy was not present until Connecticut officials enforced the statute, which they finally did in the *Griswold* case. The law could not be challenged if it was moot. Whether "hypothetical" cases are justiciable, meaning concrete and adversary cases and controversies exist, is largely a subjective matter. For example, in the Connecticut birth control case it would have been possible even before enforcement for the Supreme Court to hold that there was a concrete threat of prosecution for alleged violation of the old Connecticut law banning the use of contraceptives. But the Court's majority, by adhering to the line that such a matter was not "ripe" for judicial determination, avoided the necessity of ruling on a very delicate case. The majority was not holding that such a question was "political," and therefore not properly within the jurisdiction of the Court, but rather that the parties had not presented a real case and controversy.

The concepts of standing (the right to sue), justiciability, and the case and controversy requirement of Article III are really fused. A matter is justiciable when there is a case and controversy, which in turn automatically gives the parties standing. In general terms, in order for the courts to exercise jurisdiction, opposing interests must present the issues of the case, and a petitioner for court review must be adversely affected in a personal way which sets him apart from the community as a whole. If Congress has provided by statute that the Courts are to have jurisdiction over certain matters, then recourse to the judiciary is far easier than where no

Standing, Justiciability, and the Case and Controversy Rule

[6] Griswold v. Connecticut, 381 U.S. 479 (1965).

statute grants the right to judicial review. The Courts will not hear cases unless "legal" interests are at stake—that is, interests protected by statutory or constitutional law. Because these conditions must be met before the Courts will hear a case, access to the judiciary is extremely limited.

In recent years, as environmental groups in particular have sought judicial help to stall governmental and private actions that they consider to be detrimental to long-range environmental interests, the Courts have developed and expanded the traditional doctrine of standing. Generally they have opened their doors to greater participation on the part of legitimate environmental and other public interest pressure groups. But the courts still demand that groups or individuals seeking judicial review must have a personal interest at stake distinguishable from the interests of the public at large. They must show some injury from the government action they are challenging.

The current doctrine of standing is well illustrated by the case of *Sierra Club* v. *Morton* (1972). In this case, the Sierra Club challenged a Forest Service decision that permitted a Disney development in the Mineral King Valley, adjacent to the Sequoia National Park in the Sierra Nevada mountains of California. The Disney Corporation had submitted a plan to the Forest Service to develop a $35 million complex for recreational purposes in the valley, under a thirty-year use permit from the government. Access to the resort was to be gained by a twenty-mile highway, a part of which traversed Sequoia National Park. The Forest Service approved the plan and the Sierra Club in June of 1969 filed a suit in the district court for the Northern District of California seeking a judgment that certain aspects of the proposed development were not authorized by federal laws.

Before the courts can reach the "merits" of the case—that is, the issues upon which the petitioner is basing the case—standing to sue must be granted. Although the district court granted standing to the Sierra Club in this case, its decision was reversed by the Ninth Circuit Court of Appeals on the basis that the Sierra Club had not indicated in its complaint that its members would in any way be specifically affected by the Disney Development. The Sierra Club then appealed this decision to the Supreme Court, which granted review and upheld the court of appeals. Like the appellate court, the Supreme Court noted that the Sierra Club had failed in its complaint to indicate how the Disney Development would affect its membership.

The Sierra Club failed to allege that it or its members would be affected in any of their activities or pasttimes by the Disney Development. Nowhere in the pleadings or affidavits did the Club state that its members used Mineral King for any purpose, much less that they use it in any way that would be significantly affected by the proposed actions of the respondents.

The Club apparently regarded any allegations of individualized injury as superfluous, on the theory that this was a "public" action involving questions as to the use of natural resources, and that the Club's long-standing concern with and expertise in such matters was sufficient to give it standing as a "representative of the public."[7]

[7] Sierra Club v. Morton, 405 U.S. 727, 735–36 (1972).

The Court held that it was not enough for the Sierra Club merely to assert that the proposed development was contrary to their value preferences, without alleging specific injury.

The Court's decision in *Sierra Club* v. *Morton* should not be taken to indicate judicial intention to construct new obstacles in the way of environmental groups seeking to use the courts. But the decision did set *some* limits, and it required that at least minimum conditions of the case and controversy criteria be met. In reaction to the Supreme Court's decision, the Sierra Club merely rewrote its brief, claiming individualized injury to its membership, which was readily supportable, and refiled its complaint in the case.

A year after the Sierra Club decision the Court permitted a groups of law students at George Washington University to have standing to challenge a decision of the Interstate Commerce Commission that allegedly adversely affected environmental interests. The students claimed merely that they had used the parks and woodlands in and around the Washington, D.C. area, giving them a personal interest in the ICC's decision. The students' interest was remote, but a majority of the Court nevertheless granted them standing even though their interest was not sharply differentiated from the interests of the general public.[8]

In the mid-1970s the Supreme Court began to tighten its standing requirements by requiring citizens challenging gov-

[8] United States v. Students Challenging Regulatory Agency Procedures (SCRAP), 412 U.S. 669 (1973).

ernment action to demonstrate that they had an interest in the challenged action that was distinguishable from the general interest of all citizens. To achieve standing, plaintiffs had to show a concrete injury and a personal stake in the outcome of a case.[9] The Court began to require in addition that in order to achieve standing plaintiffs must demonstrate that their alleged injury would very likely be redressed by a favorable judicial decision.[10]

[9] Schlesinger v. Reservists' Committee to Stop the War, 418 U.S. 208 (1974).

[10] Simon v. Eastern Kentucky Welfare Rights Organization, 426 U.S. 26 (1976).

Judicial Independence in Policymaking

Since the courts interpret both constitutional and statutory law, in a sense they stand above the law. When the courts are determined, even the clearest mandates of Congress can be interpreted out of existence by a clever stroke of the judicial pen. For example, in the late 1960s heated controversy arose over the operation of the Selective Service System. The Selective Service System was attempting to punish as "delinquents" under the terms of the Selective Service Act individuals who were involved in demonstrations against the draft and the Vietnam War. The Selective Service Act at that time clearly stated that *preinduction* judicial review of classifications by draft boards was precluded. The only channels of review were within the Selective Service System itself. This was written into law to prevent mass appeals of classifications, which could have had the effect of impeding the operation of the Selective Service System.

Regardless of the specific statutory preclusion of judical review, the courts when presented with cases involving the reclassifications of demonstrators and other acts by Selective Service boards that judges considered beyond the boards' authority did not hesitate to step in and exercise judicial review. For example, in the case of *Wolff* v. *Selective Service Local Board No. 16*, two New York Selective Service boards, at the request of the New York City Director of Selective Service, reclassified two University of Michigan students for their demonstration at the offices of the Selective Service local board in Ann Arbor, Michigan, in October of 1965 to protest the Vietnam War.[11] The district court held that it did not have jurisdiction because of the legislative preclusion of judicial review, but on appeal the circuit court

[11] 372 F. 2d 817 (1967).

held that the action of the Selective Service System threatened constitutional rights. The court declared that "the threat to first amendment rights is of such immediate and irreparable consequence not simply to these students but to others as to require prompt action by the courts to avoid an erosion of these precious constitutional rights."

Holding that the Selective Service boards acted beyond their authority, the circuit court in the *Wolff* case reversed the lower court's decision. The court found that although the Selective Service Act provides explicitly that the decisions of local boards shall be final, subject only to review within the Selective Service System, what this really means is that local board decisions are final provided the boards have acted within their legal jurisdiction. When boards act beyond their jurisdiction, the courts can intervene even before administrative remedies have been exhausted (which is usually required before judicial review can be obtained). Remember that the real issue in the *Wolff* case concerned the proper stage at which courts would be involved. The statute clearly stated that if a registrant refused to be inducted, and criminal proceedings were brought against him, he would initially be tried in the federal district courts, as is customary in federal criminal proceedings. But this is quite a different matter from authorizing *preinduction* judicial review of classifications.

Congressional response to the *Wolff* case was swift and straightforward. Congress passed a new law that provided:

No judicial review shall be made of the classification or processing of any registrant by local boards, appeal boards or the president, except as a defense to a criminal prosecution instituted under Section 12 of this Title *after* the registrant has responded either affirmatively or negatively to an order to report for induction, or for civilian work in the case of a registrant determined to be opposed to participation in war in any form.[12]

[12] 50 U.S. C. Section 460 (b) (3). 81 Stat. 100, Section 10(b) (3) (1967). Italics added.

The explicitness of this language was such that no one could possibly mistake the intent of Congress. Indeed, the Armed Services Committee of the House of Representatives in recommending this change stated:

The Committee was disturbed by the apparent inclination of some courts to review the classification action of local or appeal boards before the registrant had exhausted his administrative remedies. Existing law quite clearly precludes such a judicial review until after a registrant has been ordered to report for induction. . . . In view of this inclination of the courts to prematurely inquire into the classification action of local boards, the Committee has rewritten this provision of the law so as to more clearly enunciate this principle. The Committee was prompted to take this action since continued disregard of this principle of the law by various courts could seriously affect the administration of the selective service system.[13]

Similar expressions of dissatisfaction came from the Senate.

How would the courts respond to this new law that so clearly precluded judicial review of Selective Service determinations before an order for induction? The issue was immediately raised in *Oestereich* v. *Selective Service System Local Board No. 11,* involving the reclassification of a theological school student from 4D, which granted exemption, to 1A.[14] Oestereich had returned his registration certificate to the government to express his dissent from United States participation in the Vietnam War. In response to this action, his board changed his classification from 4D to 1A. After his administrative appeal failed, he was ordered to report for induction and at that point he sought to restrain his induction by a suit in a district court. Section 10(b)(3) clearly stated that there should be no judicial review of a registrant's classification at this stage, but only as part of his defense to a criminal prosecution (which was not the case here). The Supreme Court, overruling the lower courts, held that judicial review was appropriate because the action of the board exceeded its authority under the law. Speaking for the majority, Justice William Douglas stated in part that:

> . . . to hold that a person deprived of his statutory exemption in such a blatantly lawless manner must either be inducted and raise his protest through habeas corpus or defy induction and defend his refusal in a criminal prosecution is to construe the act with unnecessary harshness.

These Selective Service cases are examples of how the judiciary can override clearly stated preferences of Congress simply by interpreting statutory language and the "intent of Congress" to be something other than what it is. This means that even though Congress has the constitutional authority to control the appellate jurisdiction of the Supreme Court, and both the original and appellate jurisdiction of lower courts, under the terms of Article III, the courts can and have exerted

[13] H.R. Rep. No. 267, 90th Congress 1st Sess. 30–31 (1967).

[14] 393 U.S. 233 (1968).

their independence and overridden congressional wishes. This is particularly true where the courts consider that constitutional rights are involved, or that clear *ultra vires* action has been taken by administrative agencies.

The Selective Service cases illustrate one aspect of the independence of the judiciary. The courts can be subject to political control and influenced by the demands of Congress. The classic retreat of the New Deal Court in the face of vehement opposition by President Roosevelt, who in turn represented a large majority of the people, is a case in point. The fact that courts do not always retreat in the face of strong political opposition, however, is illustrated by the decisions of the Warren Court. All of the innovative decisions of that Court, from *Brown* v. *Board of Education* (school desegregation),[15] *Baker* v. *Carr* (one man–one vote),[16] through the school prayer decision and the cases that incorporated the Bill of Rights under the due process clause of the Fourteenth Amendment, raised strong opposition from various sections of the country. Nevertheless, the Court did not retreat, but continued its innovative policymaking.

It is clear that the Supreme Court can pick and choose what cases it wants to hear within its appellate jurisdiction, under the provisions of the Judiciary Act of 1925, which was passed to allow the Court discretion in choosing when to grant writs of *certiorari* (writs to review the record of lower court decisions). The Court had become overburdened under the old rules, which required the granting of most appeals for writs of *certiorari*. In practice, then, the Supreme Court can choose to hear a case or not as it wishes. This is not true of lower courts, which must hear cases if jurisdiction is established.

Aside from appellate jurisdiction, the Supreme Court exercises original jurisdiction "in all cases affecting ambassadors, other public ministers and consuls, and those in which a state shall be a party . . ." (Article III). An interesting and generally unknown dimension of judicial self-restraint is that the Court can and often has refused to hear cases (particularly involving political questions) that clearly arise within its original jurisdiction. Although Chief Justice Marshall stated in *Cohens* v. *Virginia* (1821) that "we have no more right to decline the

Judicial Self-Restraint in Policymaking

[15] Brown v. Board of Education, 347 U.S. 483 (1954).

[16] Baker v. Carr, 369 U.S. 186 (1962).

[17] Cohens v. Virginia, 6 Wheaton 264, 404 (1821).

exercise of jurisdiction which is given than to usurp that which is not given,"[17] the Supreme Court has not hesitated to decline to hear cases which it does not consider appropriate.

That the Supreme Court has discretion to refuse cases that would seem to fall within its original jurisdiction is illustrated in *Ohio* v. *Wyandotte*. The Supreme Court refused to go to the merits of an appeal by the state of Ohio that sought to bring the case within the original jurisdiction of the Court. The state sought a Court order that would prevent two out-of-state corporations, as well as a Canadian corporation that was owned by one of the domestic corporations, from polluting Lake Erie by dumping mercury into its tributaries outside of Ohio. In addition, Ohio sought monetary payments for damages that had already been done to fish, wildlife, and vegetation within its borders. Clearly, this was a case between a state and citizens of another state, as well as between a state and foreign citizens, and therefore within the original jurisdiction of the Court. Nevertheless, the Court concluded that:

While we consider that Ohio's complaint does state a cause of action that falls within the compass of our original jurisdiction, we have concluded that this Court should nevertheless decline to exercise that jurisdiction.[18]

[18] Ohio v. Wyandotte Chemicals Corp., 401 U.S. 493, 495 (1971).

Various reasons were given by the Court for refusing to exercise its jurisdiction in the *Wyandotte* case. The "difficulties" of the case were cited, and the "sense of futility that has accompanied this Court's attempts to treat with the complex technical and political matters that inhere in all disputes of the kind at hand." The Court believed that this was a matter for resolution by other parts of the government, whether federal, state, or local. It did not exclude the possibility of jurisdiction being exercised by lower courts. In concluding its opinion, the Court stated:

To sum up, this Court has found even the simplest sort of interstate pollution case an extremely awkward vehicle to manage. And this case is an extremely complex one, both because of the novel scientific issues of fact inherent in it and the multiplicity of governmental agencies already involved. Its successful resolution would require primarily skills of fact finding, conciliation, detailed coordination with—and perhaps not infrequent deference to—other adjudicatory bodies, and close supervision of the technical performance of local industry. We have no claim to such expertise, nor reason to believe that, were we to adjudicate this case, and others like it, we would not have to reduce drastically our attention to those controversies for which this Court is a proper and necessary forum. Such a serious intrusion of society's interest in our most deliberate and considerate performance of our paramount role as the supreme federal appellate court could, in our view, be justified only by the strictest necessity, an element which is evidently totally lacking in this instance.[19]

[19] Ibid., pp. 504–5.

This is a clear-cut example of the way in which the Court can avoid involvement in a major policymaking area, even though it has jurisdiction and could set the directions of policy if it wanted to become involved.

The case and controversy requirement of Article III, and questions of appellate and original jurisdiction, are all part of the procedural context within which the federal judiciary functions. Beyond formal constitutional requirements and judicial interpretations of them, the courts have established elaborate procedures for the determination of cases that profoundly affect their policymaking role. Nowhere is there a more rigid chain of command in the ultimate sense than in the federal and state judiciaries. Lower courts must operate within the framework of policies set forth by the Supreme Court or face almost certainly being overturned on appeal. The lower the level of court, the less likely it is to establish broad policy principles. Trial courts, in the federal system of the district courts, must render their decisions based upon the record that is developed by the immediate parties to the proceedings.

The Procedural Context of Judicial Decision Making

In broad terms, judicial policymaking takes place within the context of the following procedural boundaries:

1. Cases are initiated by parties outside of the judiciary. The courts are helpless to take the initiative to rule and enunciate principles of public policy if an outside agent does not bring a legitimate case and controversy.
2. Assuming that the parties meet the rigid conditions of the case and controversy rule, once the case is before the court at the trial level the judge (and jury if one is involved) at least theoretically is bound by the factual record developed by the parties themselves, and cannot

take "judicial notice" of matters beyond the record unless they are of common knowledge or involve points of law. Judicial proceedings, unlike many congressional hearings, are not merely rhetorical exercises, but establish records that often determine the outcome of the case. On appeal, judges are limited to the factual record of the trial court, although they can of course overrule points of law that have been established by lower courts.

3. The process of judicial decision making is to be impartial insofar as the interests of judges are not to conflict or to be directly connected with the interests of the parties to the proceeding. Judges can have general policy biases, but cannot have a personal stake in the outcome of a decision.

4. Unless points of law have been improperly applied by lower courts, generally their decisions are upheld if there is substantial factual evidence in the record to support their opinion.

5. Where constitutional issues are involved in federal cases, at the trial level three-judge district courts are convened to hear them. Direct appeals may be made from these courts to the Supreme Court.

The case-by-case approach of the judiciary means that policy is established only insofar as cases set precedents. Since courts do not have to follow the rule of *stare decisis* (adherence to precedent), there is no way to tell how far precedents will extend, although decisions of the Supreme Court clearly bind all lower courts until the Supreme Court itself decides to overrule its prior decision.

Judicial Administration

Part of the procedural context of the judiciary involves the way in which courts are administered. This is a rarely discussed and generally misunderstood field. Who are the administrative agents of the courts? To what extent is the federal judiciary influenced by the inputs of those who are involved in various ways in administering what the courts do, but are not themselves judges? Mark Cannon, speaking as administrative assistant to the Chief Justice of the United States, has pointed out that the number of cases and their complexity has vastly increased over the last decade, but the use of managerial techniques by the judiciary has not kept pace. While complexity and volume of business have necessitated the growth of bureaucracy in other branches of the government, the federal judiciary has now followed suit. Six hundred and forty-nine federal judges and approximately the same number of clerks struggle on the federal district and appellate courts each year with a staggering volume of cases that increase by approximately ten percent each year. At the opening of the 1980s the district courts were receiving 155,000 cases each year, a 150 percent increase over 1962. At the end of each year, approximately 180,000 cases are pending before the district courts. The appellate courts receive approximately 20,000 cases per year, and the case backload has resulted in over 17,000 pending cases at the end of the court's term, a 300 percent increase from the early 1960s. On the Supreme Court, nine justices and thirty-two clerks confronted a backlog of almost 5000 cases in 1981. Each year the Court has been able to decide only a few more than 100 cases.

The inevitable result of the increasing burdens upon the judiciary has been delay and frustration for both judges and those involved in the judicial process. Judicial procedure emphasizes the central role of the independent and impartial judge, making it difficult, if not impossible, to delegate judicial tasks of any significance to lower level administrators. The most common recommendation that is made to aid the judiciary in meeting its increased responsibilities is simply to expand the number of judgeships. At the same time, there is widespread recognition within the judiciary that the simple expansion of numbers of judges will not by itself solve the problems that they face. In 1968 the Federal Judicial Center was established to conduct research into special problems of the judiciary.

One of the most far-reaching recommendations that came from a study group sponsored by the Judicial Center is for the establishment of an intermediate court of appeals between the regular appellate courts and the Supreme Court. At the present time the Supreme Court is operating with a staff that is minuscule relative to the scope of its responsibilities. The chief justice now has an administrative assistant, four law clerks, an executive secretary, and last but not least, a chauffeur. The associate justices have staffs of five—three law clerks, one secretary, and a messenger. In addition to the personal staffs of the justices, the Supreme Court employs some professional staff to aid it in handling its case loads. However, Supreme Court justices as well as their counterparts in the lower federal judiciary always personally peruse cases that come before them, because by the very nature of the judicial process it is impossible to delegate this task.

The office staff of the clerk of the Supreme Court, fewer than a dozen career employees, handles the formal requirements for applications of cases coming before the court. Of course, the clerk's staff in no way affects or participates in the decisions of the high tribunal. It is the law clerks to the justices themselves who are thought to influence the preparation and writing of decisions, both in the Supreme Court and in the lower echelons. In reality, however, the justices do not delegate final decision-making authority in any way to their clerks, and on cases appealed to them they do not even establish a division of labor among themselves. Each justice takes part in both the handling of appeals for writs of *certiorari* and other appellate writs, and in the writing of final opinions. Anthony Lewis has described the role of the clerks in the following terms:

> . . . Law clerks assist in research and may write drafts of material for the justice. They also perform the function of keeping him in touch with current trends of legal scholarship, especially the often critical views of the law schools about the Supreme Court. That is an important role in a court which could so easily get isolated in its ivory tower. But the law clerks do not judge, they can only suggest. As a practical matter, a young man [or woman] who is there only briefly is unlikely to make any significant change in the actual votes cast on cases by a judge who has been considering these problems for years.[20]

[20] Anthony Lewis, *Gideon's Trumpet* (New York: Random House, Vintage Edition, 1966), p. 32.

The proposal for a new intermediate appellate court just below the Supreme Court to screen out, hear, and decide certain cases involving conflicting rulings among the circuit courts would have the effect of reducing the work load of the Supreme Court. However, in no way would it change the nonbureaucratic approach of the Court to judicial decision

The Courts

making. The effect of such a court would certainly be to deny appellees the consideration that is now given to their cases by all of the Supreme Court justices. Some significant cases might never reach the Supreme Court, although it is not the intention of those proposing the intermediate appellate body to give to it any final authority should the Supreme Court wish to act in a particular case. Moreover, the new court is not supposed to decide cases involving significant issues of constitutional and statutory law, but is to pass such cases along to the Supreme Court. Although there is a possibility that such an intermediate appellate court might reduce the policymaking role of the Supreme Court, this is anything but certain.[21]

Various other suggestions have been made to cope with the work load of the Supreme Court and the lower federal judiciary. Proposals have been made to narrow the jurisdiction of the lower federal courts in order to reduce the number of cases coming before them. The Judicial Conference, a representative group of federal judges chaired by the chief justice of the Supreme Court, has argued that the federal courts should not have "diversity jurisdiction," which permits certain cases to be heard in federal courts if the litigants are from different states. Chief Justice Burger, who has made court reform a major issue, has proposed that the Judicial Conference rather than Congress establish new judgeships subject to a congressional veto. While the courts are valiantly striving to expand the number of judgeships and streamline their procedures to deal with the increasing caseload, Congress continues to burden the courts by expanding judicial review of administrative agency decisions and enacting legislation that encourages citizens to challenge agency action in the courts. Wisconsin Representative Robert Kastenmeier, who chairs the House subcommittee responsible for the federal courts, has stressed that "court-related problems are not merely lawyer problems, or judge problems, or law enforcement problems, they are people problems." Kastenmeier has concluded that "the needs of the poor, powerless, and underprivileged—individuals whose desires have generally been underrepresented in the legislative and executive branches and whose rights often have been vindicated in the

[21] See Nathan Lewin, "Helping the Court with Its Work," *New Republic*, 3 March 1973, for a discussion of the intermediate court proposal.

[21] *Congressional Quarterly Weekly Report,* 16 February 1980, p. 399.

antimajoritarian judicial branch, are of utmost importance."[21] House and Senate liberals like Kastenmeier have sponsored legislation to increase public access to judicial proceedings, which if passed might in fact make the courts unable to respond adequately to an increased number of lawsuits because of a work overload on judges and staff who are already overburdened.

Although an increasing emphasis is being placed upon the need to improve judicial administration, there is little doubt that judicial efficiency will always depend largely upon the actions of judges rather than administrators. The judges ultimately have to make the decisions. Case disposition may be improved by the increasing use of lower level quasi-judges, such as magistrates (formerly U.S. commissioners), who aid district courts in processing civil and criminal litigation. Magistrates conduct trials of individuals who have been accused of minor offenses, and they can impose sentences of up to one year in jail or fines up to $1,000. They conduct pretrial conferences for cases that are pending on the civil and criminal dockets of the district courts, screen pretrial motions, and recommend disposition of them. They also review Social Security appeals, screen prisoner petitions, review petitions under the Narcotic Addict Rehabilitation Act, conduct first indictment arraignments of defendants in felony cases, serve as special masters under the appointment of district judges, issue search and arrest warrants, fix bail for persons charged with criminal offenses, and issue commitment and release orders for persons charged with criminal offenses. These are not insignificant judicial responsibilities. They obviously affect the procedural policies of the courts, although they do not influence major judicial policymaking decisions.

The major task of judicial administrators and judges in the future will be to render the court system more responsible both in terms of the standards that the judges in the legal profession themselves have established, and in response to broader demands from the community. For example, the speedy disposition of cases is a major goal of the judiciary, and current procedural rules may have to be changed to expedite case disposition. Speed in the handling of cases must always be complemented by fair procedures in accordance with due process of law as defined by the judiciary itself.

One of the greatest needs in judicial policy making is for consistency and uniformity of standards that are applied within the federal court system and among the states in the adjudication of individual cases. Standards enunciated by the Supreme Court are not always followed. In cases that do not raise important issues of constitutional and statutory law, and therefore are in practice excluded from the purview of the Supreme Court, it is even more difficult to maintain consistency. This is particularly true in those areas where quasi-judges, magistrates, and referees in bankruptcy handle a large volume of cases that are not for practical purposes generally appealed, and where they are appealed do not usually raise issues that the Supreme Court feels the need to resolve. Referees in bankruptcy, for example, although agents of district courts and operating under the authority of the federal bankruptcy law, often handle cases quite differently in different sections of the country.[22]

The problems of judicial discretion and inconsistency in policy implementation are analogous to the problem of administrative discretion that arises within the bureaucracy. Wherever subordinate officials are given the responsibility and power to interpret law, even though avenues of appeal may be present, their decisions are often in fact final. Maintenance of uniformity and consistency of legal interpretation within given jurisdictions is difficult to achieve.

[22] See David T. Stanley et al., *Bankruptcy: Problem, Process, Reform* (Washington, D.C.: The Brookings Institution, 1971), for a description of how the referee system works and the attending problems.

EXAMPLES OF JUDICIAL POLICYMAKING

Although courts cannot set policy on their own initiative, and must operate within the framework of the case and controversy requirement, the number and variety of appeals give judges ample opportunity to shape public policy in many fields. Even a brief glance at American history demonstrates the profound impact that judicial policymaking has had upon our society.

Sometimes the courts shape policy by negating acts of Congress and state legislatures. In the period from approximately 1890 to 1920, the Supreme Court imposed its own views on state legislators with regard to the scope and content of eco-

Economic Policy

nomic regulations that were permissible under the due process clause of the Fourteenth Amendment. Acting in an entirely subjective manner, the Court defined "due process" as requiring "reasonable" state action in the regulation of economic interests.

It was impossible to predict the subjective feelings of the Court regarding what constituted reasonable action, and therefore exactly how it would hold in particular cases. Sometimes the Court upheld state statutes that regulated economic activity and on other occasions it did not. In *Holden* v. *Hardy* (1898), the Court by a 7 to 2 vote held constitutional a Utah statute limiting the hours of workmen in mines, smelters, and ore refineries, to a maximum of eight hours a day.[23] In that case the Court found that the state should have discretion to regulate the hours of workmen. This ruling seemed to negate the "right of free contract" (part of "liberty of due process") that had been previously established by the Court, which limited the authority of states to interfere in contractual arrangements between employers and employees. In its opinion in the *Holden* case the Court upheld state regulation because of the existence of hazardous working conditions, and also because of the unequal bargaining power of employers and employees.

Shortly after the *Holden* ruling, in the historic case of *Lochner* v. *New York* (1905), the Court in a 5 to 4 decision declared unconstitutional a New York statute that limited the hours of labor in bakery shops to sixty per week, or ten in any one day.[24] The statute, the Court said, violated the right of free contract. Employers should be free to purchase or to sell labor. The contradiction between the *Holden* and *Lochner* decisions illustrates that during this period the Court was not adhering to strict principles of the law. Rather, the Court was going beyond even its own interpretations of the Constitution in previous cases to look at the conditions under which the cases arose, and on this basis trying to make the appropriate decision. This type of substantive decision making extended into all areas of social legislation at that time, with the Court freely imposing its own values upon state legislatures and Congress alike. Where economic regulations involved hours of labor, public utility rates, taxation, or other aspects of

[23] Holden v. Hardy, 169 U.S. 366 (1898).

[24] Lochner v. New York, 198 U.S. 45 (1905).

The Courts

economic activity, the Court felt itself obliged to act as the final arbiter of the reasonableness of the substantive content of the laws. When the Court acted in this way under the due process clause of the Fourteenth Amendment, it was essentially defining due process in substantive rather than in procedural terms, and its doctrines became known as "substantive due process" in the economic realm.

Just as the courts during the latter nineteenth and early twentieth centuries were reluctant to grant much leeway to legislatures to make economic policy without careful judicial scrutiny, they were unwilling to allow the infant administrative process to act in an independent fashion. The Interstate Commerce Commission (ICC) was created in 1887, and Congress delegated to it "quasi-legislative" and "quasi-judicial" functions. At the beginning, the authority of the ICC was not as great in the exercise of legislative and judicial powers as it was to become in later years. At first the courts carefully supervised the agency, and did not hesitate to overrule it when its decisions did not agree with judicial opinion. The initial confusion over whether the agency had the power to fix rates, which seemed to be implied in its enabling statute, was resolved by the Supreme Court in 1896 in a decision holding unequivocally that the ICC could not determine reasonable rates, but only establish facts with regard to rates already in effect.[25] This meant that the ICC was limited to declaring *existing* rates unreasonable. It had no positive power to set new rates.

In 1897, the Supreme Court again declared emphatically, in *ICC* v. *Cincinnati, New Orleans, and Texas Pacific Railway Co.,* that the Commission could not determine and enforce new rates upon a railroad after having first determined that the existing rate structure was unreasonable.[26] Rate making, said the Court, is essentially a legislative function, and the separation of powers doctrine requires that if it is to be exercised by government at all it must be carried out within the legislative branch. In another decision the Court held that, although the Interstate Commerce Act of 1887 clearly declared that the findings of fact of the ICC were to be taken as conclusive by the courts when they exercised judicial review, the circuit courts of appeals that reviewed the decisions of the

[25] Cincinnati, New Orleans, and Texas Pacific Railway Company v. ICC (1896).

[26] Interstate Commerce Commission v. Cincinnati, New Orleans, and Texas Pacific Railway Co., 167 U.S. 479 (1897).

27 ICC v. Alabama Midland Ry. Co. (1897).

ICC were not to be restricted to the agency's factual record, but could accept additional evidence presented by the parties and act upon it.[27] Railroads wishing to circumvent the authority of the ICC were encouraged to withhold information purposely during the agency proceedings so that it might later be introduced before a reviewing court in such a way as to make the decision of the commission appear unreasonable.

Legislatures and administrative agencies became less beholden to subjective judicial opinions as the twentieth century progressed. The judiciary never completely retreated into a doctrine of judicial self-restraint. It tended to become more cautious about involving itself in political disputes with Congress or state legislatures on the one hand, and administrative agencies that were the chosen agents of the legislatures on the other. The invocation of the doctrine of substantive due process in the economic sphere to overrule legislative action was not abandoned by the Supreme Court until after the bitter struggle over the scheme of President Franklin Roosevelt to "pack" the Court in an attempt to overcome its opposition to the key legislative proposals of the New Deal.

The Court in the New Deal Period

The early New Deal period witnessed a conservative and activist Supreme Court holding unconstitutional major legislation designed to curb the economic ills of the country. The Supreme Court, standing alone within government but reflecting the viewpoints of powerful economic interests on the outside, was single-handedly negating presidential and congressional policy proposals. While some of President Roosevelt's advisors—for example, Secretary of the Interior Harold Ickes—felt that a constitutional amendment should be pushed that would revoke the authority of the Supreme Court to declare acts of Congress unconstitutional, the president took a less drastic course. He recommended to Congress that he be allowed to appoint one new justice for each justice on the Supreme Court over seventy years of age. In 1937 this would have meant that he would have been able to appoint up to six new Supreme Court justices, and thereby have switched the Court from a conservative to a liberal position, assuming his appointees continued to adhere to the policy preferences of

The Courts

the president (which would have by no means been a certainty).

Roosevelt's court-packing plan was doomed from the start. Beginning in 1937 the Supreme Court, due to the crossing over of Justice Roberts from the conservative to the liberal side of the bench, changed its position and began to support New Deal programs. The historic case in which the Supreme Court began to shift its position from the conservative to the liberal side was *West Coast Hotel Co. v. Parrish* (1937).[28] In this case the Court upheld a minimum wage statute for women in the state of Washington, overruling its former opinion in *Adkins v. Children's Hospital* (1923).[29]

In the *Adkins* case, the court had invalidated a minimum wage statute of the District of Columbia because it violated the principle of "freedom of contract" implied, it said, in the due process clause of the Fifth Amendment. "Freedom of contract" was an important principle that was also applied by the Supreme Court under the due process clause of the Fourteenth Amendment to invalidate a number of state statutes that regulated employer-employee relationships.

In the *West Coast Hotel* case the Court pointed out that its prior decisions upholding freedom of contract did not imply an absolute right to contract. For example, in *Muller v. Oregon* (1908),[30] the Court upheld the constitutional authority of the state to limit working hours for women. Holding the *Adkins* case to be specifically overruled, the Court found in *West Coast Hotel* that the public interest justified the regulation of working hours for women. Moreover, it pointed out that workers placed in an unequal position *vis à vis* employers can be exploited, and denied a living wage which places a burden upon the community to support them. Taking judicial notice of the Depression, the Court reasoned that states can take into account social problems and legislate accordingly. By implication this applied to the federal government also. Secretary of the Interior Ickes noted in his diary the day after the decision that "Chief Justice Hughes delivered the opinion and he used language, which, if it had been adopted earlier by the Supreme Court and consistently followed, would probably have prevented the strained relationship that now exists

[28] West Coast Hotel Co. v. Parrish, 300 U.S. 379 (1937).

[29] Adkins v. Children's Hospital, 261 U.S. 525 (1923).

[30] Muller v. Oregon, 208 U.S. 412 (1908).

[31] Harold L. Ickes, *The Inside Struggle* (New York: Simon and Schuster, 1954), p. 106.

[32] National Labor Relations Board v. Jones and Laughlin Steel Corp., 301 U.S. 1 (1937).

[33] Hammer v. Dagenhart, 247 U.S. 251, 269 (1918).

[34] Ibid., p. 271.

between the Supreme Court on the one side and the legislative and executive branches on the other."[31]

In a series of cases after *West Coast Hotel,* the Supreme Court held that the federal government had the authority to extend its power over the states in a number of fields, and thereby upheld the core of the New Deal program. In April of 1937, a month after the *West Coast Hotel* decision, the Supreme Court upheld the National Labor Relations Act in *NLRB* v. *Jones and Laughlin Steel Corporation* (1937).[32] The issue was whether or not Congress had the authority under the commerce clause to regulate labor conditions in industries that were "indirectly" involved in interstate commerce. In prior decisions the Supreme Court had held that manufacturing operations were only "indirectly" involved in interstate commerce because, although their goods were later shipped out of state and therefore were in interstate commerce, the actual manufacturing took place within a particular state and therefore did not involve interstate commerce. For example, in *Hammer* v. *Dagenhart* (1918), the Court posed the following question:

. . . Is it within the authority of Congress in regulating commerce among the states to prohibit the transportation in interstate commerce of a manufactured good, the product of a factory in which, within thirty days prior to their removal therefrom, children under the age of fourteen have been employed or permitted to work, or children between the ages of fourteen and sixteen years have been employed or permitted to work more than eight hours in any day, or more than six days in any week, or after the hour of 7 P.M. or before the hour of 6 A.M.?[33]

The Court pointed out, "the thing intended to be accomplished by this statute is the denial of the facilities of interstate commerce to those manufacturers in the states who employ children within the prohibited ages."[34] But, the Court held, only if the goods produced by the children were inherently harmful would it be legally justified to close the channels of interstate commerce to their shipment. This limited view of the commerce power of Congress strictly limited the permissible scope of federal legislation.

The National Labor Relations Act of 1935, like the child labor statute involved in *Hammer* v. *Dagenhart,* sought to regulate the relationships between labor and employers in all

The Courts

firms engaged in "interstate commerce." The National Labor Relations Board was given jurisdiction over all labor disputes that burdened or threatened to burden interstate commerce. Specifically, the board was to prevent "unfair labor practices" through the issuance of cease and desist orders, enforceable in the courts. The way the act was framed clearly indicated that it was intended to extend governmental authority over manufacturing industries that were only "indirectly" involved in interstate commerce under the terms of prior Supreme Court decisions. Nevertheless, in upholding the act, the Supreme Court overruled its previous distinction between direct and indirect interstate commerce with the statement that:

... The congressional authority to protect interstate commerce from burdens and obstructions is not limited to transactions which can be deemed to be an essential part of a "flow" of interstate or foreign commerce. Burdens and obstructions may be due to injurious actions springing from other sources. The fundamental principle is that the power to regulate commerce is the power to enact "all appropriate legislation" for "its protection and advancement . . ."; to adopt measures "to promote its growth and insure its safety . . ."; "to foster, protect, control and restrain. . . ." That power is plenary and may be exerted to protect interstate commerce "no matter what the source of the dangers which threaten it. . . ." Although activities may be intrastate in character when separately considered, if they have such a close and substantial relation to interstate commerce that their control is essential or appropriate to protect that commerce from burdens and obstructions, Congress cannot be denied the power to exercise that control.[35]

[35] NLRB v. Jones and Laughlin Steel Corp., 301 U.S. 1, 36–37 (1937).

NLRB v. *Jones and Laughlin Steel* opened the way to extensive government regulations based upon the commerce clause of Article I. Virtually any economic activity can be, and generally has been, interpreted to be part of interstate commerce because it is in some way connected. Any firm that either draws its materials from interstate commerce or ships its products back into that commerce is subject to federal regulation. Most of the federal regulatory apparatus has been legally based upon the authority of Congress under the liberally interpreted commerce clause.

Immediately following the decision in *NLRB* v. *Jones and Laughlin Steel,* the Supreme Court overruled the doctrine of "dual federalism" which had stated that the constitutional authority of Congress was limited by the reserved powers of the states. For example, the Court had declared the first Agricultural Adjustment Act of 1933 unconstitutional on the grounds that its purpose was the regulation of agriculture, which lay within the reserved powers of the states.[36] Chief Justice John Marshall would have been horrified at the doctrine of dual federalism, for it repudiated his clear-cut decisions that established the principle of national supremacy over states in cases where there was any conflict of laws. Moreover, dual federalism contradicted the doctrine of federal preemption of a policy field where uniformity is demanded and Congress can imply policy authority from its enumerated powers. Under the doctrine of dual federalism it would have been impossible for the federal government to expand its programs sufficiently to meet the emergencies of the Depression era. Eventually the Supreme Court recognized this reality and abandoned the principle of dual federalism in upholding the Social Security Act of 1935.[37] Although Justice Cardozo, who wrote the majority opinion, did not explicitly overrule the dual federalism doctrine, he nevertheless strongly supported national supremacy and by implication held that the reserved powers of the states under the Tenth Amendment could not be used to negate needed national legislation. Cardozo took judicial notice of the Depression, pointing out its disastrous effects upon the economy and employment. National action was needed, he said, and it would be intolerable for the Supreme Court to negate legislation such as the Social Security Act on the basis of abstract and questionable constitutional principles.

The shift in the position of the Supreme Court in the latter 1930s toward judicial self-restraint and a respect for the initiatives of the executive and legislature in public policymaking reflected a recognition that courts cannot stand in the way of legislation that is politically supported and clearly in the public interest. The role of the courts as negators of public policy passed by Congress ended with the New Deal, and no law dealing with economic problems has been declared unconstitutional since 1936.

[36] United States v. Butler, 297 U.S. 1 (1936).

[37] Stewart Machine Company v. Davis Case, 301 U.S. 548 (1937).

The Post–New Deal Period

Between the New Deal Court and the Warren Court, there was no significant policy innovation by the federal judiciary.

The doctrine of judicial self-restraint in political questions was the rule of the day. In the areas of civil liberties and civil rights, the Supreme Court was extremely reluctant to "nationalize" any more provisions of the Bill of Rights than it had during the 1920s and 1930s. The Supreme Court was perfectly willing to overrule state actions on an *ad hoc* basis where it felt that state action violated "fair" procedures in criminal proceedings. However, it was unwilling to upset the federal-state balance of power by holding that all of the rights accorded to defendants in federal courts were applied to the states under the due process clause of the Fourteenth Amendment.

The Supreme Court might have entered the "political thicket" of electoral reapportionment in *Colegrove* v. *Green* (1946), a case in which the congressional electoral districts in Illinois were challenged as a violation of the equal protection clause of the Fourteenth Amendment because of tremendous disparity in the number of voters from district to district.[38] Urban voters in the city of Chicago were placed at a tremendous disadvantage in relation to downstate rural voters. One Chicago congressional district had nine times more voters than one of the downstate districts. Illinois had not been reapportioned since 1901, a time when the rural areas of the state were in balance with the urban sections. The Supreme Court voted by a 4 to 3 margin not to give the courts jurisdiction over electoral reapportionment in the state of Illinois because such "political questions" are nonjusticiable. Justice Rutledge, however, who voted with the majority, did not accept this argument. He held that the issue was justiciable, but nevertheless decided to vote with the majority on other grounds. The nominees for the Illinois congressional districts had already been chosen when *Colegrove* was before the Court. Rutledge felt that judicial intervention at that time would unduly upset the forthcoming general election in Illinois. Therefore, although Justice Frankfurter's opinion for the majority is widely cited as an example of the Court's avoidance of a tricky political issue, the majority voting in that case did not accept Frankfurter's reasoning.

The Court confronted the reapportionment issue again in 1962, in *Baker* v. *Carr,* and held the case justiciable.[39] The majority of the Court in the *Baker* case noted that in *Cole-*

[38] Colegrove v. Green, 328 U.S. 549 (1946).

[39] Baker v. Carr, 369 U.S. 186 (1962). For further discussion of the *Baker* case see Chapter 5.

grove a majority did in fact hold the issue of electoral reapportionment to be a proper matter of judicial concern. The former position of the Court was ambiguous, however; in 1950 a firm majority of the Court held, in *South* v. *Peters,* the distribution of voters in state electoral districts to be a political question and therefore beyond the jurisdiction of the courts.[40] In that case the infamous county unit system of Georgia was challenged as being a violation of the equal protection clause of the Fourteenth Amendment.

Additional policy areas in the late 1940s and early 1950s in which the Supreme Court refused to innovate included the loyalty and security policies of federal and state governments. This was one of the major political issues of the time. Just as Senator Joe McCarthy was embarking upon his career to ferret out Communists in government, which was soon to terrorize many elements of the community, particularly federal employees, the Supreme Court was confronted with the question of the validity of the Smith Act in *Dennis* v. *United States* (1951).[41] The Court upheld the 1940 statute on the basis that Congress has a right to proscribe First Amendment freedoms where there is a "clear and present danger" to the security of the nation.

There is little doubt that the era of the Supreme Court from 1937 to 1954 was characterized by judicial self-restraint. As the Court abandoned the doctrine of substantive due process in the economic realm, it also retreated from active involvement in policy formulation in other areas. Judicial deference to the wishes of government was carried over into such policy fields as civil liberties and civil rights. The Supreme Court became a ratifier of government decisions, rather than an innovator in policymaking.

The Warren Court

The profound impact that courts can have upon public policy was illustrated during the era of the Warren Court. The Court injected a new spirit of activism throughout the federal judiciary, which had a spillover effect upon state courts as well. Of particular importance was the use by the Court of the due process and equal protection clauses of the Fourteenth Amendment to rationalize the establishment of federal standards requiring equal educational opportunity by abandon-

[40] South v. Peters, 339 U.S. 276 (1950).

[41] Dennis v. United States, 341 U.S. 494 (1951). For further discussion of the *Dennis* case see Chapter 4.

ment of the "separate but equal" doctrine; the one man–one vote rule that revolutionized electoral apportionment in both congressional and state legislative districts; and the extension of most of the provisions of the Bill of Rights as prohibitions upon state action.[42]

[42] See Chapter 3 for a discussion of the Bill of Rights and Chapter 5 for an examination of equal protections under the laws.

CONTEMPORARY JUDICIAL POLICYMAKING

Although President Nixon made a concerted attempt to appoint "strict constructionists" or conservatives to the Supreme Court and the lower federal judiciary, the legacy of the Warren Court was too firmly ingrained in our law to be overturned completely.

While the Burger Court retreated somewhat from liberal Warren Court doctrines—refusing, for example, to go as far as the Warren Court in ordering the busing of school children to achieve racial integration—in general the Burger Court maintained the policies of its predecessor. In some areas the Burger Court went further than the Warren Court had—for example, in extending criminal rights by granting those accused of crimes the right to counsel at preliminary judicial hearings.

Ironically, the conservative Burger Court has infuriated many conservative politicians, such as North Carolina Republican Jesse Helms, because it has insisted upon continued support for the busing of school children to achieve racial balances within school districts that had a history of past discrimination, or where the weight of the evidence suggested that there was an intent to discriminate by drawing school district lines to segregate racial minorities.

Even more important to conservatives than the busing issue is the stand the Court has taken on the issue of abortion in *Roe* v. *Wade* (1973), in which the Court upheld the absolute right of a woman to have an abortion during the first trimester of pregnancy.[43] Under the *Roe* decision, states can regulate abortions, but only during the last six months of pregnancy and then only where it is demonstrated to be necessary to preserve the health of the mother. The abortion decision spawned a nationwide right-to-life movement that put

[43] Roe v. Wade, 410 U.S. 113 (1973).

pressure upon Congress to pass and submit to the states an amendment that would ban abortions.

The victory of Ronald Reagan in 1980 encouraged the antibusing and antiabortion conservatives. The president had not hesitated during his campaign and after his election to affirm his strong views against busing and abortion, and announced at a press conference shortly after his inauguration his support for a right-to-life amendment as well as congressional legislation to prohibit abortions. Jesse Helms led a group of congressional conservatives in sponsoring legislation that would define life to begin at conception, thereby prohibiting abortions because they would constitute the taking of a human life. The passage of such legislation would undoubtedly force a confrontation between Congress and the Supreme Court over what the Court had previously proclaimed to be the constitutional right to abortion.

Another tack taken by Court opponents has been the introduction of legislation that would withdraw jurisdiction from the Court over cases relating to state laws on prayer in public schools, abortion, or school desegregation plans. The attack upon the Court mounted by congressional conservatives in the Ninety-seventh Congress was the most serious threat to judicial independence since Franklin Roosevelt's court-packing scheme of 1937.

Proponents of the legislative restrictions upon the jurisdiction of the Court argued that the Constitution clearly states that the appellate authority of the Supreme Court is under congressional control. Congress can withdraw what jurisdiction it wants from the High Court, although it cannot interfere with the Court's original jurisdiction, which is set forth in the Constitution. Opponents of the legislation argued that such severe restrictions upon the Court's jurisdiction would curb its essential constitutional role that had evolved over almost two centuries. The Court has assumed the responsibility of maintaining the supremacy of the Constitution from its very first decisions in the first decade of its operation. National supremacy over the states was established in the 1790s, and strongly reaffirmed by the Marshall Court. To assert in the 1980s that the Court cannot review state actions involving constitutional questions would render the Court impotent and make the Constitution subject to the inevitably conflicting interpretations of state courts.

The opponents of the efforts to restrict the Supreme Court also argued that the proposed legislation limiting the Court's jurisdiction was a violation of the spirit if not the letter of the separation of powers doctrine. Congress should not, they declared, attempt to force its will upon the Supreme Court on substantive issues, nor can the legislature curb the Court's legitimate constitutional powers.

The Court had in the past weathered many political storms at least as violent as those raised by its opponents during Reagan's presidency. All of the highly controversial decisions of the Court—and there have been many—resulted in vitriolic and scathing attacks upon the justices, and threats of impeachment. The Supreme Court under Marshall, Taney (the *Dred Scott* decision), Charles Evans Hughes during the New Deal, and Earl Warren was deeply embroiled in political controversy and had to withstand persistent outside attacks. There was nothing new in the plans of the Ninety-seventh Congress to limit the Court by reducing its jurisdiction. Congress had done so in the past under the most blatant of circumstances when it repealed the appellate jurisdiction of the Court over habeas corpus cases, which had been granted in an 1867 law, and prohibited appeals that had already been taken under the law in order to prevent the Court from ruling on the constitutionality of the Reconstruction Acts.[44] Congress withdrew the Court's jurisdiction as the justices were about to render their opinion in a case reviewing the denial of a writ of habeas corpus by a federal circuit court.

The Court's acquiescence to congressional withdrawal of its jurisdiction over habeas corpus cases after the Civil War, however, involved unusual circumstances and a particularly delicate political situation which the Court thought it best to avoid. Although the Court has occasionally avoided political controversy through the exercise of judicial self-restraint and acquiescence to Congress, what is remarkable about its history is the extent to which it has exercised independent power to shape the very foundations of the constitutional system in important areas of public policy, ranging from the economic sphere to civil liberties and civil rights. "Conservative" courts,

[44] Ex parte McCardle, 7 Wallace 506 (1869).

such as that of Chief Justice Charles Evans Hughes during the 1930s, have been as controversial as "liberal" courts, such as that of Chief Justice Earl Warren during the 1950s and 1960s.

THE NOMINATION OF THE FIRST WOMAN SUPREME COURT JUSTICE

A Keen Mind, Fine Judgment

[*Presidents balance political and ideological considerations in nominating Supreme Court justices. President Reagan was determined to select, first, a justice who was not a man and, second, a person with a conservative outlook.*]

Until [July, 1981,] Sandra O'Connor was an obscure judge who has served a mere eighteen months on an intermediate appeals court. She has never decided weighty constitutional issues and her *curriculum vitae* does not include a bibliography of scholarly law-review articles. What then are her qualifications for a seat on the U.S. Supreme Court? One of her mentors in Phoenix offers an answer. O'Connor brings two key qualities to the job, says Arizona Gov. Bruce Babbitt: "raw intellectual ability and a great sense of judgment."

The nation's legal community seems to concur. Stanford constitutionalist Gerald Gunther, praising President Reagan for taking "the high road" with his selection, says that O'Connor "seems by all reports to be a perfectly qualified, conservative-philosophy judge." She is hardly a towering figure in the law—few legal authorities outside Arizona know much about her work—but that has never counted for much in Supreme Court nominations. The main factor in her favor was plainly her sex. "There are women around with better credentials," says Brooklyn Law School Prof. Joel Gora, "but hers are awfully good."

Modern Woman

O'Connor's credentials as the quintessential modern woman—capable of melding family, career and civic responsibilities—are almost flawless. She and her lawyer husband, John Jay O'Connor III, have been married for 29 years and have raised three sons along the way. Friends call her a gourmet cook. She was once president of the Junior League of Phoenix and now serves on the boards of the Arizona chapters of the Salvation Army, the YMCA and the National Conference of Christians and Jews.

Sandy Day was born on March 26, 1930, and grew up on her family's Lazy B ranch in southeastern Arizona. She was such a bright child that her parents, finding no rural school nearby worthy of her, sent her to live with her grandmother in El Paso, Texas, where she attended a private school. She entered Stanford at 17, graduated with great distinction, then attended Stanford Law School, where she was an editor of the Law Review.

In law school she met John, one class behind her; they had dinner the first night they met, while working on the Law Review; it was the first of 46 straight dates. They married shortly after she graduated; when John finished school, the O'Connors worked in Germany for three years, she as a civilian lawyer for the Army, he in the Judge Advocate General's Corps. After they moved to Phoenix, O'Connor went into practice for two years before she had the first of three sons, Scott, now 23. (The others are Brian, 21, and Jay, 19.)

Politician

About the time her youngest son entered school, O'Connor returned to law, became an assistant attorney general of Arizona and entered Republican Party politics. Appointed to the state Senate in 1969, she was later elected twice, becoming Majority Leader in 1973.

The nature of political controversy surrounding the Court depends upon whose ox is being gored by the decisions of the High Tribunal.

The U.S. Supreme Court has known many former politicians, but O'Connor would be the only current Justice ever elected to legislative office. (Potter Stewart, just retired, was once a Cincinnati city councilman.)

Arizona politicians describe O'Connor as conservative, a view supported by her record on the abortion issue. But on some women's issues she often took the liberal position. She led fights to remove sex-based references from state laws and to eliminate job restrictions in order to open more positions to women. "Sandra succeeded as a political leader because she not only has intelligence and integrity, but is a warm person and very fair," says Mary Dent Crisp, a longtime Arizona friend who broke with the GOP last summer over its opposition to the Equal Rights Amendment.

O'Connor left the Senate and won election as a Phoenix trial judge in 1975. Although she was mentioned regularly as a potential Republican candidate for governor, she committed herself to the judicial branch in 1979 when she accepted an appointment from Babbitt, a Democrat, to the Arizona court of appeals. The docket of a state intermediate court consists largely of appeals from criminal convictions, workmen's and unemployment compensation cases, divorces and bankruptcies. It is a long way from *Marbury v. Madison,* and in O'Connor's 29 written opinions there are no examples of soaring constitutional rhetoric. What the opinions do show is a careful study of precedent, ample citation and a clear, no-nonsense writing style that some Justices of the Supreme Court might do well to emulate.

O'Connor probably will be comfortable with a Burger Court that pays growing obeisance to legislative decisions and the prerogatives of state courts. In an essay published in the William and Mary Law Review last January she predicted that President Reagan's election would encourage the Supreme Court's trend toward "shifting to the state courts some additional responsibility" and argued that state judges rivaled Federal judges in competence. Noting that many state-court judges become Federal judges, O'Connor said: "When the state-court judge puts on his or her Federal-court robe, he or she does *not* become immediately better equipped intellectually to do the job."

'Role Model'

The nation should soon find out if she is right. Some Justices grow on the job; some don't. It is one of the historic truths about the Supreme Court that no one can safely predict how a Justice will turn out—in either legal competence or judicial philosophy. The first judgments on O'Connor are that she will not be a great intellectual force on the Court, but rather a skilled craftsman. "She is a technician in the best sense of the word," says Ernst John Watts, dean of the National Judicial College. It is easier, perhaps, to predict the impact of her presence on the Supreme Court in nonjudicial matters. "Sandra is very clearly a role model for somewhat younger women," says her close friend Sharon Rockefeller, wife of a governor (Democrat John D. Rockefeller IV, of West Virginia) and daughter of a U.S. senator (Republican Charles H. Percy of Illinois). "She understands very well the conflict between a woman's desires to be part of the professional world and yet to be a perfect mother and wife as well." O'Connor is "serenity itself," says Rockefeller. "If anyone was born to be a judge, Sandra was."

Source: Jerrold K. Footlick with David T. Friendly, *Newsweek,* July 20, 1981, pp. 18–19. Copyright © 1981, by Newsweek, Inc. All Rights Reserved. Reprinted by Permission.

The Supreme Court is inevitably thrust into the center of political controversy. It is the responsibility of the Court to hear important constitutional cases, which always involve questions upon which there are sharp disagreements among different segments of the population. Sometimes the Court seems to be attacked from all sides, as in its busing decisions, which united liberals and conservatives throughout the nation in strong opposition to the Court.

The Court will survive the controversy surrounding it in the 1980s as it has withstood the numerous attacks made upon it in the past. It may have to bend a little to meet its political opposition by exercising more judicial self-restraint than it has exhibited in many of the contemporary opinions that have so strongly buttressed the civil liberties and rights of all citizens. It is highly unlikely, however, that the Court would reverse the course of history in civil liberties and civil rights policies that it has helped to make. If Congress forces a major confrontation with the justices over the fundamental constitutional powers of the Court and its major constitutional decisions, the Court will not back down, but in all likelihood will hold unconstitutional congressional legislation that intrudes upon its prerogatives.

Suggestions for Further Reading

Abraham, Henry J. *The Judicial Process.* 4th ed. New York: Oxford University Press, 1980. A comparative introductory analysis of the role of the judiciary in the United States, Great Britain, and France.

Jackson, Robert H. *The Struggle for Judicial Supremacy.* New York: Random House, 1941. A firsthand account of the battle between President Franklin Roosevelt and the Supreme Court.

Lewis, Anthony. *Gideon's Trumpet.* New York: Random House, 1964. The exciting story of a major Supreme Court case is told from beginning to end.

McCloskey, Robert G., ed. *Essays in Constitutional Law.* New York: Random House/Vintage, 1957. Essays by leading scholars on the Supreme Court and the Constitution.

Westin, Alan F., and Mahoney, Barry. *The Trial of Martin Luther King.* New York: Thomas Y. Crowell Co., 1974. An excellent study of a major Supreme Court case involving the right of protest.

Woodward, Bob, and Armstrong, Scott. *The Brethren.* New York: Simon and Schuster, 1979. A controversial but fascinating account of Supreme Court decision making.

APPENDIX A

The Constitution of the United States

We the People of the United States, in Order to form a more perfect Union, establish Justice, insure domestic Tranquility, provide for the common defence, promote the general Welfare, and secure the Blessings of Liberty to ourselves and our Posterity, do ordain and establish this Constitution for the United States of America.

Preamble

ARTICLE 1

Section 1. All legislative Powers herein granted shall be vested in a Congress of the United States, which shall consist of a Senate and House of Representatives.

Section 2. The House of Representatives shall be composed of Members chosen every second Year by the People of the several States, and the Electors in each State shall have the Qualifications requisite for Electors of the most numerous Branch of the State Legislature.

House Membership

No Person shall be a Representative who shall not have attained to the age of twenty five Years, and been seven Years a Citizen of the United States, and who shall not, when elected, be an Inhabitant of that State in which he shall be chosen.

Representatives and direct Taxes shall be apportioned among the several States which may be included within this Union, according to their respective Numbers, *which shall be* determined by adding to the whole Number of free Persons, including those bound to Service for a Term of Years, and excluding Indians not taxed, *three fifths of all other persons.*[1] The actual Enumeration shall be made within three Years after the first Meeting of the Congress of the United States, and within every subsequent Term of ten Years, in such Manner as they shall by Law direct. The Number of Representatives shall not exceed one for every thirty Thousand, but each State shall have at Least one Representative; and until such enumeration shall be made, the State of New Hampshire shall be entitled to chuse three, Massachusetts eight, Rhode-Island and Providence Plantations one, Connecticut five, New-York six, New Jersey four, Pennsylvania eight, Delaware one, Maryland six, Virginia ten, North Carolina five, South Carolina five, and Georgia three.

When vacancies happen in the Representation from any State, the Executive Authority thereof shall issue Writs of Election to fill such Vacancies.

The House of Representatives shall chuse their Speaker and other Officers; and shall have the sole Power of Impeachment.

[1] Throughout, italics are used to indicate passages altered by subsequent amendments. In this instance, for example, see Fourteenth Amendment.

Senate Membership

[2] See Seventeenth Amendment.

Section 3. The Senate of the United States shall be composed of two Senators from each State, *chosen by the Legislature thereof,*[2] for six Years; and each Senator shall have one Vote.

Immediately after they shall be assembled in Consequence of the first Election, they shall be divided as equally as may be into three Classes. The Seats of the Senators of the first Class shall be vacated at the Expiration of the second Year, of the second Class at the Expiration of the fourth Year, and of the third Class at the Expiration of the sixth Year, so that one third may be chosen every second Year; *and if Vacancies happen by Resignation, or otherwise, during the Recess of the Legislature of any State, the Executive thereof may make temporary Appointments until the next Meeting of the Legislature, which shall then fill such Vacancies.*[3]

[3] See Seventeenth Amendment.

No Person shall be a Senator who shall not have attained to the Age of thirty Years, and been nine Years a Citizen of the United States, and who shall not, when elected, be an Inhabitant of the State for which he shall be chosen.

The Vice President of the United States shall be President of the Senate, but shall have no Vote, unless they be equally divided.

The Senate shall chuse their other Officers, and also a President pro tempore, in the Absence of the Vice President, or when he shall exercise the Office of President of the United States.

The Senate shall have the sole Power to try all Impeachments. When sitting for that Purpose, they shall be on Oath or Affirmation. When the President of the United States is tried, the Chief Justice shall preside: And no Person shall be convicted without the Concurrence of two thirds of the Members present.

Judgment in Cases of Impeachment shall not extend further than to removal from Office, and disqualification to hold and enjoy any Office of honor, Trust or Profit under the United States: but the Party convicted shall nevertheless be liable and subject to Indictment, Trial, Judgment and Punishment, according to Law.

Section 4. The Times, Places and Manner of holding Elections for Senators and Representatives, shall be prescribed in each State by the Legislature thereof; but the Congress may at any time by Law make or alter such Regulations, except as to the Places of chusing Senators.

The Congress shall assemble at least once in every Year, and such Meeting shall be on the first Monday in December, unless they shall by Law appoint a different Day.[4]

Section 5. Each House shall be the Judge of the Elections, Returns and Qualifications of its own Members, and a Majority of each shall constitute a Quorum to do Business; but a smaller Number may adjourn from day to day, and may be authorized to compel the Attendance of absent Members, in such Manner, and under such Penalties as each House may provide.

Impeachments

Election

---

[4] See Twentieth Amendment.

Rules of Congress

Each House may determine the Rules of its Proceedings, punish its Members for disorderly Behaviour, and, with the Concurrence of two thirds, expel a Member.

Each House shall keep a Journal of its Proceedings, and from time to time publish the same, excepting such Parts as may in their Judgment require Secrecy; and the Yeas and Nays of the Members of either House on any question shall, at the Desire of one fifth of those Present, be entered on the Journal.

Neither House, during the Session of Congress, shall, without the Consent of the other, adjourn for more than three days, nor to any other Place than that in which the two Houses shall be sitting.

Compensation

Section 6. The Senators and Representatives shall receive a Compensation for their Services, to be ascertained by Law, and paid out of the Treasury of the United States. They shall in all Cases, except Treason, Felony and Breach of the Peace, be privileged from Arrest during their Attendance at the Session of their respective Houses, and in going to and returning from the same; and for any Speech or Debate in either House, they shall not be questioned in any other Place.

No Senator or Representative shall, during the Time for which he was elected, be appointed to any civil Office under the Authority of the United States, which shall have been created, or the Emoluments whereof shall have been encreased during such time; and no Person holding any Office under the United States, shall be a Member of either House during his Continuance in Office.

Enacting Bills

Section 7. All bills for raising Revenue shall originate in the house of Representatives; but the Senate may propose or concur with Amendments as on other Bills.

Veto Power

Every Bill which shall have passed the House of Representatives and the Senate, shall, before it become a Law, be presented to the President of the United States; if he approve he shall sign it, but if not he shall return it, with his Objections to that House in which it shall have originated, who shall enter the Objections at large on their Journal, and proceed to reconsider it. If after such Reconsideration two thirds of that House shall agree to pass the Bill, it shall be sent, together with the Objections, to the other House, by which it shall likewise be reconsidered, and if approved by two thirds of that House, it shall become a Law. But in all such Cases the Votes of both Houses shall be determined by Yeas and Nays, and the Names of the Persons voting for and against the Bill shall be entered on the Journal of each House respectively. If any Bill shall not be returned by the President within ten Days (Sundays excepted) after it shall have been presented to him, the Same shall be a Law, in like Manner as if he had signed it, unless the Congress by their Adjournment prevent its Return, in which Case it shall not be a Law.

Every Order, Resolution, or Vote to which the Concurrence of the Senate and House of Representatives may be necessary (except on a question of Adjournment) shall be presented to the President of the United States; and before the Same shall take Effect, shall be approved by him, or being disapproved by him, shall be repassed by two thirds of the Senate and House of Representatives, according to the Rules and Limitations prescribed in the Case of a Bill.

Section 8. The Congress shall have Power To lay and collect Taxes, Duties, Imposts and Excises, to pay the Debts and provide for the common Defence and general Welfare of the United States; but all Duties, Imposts and Excises shall be uniform throughout the United States;

Powers of Congress

To borrow Money on the credit of the United States;

To regulate Commerce with foreign Nations, and among the several States, and with the Indian Tribes;

To establish an uniform Rule of Naturalization, and uniform Laws on the subject of Bankruptcies throughout the United States;

To coin Money, regulate the Value thereof, and of foreign Coin, and fix the Standard of Weights and Measures;

To provide for the Punishment of counterfeiting the Securities and current Coin of the United States;

To establish Post Offices and post Roads;

To promote the Progress of Science and useful Arts, by securing for limited Times to Authors and Inventors the exclusive Right to their respective Writings and Discoveries;

To constitute Tribunals inferior to the Supreme Court;

To define and punish Piracies and Felonies committed on the high Seas, and Offences against the Law of Nations;

To declare War, grant Letters of Marque and Reprisal, and make Rules concerning Captures on Land and Water;

To raise and support Armies, but no Appropriation of Money to that Use shall be for a longer Term than two Years;

To provide and maintain a Navy;

To make Rules for the Government and Regulation of the land and naval Forces;

To provide for calling forth the Militia to execute the Laws of the Union, suppress Insurrections and repel Invasions;

To provide for organizing, arming, and disciplining, the Militia, and for governing such Part of them as may be employed in the Service of the United States, reserving to the States respectively, the Appointment of the Officers and the Authority of training the Militia according to the discipline prescribed by Congress;

To exercise exclusive Legislation in all Cases whatsoever, over such District (not exceeding ten Miles square) as may, by Cession of particular States, and the Acceptance of Congress, become the Seat of the Government of the United States, and to exercise like Authority over all Places purchased by the Consent of the Legislature of the State in which the Same shall be, for the Erection of Forts, Magazines, Arsenals, dock-Yards, and other needful Buildings;—And

To make all Laws which shall be necessary and proper for carrying into Execution the foregoing Powers, and all other Powers vested by this Constitution in the Government of the United States, or in any Department officer thereof.

Limits on Congressional Power

Section 9. The Migration or Importation of such Persons as any of the States now existing shall think proper to admit, shall not be prohibited by the Congress prior to the Year one thousand eight hundred and eight, but a Tax or duty may be imposed on such Importation, not exceeding ten dollars for each Person.

The Privilege of the Writ of Habeas Corpus shall not be suspended, unless when in Cases of Rebellion or Invasion the public Safety may require it.

No Bill of Attainder or ex post facto Law shall be passed.

No Capitation, or other direct, Tax shall be laid, unless in Proportion to the Census or Enumeration herein before directed to be taken.

No Tax or Duty shall be laid on Articles exported from any State.

No Preference shall be given by any Regulation of Commerce or Revenue to the Ports of one State over those of another: nor shall Vessels bound to, or from, one State, be obliged to enter, clear, or pay Duties in another.

No Money shall be drawn from the Treasury, but in Consequence of Appropriations made by Law; and a regular Statement and Account of the Receipts and Expenditures of all public Money shall be published from time to time.

No title of Nobility shall be granted by the United States: And no Person holding any Office of Profit or Trust under them, shall, without the Consent of the Congress, accept any present, Emolument, Office, or Title, of any kind whatever, from any King, Prince, or foreign State.

Section 10. No State shall enter into any Treaty, Alliance, or Confederation; grant Letters of Marque and Reprisal; coin Money; emit Bills of Credit; make any Thing but gold and silver Coin a Tender in Payment of Debts; pass any Bill of Attainder, ex post facto Law, or Law impairing the Obligation of Contracts, or Grant any Title of Nobility.

Powers of the States

No State shall, without the Consent of the Congress, lay any Imposts or Duties on Imports or Exports, except what may be absolutely necessary for executing its inspection Laws: and the net Produce of all Duties and Imposts, laid by any State on Imports or Exports shall be for the Use of the

Treasury of the United States; and all such Laws shall be subject to the Revision and Control of the Congress.

No State shall, without the Consent of Congress, lay any Duty of Tonnage, keep Troops, or Ships of War in time of Peace, enter into any Agreement or Compact with another State, or with a foreign Power, or engage in War, unless actually invaded, or in such imminent Danger as will not admit of delay.

ARTICLE II

Section 1. The executive Power shall be vested in a President of the United States of America. He shall hold his Office during the Term of four Years, and, together with the Vice President, chosen for the same Term be elected as follows:

Presidential Election

Each State shall appoint, in such Manner as the Legislature thereof may direct, a Number of Electors, equal to the whole Number of Senators and Representatives to which the State may be entitled in the Congress but no Senator or Representative, or Person holding an Office of Trust or Profit under the United States, shall be appointed an Elector.

The Electors shall meet in their respective States, and vote by Ballot for two Persons, of whom one at least shall not be an Inhabitant of the same State with themselves. And they shall make a List of all the Persons voted for, and of the Number of Votes for each; which List they shall sign and certify, and transmit sealed to the Seat of the Government of the United States, directed to the President of the Senate. The President of the Senate shall, in the Presence of the Senate and House of Representatives, open all the Certificates, and the Votes shall then be counted. The Person having the greatest Number of Votes shall be the President, if such Number be a Majority of the whole Number of Electors appointed; and if there be more than one who have such Majority, and have an equal Number of Votes, then the House of Representatives shall immediately chuse by Ballot one of them for President;

and if no Person have a Majority, then from the five highest on the List the said House shall in like Manner chuse the President. But in chusing the President, the Votes shall be taken by States, the Representation from each State having one Vote; A quorum for this purpose shall consist of a Member or Members from two thirds of the States, and a Majority of all the States shall be necessary to a Choice. In every Case, after the Choice of the President, the Person having the greatest Number of Votes of the Electors shall be the Vice President. But if there should remain two or more who have equal Votes, the Senate shall chuse from them by Ballot the Vice President.[5]

The Congress may determine the Time of chusing the Electors, and the Day on which they shall give their Votes; which Day shall be the same throughout the United States.

No Person except a natural born Citizen, or a Citizen of the United States, at the time of the Adoption of this Constitution, shall be eligible to the Office of President; neither shall any Person be eligible to that Office who shall not have attained to the Age of thirty five Years, and been fourteen Years a Resident within the United States.

In Case of the Removal of the President from Office, or of his Death, Resignation, or Inability to discharge the Powers and Duties of the said Office, the Same shall devolve on the Vice President, and the Congress may by Law provide for the Case of Removal, Death, Resignation or Inability, both of the President and Vice President, declaring what Officer shall then act as President, and such Officer shall act accordingly, until the Disability be removed, or a President shall be elected.[6]

The President shall, at stated Times, receive for his Services, a Compensation which shall neither be increased nor diminished during the Period for which he shall have been elected, and he shall not receive within that Period any other Emolument from the United States, or any of them.

Before he enter on the Execution of his Office, he shall take the following Oath or Affirmation:—"I do solemnly swear (or affirm) that I will faithfully execute the Office of President of the United States, and will to the best of my Ability,

[5] Superseded by the Twelfth Amendment.

Requirements to Be President

[6] See Twenty-fifth Amendment.

preserve, protect and defend the Constitution of the United States."

Section 2. The President shall be Commander in Chief of the Army and Navy of the United States, and of the Militia of the several States, when called into the actual service of the United States; he may require the Opinion, in writing, of the principal Officer in each of the executive Departments, upon any Subject relating to the Duties of their respective Offices, and he shall have Power to grant Reprieves and Pardons for Offences against the United States, except in Cases of Impeachment.

He shall have Power, by and with the Advice and Consent of the Senate, to make Treaties, provided two thirds of the Senators present concur; and he shall nominate, and by and with the Advice and Consent of the Senate, shall appoint Ambassadors, and other public Ministers and Consuls, Judges of the supreme Court, and all other Officers of the United States, whose Appointments are not herein otherwise provided for, and which shall be established by Law: but the Congress may by Law vest the Appointment of such inferior Officers, as they think proper, in the President alone, in the Courts of Law, or in the Heads of Departments.

The President shall have Power to fill up all Vacancies that may happen during the Recess of the Senate, by granting Commissions which shall expire at the End of their next Session.

Section 3. He shall from time to time give to the Congress Information of the State of the Union, and recommend to their Consideration such Measures as he shall judge necessary and expedient; he may, on extraordinary Occasions, convene both Houses, or either of them, and in Case of Disagreement between them, with Respect to the Time of Adjournment, he may adjourn them to such Time as he shall think proper; he shall receive Ambassadors and other public Ministers, he shall take Care that the Laws be faithfully executed, and shall Commission all the Officers of the United States.

Section 4. The President, Vice President, and all civil Officers of the United States, shall be removed from Office on Impeachment for, and Conviction of Treason, Bribery, or other high Crimes and Misdemeanors.

Section 1. The judicial Power of the United States, shall be vested in one supreme Court and in such inferior Courts as the Congress may from time to time ordain and establish. The Judges, both of the supreme and inferior Courts, shall hold their Offices during good Behaviour, and shall, at stated Times, receive for their Services, a Compensation, which shall not be diminished during their Continuance in Office.

Section 2. The judicial Power shall extend to all Cases, in Law and Equity, arising under this Constitution, the Laws of the United States, and Treaties made, or which shall be made, under the Authority;—to all Cases affecting Ambassadors, other public Ministers and Consuls;—to all Cases of admiralty and maritime Jurisdiction;—to Controversies to which the United States shall be a Party—to Controversies between two or more States;—*between a State and Citizens of another State*[7]—between Citizens of different States;—between Citizens of the same State claiming Lands under Grants of different States, *and between a State or the Citizens thereof, and foreign States, Citizens, or Subjects.*[8]

Jurisdiction of Federal Courts

[7] See Eleventh Amendment.

[8] See Eleventh Amendment.

In all cases affecting Ambassadors, other public Ministers and Consuls, and those in which a State shall be Party, the supreme Court shall have original Jurisdiction. In all the other Cases before mentioned, the supreme Court shall have appellate Jurisdiction, both as to Law and Fact, with such exceptions, and under such Regulations as the Congress shall make.

The Trial of all Crimes, except in Cases of Impeachment, shall be by Jury; and such Trial shall be held in the State where the said Crimes shall have been committed; but when not committed within any State, the Trial shall be at such Place or Places as the Congress may by Law have directed.

Treason

Section 3. Treason against the United States, shall consist only in levying War against them, or in adhering to their Enemies, giving them Aid and Comfort. No Person shall be convicted of Treason unless on the Testimony of two Witnesses to the same overt Act, or on Confession in open Court.

The Congress shall have Power to declare the Punishment of Treason, but no Attainder of Treason shall work Corruption of Blood, or Forfeiture except during the Life of the Person attained.

ARTICLE IV

**Full Faith
and Credit**

Section 1. Full Faith and Credit shall be given in each State to the public Acts, Records, and judicial Proceedings of every other State. And the Congress may by general Laws prescribe the Manner in which such Acts, Records, and Proceedings shall be proved, and the Effect thereof.

**Privileges
and Immunities**

Section 2. The Citizens of each State shall be entitled to all Privileges and Immunities of Citizens in the several States.

Extradition

A Person charged in any State with Treason, Felony, or other Crime, who shall flee from Justice, and be found in another State, shall on Demand of the executive Authority of the State from which he fled, be delivered up, to be removed to the State having Jurisdiction of the Crime.

No Person held to Service or Labour in one State, under the Laws thereof, escaping into another, shall, in Consequence of any Law or Regulation therein, be discharged from such Service or Labour, but shall be delivered up on Claim of the Party to whom such Service or Labour may be due.[9]

---

[9] See Thirteenth Amendment.

**Creation
of New States**

Section 3. New States may be admitted by the Congress into this Union; but no new State shall be formed or erected within the Jurisdiction of any other State; nor any State be formed by the Junction of two or more States, or Parts of States, without the Consent of the Legislatures of the States concerned as well as of the Congress.

The Congress shall have Power to dispose of and make all needful Rules and Regulations respecting the Territory or other Property belonging to the United States; and nothing in this Constitution shall be so construed as to Prejudice any claims of the United States, or of any particular State.

Section 4. The United States shall guarantee to every State in this Union a Republican Form of Government, and shall protect each of them against Invasion; and on Application of the Legislature, or of the Executive (when the Legislature cannot be convened) against domestic Violence.

ARTICLE V

The Congress, whenever two thirds of both Houses shall deem it necessary, shall propose Amendments to this Constitution, or, on the Application of the Legislatures of two thirds of the several States, shall call a Convention for proposing Amendments, which, in either Case, shall be valid to all Intents and Purposes, as Part of this Constitution, when ratified by the Legislatures of three fourths of the several States, or by Conventions in three fourths thereof, as the one or the other Mode of Ratification may be proposed by the Congress; Provided that no Amendment which may be made prior to the Year One thousand eight hundred and eight shall in any Manner affect the first and fourth Clauses in the Ninth Section of the first Article; and that no State, without its Consent, shall be deprived of its equal Suffrage in the Senate.

Amendment Process

ARTICLE VI

All Debts contracted and Engagements entered into, before the Adoption of this Constitution, shall be as valid against the United States under this Constitution, as under the Confederation.

Supremacy Clause	This Constitution, and the Laws of the United States which shall be made in Pursuance thereof; and all Treaties made, or which shall be made, under the Authority of the United States, shall be the supreme Law of the Land; and the Judges in every State shall be bound thereby, any Thing in the Constitution or Laws of any State to the Contrary notwithstanding.
No Religious Test	The Senators and Representatives before mentioned, and the Members of the several State Legislatures, and all executive and judicial Officers, both of the United States and of the several States, shall be bound by Oath or Affirmation, to support this Constitution; but no religious Test shall ever be required as a Qualification to any Office or public Trust under the United States.

ARTICLE VII

Ratification Process	The Ratification of the Conventions of nine States, shall be sufficient for the Establishment of this Constitution between the States so ratifying the Same.
	Done in Convention by the Unanimous Consent of the States present the Seventeenth Day of September in the Year of our Lord one thousand seven hundred and eighty seven and of the Independence of the United States of America the twelfth. In witness whereof We have hereunto subscribed our Names.
	ARTICLES IN ADDITION TO, AND AMENDMENT OF, THE CONSTITUTION OF THE UNITED STATES OF AMERICA, PROPOSED BY CONGRESS, AND RATIFIED BY THE LEGISLATURES OF THE SEVERAL STATES, PURSUANT TO THE FIFTH ARTICLE OF THE ORIGINAL CONSTITUTION.

AMENDMENT I

	[Ratification of the first ten amendments was completed December 15, 1791.]
Freedom of Religion, Speech, Press, and Assembly	Congress shall make no law respecting an establishment of religion, or prohibiting the free exercise thereof; or abridging

the freedom of speech, or of the press; or the right of the people peaceably to assemble, and to petition the Government for a redress of grievances.

A well regulated Militia, being necessary to the security of a free State, the right of the people to keep and bear Arms, shall not be infringed.

Right to Bear Arms

No Soldier shall, in time of peace be quartered in any house, without the consent of the Owner, nor in time of war, but in a manner to be prescribed by law.

Quartering Soldiers

The right of the people to be secure in their persons, houses, papers, and effects, against unreasonable searches and seizures, shall not be violated, and no Warrants shall issue, but upon probable cause, supported by Oath or affirmation, and particularly describing the place to be searched, and the persons or things to be seized.

Search and Seizure

No person shall be held to answer for a capital, or otherwise infamous crime, unless on a presentment or indictment of a Grand Jury, except in cases arising in the land or naval forces, or in the Militia, when in actual service in time of War or public danger; nor shall any person be subject for the same offence to be twice put in jeopardy of life or limb; nor shall be

Due Process of Law

compelled in any criminal case to be witness against himself, nor be deprived of life, liberty, or property, without due process of law; nor shall private property be taken for public use, without just compensation.

AMENDMENT VI

Trial Rights

In all criminal prosecutions, the accused shall enjoy the right to a speedy and public trial, by an impartial jury of the State and district wherein the crime shall have been committed, which district shall have been previously ascertained by law, and to be informed of the nature and cause of the accusation; to be confronted with the witnesses against him; to have compulsory process for obtaining witnesses in his favor, and to have the Assistance of Counsel for his defence.

AMENDMENT VII

Common Law Suits

In Suits at common law, where the value in controversy shall exceed twenty dollars, the right of trial by jury shall be preserved, and no fact used by a jury, shall be otherwise reexamined in any Court of the United States than according to the rules of the common law.

AMENDMENT VIII

Bail, Cruel and Unusual Punishment

Excessive bail shall not be required, nor excessive fines imposed, nor cruel and unusual punishments inflicted.

AMENDMENT IX

Unenumerated Right

The enumeration in the Constitution, of certain rights, shall not be construed to deny or disparage others retained by the people.

The powers not delegated to the United States by the Constitution, nor prohibited by it to the States, are reserved to the States respectively, or to the people.

[January 8, 1798]

The Judicial power of the United States shall not be construed to extend to any suit in law or equity, commenced or prosecuted against one of the United States by Citizens of another State, or by Citizens or Subjects of any Foreign State.

[September 25, 1804]

The Electors shall meet in their respective states and vote by ballot for President and Vice President, one of whom, at least, shall not be an inhabitant of the same state with themselves; they shall name in their ballots the person voted for as President, and in distinct ballots the person voted for as Vice President, and they shall make distinct lists of all persons voted for as President, and of all persons voted for as Vice President, and of the number of votes for each, which lists they shall sign and certify, and transmit sealed to the seat of the government of the United States, directed to the President of the Senate;—The President of the Senate shall, in the presence of the Senate and House of Representatives, open all the certificates and the votes shall then be counted;—The person having the greatest number of votes for President, shall be the President, if such number be a majority of the whole number of Electors appointed; and if no person have such majority, then from the persons having the highest numbers not exceeding three on the list of those voted for as President, the House of Representatives shall choose immediately, by ballot, the President. But in choosing the President, the votes shall be taken by states, the representation from each state having one vote; a quorum for this purpose shall consist of a member or members from two thirds of the states, and a majority of all the states shall be necessary to a choice. And if the House of Representatives shall not choose a President whenever the right of choice shall devolve upon them, *before the fourth day of March next following,*[10] then the Vice President shall act as President, as in the case of the death or other constitutional disability of the President.—The person having the greatest number of votes as Vice President shall be the Vice President, if such number be a majority of the whole number of Electors appointed, and if no person have a majority, then from the two highest numbers on the list, the Senate shall choose the Vice President; a quorum for the purpose shall consist of two-thirds of the whole number of Senators, and a majority of the whole number shall be necessary to a choice. But no person constitutionally ineligible to the office of President shall be eligible to that of Vice President of the United States.

[10] Altered by the Twentieth Amendment.

AMENDMENT XIII

[December 18, 1865]

Slavery Prohibited

Section 1. Neither slavery nor involuntary servitude, except as a punishment for crime whereof the party shall have been duly convicted, shall exist within the United States, or any place subject to their jurisdiction.

Section 2. Congress shall have power to enforce this article by appropriate legislation.

[July 28, 1869]

Section 1. All persons born or naturalized in the United States, and subject to the jurisdiction thereof, are citizens of the United States and of the State wherein they reside. No State shall make or enforce any law which shall abridge the privileges or immunities of citizens of the United States; nor shall any State deprive any person of life, liberty or property, without due process of law; nor deny to any person within its jurisdiction the equal protection of the laws.

Citizenship for Slaves
Due Process
Equal Protection

Section 2. Representatives shall be apportioned among the several States according to their respective numbers, counting the whole number of persons in each State, excluding Indians not taxed. But when the right to vote at any election for the choice of electors for President and Vice President of the United States, Representatives in Congress, the Executive and Judicial officers of a State, or the members of the Legislature thereof, is denied to any of the male inhabitants of such State, being twenty-one years of age, and citizens of the United States, or in any way abridged, except for participation in rebellion, or other crime, the basis of representation therein shall be reduced in the proportion which the number of such male citizens shall bear to the whole number of male citizens twenty-one years of age in such State.

Section 3. No person shall be a Senator or Representative in Congress, or elector of President or Vice President, or hold any office, civil or military, under the United States, or under any State, who, having previously taken an oath, as a member of Congress, or as an officer of the United States, or as a member of any State legislature, or as an executive or judicial officer of any State, to support the Constitution of the United States, shall have engaged in insurrection or rebellion against the same, or given aid or comfort to the enemies thereof. But Congress may by a vote of two thirds of each House, remove such disability.

Section 4. The validity of the public debt of the United States, authorized by law, including debts incurred for payment of pensions and bounties for services in suppressing insurrection or rebellion, shall not be questioned. But neither the United States nor any State shall assume or pay any debt or obligation incurred in aid of insurrection or rebellion against the United States, or any claim for the loss or emancipation of any slave; but all such debts, obligations, and claims shall be held illegal and void.

Section 5. The Congress shall have power to enforce, by appropriate legislation, the provisions of this article.

AMENDMENT XV

[March 30, 1870]

Right to Vote

Section 1. The right of citizens of the United States to vote shall not be denied or abridged by the United States or by any State on account of race, color, or previous condition of servitude.

Section 2. The Congress shall have power to enforce this article by appropriate legislation.

AMENDMENT XVI

[February 25, 1913]

Income Tax

The Congress shall have power to lay and collect taxes on incomes, from whatever source derived, without apportionment among the several States, and without regard to any census or enumeration.

AMENDMENT XVII

[May 31, 1913]

**Popular Election
of Senators**

The Senate of the United States shall be composed of two Senators from each State, elected by the people thereof, for six years; and each Senator shall have one vote. The electors in each State shall have the qualifications requisite for electors of the most numerous branch of the State legislatures.

When vacancies happen in the representation of any State in the Senate, the executive authority of such State shall issue writs of election to fill such vacancies: *Provided,* That the legislature of any State may empower the executive thereof to make temporary appointments until the people fill the vacancies by election as the legislature may direct.

This amendment shall not be so construed as to affect the election or term of any Senator chosen before it becomes valid as part of the Constitution.

AMENDMENT XVIII

[January 29, 1919]

Section 1. After one year from the ratification of this article the manufacture, sale, or transportation of intoxicating liquors within, the importation thereof into, or the exportation thereof from the United States and all territory subject to the jurisdiction thereof for beverage purposes is hereby prohibited.

Prohibition of Liquor

Section 2. The Congress and the several States shall have concurrent power to enforce this article by appropriate legislation.

Section 3. This article shall be inoperative unless it shall have been ratified as an amendment to the Constitution by the legislatures of the several States, as provided in the Constitution, within seven years from the date of the submission hereof to the States by the Congress.[11]

[11] Repealed by the Twenty-first Amendment.

AMENDMENT XIX

[August 26, 1920]

The right of citizens of the United States to vote shall not be denied or abridged by the United States or by any State on account of sex.

Women's Right to Vote

Congress shall have power to enforce this article by appropriate legislation.

AMENDMENT XX

[February 6, 1933]

Section 1. The terms of the President and Vice President shall end at noon on the 20th day of January, and the terms of Senators and Representatives at noon on the 3rd day of January, of the years in which such terms would have ended if this article had not been ratified; and the terms of their successors shall then begin.

Section 2. The Congress shall assemble at least once in every year, and such meeting shall begin at noon on the 3rd day of January, unless they shall by law appoint a different day.

Section 3. If, at the time fixed for the beginning of the term of the President, the President elect shall have died, the Vice President elect shall become President. If a President shall not have been chosen before the time fixed for the beginning of his term, or if the President elect shall have failed to qualify, then the Vice President elect shall act as President until a President shall have qualified; and the Congress may by law provide for the case wherein neither a President elect nor a Vice President elect shall have qualified, declaring who shall then act as President, or the manner in which one who is to act shall be selected, and such person shall act accordingly until a President or Vice President shall have qualified.

Section 4. The Congress may by law provide for the case of the death of any of the persons from whom the House of Representatives may choose a President whenever the right of choice shall devolve upon them, and for the case of the death of any of the persons from whom the Senate may choose a Vice President whenever the right of choice shall have devolved upon them.

Section 5. Sections 1 and 2 shall take effect on the 15th day of October following the ratification of this article.

Section 6. This article shall be inoperative unless it shall have been ratified as an amendment to the Constitution by the legislatures of three fourths of the several States within seven years from the date of its submission.

AMENDMENT XXI

[December 5, 1933]

Section 1. The eighteenth article of amendment to the Constitution of the United States is hereby repealed.

Repeals Prohibition

Section 2. The transportation or importation into any State, Territory, or possession of the United States for delivery or use therein of intoxicating liquors, in violation of the laws thereof, is hereby prohibited.

Section 3. This article shall be inoperative unless it shall have been ratified as an amendment to the Constitution by conventions in the several States, as provided in the Constitution, within seven years from the date of the submission hereof to the States by the Congress.

AMENDMENT XXII

[February 26, 1951]

Section 1. No person shall be elected to the office of the President more than twice, and no person who has held the office of President, or acted as President, for more than two years of a term to which some other person was elected

Two-term Limit for President

President shall be elected to the office of President more than once. But this Article shall not apply to any person holding the office of President when this Article was proposed by the Congress, and shall not prevent any person who may be holding the office of President, or acting as President, during the term within which this Article becomes operative from holding the office of President or acting as President during the remainder of such term.

Section 2. This article shall be inoperative unless it shall have been ratified as an amendment to the Constitution by the legislatures of three fourths of the several States within seven years from the date of its submission to the States by the Congress.

AMENDMENT XXIII

**Right to Vote
for Residents of
the District of Columbia**

[March 29, 1961]

Section 1. The District constituting the seat of Government of the United States shall appoint in such manner as the Congress may direct:

A number of electors of President and Vice President equal to the whole number of Senators and Representatives in Congress to which the District would be entitled if it were a State, but in no event more than the least populous State; they shall be in addition to those appointed by the States, but they shall be considered, for the purposes of the election of President and Vice President, to be electors appointed by a State; and they shall meet in the district and perform such duties as provided by the twelfth article of amendment.

Section 2. The Congress shall have power to enforce this article by appropriate legislation.

[January 23, 1964]

Section 1. The right of citizens of the United States to vote in any primary or other election for President or Vice President, for electors for President or Vice President, or for Senator or representative in Congress, shall not be denied or abridged by the United States or any state by reason of failure to pay any poll tax or other tax.

Prohibits Poll Taxes

Section 2. The Congress shall have the power to enforce this article by appropriate legislation.

[February 19, 1967]

Section 1. In case of the removal of the President from office or of his death or resignation, the Vice President shall become President.

Presidential Disability
and Replacement
for Vice President

Section 2. Whenever there is a vacancy in the office of the Vice President, the President shall nominate a Vice President who shall take office upon confirmation by a majority vote of both Houses of Congress.

Section 3. Whenever the President transmits to the President pro tempore of the Senate and the Speaker of the House of Representatives his written declaration that he is unable to discharge the powers and duties of his office, and until he transmits to them a written declaration to the contrary, such powers and duties shall be discharged by the Vice President as Acting President.

Section 4. Whenever the Vice President and a majority of either the principal officers of the executive departments or of such other body as Congress may by law provide, transmit to the President pro tempore of the Senate and the Speaker of the House of Representatives their written declaration that the President is unable to discharge the powers and duties of his office, the Vice President shall immediately assume the powers and duties of the office as Acting President.

Thereafter, when the President transmits to the President pro tempore of the Senate and the Speaker of the House of Representatives his written declaration that no inability exists, he shall resume the powers and duties of his office unless the Vice President and a majority of either the principal officers of the executive departments or of such other body as Congress may by law provide, transmit within four days to the President pro tempore of the Senate and the Speaker of the House of Representatives their written declaration that the President is unable to discharge the powers and duties of his office. Thereupon Congress shall decide the issue, assembling within forty-eight hours for that purpose if not in session. If the Congress, within twenty-one days after receipt of the latter written declaration, or, if Congress is not in session, within twenty-one days after Congress is required to assemble, determines by two thirds vote of both Houses that the President is unable to discharge the powers and duties of his office, the Vice President shall continue to discharge the same as Acting President; otherwise, the President shall resume the powers and duties of his office.

AMENDMENT XXVI

**Voting Age Lowered
to Eighteen**

[June 30, 1971]

Section 1. The right of citizens of the United States, who are eighteen years of age or older, to vote shall not be denied or abridged by the United States or any State on account of age.

Section 2. The Congress shall have the power to enforce this article by appropriate legislation.

Section 1. Equality of rights under the law shall not be denied or abridged by the United States or by any State on account of sex.

Proposed Equal Rights Amendment

Section 2. The Congress shall have power to enforce, by appropriate legislation, the provisions of this article.

Section 3. This amendment shall take effect two years after date of ratification.

Section 1. For purposes of representation in the Congress, election of the President and Vice President, and article V of this Constitution, the District constituting the seat of government of the United States shall be treated as though it were a State.

Proposed Voting Representation for the District of Columbia

Section 2. The exercise of the rights and powers conferred under this article shall be by the people of the District constituting the seat of government, and as shall be provided by the Congress.

Section 3. The twenty-third article of amendment to the Constitution of the United States is hereby repealed.

Section 4. This article shall be inoperative, unless it shall have been ratified as an amendment to the Constitution by the legislatures of three-fourths of the several States within seven years from the date of its submission.

ACKNOWLEDGMENTS (continued from page iv)

Congressional Quarterly Weekly Report, vol. 30, no. 11 (March 11, 1972), pp. 524, 567 and vol. 30, no. 42, (October 14, 1972), pp. 2692–2694. Reprinted by permission.

"Voters Are Adults," in *The Wall Street Journal,* October 28, 1980. Reprinted by permission of *The Wall Street Journal,* © Dow Jones & Company, Inc. All rights reserved.

Gerald Gunther, *Cases and Materials on Constitutional Law,* 9th edition. Copyright © 1975 The Foundation Press. Reprinted by permission.

Index

U.S. Supreme Court. *See also* Judicial review; Judicial self-restraint; and specific cases, issues, and doctrines
administration and staff, 429–431
appointments, 244, 258, 436–437
and Congress, 60, 319–323
constitutional powers of, 4–5, 6, 7
early, 39
FDR's attempt to pack, 112, 112n, 281, 320, 436–437
and federalism, 81–82, 102, 105–106, 108–116
first woman justice, 445–446
and interest groups, 204–205, 207–209
Madison on, 26, 34
nationalization of constitutional rights by, 52, 54–58, 60–62, 64–71, 74–76, 78–79, 82–87, 115–116
policy making by, 413–428, 435–448
powers of, 15–16, 37
and president, 259, 261–268, 436–437
United States v. *Curtiss-Wright Export Corporation,* 264–265
United States v. *Harriss,* 204
United States v. *Miller,* 52
Unit rule, 145

Veterans, 312–313
Vice-president, 11, 14
Vietnam War, 138, 143–144, 257, 260, 264, 269–270, 274–275, 281–282, 290, 292, 294–298, 301–302, 309, 422, 423, 424
Vinson, Chief Justice Frederick, 268
Virginia Bill of Rights, 44
Virginia plan. *See* Randolph plan
Virginia v. *Rives,* 71
Voluntary associations, 211–212
Voting Rights Act (1965), 90, 159, 161, 260, 394

Wagner Act (1935). *See* National Labor Relations Act
Wallace, George, 185
Wallace, Henry A., 155
Wallace, Mike, 229
Wall Street Journal, 173, 184–185
War power, 28
War Powers Resolution (1973), 297–298, 210
Warren, Charles, 109
Warren, Chief Justice Earl, 66, 86, 116, 204–205, 447
Warren Court, 88, 89–90, 110, 116, 417, 425, 442–443
Washington, George, 38, 39, 49, 105
Watergate scandal, 151, 164, 260, 282, 285, 408
Water Pollution Control Act (1972), 370–373
Watt, James G., 219
Watts, Ernst John, 446
Weber v. *Aetna Casualty and Surety Co.,* 89
Wednesday Club, 357
Weinberger, Caspar, 219
Welfare, 123, 126

Wesberry v. *Sanders,* 88
West Coast Hotel Company v. *Parrish,* 112n–113n, 321, 437
Whigs, 118, 119
White, Justice Byron, 68, 70, 74n, 75, 114, 263
White House staff, 285, 287–288, 289, 324–325
Will, George F., 263
Willoughby, W. F., 405, 407
Wills, Gary, 93
Wilson, James, 45–46, 47, 48
Wilson, Woodrow, 40, 264, 268, 280, 293, 298
"Winner-take-all" primaries, 146
Wiretapping, 55–56
Wolff v. *Selective Service Local Board No. 16,* 422–423
Women
and jury selection, 71, 89, 89n
McGovern Commission and, 146, 147
minimum wage, 321
and party politics, 158, 159
Wong Yang Sung v. *McGrath,* 61n–62n
Workmen's compensation laws, 385–386
World War I, 298
World War II, 158, 266–267, 299, 387
Wright, James, 352
"Writing to Members of Congress," 334–335
Writs of assistance, 53–54
Writs of *certiorari,* 425

Youth, and Democratic convention of 1972, 145, 146